Foun
and
Accou

Foundations of Cost and Management Accounting

Roy Dodge

Faculty of Business and Management, University of Westminster

CHAPMAN & HALL
University and Professional Division

London · Glasgow · Weinheim · New York · Tokyo · Melbourne · Madras

Published by
Chapman & Hall, 2–6 Boundary Row, London SE1 8HN, UK

Chapman & Hall, 2–6 Boundary Row, London SE1 8HN, UK

Blackie Academic & Professional, Wester Cleddens Road, Bishopbriggs, Glasgow G64 2NZ, UK

Chapman & Hall GmbH, Pappelallee 3, 69469 Weinheim, Germany

Chapman & Hall Inc., One Penn Plaza, 41st Floor, New York NY 10119, USA

Chapman & Hall Japan, Thomson Publishing Japan, Hirakawacho Nemoto Building, 6F, 1–7–11 Hirakawa-cho, Chiyoda-ku, Tokyo 102, Japan

Chapman & Hall Australia, Thomas Nelson Australia, 102 Dodds Street, South Melbourne, Victoria 3205, Australia

Chapman & Hall India, R. Seshadri, 32 Second Main Road, CIT East, Madras 600 035, India

First edition 1994

© 1994 Roy Dodge

Typeset in 11/12pt Goudy by EXPO Holdings, Malaysia
Printed in Singapore by Kin Keong Printing Co. Pte. Ltd

ISBN   0 412 58820 X

Printed on permanent acid-free text paper, manufactured in accordance with ANSI/NISO Z39.48–1992 and ANSI/NISO Z39.48–1984 (Permanence of Paper).

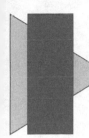

Contents

Preface

It is only natural that students embarking on a course of cost and management accounting will imagine that within a short while they will learn how to work out the cost of something. When they are told that there is no single concept of cost, and that the cost of something depends on the purpose for which the cost is needed, their reaction is sometimes one of open-mouthed disbelief. It might help if students started their studies by considering the following quotation from the work of an eminent researcher, J. Maurice Clark:

> If cost accounting sets out, determined to discover what the cost of everything is and convinced in advance there is one figure which can be found which will furnish exactly the information which is desired for every possible purpose, it will necessarily fail because there is no such figure. If it finds a figure which is right for some purposes, it must necessarily be wrong for others.

What is so impressive about this quotation, apart from the eloquent language, is the fact that it was written in 1923. Seventy years later we still hear politicians talking about the cost of goods and services supplied by national institutions as if cost were a certainty. This is very odd. The public have learned to question the word profit, but cost is assumed to be a fact.

The work published by J. Maurice Clark (University of Chicago Press, 1923) addressed the problem of cost accounting systems being dominated by the need to produce information for financial accounting. The requirement to report profits and assets to shareholders meant that companies in the manufacturing sector needed systems for measuring the cost of their finished products so that they could construct an income statement and a balance sheet. The methods developed (which are still being used today) have cost accounting and financial accounting as integrated parts of a single double-entry book-keeping system.

Clark was not criticizing these methods in terms of their usefulness for measuring profit; he was putting forward arguments in favour of separating cost analysis for managers from a system that was producing routine cost information for financial accounting. Clark had identified several reasons why managers needed cost information apart from the legal requirement of reporting profit to shareholders. He argued that these diverse needs could not be satisfied by information produced from a single integrated system designed to support the financial accounting function.

It is also remarkable that the work of people like Clark (and his successor at the University of Chicago, William Vatter) has been ignored for such a long time. I had not heard of it when I was a student and I doubt if many of my contemporaries had either. We probably questioned whether many of the cost accounting techniques were really designed for helping managers to run the business, but these were presented as a part of the syllabus and so we had to make sense of them if we wanted to pass the exam. It was only after the publication of books such as *Relevance Lost* by H. Thomas Johnson and Robert S. Kaplan (Harvard Business School Press, 1987) that many of us became aware of these earlier studies and realized that our own reservations were well founded.

Criticizing the traditions of cost accounting has now become the order of the day. So many new ideas are espoused that it is almost as if we are being asked to change the way we think from one month to the next. In some ways this is reminiscent of the revolution that financial accounting went through during the late 1960s. It could go even further. It might not be possible to manage a free market economy without the discipline of financial accounting, but there are writers, notably H. Thomas Johnson (co-author of *Relevance Lost*), who believe that accounting information is no longer relevant for the purposes of managing business operations. In his book *Relevance Regained* (Free Press, 1992), Johnson states that 'if companies are to compete effectively, they must remove accounting information from their control systems and relieve their accounting departments of responsibility for providing information to control business operations'.

If Johnson's ideas are turned into reality, my book (and many others) will have a relatively short life cycle. In the meantime, we have to get on with the task of using information from existing systems. We also have the task of encouraging change so that the information produced by cost accounting is more relevant to the needs of managers. In some ways this makes writing a text book on cost and management accounting exciting, in others it is slightly awkward. Students must learn about the traditional techniques because these are still being used by the majority of companies. Yet at the same time students must be made aware of the limitations of product cost information if it has been produced on a routine basis by those parts of the system that are designed to support financial accounting. Whether I have been able to achieve this balance is for readers to judge.

It is mainly in the area of product costs (thinking of products as being goods or services) that we encounter most of the problems of making cost information useful. To some extent these problems are being redressed by the introduction of techniques such as activity-based costing. There are many other aspects of cost and management accounting where the techniques are used for the sole purpose of helping managers to plan and make decisions. Cost/volume/profit analysis for evaluating short-term opportunities, relevant costs for decision making, and techniques for working capital management are a few examples of where the subject is not stifled by the dictates of financial accounting.

I have attempted to make the book useful for non-specialists as well as for students aiming at an accounting qualification. Some courses require students to develop competence in the interpretation and use of accounting information rather than in producing it. These students are usually attending some kind of general management course (such as DMS) that includes an accounting and finance module. It is quite difficult to make use of accounting information without learning how it is produced. Consequently, the approach taken is to get all readers involved in the underlying techniques but to provide some kind of signpost to show where the non-specialist can stop reading and accountancy students should continue. Sometimes this is dealt with by a codicil at the end of the chapter, and sometimes by an appendix that deals with any book-keeping or other specialist aspects. The result is intended to be a book that should satisfy a wide variety of needs for students preparing for a foundation qualification in cost and management accounting.

The general level of competence that readers should be able to achieve is at least equal to that required by the Chartered Association of Certified Accountants for the relevant papers (management accounting and parts of financial management) in their Certified Diploma in Accounting and Finance. But this is only a general guide, some of the specialist topics take the subject well beyond the technical requirements of these examinations.

Sources and acknowledgements

There cannot be very many teachers of cost and management accounting whose thoughts have not been influenced at some time by the standard text books on the subject, such as *Cost Accounting: A Managerial Emphasis* by Charles T. Horngren and George Foster (Prentice Hall International) and *Management and Cost Accounting* by Colin Drury (Chapman & Hall). The fact that these two books become larger with each new edition is an indication of how the subject is growing. I have very rarely made any direct reference to these books in my own work but I must confess that I frequently use them when I need a source of inspiration or reference.

I imagine that the whole profession must be indebted to the authors of *Relevance Lost* and *Relevance Regained* (see Preface for publication details), for having brought a breath of fresh air to the subject. We might not agree with all of their ideas but they made us stop and think about what we were doing. Although I have made several references to these works throughout my book, any serious student of cost and management accounting is advised to read them in their entirety.

There are so many organizations and people to whom one owes a debt of gratitude on a project like this that it is impossible to mention them all. There is the National Extension College, Cambridge, who gave me my first opportunity of writing on the subject; my colleagues (Usha Mehta, Jagdish Radia and Gordon Gloor), who never complained when I interrupted their concentration in order to bounce ideas off them, even though they knew that I needed the benefit of their counsel for my book (in other words, sorry for getting on your nerves); and a score of publications such as the study manuals published by Brierly Price Prior, from which one picks up ideas.

I am also grateful to the following examination boards for permission to reproduce questions from their examination papers:

- The Chartered Association of Certified Accountants (ACCA), including questions from the examination for the Certified Diploma in Accounting and Finance
- The Chartered Institute of Management Accountants (CIMA)
- The Association of Accounting Technicians (AAT)
- The Chartered Institute of Bankers (CIB)

- The Associated Examining Board for GCE A Level (AEB)
- The University of London School Examination Board for GCE A Level (ULSEB)

None of the answers (nor any hints on answers) within this book has been provided by any examination board; they are entirely my own responsibility.

Using this book

Activity-based learning

The publication of student text books that use an activity (or discovery) learning approach is now more common than it was a few years ago. In view of this, authors can probably stop wasting everyone's time by explaining (or justifying) the method.

If you have not encountered this type of text book previously, you will find that they differ from traditional text books in that the explanatory text is frequently punctuated by activities. Some of these are intended to be thought provoking, others require you to explore the subject by experimenting with figures. In most cases there is somewhere for you to write down the result of your work. This might be a space in the activity box, completing an outline format below the box, or completing a worksheet at the end of the chapter. In some cases you might find it preferable to draft out an answer on your own paper before writing anything in the book. Each activity has a reference number from which you can find my answer (or feedback) from the Key at the end of the chapter.

The basic idea is to get you actively involved in the learning process, in the same way as teachers in a classroom try to get you involved by throwing out questions as the subject is gradually explored. In many cases you will be creating illustrations that are presented by the author in a traditional text book. It is important to do something with each activity as you come to it because in many cases it will form an essential link in the flow of explanatory text. It does not matter if you make mistakes when working through these activities; we all learn by making mistakes. In any case, the subject of an activity might be 'open-ended', in which case there is no such thing as a mistake, merely a difference of opinion.

Flexibility of use

Teachers adopting this book as classroom material will find many different ways of using it. Having spoken to a number of tutors who have used the companion volume (*Foundations of Business Accounting*) it seems that the most popular approach is to construct a lecture around the subject area and then ask students to complete the activities as they become appropriate to the matter being explored. In other words, there is an interaction between the tutor and student (rather than between the text and reader), with the activities forming the basis of classroom work. The students then have an opportunity of working through the text later, should they wish to do so.

In some cases, particularly with the large groups that we have to cope with nowadays, it might be more appropriate to deliver a shorter lecture giving an outline of the subject area and then require students to work through the relevant chapter on their own. Seminars and tutorial guidance can then be directed towards helping students with their individual study problems. There is a wide range of material at the end of each chapter that can be used for course assignments, although many tutors will probably wish to supplement this with their own ideas in some cases.

If you are using the book without tutorial guidance, you are strongly advised to work through the chapters in the sequence provided. We have to use chapters in order to divide the subject into easily manageable chunks for study purposes, not because each chapter represents a unique subject that can be studied in isolation. There are a few topics that can be studied in isolation but, generally speaking, you will find that the material in one chapter builds on the material covered in earlier chapters. There is some guidance in certain chapters showing where the non-specialist can stop reading (see Preface). The remaining material in those chapters has been included for the benefit of accounting students. There is similar guidance on this in the question section at the end of each chapter.

End of chapter questions

The questions at the end of each chapter have been carefully selected so that it should be possible to complete them from the study material provided up to that point. In some of the earlier chapters I was aware that some students might not have progressed very far with related subjects such as financial accounting. This can happen on some first-year courses where students are expected to study both cost accounting and financial accounting as parallel subjects. In view of this, some of the questions (and some of the text) include explanations of technical terms that students might not have encountered previously. As the book proceeds, it was assumed that this would become less and less of a problem.

If you are using the book for private study you are strongly advised to complete some of the questions at the end of each chapter. The text and learning activities tend to concentrate on building up the basic principles; you will not be able to assess your competence very well without working on some of the more detailed problems. For most chapters, eight questions have been set. The answers to the first four can be found at the end of the book; answers to the remaining questions are published in a separate *Teacher's Manual*. In some cases the answers provide additional tutorial guidance.

The influence of manufacturing entities

The techniques of cost accounting were originally developed for manufacturers but they have been adapted for use in service industries. Unfortunately, this does mean that some of the inadequacies of traditional cost accounting have found their way into the service sector. Despite the decline of manufacturing, and the rise of service industries, in the UK, it is still helpful to use a manufacturer as a model for learning some of the principles, particularly those that relate to the way in which product costs are determined. There is nothing wrong with this providing readers are given some indication of how these principles can be applied to other industries.

You will find ample reference to this matter as you proceed through the book. You will even find instances where the cost accounting techniques as used in (say) car manufacturing can be applied to many different types of entity, including hospitals, colleges and poultry farming. The alternative to using a manufacturer as a kind of generic model is to write a separate text book on cost accounting for each type of entity. This is unnecessary: there is basically no difference between the problem of determining the cost of a case of baked beans, and determining the cost of providing a hospital bed for one day. The main difference is in identifying the cost object, not in the technique.

In any case, many of the subjects dealt with in the study of cost and management accounting are not concerned with techniques for working out the cost of products (the units of goods or services produced). In these cases we can look at other types of entity when learning the principles. The ability to apply these principles to a wide range of economic activity is an important soft skill that students have to develop.

Abbreviations

At the moment the subject of cost and management accounting is so dynamic that a new abbreviation seems to emerge every few months. These abbreviations have even been grouped under an abbreviated label, TLA (three-letter acronym)! Many of these TLAs relate to topics that are outside of the scope of subjects covered by this book.

Throughout this book the normal convention on abbreviations for technical terms has been followed: a full description is given when the term is first introduced, followed by the abbreviation in brackets. Thereafter, the abbreviation is used on the assumption that readers will know what it means. If there is a substantial distance between infrequently used abbreviations, the full description is repeated. In cases of doubt you should refer to the following list:

ABC	Activity-based costing
ARR	Accounting rate of return
AVCO	Average cost
BOAR	Budgeted overhead absorption rate
CSR	Contribution to sales ratio
CVP	Cost/volume/profit
DOG	Degree of operational gearing
EBIT	Earnings before interest and tax
EOQ	Economic order quantity
EPS	Earnings per share
EU	Equivalent unit
FIFO	First in, first out
IRR	Internal rate of return
JIT	Just-in-time
LIFO	Last in, first out
NFI	Non-financial indicator
NPV	Net present value
RI	Residual income
ROCE	Return on capital employed
ROI	Return on investment
SSAP	Statement of standard accounting practice

TQM   Total quality management
WACC   Weighted average cost of capital

Abbreviations used to identify the source of past examination questions are given in the Sources and Acknowledgements section.

1 ▷ Concepts of cost

Objectives

After you have completed this chapter, you should be able to:
- explain why the word 'cost', by itself, is meaningless when referring to measurements of economic activity
- describe how different concepts are used for identifying costs according to the purposes for which those costs are needed
- explain why managers might be given misleading cost information unless they state the purposes for which that information is needed
- demonstrate why it is necessary to be sceptical over the word 'cost' when it is used by those who give little thought to its meaning

Introduction

We frequently hear politicians discussing the cost of goods and services provided by our national institutions, usually in the context of introducing some kind of market mechanism to the system. The news media tend to focus on the social issues involved; the way in which the word 'cost' has been used is very rarely questioned. This lack of curiosity can probably be attributed to the word 'cost' itself, because it seems to imply something that an accountant should be able to measure with a reasonable degree of accuracy.

In this chapter you will learn to question the way in which the word 'cost' is used in relation to measurements of business activity. You will soon discover that it quite reasonable to ask questions like: what do you mean by cost? What kind of cost are you talking about? For what purpose are you using the cost? We cannot talk about the cost of a product as if it represents some kind of certainty. There are many different concepts of cost and quite often the way in which costs are measured will depend upon the reason for which that cost is needed.

As you work your way through the chapter you will start to accumulate some of the concepts and technical terms used in cost accounting. You will also gain an overview of the different ways in which costs are classified according to the circumstances in which they are used. In most cases the subject is dealt with at an introductory level; details of the specific techniques are covered in subsequent chapters.

1.1 Different costs for different purposes

The issue that precipitated the 1984/85 coal miners' strike was the proposed closure of the Cortonwood pit in Yorkshire. The National Coal Board (NCB) claimed that the pit was unprofitable: the accounting statements used in support of this argument showed that the operating costs of producing a tonne of coal were £50.50 whereas the net sale proceeds were £44.30 per tonne, an apparent loss of £6.20 per tonne.

During the strike these figures were challenged and in November 1984 it was argued that the basis used for calculating the loss per tonne was wrong. The operating costs per tonne included various amounts (totalling £11.95 per tonne) that would probably not be saved by closing down the mine. When these costs were excluded from the calculation the mine was shown to be contributing to NCB's profits at the rate of £5.75 per tonne.

The argument over whether the mine was losing £6.20 per tonne or was contributing to profits at the rate of £5.75 per tonne centred around a common misconception of the word 'cost'. It is quite likely that most people (unless they have studied accounting) will think of the word 'cost' as representing something that is certain. This idea probably stems from the way we experience cost in our everyday lives; if we buy a television for £300 we can say (with certainty) that the cost was £300. Consequently, we tend to attach the same notion of precision when we hear the business community and politicians talking about the cost of a product.

But the ingredients of cost become somewhat more complicated when dealing with organizations that produce things such as a tonne of coal, a case of baked beans, or a service such as a hospital bed for one day. If the cost of these things could be determined by simply adding up all the money spent, there would be no reason to make a study of cost accounting. In many cases we need to know the specific purpose for which costs are required before we can start to measure them. The way in which costs are determined for routine accounting purposes (such as reporting profits) might not be appropriate for making decisions.

In the case of Cortonwood, the original amount of £50.50 per tonne for operating costs was based on the figures used in the profit and loss account for that particular mine. These costs included a share of NCB's central office overheads that were apportioned to each mine on a standard basis. There is nothing wrong with this idea when producing a profit statement for the purposes of accounting control. Each mine receives some benefit from the provision of central services by the NCB and so it is a reasonable accounting practice to charge these costs to the various mines on a pro rata basis. But the reason why cost information was needed for Cortonwood was not for the purpose of accounting control, it was for the purpose of making a decision.

Activity 1

The costs apportioned to Cortonwood for general overheads and services provided by the NCB amounted to £3.79 per tonne. Try to describe why it might have been wrong to include these if the purpose for which cost information was needed was to determine whether the mine was uneconomic.

Accountants call this type of cost an 'unavoidable' cost and it is one of several concepts used for identifying costs when producing information to help managers to make decisions.

The figures for Cortonwood included several types of unavoidable cost but it is not necessary for you to understand all of them at this stage. It is more important that you embark on your study of cost and management accounting with an open mind regarding the way in which the word 'cost' is used. If you keep in mind that the cost of something can differ according to the purpose for which that cost is needed, you will not find it so confusing when, for example, one chapter shows you how to include overheads in the cost of a product and another chapter tells you that these overheads are not relevant and should be ignored. The subject of cost accounting appears to be full of contradictions like this unless you accept the axiom 'there are different costs for different purposes'.

1.2 The information system

Accounting systems are designed to produce financial information about an economic entity to those who need it and to those who have a right to receive it. If you have studied 'financial accounting' (even at an elementary level) you will know that the accounting system is designed to produce periodic financial statements to those who have invested money in the business.

If the business is owned by a limited company, the shareholders participate in the risks and rewards of ownership through their investment (owning shares) in that company. Most of these shareholders are not directly involved in the daily management of the business, so the law seeks to keep them informed by ensuring that the directors produce annual financial statements to show the company's operating results (a profit and loss account) for each year and its financial position (a balance sheet) at the end of each year.

These statutory accounts are highly regulated by legislation and professional accounting standards. As a result, the annual financial statements presented to shareholders must:

- be presented in a specific form
- contain all the information stipulated by law and professional standards
- measure the results of certain types of transaction in a way that does not contravene either legislation or professional accounting standards

Activity 2

Accounting information produced for shareholders is highly regulated by both law and professional accounting standards. There are no regulations regarding accounting information produced for management except those that are dictated by the needs of the business itself. Make a note of why you think that accounting information for shareholders is subject to such strict regulations.

In view of the rigorous nature of the regulations designed to protect the interests of shareholders, it is not surprising to find that the design of most accounting systems is driven by the need to satisfy these requirements. Yet such systems must also produce information to assist management with their daily task of controlling the business, making decisions and ensuring that the shareholders' funds are used in the most profitable way. The requirement to satisfy the needs of two separate user groups can sometimes create conflicts in the way that cost information is produced by the accounting system.

If we take a manufacturing entity as an example, the accounting system must ensure that information is available regarding the cost of goods produced. This is necessary because the financial statements submitted to shareholders (profit and loss account and balance sheet) must treat the cost of goods on hand at the end of the period as an asset. Since there are various principles that could be adopted for calculating the cost of these products, financial accounting regulations insist that the cost of closing stock is determined in a particular way. This helps to ensure that all manufacturing companies calculate their results on a uniform basis. Unfortunately, the basis adopted for calculating product costs in financial accounting can mislead managers when cost information is needed for the purposes of making decisions.

Activity 3

Management will need to know the cost of goods produced for various reasons other than to satisfy the requirements of financial accounting regulations. Make a note of any reasons that occur to you as to why management might need this information.

Financial accounting has much earlier origins than cost accounting. In the early days of manufacturing, profit margins were so excessive that businesses did not really need a reliable system for determining the costs of individual products. In order to produce annual financial statements for shareholders, it would have been necessary to work out the cost of unsold stock at the end of the year but this was done as a separate clerical exercise – the figures were not produced automatically by the double-entry book-keeping system.

When competition became more intense, managers needed a more reliable system to determine individual product costs. The First World War (1914–1918) also gave an impetus to the development of cost accounting because weapons were purchased by the government at a price which was calculated by adding a profit margin to the manufacturer's cost. These influences resulted in cost accounting being developed as a separate information system (i.e. separate from the normal financial accounting system). Eventually, techniques were devised to integrate cost and financial accounting as one single system. The cost accounting systems that we find being operated today are based on techniques that had already become established by the 1950s.

These techniques have changed very little over the years although a recent innovation has been to take a more scientific approach when accounting for overheads. You will learn about this in Chapter 5. You will also discover that although the techniques were developed for manufacturers, various aspects can easily be applied to the service sector. The same approach can be used whether we are calculating the cost of a tonne of coal or the cost of providing a hospital bed for one day.

For the moment it is sufficient to understand that although we usually separate financial accounting from cost accounting for the purposes of study, in terms of double-entry book-keeping they each form part of one integrated system. This single system, as stated earlier, tends to be dominated by the need to satisfy the financial accounting regulations and will produce figures for the cost of goods produced based on those regulations. If managers require information for decision making, the accountant might have to ignore the figures used in routine accounting reports and select those that are relevant to the specific decision. This often involves treating costs (and revenues) used in profit measurements as irrelevant, and sometimes in using costs that are not even classified as costs in the accounting records.

1.3 Purposes for which costs are needed

A useful starting point in trying to make sense of the different concepts of cost is to consider the various purposes for which cost information is needed. In the majority of cases, these purposes will fall under one of the following headings:

- stock valuation and profit measurement (for financial accounting)
- decision making
- planning and control

The problem of determining costs for **stock valuation and profit measurement** is specific to certain types of industry such as manufacturing and mining. As stated earlier, the basis used is regulated by legislation and professional accounting standards. In most cases the accounting system is designed to produce this cost information on a regular basis. This subject is introduced in Chapter 3 (The influence of manufacturing) and certain components of the system are covered in more detail in Chapters 4, 5 and 6. The concepts and techniques are explained in the context of a manufacturing entity (for which they were developed) but certain aspects can be applied to service industries, where the problem of calculating the cost of closing stock does not apply.

Costs for **decision making** are usually produced as and when required by managers. The cost accountant uses skills and judgement in order to select cost information that is relevant to the decision. Some of this information will be available from the routine accounting system but in most cases a specific analysis is required. A detailed study of this subject is postponed until Chapter 11. It is an interesting subject but it does require knowledge of the language, concepts and techniques that you will gradually accumulate by working through the earlier chapters.

Costs for **planning and control** will include both predicted costs and costs actually incurred. Planning future operations involves predicting future income and expenditure; control takes the form of comparing actual results with the targets that were set when the plan was devised. The process of budgeting (covered in Chapter 9) is the most obvious example. But the subject of planning and control is not restricted to budgeting. In decentralized organizations, central management needs information systems that allow local managers to have a reasonable degree of local autonomy providing they keep within the overall goals of the company. Specific techniques have been developed for this purpose (discussed in Chapter 8), which are designed to motivate divisional managers and encourage initiative.

The thorny problem of product costs recurs with divisionalized companies, this time for the purpose of setting a price for goods or services transferred from one division to another. The same concepts of cost control can be applied in any organization where one department provides services to another, such as a centralized computer department providing services to various user groups. You will need to keep in mind that costs used for internal accounting controls are not likely to be the relevant costs for decision making.

Activity 4

Assume that a local authority is trying to decide whether it should continue to provide its own day-care services or use an external agency which has quoted a fee of £10 per hour for each attendant provided. For internal accounting purposes, the local authority has calculated its own cost of providing an attendant at £14 per hour. It might not be relevant simply to compare these two costs when making the decision. See if you can think of some costs that the local authority might have included in its internal rate of £14 that might not be relevant to the decision.

1.4 Classifications of cost

We can now try to relate different concepts of cost to the purposes for which the cost is needed. The concepts dealt with in this chapter are not by any means a complete list of the different ways in which costs can be classified, but they form a useful key to the cost accountant's language. It does not matter if you find some of the terms difficult to remember; you will soon be using them in much more detail in later chapters.

The relationship between cost classification and its purpose is not always neat and tidy. Some cost classifications are relevant to more than one purpose. The cost accounting system (meaning the system by which costs are classified and recorded in the books) will be designed to produce the cost of what is known as a 'cost object'. The cost object can be one of several things. For example, it could be a unit of product or service (produced for external marketing or internal transfer), or it might be the cost of running a department or a machine. Sometimes costs are initially collected for a cost object such as a production department and then later attributed to other cost objects such as the manufactured goods processed by that department.

These cost objects are not quite the same thing as the purpose for which the cost is required. Costs for decision making is one example of where costs are determined for a purpose rather than for an object. Consequently, looking at cost concepts from the viewpoint of cost objects tends to be a narrow perception of the subject, although the two viewpoints (object and purpose) will overlap to some extent.

An interesting feature of cost classification is that the labels used to identify different concepts can often be considered in pairs. Table 1.1, which attempts to link different cost classifications to the circumstances in which they are used, provides an example of this pairing.

Table 1.1

Cost classifications in pairs	Circumstances in which used
Marginal cost and absorbed cost Direct cost and indirect cost	Stock valuation and profit measurement (for financial accounting)
Sunk cost and committed cost Opportunity cost and incremental cost Avoidable cost and unavoidable cost	Decision making
Fixed cost and variable cost Standard cost and incurred cost Controllable cost and uncontrollable cost	Planning and control

The link between classification and purpose is not as watertight as might be suggested by Table 1.1. For example, some of the concepts used to classify costs for stock valuation and profit measurement might be used when producing costs for decision making. But the idea of linking different concepts of cost with the purpose for which they are needed forms a helpful way of structuring the subject and is used for the remainder of this chapter.

Table 1.1 shows two pairs of cost classifications:

- marginal cost and absorbed cost
- direct cost and indirect cost

Marginal cost and absorbed cost

If you have studied financial accounting you will know that accounting profit is determined on a periodic basis by matching the income from the sale of the company's products with all of the costs consumed in generating that income.

The 'costs consumed' will not be the same as the costs incurred. For example, if a company buys some goods for £100 intending to sell them for, say, £150, the company has incurred a cost of £100 but (in accounting jargon) that cost will not be 'consumed' until the goods are sold. If the goods have not been sold at the end of the accounting period the cost of £100 is not treated as a cost to be matched with sales income for that period, it is carried forward as an asset. In this example, the process of matching income and expenditure in order to calculate profit will recognize that no expense has been incurred by spending £100. The only thing that has occurred is that the composition of the company's assets has changed; one of the assets (cash) has been replaced by another asset (stock). The cost of that stock will be treated as an expense when the goods are sold.

The same process of matching must be used when measuring the profits of a manufacturer. The main difference is that manufacturers do not simply buy things for sale; they buy raw materials and convert them into finished goods. The manufacturer will incur various costs in producing these finished goods.

Activity 5

Think about any kind of manufacturing entity and describe (using your own words) some of the costs that will be incurred in the manufacturing process. Concentrate on costs incurred by the factory where the goods are made and ignore other operating costs of the business such as administration, selling and distribution. It does not matter if the descriptions in your list differ from those in the Key, the object of the activity is to focus your attention on the different types of manufacturing cost.

The key point to keep in mind at the moment is that none of these costs is treated as an expense to be matched with sales income until the finished goods have been sold.

Newcomers to cost accounting often find this point confusing because they are accustomed to thinking of costs such as rent and insurance as being expenses that are deducted from sales income when calculating profit. But financial accounting regulations insist that the cost of finished goods should include all manufacturing costs, including all expenses that can be related to the manufacturing process such as rent, rates and insurance of the factory building. Consequently, a manufacturer could spend (say) £1,000,000 on running the factory and the whole of this cost will be carried forward as an asset (as part of the cost of stock) if none of the goods produced have been sold by the end of the period. Manufacturing expenses are simply being turned into assets. The cost of these assets becomes an expense (called cost of sales) when the goods are sold.

It is the treatment of manufacturing expenses, such as rent and insurance of the factory, that accounts for the difference between marginal cost and absorbed cost. The starting point is to consider marginal cost. Anyone who has studied economics will be able to define marginal cost as the cost of producing one more unit. If this unit were not produced, the cost would not be incurred. Some costs of running the factory will be the same whether 100 units or 1,000 units are produced. Such costs do not form part of the marginal cost.

Activity 6

Try to identify whether the following costs will (by answering yes) or will not (by answering no) form part of the marginal cost of a manufactured product. If you have any doubts (and doubts are quite reasonable in this subject) you can answer 'not sure'.

	Delete as appropriate
Cost of raw materials	yes/no/not sure
Cost of bought in components	yes/no/not sure
Insurance of the factory building	yes/no/not sure
Cost of employing people to assemble the components	yes/no/not sure
Cost of the factory supervisor	yes/no/not sure

The introduction of uncertainties in this activity shows that the classification of cost will not always be precise, and sometimes a pragmatic approach must be used. The way in which costs are classified will also change as changes are made in the way that goods are produced. In the early days of manufacturing, production methods tended to be labour intensive. In these circumstances, the cost of employing workers to produce the goods could be considered to be part of the marginal cost of a product. Modern production methods tend to be so highly automated that the role of many factory employees is to monitor the machines that do the work. Should the cost of a machine-minder be treated as part of the marginal cost? Probably not; the cost of a machine-minder is likely to be the same whether 100 units or 1,000 units are produced.

By tradition more than anything else, the cost of employees who are directly involved in the actual production process are treated as a part of the marginal cost of a manufactured product. The cost of employing this type of person must be separated from the cost of other employees in the factory such as fork-lift truck drivers, cleaners and maintenance staff. The cost of these types of staff will be treated as factory overheads and do not form a part of the marginal cost.

For the sake of simplicity we will assume that the marginal cost of a product consists of the cost of its raw material ingredients and the cost of factory employees who are directly involved in assembling the product. All other costs such as rent and insurance of the factory building, depreciation of the plant, and heating and maintenance costs are classified as factory overheads.

The total of all of these overheads will be accumulated in a specific way and attributed to the unit cost of all goods produced on some kind of pro rata basis. The process of attaching factory overheads to the cost of units produced is known as 'overhead absorption' and you will see how it is done in Chapter 5. By way of a simple example, if the total factory overheads amount to £10,000 and 10,000 units of a single product are made, the overhead cost per unit will be £1. This is an oversimplification of a complex problem, because most companies produce more than one type of product and the demands made on factory resources will vary from one product to another. However, we can now see the relationship between marginal cost and absorbed cost. In simple terms this relationship can be presented as follows:

	per unit
Marginal cost (e.g. raw material ingredients and direct labour)	X
Factory overheads absorbed	X
Absorbed cost	X

As stated earlier, the cost of closing stock is carried forward as an asset when calculating profits. The effect of this is to carry forward costs that were incurred in one period to the period in which the goods are sold. As you can see, absorbed cost per unit is greater than marginal cost per unit. In the days when companies were free to select their own basis for valuing closing stocks (prior to 1970) reported profits depended upon whether closing stock was valued at marginal cost or absorbed cost. Today, companies do not have this choice; closing stock must be valued on the basis of absorbed cost.

However, we are discussing here the basis that must be used for financial accounting purposes (i.e. reporting profits and assets to shareholders). Until quite recently, the methods used for attaching overheads to manufactured products tended to be somewhat arbitrary. Taking the earlier illustration as an example, if 10,000 units were produced the overhead cost per unit would be £1.00, but if 5,000 units were produced the overhead cost per unit would be £2.00. Financial accounting regulations have a way of coping with these fluctuations but we will ignore this for the time being. The point that managers need to keep in mind is that absorbed cost per unit (as produced by the accounting system) can be misleading unless it is properly understood. Absorbed cost per unit will depend on various factors, including the number of units produced.

Direct cost and indirect cost

Although these two concepts of cost have been included under stock valuation and profit measurement, they must often be considered when producing cost information for decision making. You can get some idea of how the terms are used by considering the Cortonwood mine illustration in section 1.1. The cost of employing miners to extract the coal is a direct cost of working the mine, but the share of NCB's head-office expenses that were apportioned to the mine are indirect costs.

In classifying costs between direct and indirect, it is necessary to identify the cost object (i.e. the thing for which the costs are needed). The cost object could be one of several things such as a mine, a department or a unit of finished product. In many cases a cost which is initially classified as a direct cost of one cost object will subsequently become an indirect cost of another object. Calculating the cost of manufactured products is a good example of where this happens. Direct costs are those that can be identified specifically with a cost object in an economically feasible way. The expression 'economically feasible' is quite important; it implies that a pragmatic approach must be taken. If you look at a simple manufactured product such as an office table, you can see that most of the raw materials used in its manufacture will be classed as a direct cost of that table.

Activity 7

Some of the raw materials used in making the table cannot be measured as a specific cost of that particular table in an economically feasible way. Describe some of the raw materials to which this might apply.

The raw materials that can be conveniently identified as a specific cost of the table (such as the timber) are classified as direct materials. Raw materials that cannot be measured in this way are classed as indirect materials.

In order to attach the indirect material costs to the table it will be necessary to accumulate the total amount spent in an accounting period and spread this total over all the units made in that period. The process of accumulating these indirect costs will involve treating some of them as direct costs of a particular department. For example, if the table manufacturer has a separate department in the factory called (perhaps) the finishing department, the cost of the varnish used will be a direct cost of that department. There will be other costs of running the finishing department that are classed as indirect, for example a share of the insurance cost of the whole factory. The total costs of running the finishing department will, therefore, consist of direct costs and indirect costs. This total will be spread over all the units passing through the finishing department and will form a part of the indirect cost of the product.

The main purpose of classifying costs between direct and indirect is to facilitate the way in which costs are recorded in the book-keeping system. Direct costs can be accounted for as specific costs of the goods produced; indirect costs are accumulated for production departments and spread over all the units passing through those departments. This is necessary in order to determine unit costs on the basis of their 'absorbed cost', as discussed previously. It will, however, be necessary for managers to consider indirect

The major part of administration expenses is likely to be a fixed cost (at least in the short term) although there will be a variable element. For example, stationery, telephone and postage costs are likely to increase as business activity increases.

Activity 9

The two factors are: (1) material usage (the quantity of material used was different to the amounts specified in the standard) and (2) material price (the price of raw materials differed from the price used in the standard).

Questions

Questions for self assessment

Answers to self-assessment questions are given at the end of the book.

1.1 Neverwait Ltd, a departmental store, has three separate sales departments. Routine accounting reports are produced at regular intervals to determine the profit of each department. Profit statements for the past month reveal the following:

	Dept 1	Dept 2	Dept 3	Total
Sales income	100,000	80,000	40,000	220,000
Direct costs (cost of goods sold and specific costs of running the department)	70,000	50,000	35,000	155,000
	30,000	30,000	5,000	65,000
Apportionment of general overheads	15,000	12,000	6,000	33,000
Profit/(loss)	15,000	18,000	(1,000)	32,000

A manager reviewing these figures has suggested that Department 3 should be closed down because it is uneconomic.

Required:
(a) Discuss whether closing down Department 3 will be of benefit to the company. Make any assumptions that you consider to be appropriate.
(b) If the general overheads apportioned to each department include an amount for rent of the whole building, state a basis that might have been used to apportion the rent to each department.
(c) Make the following two assumptions:
   • none of the general overheads apportioned to Department 3 can be saved as a result of closing it down
   • future operating results of Departments 1 and 2 will be the same as for the past month.

On these two assumptions, estimate what the profit of the whole business will be for the next month if Department 3 is closed down.

(d) Describe factors other than those relating to the accounting measurements that might have to be considered when deciding whether or not close down Department 3.

producing cost information for decision making. You can get some idea of how the terms are used by considering the Cortonwood mine illustration in section 1.1. The cost of employing miners to extract the coal is a direct cost of working the mine, but the share of NCB's head-office expenses that were apportioned to the mine are indirect costs.

In classifying costs between direct and indirect, it is necessary to identify the cost object (i.e. the thing for which the costs are needed). The cost object could be one of several things such as a mine, a department or a unit of finished product. In many cases a cost which is initially classified as a direct cost of one cost object will subsequently become an indirect cost of another object. Calculating the cost of manufactured products is a good example of where this happens. Direct costs are those that can be identified specifically with a cost object in an economically feasible way. The expression 'economically feasible' is quite important; it implies that a pragmatic approach must be taken. If you look at a simple manufactured product such as an office table, you can see that most of the raw materials used in its manufacture will be classed as a direct cost of that table.

Activity 7

Some of the raw materials used in making the table cannot be measured as a specific cost of that particular table in an economically feasible way. Describe some of the raw materials to which this might apply.

The raw materials that can be conveniently identified as a specific cost of the table (such as the timber) are classified as direct materials. Raw materials that cannot be measured in this way are classed as indirect materials.

In order to attach the indirect material costs to the table it will be necessary to accumulate the total amount spent in an accounting period and spread this total over all the units made in that period. The process of accumulating these indirect costs will involve treating some of them as direct costs of a particular department. For example, if the table manufacturer has a separate department in the factory called (perhaps) the finishing department, the cost of the varnish used will be a direct cost of that department. There will be other costs of running the finishing department that are classed as indirect, for example a share of the insurance cost of the whole factory. The total costs of running the finishing department will, therefore, consist of direct costs and indirect costs. This total will be spread over all the units passing through the finishing department and will form a part of the indirect cost of the product.

The main purpose of classifying costs between direct and indirect is to facilitate the way in which costs are recorded in the book-keeping system. Direct costs can be accounted for as specific costs of the goods produced; indirect costs are accumulated for production departments and spread over all the units passing through those departments. This is necessary in order to determine unit costs on the basis of their 'absorbed cost', as discussed previously. It will, however, be necessary for managers to consider indirect costs quite carefully when making certain types of decision. Some indirect costs might have to be classified as unavoidable costs in the sense that the cost will continue to be incurred irrespective of the decision.

1.6 Costs for decision making

The three pairs of cost classification mentioned in Table 1.1 are:

- sunk cost and committed cost
- opportunity cost and incremental cost
- avoidable cost and unavoidable cost

In producing cost information that will help managers to make decisions, a change of viewpoint is needed. A decision taken today will affect what happens in the future. Although this sounds like stating the obvious, it is quite important because it means that past costs can be ignored in most decisions. The past cannot be altered by a decision that affects the future.

To take a simple (naive) example, if a manager is deciding whether to sell a product to one person for £100, or to another person for £120, the manager will obviously chose to sell it for £120. But notice how the past has been ignored in this example. The accounting records might show that the firm incurred costs of £200 in making this product but if the only options open are to sell it for either £100 or £120, past cost can be ignored when making the decision. (Notice that although past costs can be ignored for the purposes of making the decision, they cannot be ignored for the purposes of reporting profits to the shareholders.) The three pairs of cost classification mentioned above are all based on the concept of considering how future cash flows are affected by the decision.

Sunk costs and committed costs

Sunk costs are costs that have already been spent (such as the cost of £200 in the above example) and cannot be changed by the decision. **Committed costs** are those that will have to be incurred (in the future) because of a current commitment such as rent of a factory building. In many cases, committed costs cannot be changed by a decision and if this is the case they are not relevant to that decision.

Opportunity costs and incremental costs

Opportunity cost is an interesting concept because, as a cost, it will never be recorded as a cost in the accounting records. Assume that a university has a spare lecture room where the accounting records show that the costs of that room (insurance, heating, lighting, etc.) are £100 a day. (Incidentally, these costs will all be indirect costs that have been apportioned to that room out of a total for the whole building.)

An external organization has indicated that it would be prepared to pay £200 per day for use of the room. The problem being faced by the university is to work out a tuition fee for a special course that it could offer to a particular section of the public. How much should it include in the costing for use of the room? The accounting records show that the room costs £100 a day, but by using the room for its own purposes, the university has lost the opportunity of earning £200 a day by hiring it to another organization. The relevant cost in this case is, therefore, £200 per day.

The £200 per day is called an opportunity cost; it represents a benefit given up as a result of making a decision. By using the room for its own purposes, the university has lost the opportunity of hiring it to another organization for £200 per day.

Incremental cost is the extra amount that will have to be spent as a result of making a decision. In the case of the university with its spare lecture room, it could be that the special course would involve paying £100 a day to a visiting lecturer. This additional cost is known as an incremental cost. You will see how incremental costs (and incremental revenues) are used in decision making when working through Chapter 6. The important point for now is to realize that incremental costs involve looking at how costs will change in the future according to a decision that is made today.

Avoidable costs and unavoidable costs

The underlying concept of these two types of cost is fairly apparent from the names used to describe them. They tend to be relevant when the decision problem faced by managers is whether a particular segment of the business should be closed, or whether a particular product should be withdrawn from sale. In both cases, this problem usually arises because the accounting reports show that the segment or product is losing money.

Closing down a segment of the business does not mean that all of the costs associated with it in the accounting reports will be saved. Some of the costs that have been apportioned to the segment for accounting purposes will continue to be incurred at the same rate irrespective of whether the segment exists or not. Costs that can be saved by making a decision are called avoidable costs, those that cannot be saved are called unavoidable costs.

1.7 Costs for planning and control

The three pairs of cost classification mentioned in Table 1.1 are:

- fixed cost and variable cost
- standard cost and incurred cost
- controllable cost and uncontrollable cost

Fixed cost and variable cost

Although these concepts of cost have been included under planning and control, they might also be applicable to decision making. The reason why it is useful to relate them to planning is because planning involves predicting future results and this requires an understanding of how total costs will respond according to changes in the level of business activity.

Predictions are usually made for relatively short periods, such as one year. When we look at the total costs to be incurred for that period we will find that some of them are fixed in the sense that the amount to be spent will be the same irrespective of the number of units produced and sold. In other cases, the total cost incurred for the period will vary with the number of units produced and sold. The factors that cause total costs to vary according to activity are known as 'cost drivers'. Cost drivers can be various things, such as production quantities, sales quantities or the number of miles travelled by the delivery fleet.

Activity 8

Identify whether the following costs for an accounting period are likely to be classed as fixed or variable. Remember that we are talking about the total costs for a period, not the cost per unit.

	Delete as appropriate
Rent of the office and factory building	fixed/variable
Sales commissions based on 1% of price received	fixed/variable
Administration expenses	fixed/variable
Cost of raw materials used in manufacture	fixed/variable

Unfortunately, it is not always easy to classify costs between fixed and variable because some costs are a mixture of both. Take delivery costs as an example: running costs of the delivery fleet will vary with the number of miles run, other costs such as road tax and insurance are fixed. You will learn in Chapter 2 how costs such as these must be analysed in order to make use of the distinction between fixed and variable costs.

Standard cost and incurred cost

The term 'standard cost' is usually associated with a manufactured product although it can relate to a service. The basic approach is to work out (in advance of the accounting period) how much a particular product should cost in terms of its various components such as material, labour and overhead. This cost represents a standard against which the actual costs incurred will be compared. The difference between standard cost and incurred cost can then be analysed according to its cause. You will learn how the analysis is done in Chapter 7 but you will get an idea of the approach from the following activity.

Activity 9

The standard material cost for each unit to be manufactured is set at £8. The actual costs incurred work out at £9 per unit. In accounting jargon there is an adverse variance of £1 per unit. There are likely to be two factors that have contributed to this variance. See if you can identify the two factors and make a note of them here.

It is this analysis of the total variance that enables central management to exercise control. The two factors that contributed to the total will require an explanation by two different departmental managers; material price by the purchasing department and material usage by the production department. Without this analysis the company has no means of identifying which aspects of the firm's operations are causing actual results to differ from those that were planned.

Controllable cost and uncontrollable cost

These concepts of cost are used in various ways but their most frequent application relates to monitoring and assessing departmental performance. If you consider any section of a business (whether it be a small department, or a complete division of a diversified company) there will be some costs attributable to that section over which the local manager has no control. Such costs often stem from decisions made by central management. In assessing the performance of local managers, a distinction must be made between controllable and uncontrollable costs. Failure to do this could result in poor motivation because local managers are being asked to account for something that is beyond their control.

Summary

The key learning points in this chapter can be summarized as follows:
- there is no single concept of cost; the way in which costs are measured will usually depend upon the purpose for which the cost is required
- there is usually one integrated accounting system that is designed to produce information for both cost accounting and financial accounting; the need for companies to satisfy financial accounting regulations tends to dominate the design of that system
- cost information produced for routine accounting reports is often not the relevant information needed by managers for making decisions
- the purposes for which cost information is needed can be identified under three main headings: stock valuation and profit measurement for financial accounting; decision making; planning and control
- marginal cost and absorbed cost are two separate principles that could be used for determining the cost of closing stock; marginal cost consists of the extra costs that will have to be incurred if another unit is made, absorbed cost comprises marginal cost plus factory overheads that are attributed to manufactured units by some accounting process
- financial accounting regulations require companies to value closing stocks on the basis of absorbed cost, but in many cases information on marginal cost is more useful to management
- direct costs and indirect costs are ways of looking at costs from the viewpoint of cost objects, such as products or departments

- for accounting purposes, the distinction between direct and indirect costs facilitates the recording process; costs that can be identified easily as a specific cost of the cost object are treated as direct, any other costs that are to be attributed to the cost object are treated as indirect
- various accounting techniques are used to attribute indirect costs to cost objects
- costs for decision making are usually established by considering how future cash flows will change as a result of making the decision
- sunk costs represent money already spent, committed costs are future costs that will be incurred because of a current commitment; these costs are not usually relevant to a decision because they cannot be changed by the decision
- opportunity costs represents a benefit forgone as a result of making a decision, incremental costs are the extra costs that will be incurred as a result of a decision
- avoidable costs and unavoidable costs are concepts used to establish how future cash flows will change as a result of making a decision
- costs for planning and control can be identified under several headings, such as: fixed cost and variable cost, standard cost and incurred cost, controllable cost and uncontrollable cost
- control is often established by predicting future results and setting performance targets, actual performance is compared to these targets; any significant variances must be analysed and then explained by those responsible for them
- in predicting future results, the distinction between fixed costs and variable costs is important
- activities that cause total costs to change are known as cost drivers: in some cases, total cost will remain fixed irrespective of the level of activity; in others, total costs will vary with the level of activity

Activity 1

They represent costs that cannot be saved by closing down a segment of the business. It is most likely that NCB's central costs would continue to be incurred at the same level whether the mine was closed or not.

Activity 2

Various reasons, such as: (1) the majority of shareholders will be members of the general public (including those who have an interest in shares through institutional investors such as pension funds). Since shareholders provide the risk capital, they must be properly informed of the company's affairs; (2) many business transactions can be measured in different ways for accounting purposes and unscruplous directors could take advantage of this in order to manipulate the figures. Accounting regulations specify the ways in which these measurements must be made.

Activity 3

Various reasons such as: (1) to detemine selling prices (unless prices are dominated by market forces); (2) to control costs where current profit margins considered inadequate and cannot be changed by price increases; (3) to make forecasts and plans for the future.

Activity 4

The £14 might include various internal costs (such as the provision of central computer services, office accommodation and so on) that have been apportioned to the day care section. To some extent the total amount of money spent by the authority on these services will not be reduced if the section is closed. The decision should be based on comparing the external agency's fees with the costs that can be saved by closing the section.

Activity 5

You could have included various things such as: raw materials (or bought in components) used in manufacturing products; factory labour costs; a share of rent, rates and insurance of the whole building; electricity used in the factory; repairs and maintenance of equipment; costs of maintaining a stores department; cleaning and security.

Activity 6

Cost of raw materials – yes. Cost of bought in components – yes (the same concept as raw materials). Insurance of the factory building – no. Cost of employing people to assemble the products – either yes or not sure (see comments following the activity). Cost of a factory supervisor – no.

Activity 7

You could have included items such as paints, varnish, glue, screws and nails.

Activity 8

Rent of office and factory building – fixed. Sales commissions – variable. Administration expenses – probably fixed (but see note below). Cost of raw materials – variable.

The major part of administration expenses is likely to be a fixed cost (at least in the short term) although there will be a variable element. For example, stationery, telephone and postage costs are likely to increase as business activity increases.

Activity 9

The two factors are: (1) material usage (the quantity of material used was different to the amounts specified in the standard) and (2) material price (the price of raw materials differed from the price used in the standard).

Questions

Questions for self assessment

Answers to self-assessment questions are given at the end of the book.

1.1 Neverwait Ltd, a departmental store, has three separate sales departments. Routine accounting reports are produced at regular intervals to determine the profit of each department. Profit statements for the past month reveal the following:

	Dept 1	Dept 2	Dept 3	Total
Sales income	100,000	80,000	40,000	220,000
Direct costs (cost of goods sold and specific costs of running the department)	70,000	50,000	35,000	155,000
	30,000	30,000	5,000	65,000
Apportionment of general overheads	15,000	12,000	6,000	33,000
Profit/(loss)	15,000	18,000	(1,000)	32,000

A manager reviewing these figures has suggested that Department 3 should be closed down because it is uneconomic.

Required:
(a) Discuss whether closing down Department 3 will be of benefit to the company. Make any assumptions that you consider to be appropriate.
(b) If the general overheads apportioned to each department include an amount for rent of the whole building, state a basis that might have been used to apportion the rent to each department.
(c) Make the following two assumptions:
  • none of the general overheads apportioned to Department 3 can be saved as a result of closing it down
  • future operating results of Departments 1 and 2 will be the same as for the past month.

On these two assumptions, estimate what the profit of the whole business will be for the next month if Department 3 is closed down.

(d) Describe factors other than those relating to the accounting measurements that might have to be considered when deciding whether or not close down Department 3.

1.2 Hypertech Ltd produces and markets one type of product. The accountant has produced the following cost analysis of this product based on the past results:

	£
Variable cost perunit	10
Fixed cost per unit	12
Selling price per unit	30
Profit per unit	8

The fixed cost per unit represents all fixed costs incurred in running the business and has been calculated on the basis that the company will produce and sell 100,000 units of the product.

Required:
Calculate (in whatever form occurs to you) the profit of the company if the following occur:
(a) 80,00 units are made and sold
(b) 100,000 units are made and sold
(c) 120,000 units are made and sold

1.3 Magiboard Ltd set up business on 1 January 1994 to manufacture and sell one type of product. The following operating figures relate to year ending 31 December 1994:

	£
Sales income	100,000
Cost of raw materials used	20,000
Cost of direct labour	10,000
Factory overheads	15,000
Selling and administraation overheads	35,000

The number of units manufactured in 1994 was 30,000 but the number of units sold was 25,000.

Required:

(a) For the purposed of closing stock valuation, calculate the cost per unit on the following two bases:
   (i) marginal cost
   (ii) absorbed cost.

You may assume that direct labour is a part of the marginal cost.

(b) Produce a statement to show the company's profit in its first year on the basis that:
   (i) closing stock is valued at marginal cost
   (ii) closing stock is valued at absorbed cost.

You may use any format that occurs to you for this statement.

Question without answer

The answers to this question is published separately in the *Teacher's Manual*.

1.4 Skirb Ltd manufactures bricks. In 1992 they manufactured and sold 10 million bricks. All bricks are packed on pallets for ease of handling and each pallet contains 1,000 bricks.

In year ending 31 December 1992 all the bricks manufactured were sold at £100 per pallet. The unit cost of a pallet of bricks based on the 1992 level of output were:

	£
Direct materials	30
Direct labour	20
Factory costs: variable	11
fixed	5
Selling and distribution costs: variable	8
fixed	4
Other fixed costs	7

The managing director is currently considering two different courses of action for 1993. There are two production possibilities, as follows:

(i) To take advantage of an offer from an international company to manufacture under licence a special facing brick. Skirb Ltd would be required to pay a royalty (for licence to manufacture) of £5 for every pallet of bricks produced and sold. The new brick would cost £3 less per pallet in direct materials than the present brick, but would involve an increase of factory fixed costs of £40,000 annum.

It is expected that 12 million of the new bricks could be produced and sold at £120 per pallet.

(ii) To maintain production of the present brick but also to attempt to increase sales.

It is expected that sales could be increased to 15 million bricks if the price per pallet were reduced to £90. The increased output would increase direct labour costs by 20% and factory variable costs by 10% over the present level of pallet unit costs.

You may assume that all other cost–revenue relationships will not change.

Required:
Prepare forecast profit estimates for 1993 for each of the proposals in (i) and (ii) above.

(Adapted from an AEB A level question)

2 Cost/volume/profit analysis

Objectives

After you have completed this chapter, you should be able to:
- describe and illustrate how various costs behave in response to changes in the level of activity as measured by the cost driver
- differentiate between fixed, variable and partly-variable costs
- use basic techniques for analysing partly-variable costs into their fixed and variable components
- discuss the concept of contribution per unit and calculate a measure of contribution that can be used by multi-product firms
- identify situations where decisions should be based on measuring performance according to contribution rather than accounting profit
- produce calculations and graphical illustrations to show the relationship between costs and profit at various levels of sales volume
- calculate and discuss the relevance of measures such as break-even point and margin of safety
- discuss some of the limitations of break-even analysis as used by accountants
- use cost/volume/profit analysis to assist management in making decisions

Introduction

Cost/volume/profit (CVP) analysis is an extremely interesting subject and one of the most useful for helping managers with short-term planning and decision making. It is also very popular with examiners; it is quite difficult to find any examination paper on cost accounting where CVP analysis does not appear in one form or another. The techniques involved require costs to be separated into their fixed and variable elements. The text and activities have been written on the assumption that you will have a broad idea of the difference between fixed and variable costs following a study of Chapter 1. CVP analysis considers the way in which total costs will behave over a relatively short time period, such as one year. In the long term, all costs are variable and so CVP analysis is not an appropriate tool for evaluating long-term (strategic) plans and decisions.

CVP analysis is concerned with using cost information rather than with recording costs in the accounting records. As a subject it is sometimes (incorrectly) called 'marginal costing'. This is misleading because marginal costing is an accounting principle whereby the cost of finished goods are determined on the basis of their variable (marginal) cost. There is nothing to stop a company from setting up its recording system to determine product costs on a marginal cost basis, although it will be necessary to recalculate the cost of closing stocks when producing the annual financial statements for shareholders. This is necessary because (as discussed in Chapter 1) financial accounting regulations require the cost of closing stock to be reported on the basis of absorbed cost, not marginal cost. The point that you need to keep in mind is that the marginal cost of a manufactured product is only one of the variable costs that need to be considered in CVP analysis.

Although most of the explanations in this chapter are given in the context of a business selling a physical product that has been bought or manufactured, CVP analysis is equally applicable to businesses that provide services.

2.1 Short-term cost behaviour

It is reasonable for managers to request information that will enable them to assess whether the selling price of a product provides an adequate profit margin over its total cost. The request is reasonable enough but because the total cost of a product will include some costs that are fixed and some that are variable, the information can be misleading unless it is used with care. The terms 'fixed cost' and 'variable cost' are a reference to the way in which total costs for a period behave according to changes in the level of activity. As mentioned in the introduction, CVP analysis will consider a cost to be fixed if it is not likely to change in total over a relatively short time period, such as one year.

Furthermore, the concept of total cost per unit can be ambiguous because there is no precise way of attributing fixed overheads to each unit produced. Whatever methods are used, in practice there will be some arbitrary allocations of overheads to individual products. In this chapter we are not concerned with the various techniques of attributing fixed overheads to each product (these are covered in Chapter 5); we are more concerned with excluding fixed overheads from product costs in order to help managers see the effect of their decisions on future results. You will get an idea of the deception of total cost per unit when making forecasts by working through the activities based on the following data:

Data for the activities

A manufacturing company produces and sells two types of product. The following forecast data is available:

	Product 1	Product 2
Number of units to be produced and sold	40,000	20,000
Selling price per unit	£10	£4
Variable cost per unit	£6	£3

Total fixed overheads for the next accounting period are budgeted at £120,000.

The managing director is concerned about profit margins and has asked the cost accountant to produce information showing the total cost of each unit and the profit earned by each unit. The cost accountant decides that the most appropriate basis for calculating the fixed overhead cost per unit is to average the total of £120,000 evenly over the 60,000 units (this is not very scientific but it will suffice for the purposes of the current activities). The fixed overhead cost per unit (for both products) is, therefore, £2 and the cost accountant submits the following data to the managing director:

	Product 1		Product 2	
Selling price per unit		£10.00		£4.00
Variable cost per unit	£6.00		£3.00	
Fixed cost per unit	2.00		2.00	
Total cost per unit		8.00		5.00
Profit/(loss) per unit		2.00		(1.00)

The sales director has indicated to the board that, because of competition, it is not possible to increase the selling price of Product 2.

Activity 1

The managing director concludes that Product 2 should be withdrawn from sale because it is causing the company to lose money at the rate of £1.00 per unit. On the assumption that fixed overheads will not change in total as a result of the decision, calculate forecast profits for the circumstances described below. Use your own paper (and format) for the calculations but make a note of the profit against each alternative.

1. Product 2 is withdrawn from sale.

2. The company continues to produce and sell Product 2.

Although this was a relatively simple activity, it does illustrate how easy it is to be deceived by the idea of a total cost per unit. We can look at this deception in another way. Assume that the scenario described in the next activity is independent of that for Activity 1.

Activity 2

The company is aiming to make a profit of £70,000 for the next accounting period. The figures show that the profit earned by Product 1 is £2.00 per unit whereas Product 2 is making a loss. The managing director concludes that Product 2 should be withdrawn from sale and then works out that the company must sell (£70,000 ÷ £2) 35,000 units of Product 1 in order to meet the forecast profit of £70,000. The sales director confirms that the sales target of 35,000 units of Product 1 can easily be achieved.

Calculate the profits that will be earned if Product 2 is withdrawn and 35,000 units of Product 1 are sold.

As you can see, this is nowhere near the target profit of £70,000. However, the activity was fictitious and assumed that the managing director was illiterate in matters of cost accounting. It is not difficult to work out how many units of Product 1 must be sold (if Product 2 is withdrawn) in order to earn a profit of £70,000. The approach is to ignore the fixed overhead cost per unit and to make use of the difference between sales price and variable cost per unit.

If you look at the figures for Product 1 again you can see that the difference between sales price and variable cost per unit is (£10 – £6) £4.00. This amount is known as the 'contribution' per unit. The word 'contribution' is used in the sense that each time a unit of Product 1 is sold it contributes £4.00 towards payment of fixed overheads. After selling a certain quantity, the total contribution from the sales of Product 1 will equal the fixed overheads of £120,000 and so each unit sold thereafter will contribute £4.00 towards the profit of £70,000. Consequently, the number of units that must be sold will be a quantity that earns a total contribution equal to the fixed overheads and the target profit.

Activity 3

Using the above explanation, work out the number of units of Product 1 that must be sold in order to earn a profit of £70,000. Assume that Product 2 is withdrawn from sale and that fixed overheads for the period will not alter as a result of the decision.

The figures can be proved by setting out a conventional profit statement in the following form:

Sales (47,500 units at £10 per unit)	475,000
Less variable costs (47,500 units at £6 per unit)	285,000
Total contribution	190,000
Less fixed costs for the period	120,000
Profit	70,000

Activity 3 illustrates the basic approach to CVP analysis. It considers how total **costs** will respond to changes in **volume** so that **profit** at any particular level of volume can be estimated. As with many aspects of cost accounting, the process can be reduced to a formula. In its simplest form, the formula is as follows:

$$\frac{\text{Fixed overheads} + \text{Desired profit}}{\text{Contribution per unit}}$$

The problem with most formulae is that they represent simple models of a real world that is riddled with practical difficulties. For example, how can the above formula be used when analysing the figures of a company that trades with many different types of product? There is no concept of contribution per unit in this case. And how are we going to be able to identify whether a cost is fixed or variable, particularly as some costs are a mixture of both? Practical solutions can be found to these problems, some of which are based on crude techniques and some that are quite sophisticated. Whatever approach is used, you must keep in mind that the objective is to help managers to make better decisions by producing information that shows the relationship between cost volume and profit: we are not trying to make accurate predictions of future results.

2.2 Cost drivers and mixed costs

Variable costs are those where the total amount incurred for a period is a direct result of changes in the level of an activity affecting that cost. The activities that cause total costs to change are called the cost drivers. In a simple model, such as a business that buys things and sells them, the most obvious variable cost is the cost of goods sold, and in this case the cost driver is sales activity. Over a relatively short period (such as one year) most of the other costs incurred by this business will not be influenced by the level of sales activity and will be classed as fixed.

The term 'sales activity' is, however, slightly ambiguous because it could be a reference to sales quantities or sales value. If we simplify the model even further and relate it to a business that deals in one type of product, we can be more precise over the term 'sales activity' and identify the cost driver as sales quantities (as you did in Activity 3). When we come to deal with multi-product firms we will have to find a way of using sales value as the cost driver, but we will leave that for now and look at cost drivers in a more general way.

A cost driver is any activity that generates costs. A change in the level of that activity causes the total cost to change. Some activities (such as running a machine) cause total costs to vary in the short term; others (such as quality control inspections) cause total costs to vary in the long term. The term 'cost driver' is relatively new to cost accounting, and became part of our language when a technique called 'activity-based costing' (ABC) was exhorted as being more useful than traditional costing for identifying product costs. Despite being one of the few innovations in cost accounting over the past 50 years, ABC has not (at the time of writing this edition) been adopted by very many companies in the UK. There is clearly a lively interest in the subject because a number of surveys have been done which show that about 20% of the companies surveyed have adopted ABC and about 90% are considering it. One of the practical problems of adopting ABC is that it requires an extensive study and analysis of overheads in order to isolate the activities that generate costs.

The reason why manufacturers are taking such a keen interest in ABC can be related to the way in which production methods have changed over the past 50 years. If we look back to the 1930s we will find that production methods were labour-intensive. In those circumstances, production overheads were a very small part of total costs and there was no need to be very scientific when calculating the overhead cost per unit. The methods developed were based on accumulating the total production overheads for a period and then using some general activity measure (such as total direct labour hours) to spread this total over all the products made in that period. This approach (which is still used by most companies) makes no attempt to identify how each type of product consumes the benefits provided by various activities.

Today, production methods are such that overheads form the largest part of the cost of a product. The use of a broad (often time-related) average for attributing overheads to each product is misleading when the demands made on production resources (as represented by the cost of overheads) will vary from one product to another. For example, a part of the cost of running a raw materials stores department is driven by the number of times that materials are issued to production. If the manufacturing process of a particular product involves frequent issues of various materials, that product should be attributed with a higher proportion of the cost of running the stores department than another product that requires (say) one single issue at the start of the process.

By associating costs with cost drivers, ABC treats more costs as variable than when traditional costing is used (albeit that some are classed as long-term variable costs). You will learn how ABC works, and how the cost information can be used, when studying overhead absorption in Chapter 5. Some of the variable cost information produced by an ABC system could probably be used in CVP analysis but because not very many companies have adopted ABC it is difficult to assess the extent to which the two techniques are compatible. We will, therefore, continue the study of CVP analysis on the assumption that a detailed analysis of overheads is not available to most companies. In these cases we will have to use some of the less sophisticated techniques in order to split overheads between fixed and variable for the purposes of CVP analysis. In order to do this it will be necessary to identify a cost driver.

Activity 4

See if you can identify likely cost drivers for the following types of cost. Remember that a cost driver is an activity of some kind that causes the total cost to vary with the level of that activity.

1. Cost of power for running a particular machine
2. Sales commissions
3. Cost of running a delivery fleet
4. Cost of running a finished goods department
5. Cost of running a hospital X-ray department

Activity 4 includes examples of where the total cost for a period will contain both fixed and variable costs. Delivery costs is a good example because (as mentioned in Chapter 1) running costs will vary with the number of miles run, whereas tax and insurance costs are fixed. In CVP analysis, costs must be classed as either fixed or variable – without this split the technique is impossible. If the cost accounting system has not been set up on an ABC basis, there will be one total cost for the period and some method will have to be found for separating this total into its fixed and variable elements.

Various mathematical techniques are used for this purpose; some of the more sophisticated are usually studied under the heading of 'regression analysis'. It has become more practical to make use of these techniques in recent times because computer programs are readily available that remove the need to perform complex mathematical calculations. The subject of regression analysis is not covered by this book; instead, we will use a fairly simple technique that produces adequate results in most cases. We will call it 'high/low analysis.' The use of this technique is frequently required in cost accounting exams at a foundation level.

The basic idea of high/low analysis is to observe the changes in total costs between two levels of activity, a high level and a low level, recorded for two separate time periods. By observing the change in total costs between these two levels we can estimate the variable element in the total cost. If we can estimate the variable element, the fixed cost can be deduced as a balancing figure. You will see how it works by completing a few activities based on the following data:

Details for the activities

A company has charged all production overheads to a single account. It now needs to ascertain a variable overhead cost per unit and has decided that the most appropriate cost driver is machine hours. In order to try to identify the variable cost per machine hour, the following series of figures have been extracted from the accounting records for the past 6 years:

Year	Machine hours	Total overheads
1992	110,000	£330,000
1991	100,000	£305,000
1990	90,000	£280,000
1989	87,000	£272,500
1988	105,000	£317,500
1987	80,000	£255,000

(These details are based on part of an examination question set by the Association of Accounting Technicians.)

Computer programs that process data for regression analysis will require an input of the entire series of figures. In high/low analysis we ignore everything apart from the highest (110,000 machine hours) and lowest (80,000 machine hours) levels of activity.

Activity 5

Complete the following table. This merely requires you to enter relevant data from the above schedule and to calculate figures for the column labelled 'increase' for both machine hours and total cost.

	Activity levels		
	Low level	High level	Increase
Activity (machine hours)			
Total costs			

Make sure that your figures agree with the Key before moving on to the next activity.

Activity 6

Observation of the 'increase' column should tell us something. Notice that an increase of 30,000 machine hours has caused total costs to increase by £75,000. Make a note here of any information that can be assumed from this observation.

Having determined the variable cost per hour, the fixed cost can be found by deducting the variable cost from the total cost. As a check on the arithmetic, we can find this balance at each level of activity.

Activity 7

Complete the following table. This requires you to deduct the variable cost from total costs (at each level of activity) in order to derive fixed costs as a balancing figure.

	Activity levels	
	Low level	High level
Activity (machine hours)	80,000	110,000
Total costs Deduct variable costs (at £2.50 per hour) Fixed cost (balance)	£255,000	£330,000

The fact that fixed costs work out to be the same at both levels of activity is not conclusive proof of the actual amount, it merely proves that the arithmetic is correct. The high/low analysis makes broad assumptions over a wide range of activity, but it is usually adequate for the purposes of CVP analysis unless there are some extraneous factors affecting the figures. You will be using the technique in various situations throughout this chapter.

2.3 Contribution to sales ratio

The reason why we have devoted so much time to identifying variable cost per unit is because CVP analysis makes use of something called contribution (the difference between sales price and variable cost). In section 2.1 you used the idea of contribution per unit to work out how many units had to be sold in order to earn a specified profit. In that case you were dealing with a business that was selling one type of product. This is not very realistic, since most businesses trade with a variety of different products.

In order to use CVP analysis for multi-product firms some method is needed to determine the contribution for a typical mix of products sold by that firm. There are various approaches to this problem but one of the most useful is to use something known as the 'contribution to sales ratio' (sometimes abbreviated to CSR). The ratio between contribution and sales is usually expressed as a percentage. Consider the following figures for a period:

Sales	£100,000
Variable cost of sales	60,000
Contribution	40,000
Fixed costs	30,000
Profit	10,000

In this case, the contribution to sales ratio is 40% (40,000/100,000 × 100/1). In other words, contribution is 40% of sales. If you have studied financial accounting to any extent you will see some similarity between the CSR and the gross profit margin. In financial accounting, gross profit represents the difference between sales and the cost of goods sold; gross profit margin is an expression of gross profit as a percentage of sales. If the only variable cost in a business is the cost of goods sold, gross profit and contribution are the same.

An awareness of the gross profit margin might help with an understanding of CSR but it is important to think about how the two can differ. In most businesses there will be costs that vary with sales activity other than the cost of goods sold. A clear example is sales commissions. In financial accounting the total amount spent on sales commissions is not treated as a part of the cost of goods sold, it is classified as a selling and distribution cost. Consequently, sales commissions are not taken into account when calculating gross profit for financial accounting but they are when calculating contribution for CVP analysis.

We must now consider how the contribution to sales ratio can be used in CVP analysis. In most firms there will be a variety of products being sold, and the CSR for each type of product will differ. For example, some products might be earning a contribution of 50%, others will be earning 30% and some 20%. There could be quite a wide range of CSRs depending on the variety of products being sold. However, if we take an average sales mix of these products, we will find an average CSR. The term 'sales mix' is a technical term used to express how total sales is made up in terms of a typical mixture of the quantities of different products, such as 30% of product A, 45% of product B and 25% of product C. In many firms, this sales mix is relatively constant, so the average CSR will also be relatively constant from one year to the next.

If the contribution to sales ratio for a typical sales mix is 40%, it means that (on average) each £1.00 in sales will bring in a contribution of £0.40. In the earlier explanation of CVP analysis (section 2.1) we thought of contribution in terms of an amount per physical unit of sales; we must now think about it in terms of an amount per monetary unit (i.e. £1.00) of sales. In section 2.1 we were thinking about how many physical units needed to be sold in order to earn a specified profit; we must now think about how many £1.00 units must be received in order to earn a specified profit. The basic formula stated in Section 2.1 can be restated as follows:

$$\frac{\text{Fixed overheads} + \text{Desired profit}}{\text{Contribution per £1.00 of sales (expressed as a decimal of £1.00)}}$$

This formula will provide an answer in terms of sales value.

Activity 8

A company trades in a variety of products and the average contribution to sales ratio for the last year was 30%. Total fixed overheads for the next year are estimated at £60,000. Calculate the total value of sales that must achieved in order to earn a profit of £30,000 for the next year. You can assume that there will be no significant change in the sales mix during the next year.

As with most of these activities, it is always useful to check your calculations by setting out the relevant figures in a profit statement. The answer to Activity 8 can be proved as follows:

Sales (£90,000/0.30)	300,000
Less variable costs (70% × 300,000)	210,000
Contribution (30% × 300,000)	90,000
Less fixed costs	60,000
Profit	30,000

We can now combine the idea of CSR with high/low analysis in order to solve a particular type of problem. Suppose we are presented with the following figures for two recent periods in respect of a multi-product firm:

	Low level	High level
Sales	200,000	400,000
Profit	50,000	150,000

The problem is to determine the sales value that must be achieved in order to earn a profit of £200,000. In doing this we will assume that prices have been (and will continue to be) relatively stable, and that no significant changes in the sales mix will occur during the next period.

At first sight the problem might seem to be insoluble. On reflection, you will realize that the difference between sales value and profit is represented by total costs, and that these total costs will consist of both variable costs and fixed costs. If we can work out the variable costs (as a percentage of sales) by using high/low analysis, we can derive the fixed costs as a balancing figure. We will also know the CSR because if variable costs are (say) 60% of sales then the CSR will be 40%. You will be able to solve the problem by working through Activities 9–12.

Activity 9

Complete the table below. You did something similar in Activity 5: the main difference here is that the cost driver is sales value, whereas the cost driver in Activity 5 was machine hours. The data provided above does not give total costs but the amount can be derived from the information given. Figures for the 'increase' column will have to be calculated.

	Activity levels		
	Low level	High level	Increase
Activity (sales value)			
Total costs			

Check your figures with the Key before proceeding to the next activity.

Activity 10

You must now use the information provided by the 'increase' column. Notice that an increase in sales of £200,000 has caused costs to increase by £100,000. This should tell you something about the variable costs (as a percentage of sales). Make a note of the relevant information here.

Activity 11

You should now be able to determine fixed costs by deducting variable costs from the total costs. You should do this at both levels in order to check the arithmetic. You will find the answer by completing the table below.

	Activity levels	
	Low level	High level
Activity (sales value)	£200,000	£400,000
Total costs Deduct variable costs (50% of sales) Fixed cost (balance)	£150,000	£250,000

We now have all the information needed to solve the problem. If variable costs are 50% of sales then the CSR is 50%. Fixed costs are £50,000 per period. The original problem was to determine the sales level that would produce a profit of £200,000. You have already seen how the basic formula can be adapted for use with the CSR.

Activity 12

Solve the problem by calculating the sales value needed to earn a profit of £200,000.

2.4 Break-even analysis

By tradition, the subject of CVP analysis tends to be built around something known as the 'break-even point'. The term 'break-even' means that neither profit nor loss will occur, and the level of sales at which this happens is known as the 'break-even point'. Although the break-even point is quite an important indicator in analysing alternative business strategies, it should not be thought of as the central issue in the subject of CVP analysis.

Arithmetically, the break-even point can be calculated quite simply by using the basic formula for CVP analysis (as discussed earlier) but with the 'desired profit' being set at zero. In other words, we need to calculate the level of sales at which the total contribution will be equal to the fixed costs for the period (fixed costs plus zero = fixed costs). The components used in the formula will depend on whether the situation being analysed can be based on contribution per unit (as with a single product) or contribution per £1.00 (as when using the CSR for a multi-product concern).

In the case of an analysis for a single product, the formula will be as follows:

$$\frac{\text{Fixed costs}}{\text{Contribution per unit}}$$

In situations where the analysis is concerned with a mix of products and the approach used is based on the CSR, the formula becomes:

$$\frac{\text{Fixed costs}}{\text{Contribution per £1.00 of sales (as a decimal of £1.00)}}$$

Activity 13

1. Calculate the break-even point for the situation described in Activity 3. In this case your answer will be expressed as a number of units (sales quantity).

2. Calculate the break-even point for the situation described in Activity 8. In this case your answer will be expressed in £s (sales value).

It might seem a little strange for a subject to focus on a level of sales at which neither profit nor loss will be made, but the break-even point is quite an important indicator in short-term planning and decision making. In a simple situation, the break-even point shows the minimum level of sales that must be achieved if the business is to avoid incurring losses. This can then be considered alongside other information such as projected sales for the period. Lending institutions (such as banks) quite often consider the break-even point on any new project for which funding is being sought. It gives them an idea of the risks attached to the project.

In most cases, the break-even point is associated with another indicator known as the 'margin of safety'. Bearing in mind that CVP analysis is concerned with forward looking projections, the margin of safety can be stated as the range of sales between the break-even point and the forecast (or budgeted) level of sales. As a measurement, the margin of safety can be expressed in different ways; for example, it could be stated as being a number of units (if the project relates to one type of product), as a sales value, or as a percentage of the forecast level of sales. It is usually more helpful if the margin of safety is expressed as a percentage of forecast sales. You will see why after working through the following illustration.

Illustration

A summary of the information relating to Activities 3 and 13 (part 1) is as follows:

	Units	Sales
Forecast sales	47,500	£475,000
Break-even point	30,000	300,000
Margin of safety	17,500	£175,000

In the above, the margin of safety has been expressed in absolute terms (as either 17,500 units or sales of £175,000) and although information in this form has some value, it is difficult to use. It is preferable to express the margin of safety in relative terms by comparing it to the forecast sales and stating the relationship as a percentage. In the above example, the margin of safety (whether we use units or sales value) is 36.8% of forecast sales. In view of the high level of approximation associated with CVP analysis, it would be quite reasonable to refer to the margin of safety in this example as 37%. We now know that actual sales can be anything up to 37% less than forecast before the business starts to incur a loss.

Activity 14

A summary of the information from Activities 8 and 13 (part 2) is as follows:

	Sales value
Forecast sales	£300,000
Break-even point	£200,000

Calculate the margin of safety as a percentage of sales.

The break-even point and margin of safety are quite useful indicators when managers are faced with having to chose between two (or more) different projects. In this context the measurements help with assessing the risks associated with each project. You can get an idea of how they are used by considering the following.

A manager must decide whether the company should invest in either Project A or Project B. The following information has been obtained for the two projects:

	Project A	**Project B**
Forecast sales	£400,000	£600,000
Break-even point	200,000	450,000

As you can see, Project A will break even when only 50% of the forecast sales have been earned (the margin of safety is 50%) whereas Project B has a margin of safety of 25% and will not break even until 75% of forecast sales have been earned. From a safety point of view it looks as if Project A would be preferred. Unfortunately this is only one factor in the whole thorny problem of risk assessment. The word 'risk' has a technical meaning in business language and it is related to the range of possible returns from an investment. You will get some idea of risk assessment from section 2.7 and you will be studying it again in Chapter 12.

2.5 Graphical presentation

Since CVP analysis is concerned with measuring how variables (such as costs and revenues) change in response to changes in activity, it readily lends itself to presentation in graphical form. The graphs that we will be producing here are sometimes referred to as accountants' graphs in order to distinguish them from similar models produced by economists.

In the accountant's graph we make a number of simplistic assumptions which tend to be scorned by economists because these assumptions do not correspond to the way things work in real life. For example, we will be assuming that the variable cost per unit (or per £1.00 of sales) remains the same throughout the whole range of sales activity, yet in real life the variable cost per unit is likely to be reduced at the higher levels of activity due to the economies of scale. The main point to keep in mind on these arguments is that we are not trying to produce accurate predictions of future results; we are merely trying to show the relationship between cost, volume and profit so that managers can make decisions that are better than those they might make without this information. The limitations of CVP analysis are discussed more fully in section 2.6.

There are three types of graph in popular use: two of them are alternative ways of presenting what are usually called 'break-even graphs', the third type is usually called a 'profit/volume graph'. We will start with a simple break-even graph. The X axis (the one at the bottom) is scaled for the different volume levels, usually sales volume, either in physical units (for a single product) or sales value. The Y axis (the one on the left) is scaled in monetary values and will measure the costs or revenues for different levels of sales volume. It is easier for beginners to prepare these graphs for a single product concern and so our graphs will be based on the following data:

Selling price per unit: £30
Variable cost per unit: £10
Fixed costs for the period: £300,000
Budgeted sales level: 30,000 units.

The graph will be set up so that the X axis has a maximum output of 30,000 units. Since the highest monetary value relates to sales, the Y axis will have a maximum value of (30,000 × £30.00) £900,000. Before entering any lines for the variables on the graph, the two axes will appear as in Figure 2.1.

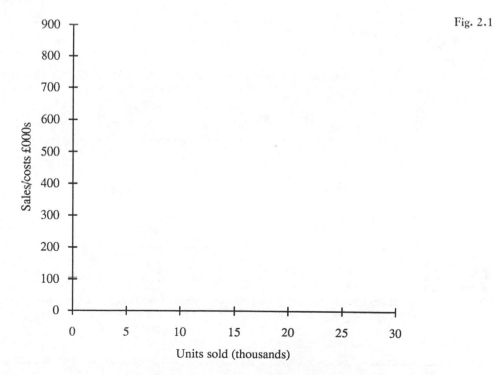

Fig. 2.1

Break-even graphs have three lines: two are for costs and one is for sales revenue. Suppose we were to draw the graph shown in Figure 2.2.

Fig. 2.2

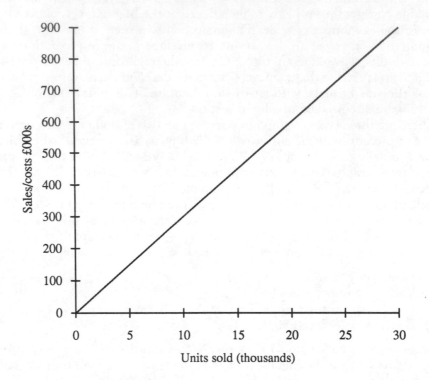

Activity 15

Identify what this line represents and (after checking with the Key) label it on Figure 2.2. Notice that with output at zero, the value is zero; with the output at 30,000 units, the value is £900,000.

Now we will add one of the two cost lines; this can be drawn as shown in Figure 2.3.

Activity 16

Identify what this line represents and (after checking with the Key) label it on Figure 2.3. Notice that the amount stays the same throughout all levels of activity.

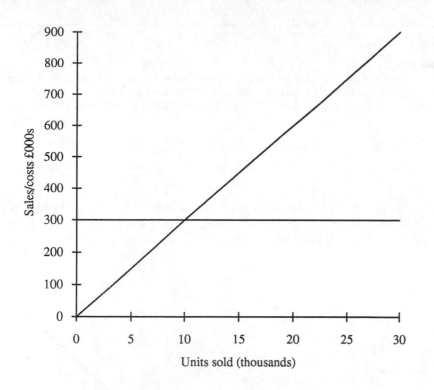

Fig. 2.3

If we now add the second cost line (the last of the three lines) the completed graph will appear as in Figure 2.4.

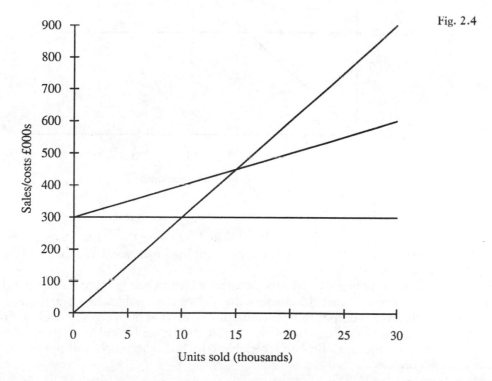

Fig. 2.4

Activity 17

Identify what this third (and final) line represents. Be careful with this before you answer because it easy to jump to the wrong conclusions. Notice that at zero sales, the cost is £300,000; at 30,000 units of sales, the cost is £600,000. After identifying the line (and checking with the Key) label all three lines on Figure 2.4.

The point at which the sales line crosses over the total costs line is the break-even point. If you drop a perpendicular from the break-even point to the X axis you will find that it occurs at 15,000 units, as shown in Figure 2.5.

Fig. 2.5

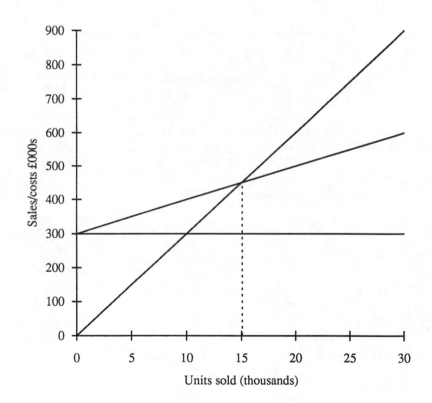

The break-even point can be checked by using the basic formula (fixed costs divided by contribution per unit), as follows: £300,000 ÷ £20 = 15,000 units.

You will notice that the above form of break-even graph does not include a variable cost line. Consequently, it does not enable the contribution at each level of output to be measured. A variation of this graph excludes the fixed cost line but shows the variable cost and total cost lines. After drawing the sales line and variable cost line, the graph will appear as in Figure 2.6.

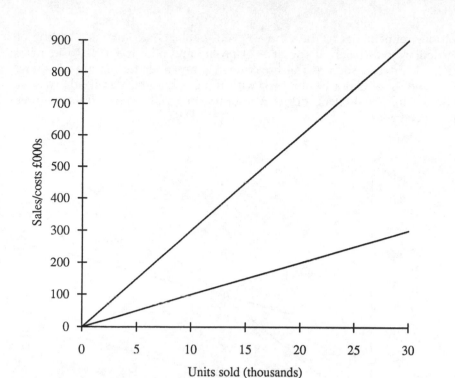

Fig. 2.6

Notice that the area between these two lines represents the contribution at different levels of sales. If we now draw the total cost line it will start at £300,000 (the fixed costs). At 30,000 units the total cost will be (£300,000 + (30,000 × £20)) £600,000. A line connecting these two points will run parallel to the variable cost line and the completed graph is as shown in Figure 2.7.

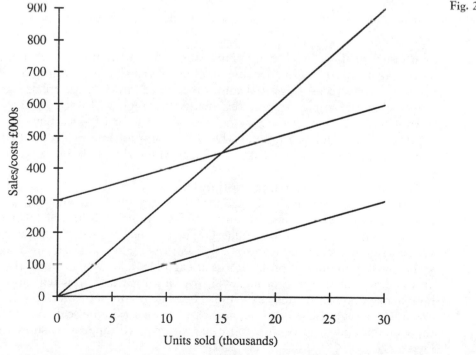

Fig. 2.7

Various refinements to these break-even graphs could include shading of particular areas (such as the area of profit) and adding labels to identify items of interest such as the break-even point and the margin of safety. The graph should not be cluttered with too much verbal detail otherwise it will lose its visual effect. Figure 2.8 shows the graph after certain features have been added.

Fig. 2.8

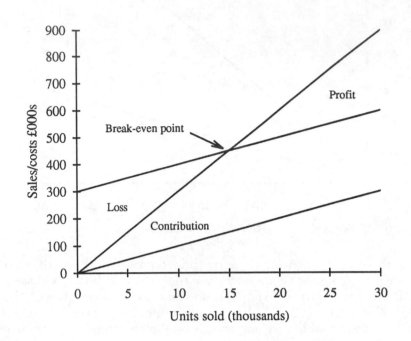

The visual focus of break-even graphs tends to be the break-even point. This can be quite useful because it gives a visual presentation of the proportion of forecast sales that must be achieved in order to break even. In the above example, anyone reviewing the graph will notice that the break-even point occurs when one half of the forecast sales have been achieved. This might be helpful when the graph for one project is being compared to one for an alternative project where the break-even point is seen to occur earlier or later.

Although break-even graphs do show the area of profit (and loss) it is almost impossible to read the amount of forecast profit at different sales levels. A graph which makes it easier to read profit at different levels of output is known as a profit/volume graph. In this case the X axis is still scaled to show increasing levels of sales, but the scale points on the Y axis will show the amount of profit or loss at each level. If (as is normal) the X axis is drawn at the zero profit level, the line for the Y axis will appear both above and below the X axis line. The scale points above zero on the Y axis are for profit, those below are for losses. If we set up the scale points for the example we have been using, the two axes will appear as shown in Figure 2.9.

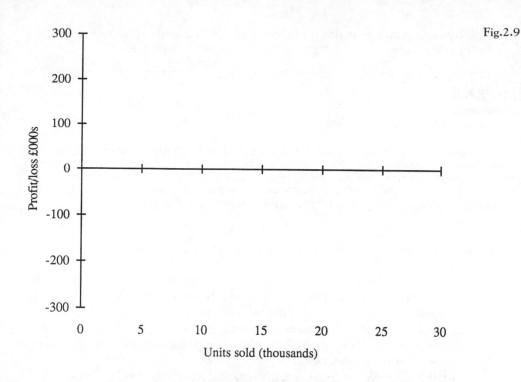

Fig.2.9

One line is drawn on the graph to enable the profit (or loss) at each sales level to be read from the scale on the Y axis. This line (in our example) will connect the loss at zero sales with the profit at sales of 30,000 units. At zero sales, the loss will equal the fixed overheads of £300,000; at 30,000 units the profit will be £300,000 (i.e. (30,000 × £20) – £300,000). When this line is drawn, the completed graph will appear as shown in Figure 2.10.

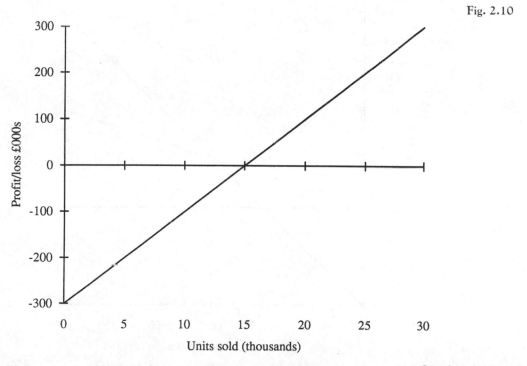

Fig. 2.10

You will notice that the line crosses the X axis at the break-even point of 15,000 units.

Activity 18

Review the graph in Figure 2.10 and answer the following:

Although the line has been drawn to enable profit (or loss) at each level of sales to be read, it is a specific variable dependent upon sales volume. This particular variable has not been plotted on any of the earlier graphs. See if you can identify what this variable is and after checking with the Key, label the line on the above graph by giving it a name. If you find this difficult, think about the fact that from zero units to 15,000 units, the point at which the line intersects with the Y axis, there is an increase of £300,000.

The three types of graph dealt with in this chapter have been illustrated by measuring sales activity in terms of physical units. We could do this because we were dealing with the sales of an individual product. If we were producing a graph for a multi-product concern we would construct it on the basis of the CSR. In this case the scale points on the X axis would be stated in terms of sales value.

In the example we have been using, forecast sales are (30,000 × £30) £900,000 and the CSR is 66.67% (or 2/3). When plotting the total cost line we will not think about variable cost as £10.00 per unit, we will think of it as 33.33% (or 1/3) of sales. Consequently, total costs at a sales level of £900,000 will be found by adding 1/3 of £900,000 to the fixed costs of £300,000. The total cost at a sales level of £900,000 is, therefore, £600,000 (the same as when we added the variable cost per unit to the fixed costs).

Fig. 2.11

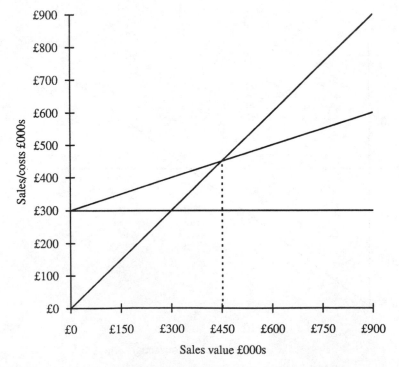

A graph produced on this basis will look exactly the same as before except that the scale points on the X axis are expressed as a sales value. The first of the two types of break-even graph would appear as shown in Figure 2.11.

2.6 Limitations of CVP analysis

Most of the limitations (and criticisms) of CVP analysis stem from the assumptions on which the techniques are based. These limitations were mentioned briefly in section 2.5 but they are easier to see following a study of break-even graphs. The main assumptions regarding costs and revenues which can be criticized are:

1. Fixed costs will remain the same throughout all levels of activity
2. Variable cost per unit is the same throughout all levels of activity
3. Selling prices will remain the same throughout all levels of activity.

These three assumptions are considered to be unrealistic for the following reasons:

1. Fixed costs are likely to show a stepped increase as business activity increases. For example, there could be a point at which it might be necessary to employ more admin and sales staff in order to cope with a higher level of sales activity.
2. At the higher levels of activity, variable costs per unit are likely to decrease because of factors such as higher discounts for bulk buying.
3. In order to achieve the higher level of sales it might be necessary to reduce selling prices by offering special trade discounts.

The counter argument to these criticisms is that the assumptions on which we base CVP analysis are likely to hold good for a relevant range of activity. Providing it is understood that our figures (and charts) are limited to a particular range of activity, the information produced will be of benefit to managers for short-term decisions. We could construct break-even charts by recognizing changes that might occur outside of the relevant range but information in this form starts to become so complex that it is difficult for managers to use.

A further criticism of CVP analysis is probably due to a misunderstanding over what the procedure attempts to achieve. It is often stated that the figures assume that everything produced (in the case of a manufacturer) will be sold. In other words, there will be no change in stock levels between two accounting dates. This is a reference to the fact that when profits are measured for financial accounting, the effect of including fixed overheads in the value of closing stock is to carry these overheads forward from one period to the next (see Chapter 1).

The implication of this criticism is that the figures for projected profit produced by CVP analysis will not hold true if there is a change in the quantity of closing stocks between two accounting dates. The counter argument to this is that CVP analysis does not pretend to be an accurate barometer of what the reported profits will be, it merely tries to help managers make better decisions by setting out the relationships between cost, volume and profit.

2.7 CVP analysis and risk assessment

Since CVP analysis deals with matters such as the margin of safety, and also identifies how profits will respond to changes in sales activity, it clearly plays some part in helping managers to identify the risks associated with a new proposal. Risk assessment is a fascinating subject but it cannot be studied fully at a foundation level. There are various factors affecting the risk of a particular project. One of these is called financial risk because it deals with the way that the project is being financed (in the form of loans and share capital). You will learn about financial risk in Chapter 12. Another aspect of risk analysis is called 'business risk' and this is related to the returns from the project itself. We can look at one aspect of business risk in this chapter.

The word 'risk' has a technical meaning when referring to the assessment of alternative projects in which money could be invested. It is related to the volatility of returns from the investment. You can get some idea of how risk might be measured by working through Activity 19.

Activity 19

A company has a choice of investing in one of two new projects. The returns (in the form of profits) from each project have been assessed as follows:

Project 1: The profits are likely to be somewhere between £10,000 and £12,000

Project 2: The profits are likely to be somewhere between £50 and £100,000

Make a note here of which project seems to carry the greatest risk.

You probably think that your reaction to this activity was little more than common sense. After all, the returns from Project 1 do seem to be fairly certain by comparison to those for Project 2. It was the absence of certainty in Project 2 that influenced your assessment of the risks associated with it. At a more scientific level, you have noticed the range (or volatility) of possible returns from the two projects; this range is fairly narrow in Project 1 but quite wide in Project 2. Measurements relating to this range form the basis of any scientific measurement of risk.

The volatility of possible returns from competing projects might be related to the relationship between fixed and variable costs for each project. Consider the following data which has been prepared for two alternative strategies of producing a particular product. Scheme A involves using relatively cheap equipment whereas Scheme B uses highly sophisticated equipment (people who like using jargon would describe these alternatives by stating that Scheme A is 'low-tech' and Scheme B is 'high-tech'). As a result, the variable cost per unit is higher under Scheme A (the low-tech strategy) than it is under Scheme B. The fixed costs for each strategy are mainly influenced by the annual depreciation charge of the equipment used, and so fixed costs are lower under Scheme A than they are for Scheme B.

	Scheme A (low-tech)	Scheme B (high-tech)
Selling price per unit (at all levels sales)	£200	£200
Variable of cost per unit	150	100
Fixed costs (including depreciation) per period	£100,000	£300,000
Forecast level of sales (for the period)	7,000 units	7,000 units

In order to find some way of calculating an indicator that can be used in risk analysis, we need to establish the level of sales at which the profits under each scheme will be identical. This information is useful in its own right but we need it in order to calculate a particular ratio. There are various ways of finding this level of sales: we could, for example, draw up a profit volume graph with a contribution line for each scheme. Profits will be equal under either scheme where the two lines cross each other. We could then read the level of sales at which this occurs from the X axis. If this approach were taken, the graph would be as shown in Figure 2.12.

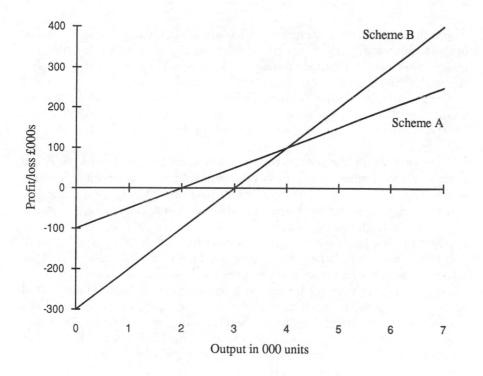

Fig. 2.12

You will notice that profits under each scheme are equal at 4,000 units. Mathematically, this could have been calculated in several ways but the most useful approach is to use our basic knowledge of CVP analysis. Notice that under Scheme B the contribution per unit is £50 greater than it is under Scheme A. The profits under either scheme will be identical when the additional contribution from Scheme B (£50.00 per unit) covers the additional fixed costs of operating Scheme B. The fixed costs under Scheme B exceed those under Scheme A by £200,000, and so equilibrium in profits occurs at (£200,000 ÷ £50.00) 4,000 units.

Activity 20

You can prove that the profits under each scheme are equal at sales of 4,000 units by completing the table below. Apart from proving the calculation, these figures will be used in calculating a ratio for the analysis of risk.

	Scheme A (low-tech)	Scheme B (high-tech)
Sales (4,000 units at £200 each)	800,000	800,000
Variable costs		
Fixed cost	100,000	300,000
Profit ( )		

The ratio that we are now going to calculate is usually called the 'degree of operational gearing' (DOG). Various other names are used to describe this ratio: sometimes it is called operational leverage. Whatever name is used, the underlying concept is to find a measure that will enable us to express how profits will change (between the two alternatives) according to changes in the level of sales. But before we see how this ratio is calculated we should take a closer look at the word 'profit' as used in the table for Activity 20.

When we identify the returns from a business project, the word 'profit' by itself is always ambiguous. This is because profit can be struck at various levels. If you look at the published profit and loss account of a company, you will see various figures being described as profit. As you read through the account from top to bottom, you will see things like: gross profit, operating profit, profit before tax, profit after tax and perhaps other types of profit in some cases. When measuring the DOG ratio we always look at profits before tax and before interest charges. This ensures that we consider the returns purely at an operating level, ignoring any influence on reported profits that might arise from the way that the project is financed. In management accounting, profit at the operating level is called 'earnings before interest and tax', usually identified by the acronym EBIT. You can remind yourself of this by writing the letters EBIT (in the brackets) after the word 'profit' in the above table.

The DOG ratio is calculated by using the following formula:

$$\frac{\text{Sales less variable costs}}{\text{EBIT}}$$

Notice that the numerator is the same as contribution. For the purposes of comparing these two projects, the DOG ratio will be calculated using the figures for sales of 4,000 units (i.e. the point at which profits under each scheme are identical). The result of the fraction is expressed as a number of times (i.e. the number of times that the denominator goes into the numerator).

Activity 21

Calculate the DOG ratio for Scheme A and Scheme B using the figures that apply when sales are at 4,000 units. Express the ratio as a number of times.

Scheme A   Scheme B

These indicators are a mathematical expression of the sensitivity of EBIT to changes in sales levels. The DOG ratio for Scheme A is 2 times, whereas for Scheme B it is 4 times. This means, for example, that if sales quantities increase by 10% (to 4,400 units) the EBIT under Scheme A will increase by (2 × 10%) 20%, whereas under Scheme B it will increase by (4 × 10%) 40%. The same rate of change will occur if there is a decrease in sales, except that here we would be describing the rate of decrease in profit.

Activity 22

You can prove the above argument by working out what the EBIT will be under each scheme If sales quantities decrease by 10% to 3,600 units. You should then compare the EBIT at 3,600 units (for each scheme) with that for 4,000 units and calculate the rate of change. Use the table below.

	Scheme A (low-tech)	Scheme B (high-tech)
Sales (3,600 units at £200 each)	720,000	720,000
Variable costs (3,600 units)		
Fixed costs	100,000	300,000
EBIT		
EBIT at 4,000 units	£100,000	£100,000
Percentage decrease in EBIT by comparison to EBIT at 4,000 units		

Scheme B has a much higher degree of operational gearing than Scheme A and, therefore, the profit under Scheme B is much more sensitive to changes in the level of sales. Since the assessment of business risk is related to the volatility of returns, Scheme B carries much more risk than Scheme A. This is also supported by the profit volume graph for the two schemes, where you will see that Scheme A breaks even much earlier in the sales cycle than Scheme B and also has a much higher margin of safety.

None of these figures is intended to provide a definitive answer to the question: which of the two schemes should the company adopt? All we have done is to analyse the figures and provide managers with information that will help them to make a decision. They will consider this information alongside many other factors – perhaps one of the most crucial in this case would be the degree of confidence they have in reaching the target sales of 7,000 units.

2.8 Contribution and decision making

The concept of contribution (the difference between sales price and variable cost) is quite often the relevant data that should be used when providing managers with information for making decisions. In this chapter we have seen how contribution could be relevant to a decision on whether or not to withdraw a product from sale. The same approach is needed when deciding whether or not to close down a segment of the business. We have also seen how CVP analysis can help with the problem of identifying the risks associated with alternative strategies. There are several other decision problems where contribution is the key factor but it is not appropriate to deal with them in a chapter on CVP analysis. They are covered in Chapter 11, where the following situations are included:

- special orders when the firm has (or does not have) spare capacity
- optimum product mix when production resources are in short supply
- closing a business segment.

On balance, it is preferable to leave these problems until you reach Chapter 11 but you could study them now if you wish.

Summary

The main learning points in this chapter can be summarized as follows:
- CVP analysis is concerned mainly with providing forecast inform-ation, it is not concerned with the principles that are used for recording product costs in the books
- the techniques used require costs to be separated into their fixed and variable elements; the variable production cost (marginal cost) is only one example of a variable cost
- the concept of total cost per unit is ambiguous and can cause wrong decisions to be made
- the basic approach to CVP analysis is to treat fixed costs as cost for the period rather than as a part of the cost of a product
- CVP analysis requires all costs to be classified as either fixed or variable
- costs that are a mixture of both fixed and variable can be separated by using the high/low technique (unless costing methods such as ABC have ensured that the split has been recorded in the accounting records)
- the basic formula of CVP analysis is to divide fixed costs plus desired profit by the contribution per unit, or by the contribution per £1.00 of sales

- when determining the break-even point, the desired profit is zero
- in mixed product companies, the contribution to sales ratio is usually used as a substitute for contribution per unit
- the data produced by CVP analysis can be presented in graphical form: there are two common types of break-even graph and one type of profit/volume graph
- it is important for managers to understand that the data on which CVP analysis is based will only be reliable within a certain range (the relevant range) of activity
- some of the criticisms of CVP analysis stem from a misunderstanding of what the procedure attempts to do: the main objective is to analyse the relationship between cost, volume and profit
- CVP analysis plays an important part in the assessment of risk of any proposed business project
- the DOG ratio provides a measure of the sensitivity of EBIT to changes in sales levels
- contribution is often the relevant data that should be used in providing managers with information for making decisions

Throughout this chapter we have been dealing with the basic principles of CVP analysis. It is important that you should attempt to use these principles for solving various kinds of business problem. The questions at the end of this chapter illustrate the wide variety of examination question that can be set on this topic, and provide you with an opportunity to practise using these principles.

Activity 1

1. The profit will be £40,000, which you could have calculated as follows:

Sales (40,000 × £10)	400,000
Less variable cost (40,000 × £6)	240,000
	160,000
Less fixed costs for the period	120,000
Profit	40,000

2. The profit will be £60,000, which you could have calculated as follows:

Sales (40,000 × £10) + (20,000 × £4)	480,000
Variable costs (40,000 × £6) + (20,000 × £3)	300,000
	180,000
Fixed costs for the period	120,000
Profit	60,000

Note that the difference of £20,000 between the two profits arises because strategy 1 will cause the company to lose the contribution (see later text) of £1.00 per unit from the sales of Product 2.

Activity 2

Sales (35,000 × £10)	350,000
Variable costs (35,000 × £6)	210,000
	140,000
Fixed costs for the period	120,000
Profit	20,000

Activity 3

The answer is 47,500 units, which can be calculated as follows. The total contribution required is £190,000. This amount is needed to cover the fixed costs of £120,000 and the target profit of £70,000. If the contribution is 4.00 per unit, the company must sell (£190,000 ÷ £4.00) 47,500 units.

Activity 4

1. Machine hours (the number of hours that the machine is used).
2. Sales value (note that sales quantity is unlikely to be the driver because commissions are usually based on a percentage of the sales price).
3. Number of miles run.
4. This is rather difficult. The annual sales demand for individual products might not be appropriate because it does not necessarily correlate to the frequency of despatches. For example, there could be a higher demand for Product A than Product B but Product A might be despatched once a year whereas Product B involves a despatch every week. The frequency of despatches is the most likely cost driver.
5. Number of X-rays performed.

Activity 5

	Low level	High level	Increase
Activity (machine hours)	80,000	110,000	30,000
Total costs	£255,000	£330,000	£75,000

Activity 6

We can assume that variable costs are (£75,000 ÷ 30,000) £2.50 per machine hour.

Activity 7

	Low level	High level
Activity (machine hours)	80,000	110,000
Total costs	£255,000	£330,000
Deduct variable costs (at £2.50 per hour)	200,000	275,000
Fixed cost (balance)	55,000	55,000

Activity 8

The answer is £300,000. The calculation is: (£60,000 + 30,000) ÷ £0.30 = £300,000.

Activity 9

	Low level	High level	Increase
Activity (sales value)	£200,000	£400,000	£200,000
Total costs	150,000	250,000	100,000

Activity 10

Variable costs are (100,000/200,000) 50% of sales.

Activity 11

	Low level	High level
Activity (sales value)	£200,000	£400,000
Total costs	£150,000	£250,000
Deduct variable costs (50% × sales)	100,000	200,000
Fixed costs (balance)	50,000	50,000

Activity 12

The answer is sales of £500,000. The calculation is (£50,000 + £200,000) ÷ £0.50.

The profit statement to prove the answer is as follows:

Sales	£500,000
Less variable costs (50% × 500,000)	250,000
Contribution	250,000
Fixed costs	50,000
Profit	200,000

Activity 13

1. The answer is 30,000 units. The calculation is £120,000 ÷ £4.00.
2. The answer is £200,000. The calculation is £60,000 ÷ £0.30.

Activity 14

The answer is 33.33% (or 1/3). The calculation is £100,000/300,000 × 100/1.

Activity 15

The sales line.

Activity 16

Fixed costs.

Activity 17

Total costs (it is not variable cost).

Activity 18

It is the contribution line. Note that the contribution is £20.00 per unit and that the total contribution at 15,000 units is £300,000.

Activity 19

In the technical sense of risk analysis, Project 2 carries a greater risk than Project 1.

Activity 20

		Scheme A (low-tech)		Scheme B (high-tech)
Sales (4,000 units at £200)		£800,000		£800,000
Variable costs (4,000)	600,000		400,000	
Fixed costs for period	100,000		300,000	
		700,000		700,000
Profit		100,000		100,000

Activity 21

The answer is Scheme A = 2 times and Scheme B = 4 times.
The calculations are: Scheme A (800,000 – 600,000) ÷ 100,000; Scheme B (800,000 – 400,000) ÷ 100,000

Activity 22

	Scheme A		Scheme B	
Sales		£720,000		£720,000
Variable costs	540,000		360,000	
Fixed costs	100,000		300,000	
		640,000		660,000
EBIT		80,000		60,000
EBIT at 4,000 units		100,000		100,000
Percentage decrease	(20,000/100,000)	20%	(40,000/100,000)	40%

? Questions

Questions for self assessment

Answers to self-assessment questions are given at the end of the book.
The sequence of questions in this section are graded, starting at a basic level and gradually proceeding to more complex problems.

2.1 A shop is currently selling 25,000 pairs of shoes each year. The relevant data is as follows:

Selling price per pair of shoes	£40
Purchase cost per pair of shoes	£25

Total annual fixed costs are:

Salaries	£100,000
Advertising	£40,000
Other fixed expenses	£100,000

Required:
(Answer each part independently of data contained in other parts of the requirement.)
(a) Calculate the break-even point in number of pairs of shoes sold.
(b) Calculate the shop's margin of safety.
(c) If a selling commission of £2 per pair of shoes was to be introduced, how many pairs of shoes must be sold to earn an annual profit of £20,000?
(d) As an alternative to the sales commission, an additional advertising campaign costing £30,000 is proposed, while at the same time selling prices are to be increased by 12 1/2 %. What would be the break-even point in number of pairs of shoes?

(AAT Final)

2.2 The sales and profit figures of Company A for two consecutive years are given below:

	Year 1	Year 2
Sales	£220,000	£280,000
Profit	£21,000	£36,000

Required:
(a) Calculate the sales necessary to earn a profit of £42,000.
(b) What would the profit be if sales were £188,000?
(c) State the assumptions you have made in producing your answers to (a) and (b).

(Adapted from question in AAT Final, part (c) added)

2.3 Cavalaire Ltd

Note: Some students might find it helpful to read the author's guidance notes (see below) before attempting this question.

The research department of Cavalaire Ltd has recently developed a new product which can be manufactured using either of two methods. The costs involved under each of these methods are:

- Method 1: Plant with an estimated useful life of five years and nil scrap value would be acquired for £200,000. Fixed expenses (other than depreciation) would amount to £60,000 per annum and variable costs per unit would be £35.
- Method 2: Plant with an estimated useful life of five years and nil scrap value would be acquired for £80,000. Fixed expenses (other than depreciation) would amount to £29,000 per annum and variable costs per unit would be £45.

The product is to be marketed at £60 per unit irrespective of the level of sales achieved. The maximum feasible production capacity under either method is 10,000 units. Working capital requirements are £40,000 under either method of production and the company depreciates plant on the straight line basis.

Required:
(a) Calculations of the number of units which must be produced and sold under either method each year in order to break even.
(b) Calculations of the number of units which must be produced and sold under either method each year in order to achieve a target return of 20% on capital invested.
(c) A full discussion of the two alternative production methods, using the calculations made under (a) and (b) and any other figures and/or diagrams you consider relevant.

Author's guidance notes:
1. **Depreciation**: for students who have not yet encountered this term in their course of study, you should note that depreciation is the name given to an annual expense found by spreading the cost of an asset (less its scrap value) over all the years that the asset is used. When the asset is acquired, the company will have to estimate the number of years that it intends to use it in order to calculate an annual expense – the expression 'estimated useful life' relates to this estimate. There are various ways of spreading the cost over the years; if you are told that a 'straight line basis' is used then an equal amount is treated as an expense for each year. The annual depreciation expense will be treated as one of the fixed expenses for CVP analysis.
2. **Capital invested**: the amount of capital invested in each method will comprise the cost of plant plus the amount of working capital. The term 'working capital' relates to the amount invested in items such as stocks and debtors that will be necessary in order to manufacture and sell the new product.

(CIB Accountancy)

2.4 Giles Radio
Note: See author's guidance notes at end of question before attempting this problem.

Giles Radio Ltd operates from several retail outlets and also owns premises which it has leased to other businesses. The tenancy in one of the leased properties will end on 30 June 1993 and the company is considering the possibility of using the premises to market personal computer equipment and software packages. Giles Radio Ltd purchased the premises for £70,000 in 1980. If the property is not going to be used for the computer retail project, it is estimated that it could be sold with vacant possession for £120,000.

The company's projects manager has prepared the following financial forecasts:
(i) The premises will have to be refurbished at a cost of £30,000 which will be paid by cash in June 1993. This cost will be written off over five years on a straight line basis.

(ii) All sales will be on a cash basis and are expected to be at the rate of £40,000 per month commencing in July 1993. The average contribution to sales ratio (CSR) is 20%.

(iii) The amount to be invested in working capital will relate entirely to trading stock. The company intends to carry sufficient stocks to cover sales for 1 month. The initial stocks will be purchased and paid for in June 1993, and will be maintained at this level throughout the year.

(iv) Annual running costs (excluding depreciation) are estimated at £44,000.

(v) The company aims to achieve, annually, a target return of 20% (before tax) on the initial investment in any project undertaken.

Required:

(a) Calculations of:
    (i)   The amount of the initial investment at 30 June 1993
    (ii) The sales level at which the company will break even
    (iii) The forecast profit per annum
    (iv) The margin of safety
    (v) The level of sales required to achieve the target return of 20% on the initial investment

(b) A brief discussion of the project based on your calculations and the information provided.

Author's guidance notes:
Initial investment: use the concept of 'opportunity cost' (discussed in Chapter 1) in order to determine the initial amount invested in the premises. The amount to be invested in working capital can be calculated from the information in item (iii).

(BABS, University of Westminster)

Questions without answers

Answers to these questions are published separately in the *Teacher' Manual*.

2.5 Marketing strategy
Note: This question requires you to interpret a graph rather than to prepare one. You should read the author's guidance note at the end of the question before attempting to solve the problem.

A marketing consultant is engaged to advise on alternative promotion strategies for a client. The estimates of annual costs and revenues applicable to each strategy enable the following chart to be produced.

(a) For each strategy:
    (i) determine the value of total fixed costs and total contribution at £14,000 sales value
    (ii) calculate the profit/volume ratio and the break-even sales value.

(b) From the information given, and the content of (a) above, make some brief recommendations about strategy choice.

(c) How would you respond to a proposal to incorporate into a product profit/volume or break-even chart an apportionment of general corporate fixed overhead?

Author's guidance note:
Profit/volume (P/V) ratio: the P/V ratio mentioned in (a) is merely another name for the ratio called contribution to sales ratio (CSR) in the text of Chapter 2. It is an old (and somewhat misleading) name for this ratio, although it is still used by some people.

(Certified Diploma in Accounting and Finance)

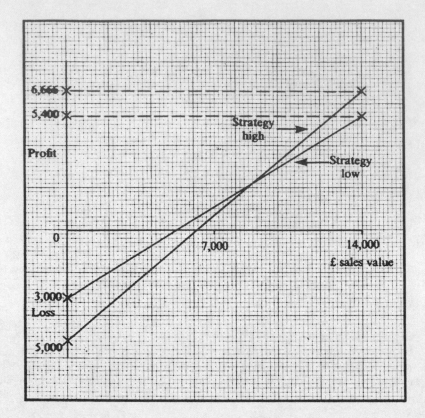

2.6 Compu (Software) Ltd.

Compu (Software) Ltd. is a small company engaged in the marketing of educational computer packages. 'Funds Flow' is one such package and the costs and revenues relating to this are shown below:

Fixed costs including the author's fee, advertising and a share of general overheads, £15,000.

Production costs involving copying onto disk and printing of a comprehensive manual, £2,400 per 100 copies up to 500 copies, £1,200 per 100 copies for copies beyond 500 copies of the package. The bulk purchase of disks and paper is £600 per 50 packages produced at any volume level.

Distribution costs involving postage and the impressive packaging, £400 per 50 packages.

Sales are made at a fixed price of £80 each.

Required:
(a) Produce a table to show revenue, costs and profit loss for 300, 500 and 700 packages produced and sold. What is the marginal cost of each increment of 200 packages in the above ranges.
(b) Draw a chart to depict the results tabulated in (a) above.
(c) Assume that 700 packages have been produced, sales of only 500 have occurred and doubts have been expressed about the marketability of the remaining 200 packages. Using the cost information provided, and generally, comment upon a proposal to sell the remainder for £20 each.

Author's guidance note: With **the graph for part (b)**, you will find that the lines for both variable cost and total cost will bend at the point of 500 packages. This is because the variable production cost per 100 copies changes at 500 copies of the package.

(Certified Diploma in Accounting & Finance)

3 The influence of manufacturing

Objectives

After you have completed this chapter, you should be able to:
- discuss and illustrate the financial accounting problems of a manufacturer
- explain why manufacturers developed cost accounting systems to support the financial accounting function of reporting profits to shareholders
- illustrate how alternative principles for calculating the cost of finished goods will affect the measurement of profit, and describe the requirements of the accounting standard relating to this problem
- discuss how information systems for managers have been influenced by the statutory requirement of reporting profits to the shareholders
- contribute to the debate about why current management information systems must be changed in order to meet the needs of prevailing business activity
- describe in general terms how various types of cost are routed through an integrated cost and financial accounting system
- describe the concept of a cost unit and a cost centre, and outline the role of production cost centres in traditional methods of overhead absorption

Introduction

Accounting practices have evolved in such a way that management accounting information is usually extracted from systems that are designed to produce annual financial reports for the shareholders. Quite often the periodic reports used by managers for internal control are little more than periodic slices of the annual report sent to shareholders. The reporting period for managers is much shorter (usually one month) but the information provided tends to focus on the same set of numbers as those used for reporting to shareholders, i.e. profit for the period and the financial position at the end of the period. Management reports contain more detail than shareholder reports, and there might be additional information such as variations from budget, but the fact remains – all of the information results from a system driven by the demands of reporting results to shareholders.

There is a great deal of contemporary research and literature which suggests that information obtained from systems designed for financial reporting to shareholders is not likely to be relevant for the purposes of helping managers to run the business. Perhaps the most notable work in this area is by Johnson and Kaplan in their book *Relevance Lost* published by the Harvard Business School (see Preface). The reason for mentioning the subject here is that most of the techniques currently used for recording cost information in the books were developed for manufacturing companies. There is little doubt that most of the recording systems currently used by these companies are strongly influenced by the need to produce information for measuring and reporting profits to shareholders.

Accounting systems designed for manufacturers must include procedures for recording cost information because there is a continuous process of creating assets (finished goods) out of various resources such as raw materials, factory labour, and the use of machinery and other resources needed to run a factory. Some of the assets produced will be sold and some will remain in stock at the end of the year. One of the problems that must be resolved by the accounting system is how to divide production costs between the finished goods sold (so that profits can be measured) and those that remain in stock (so that assets can be reported).

3.1 The financial accounting problem

If we use the first year of a new company as a model, and then take a simplistic view over how to divide costs between the cost of goods sold and the cost of closing stock, we might conclude that the problem can be resolved in the following way:

1. add up the total production costs for the year
2. deduct the cost of the finished goods on hand at the end of the year from this total
3. the difference between 1 and 2 represents the cost of the goods sold and can be used for calculating profit; the cost of closing stock is then shown as an asset.

Notice how the profit reported depends on the proportion of costs attributed to the closing stock of finished goods. For financial accounting purposes (reporting profits and net assets to shareholders) the central issue becomes one of how to determine the cost of this closing stock.

In the first place, there are different principles that could be used to identify the elements of cost. It could be argued that production costs which are usually thought of as fixed factory overheads (such as rent, rates and insurance of the factory building) should be treated as costs for the period rather than costs of the product. If you take this view then you are suggesting that closing stock should be based on 'marginal cost' (the extra cost of producing another unit) and fixed production costs (which are not influenced by the quantity produced) should be treated as expenses for the period. An alternative argument is that the factory would not exist if it were not producing goods and so the cost of closing stock should include all the costs (both direct and indirect) of bringing the stock of finished goods into existence. If you take this view then you are suggesting that stock should be based on 'absorbed cost' (marginal cost plus a proportion of fixed production overheads). You can see how the two bases produce different profits by working through Activity 1.

Activity 1

The sales of a manufacturing company in its first year of trading were £1,000,000. Manufacturing costs during this period were as follows:

	£
Cost of raw materials used	300,000
Cost of factory labour	100,000
Factory overheads	500,000

The cost of the closing stock of finished goods has been computed as follows:

Based on marginal cost	£100,000
Based on absorbed cost	£200,000

For the time being, forget about how the costs of closing stock might have been determined and simply accept the figures as given data. Using your own paper, calculate gross profit under each stock valuation method and, after checking with the key, note the amounts here.

Marginal cost	**Absorbed cost**

Gross profit for Year 1

The closing stock at the end of one year becomes the opening stock at the start of the next If we extend our simple model into the second year we can gain a different view of the same problem. In order to make it easier to see what happens, we will assume that at the end of the second year there was no closing stock of finished goods – all of the goods brought forward from the first year and all of the goods produced during the second year were sold. If you are relatively new to accounting calculations then you might need to know (in order to do the activity) that the cost of goods sold is computed as follows:

Cost of opening stock of finished goods	X
Add: manufacturing costs in the period	X
	X
Less: cost of closing stock of finished goods	(X)
Cost of goods sold	X

Activity 2

During the second year of the company in Activity 1, the sales income was £1,450,000. Manufacturing costs during this year were as follows:

	£
Cost of raw materials used	200,000
Cost of factory labour	100,000
Factory overheads	500,000

There was no closing stock of finished goods at the end of the second year.

Using your own paper, produce two calculations of gross profit for Year 2 on the basis that the stock at the end of Year 1 was costed at (a) marginal cost, and (b) absorbed cost. Note the amounts here.

	Marginal cost	Absorbed cost
Gross profit for Year 2		

A summary of the profits under each basis for the two years is as follows:

	Stock valuation basis	
	Marginal cost	Absorbed cost
Profit for Year 1	£200,000	£300,000
Profit for Year 2	£550,000	£450,000
Total	£750,000	£750,000

As you can see, total profits over the two years are equal. The different bases for calculating the cost of closing stock merely alters the accounting period in which those profits fall.

Activity 3

Review the details of Activities 1 and 2 again to see if you can identify what happens in profit calculations when closing stock is based on absorbed cost. This might sound like a silly task which can be answered by stating that stock valuations are higher than marginal cost, but you must try to be a little more specific than this. Keep in mind that absorbed cost is based on marginal cost plus a proportion of fixed production overheads. Make a note here of any points that occur to you and then check with the Key.

As far as financial accounting is concerned, the issue of whether the closing stock of finished goods should be based on marginal cost or absorbed cost has been settled in the UK by an accounting regulation known as SSAP 9. The abbreviation 'SSAP' (as an acronym it is pronounced 'sap') stands for Statement of Standard Accounting Practice and although SSAPs are developed by the accounting profession they are strongly supported by legislation. Companies are obliged to comply with SSAPs when submitting their annual financial report to the shareholders. SSAP 9 requires that the cost of closing stock should be determined on the basis of absorbed cost.

This does not mean that the time spent experimenting with the effect of the two bases (in Activities 1 and 2) has been wasted. These simple exercises clearly show how the principles used for profit measurement (matching revenues with costs) can result in costs for an earlier period being included with those for the current period. For this reason (and others not mentioned here) it might be invalid for managers to assess current performance based on measurements of profit.

Although SSAP 9 has settled a matter of principle for financial accounting, it does leave the company with a number of practical difficulties. The main problem relates to the overheads. It is relatively easy to set up a recording system to identify the direct costs of a product, such as direct materials and direct labour, but overheads are a different matter. There are many different kinds of factory overhead and many different types of product consuming the benefits represented (in accounting terms) by the cost of these overheads. A fairly complex system of tracking the different types of overhead, and for measuring how different products make demands on overhead services, will be required if we wish to arrive at a realistic overhead cost per unit. Yet very few companies have adopted such complex systems; instead, most companies continue to rely on fairly crude techniques that were developed in a bygone era (Johnson and Kaplan consider that these techniques were already in place by 1925).

Several factors have contributed to this state of affairs. In the early days of manufacturing (as mentioned in Chapter 2) factory overheads represented a relatively small part of the total cost of a product. Most accounting records had to be written up manually. Managers were, it seems, content to use information based on the simple techniques employed and, presumably, considered that the additional cost of a more refined system would not produce anything by way of greater benefits. In addition to this, the professional accountants who are responsible for ensuring that the annual report sent to shareholders gives a 'true and fair view' (a role performed by the company's external auditors) have always been prepared to accept fairly simplistic methods for attributing production overheads to the cost of finished goods.

One of the reasons why a simplistic approach is acceptable for profit measurement is because stocks have a plus and minus effect on the calculation of cost of goods sold – opening stock is added and closing stock deducted. Even the most sophisticated system of attributing factory overheads to the cost of stock is unlikely to result in a material change of results. We can see this by re-working Activity 2 (the company's second year) on the basis that the quantity and composition of the closing stock at the end of that year was exactly the same as the opening stock. On this basis the two profit calculations for Year 2 would be as follows:

	Marginal cost		**Absorbed cost**	
Sales		£1,450,000		£1,450,000
Opening stock	100,000		200,000	
Manufacturing costs	800,000		800,000	
	900,000		1,000,000	
Less closing stock	100,000		200,000	
		800,000		800,000
Gross profit		650,000		650,000

Although the two different bases cause a difference of £100,000 in the cost of opening and closing stock, the effect on profit is nil. You can see the same effect by looking at the figures for the two-year period following Activity 2. The profits for those two years were exactly the same simply because the quantity of stock at the beginning of the two-year period was the same as the quantity at the end of that period – nil in both cases. It requires a significant change in quantity (and/or composition) between opening and closing stocks for the costing basis to have a material effect on results for the period.

Activity 4

Assume that the stock quantities of a company are falling. In this situation, state which of the two bases (marginal cost or absorbed cost) for calculating the cost of closing stock will produce the higher profits.

3.2 The single information system: A call for change

As stated earlier, there are a number of academic studies to show that managers could easily make bad decisions if these are based on information produced by a system designed to measure profits: particularly in the case of decisions based on product costs. In the past, it might have been acceptable for both profit measurement and (say) pricing decisions to be based on a single concept of a product's cost. This is no longer acceptable in a highly competitive global economy. Product costs used for financial accounting include an arbitrary allocation of production overheads and ignore overheads beyond the production stage such as marketing, distribution and administration. Product costs for decision making need to be more scientific as regards production overheads and must recognize the demands made by individual products on the facilities provided beyond the production stage.

Manufacturing today is highly automated and overheads form the largest part of production costs. Information technology is relatively cheap and computerized systems are capable of analysing data in a variety of ways in order to meet the various needs of managers. Manufacturers are increasingly making use of computer-aided automation and such systems are capable of generating quantifiable data that could be used as input to a common database. Competition is much more intense and managers making pricing or cost control decisions can no longer rely on cost information produced by a system that was designed for reporting profits to shareholders.

Johnson and Kaplan (in *Relevance Lost*) consider that in the near future it will not be possible to design a single comprehensive system to satisfy conflicting demands for cost information. They identified three functions for which separate cost information systems are needed, namely:

- process control (for the moment, think of this as controlling departmental costs)
- product costs (for management control and decision purposes)
- financial reporting.

It is conceivable that certain parts of the three systems could be integrated. For example, the new methods being suggested for determining product costs could, with some adjustment to the figures, be used in determining the cost of closing stock for financial reporting. These new methods are generally labelled Activity-Based Costing (ABC) and you will learn about this in Chapter 5. The main difference between ABC and the traditional methods of attributing overheads to products can be stated as:

1. the treatment of production overheads is much more scientific under ABC
2. product costs under ABC include overheads beyond the production stage such as marketing, distribution and administration.

Presumably the external auditors will have no serious objection to the first of these two refinements. The second, however, involves a contravention of financial reporting regulations since the cost of closing stock must only include production overheads – costs beyond the production stage are written off as expenses for the period. But the information system should be capable of identifying the amount of post-production overheads included in product costs and these could easily be eliminated for financial reporting. If we reach this stage we will have developed systems whereby financial accounting information is extracted from a system designed for management accounting. Generally speaking, current procedures work in the opposite direction.

Unfortunately, this does mean that students of present day practices in cost and management accounting are required to learn procedures that have lost their relevance to contemporary business activity. But it will not be possible for accounting students to contribute to the debate for change without understanding present systems. Providing you can understand the current procedures, and their defects, you should be able to make better use of cost information and also contribute to the task of ensuring that information systems designed for future generations of managers are more relevant to their needs. Current systems will also form the basis of examination questions for many years to come.

The remainder of this chapter is based on the procedures currently used by the majority of manufacturing companies. The procedures are covered in outline so that you can gain an overall view of the system. This should make it easier for you to see how certain aspects, which are covered in more detail by Chapters 4 and 5, fit into this system. In particular, Chapter 5 looks at the problem of overhead absorption, including ABC.

The matching process

In financial accounting, profit is determined for each accounting period by using a number of conventional procedures. One of these procedures – 'matching' – attempts to match the sales income for the period with all the expenditure incurred in earning that income. In some cases, the costs incurred in one accounting period will produces benefits (in the form of sales income) in a subsequent period. In these cases the cost is not treated as an expense to be matched with sales income for the period when the cost was incurred; instead, the cost is carried forward as an asset and treated as an expense in the period when the benefit is earned (usually in the form of sales income). The cost of manufacturing goods for sale is one example of where this happens: if the goods are sold their cost is charged to 'cost of sales' (to be matched with sales income); if they have not been sold, the cost is carried forward as an asset.

Activity 5

In most businesses there is one type of cost that occurs quite frequently where the expenditure is divided up into annual slices and matched with sales income over a series of years (including the year when the expenditure was incurred). Make a note here of the type of expenditure concerned, and how the annual expense is usually described.

In many cases the benefits arising from expenditure are consumed immediately and there is no measurable amount that can be carried forward to subsequent periods. This will be so, for example, in the case of most administration expenses (staff salaries, stationery, light and power, etc.). In these cases, the benefits are said to be consumed and the costs are written of as expenses (to be matched with sales income) in the period they are incurred.

The result of the matching process is that all expenditure incurred by a business during the accounting period will be reported as either:

- an expense in the profit and loss account for that period, or
- an asset in the balance sheet at the end of that period.

In a number of cases (such as the cost of fixed assets, and costs of product development) the extent to which current expenditure produces benefits (by way of revenue) in subsequent years is a matter of judgement, and so the allocation of costs to accounting periods is subjective. There are very many regulations (and guidelines) for dealing with this type of problem in the annual report to shareholders. The matching process is illustrated by Figure 3.1.

Fig. 3.1

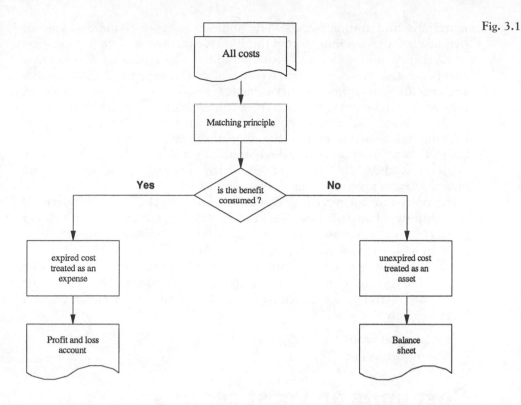

Activity 6

In profit measurement, the matching process determines the timing of when a cost is treated as an expense. Try to describe when (at what point in the passage of time) the following types of cost are treated as expenses to be matched with sales income:

1. Salary of the managing director's secretary.

2. Cost of goods manufactured.

3. Cost of purchasing a delivery van.

Period costs and production costs

In financial accounting, almost all of the costs incurred outside of the manufacturing department are treated as 'period costs' (i.e. costs to be written off as expenses for the period in which they were incurred). There are a few exceptions, notably those where the cost is treated as an expense over a number of years such as the cost of fixed assets (this refers to fixed assets outside of the manufacturing department) and product development costs.

But none of the costs incurred in the manufacturing department are treated as period costs. This applies to both the direct costs (such as raw materials) and indirect costs. The indirect costs will include various overheads which beginners often think of as expenses, such as depreciation of the plant and rent of the factory building. The entire set of costs that can be related to running the factory and producing manufactured goods are sometimes described as inventoriable costs. This expression stems from how the word 'inventory' is used (particularly in the USA) to mean stock. In other words, all factory costs result in an asset (stock). The book-keeping is designed to ensure that all of these factory costs are ultimately charged to an asset account called 'finished goods'. When goods are sold, the cost of those sold is taken out of the finished goods account and charged to an expense account called 'cost of sales'.

The procedure for recording cost information in the books is relatively straightforward in the case of direct costs (direct materials and direct labour). It is the treatment of overheads that causes most of the difficulty, in both a conceptual and practical sense. You will see shortly that over-heads are shuffled around in various ways before they eventually finish up as a part of the cost of finished goods. In order to understand how all costs are routed through the system, you need to understand two technical terms, namely:

- a cost unit, and
- a cost centre.

Cost units and cost centres

A **cost unit** is defined by the Chartered Institute of Management Accountants (CIMA) as: '*a quantitative unit of product or service for which costs are ascertained*'. Think of cost units as being the 'things' produced. Each company (or public service) will determine its own cost units; in some cases it might be a small quantity of homogeneous items such as a six-pack of lager, or a single item such as a particular model of computer, or (in the service sector) a measurable service such as the provision of a hospital bed for one day.

Activity 7

Try to imagine what the cost units might be in the cases mentioned below and make a note of them against each item. There is no right or wrong answer to this activity because each entity will have its own rules as to what constitutes a cost unit.

1. The provision of accountancy services by a practising accountant.

2. Manufacturer of photocopying paper.

3. A haulage contractor.

A **cost centre** is defined by CIMA as: '*a location or function for which costs are ascertained before relating them to cost units*'. Think of cost centres as being departments in the factory. A cost centre could be any identifiable department (or even a single machine) in the factory. When we look at cost centres in the production department we will find that there are basically two types:

- a production cost centre, and
- a service cost centre.

Production cost centres are those where the actual production process is taking place, such as the assembly department and the packaging department. A service cost centre is one that is providing various services to the production cost centres, such as the stores department or even a canteen for the factory staff.

Activity 8

Identify whether the following cost centres (in the production department) are likely to be production cost centres or service cost centres:

1. Maintenance department of a computer manufacturer.

2. Finishing department (varnishing and polishing) of a furniture manufacturer.

3. Quality control department for a frozen food manufacturer.

4. Weaving department of a textile manufacturer.

The way in which factory overheads are dealt with in the accounting records must ensure that all overheads are eventually attributed to production cost centres. They can then be related to the cost units processed by those cost centres. Overheads that are initially treated as the cost of running a service cost centre must be apportioned to the production cost centres using some kind of proxy for measuring the benefits that each production cost centre receives from the provision of those services. When all factory overheads have been attributed to production cost centres, some kind of measurement of activity (such as the number of direct labour hours or machine hours) in each production cost centre is used to relate overheads to the cost of finished goods passing through that cost centre.

The procedure of relating total overheads to the units processed by a production cost centre is known as overhead absorption (the total overheads for a production cost centre are 'soaked up', or absorbed, by the units processed in that centre). For example, if the total overheads attributable to the finishing department of a furniture manufacturer for a period are £64,000, and the total direct labour hours in the finishing department for that period are 32,000 hours, the overhead cost per direct labour hour is (£64,000 ÷ 32,000) £2.00 per hour. This is known as the absorption rate for the finishing department. Consequently, a unit that was processed in the finishing department for 2 labour hours will absorb (2 × £2) £4.00 as overhead. (Note that the expression: '2 labour hours' could be a reference to various combinations of labour time such as: 1 person working on the unit for 2 hours, 2 persons working on the unit (concurrently or consecutively) for 1 hour each, and so on.)

Activity 9

The overhead cost of £4.00 (as discussed in the above paragraph) will not be the total overhead cost of the unit produced. See if you can explain why this is so.

In the answer to Activity 9 it was assumed that the furniture manufacturer had a sequence of processes such as cutting, assembly and finishing. If this was the case, the overheads for each of these production cost centres must be absorbed by the units produced; the cost unit will accumulate overheads from each department in the sequence. Modern production methods are, however, moving away from this type of processing in favour of what is generally called 'cellular' manufacturing. In these cases production workers are multi-skilled and there is less physical separation of the different processes. It is quite likely that companies adopting this type of production will also have abandoned the traditional methods of overhead absorption.

You will learn about the mechanics of overhead absorption in Chapter 5 (both traditional and ABC). For the time being you need some kind of overview of how all costs are routed through the book-keeping system where traditional overhead absorption is used. Figure 3.2 should help. When you first look at this diagram it appears to be quite complex, yet it is little more than an explosion of the earlier diagram used to illustrate the matching process. You will notice that costs enter the system at the top (1) and finish up (in the bottom right-hand corner) as either an asset (14) or an expense (4). The reason why it looks more complex than the earlier diagram is because production costs (particularly the overheads) have to meander through a number of processes before they finish up as assets or expenses.

One of the problems of presenting a completed diagram in a book is that it appears as a static representation of something dynamic. Since there is no suitable way of getting you to build up the diagram in stages, the version presented here includes some blank boxes that you can complete from instructions in the activities. By doing this you should be able to see the various movements involved.

Activity 10

Try to follow the cost path by finding the sequence of symbol numbers in Figure 3.2. Notice how the first stage at which the pathway differs is at (2) where, if the cost is not a production cost, it is treated as a period cost (3) and reported in the profit and loss account (4) as an expense.

In the box for (3), make a list of three examples of period costs. When doing this, describe each example by its function, such as 'administration', rather than by the type of expense, such as 'stationery'.

Fig. 3.2

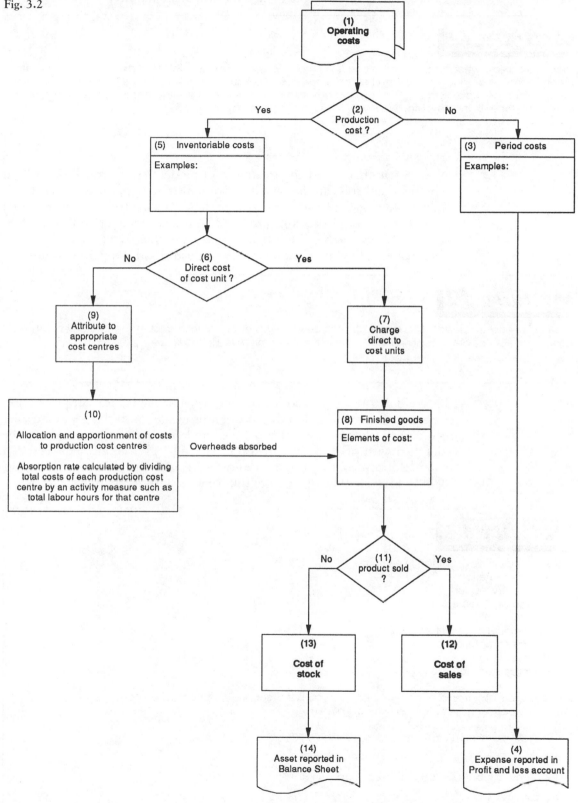

Activity 11

Now try to follow what happens if the cost is a production cost. Box (5) is labelled as 'inventoriable costs', meaning that all production costs are treated as the cost of producing stock. There are three main classes of production cost; make a note of them in the box. In this case, it is important to ensure that your examples agree with those in the Key, otherwise Activity 13 will not make any sense.

Now notice that at (6) the treatment of production costs will depend on whether the cost is classified as a direct or indirect cost of the cost unit. If it is a direct cost (such as direct materials or direct labour) the amount is treated as a discrete cost of the units produced. If it is an indirect cost of the cost units (a factory overhead) it is treated initially as the cost of a cost centre but eventually washes into the amount of overhead absorbed by the cost units.

Activity 12

The cost of finished goods (8) is made up of three elements of cost. Make a list of the three elements but check with the Key before writing them down in the space provided in the figure.

Before doing the next activity, notice what happens after all production costs have been charged to the cost of finished goods. If the goods are sold, the cost is taken out of finished goods and charged to cost of sales to be matched with sales income in the profit and loss account. This leaves a balance of costs in the account for finished goods which represents the cost of closing stock to be reported in the balance sheet as an asset.

Activity 13

In (5) you should have written three items:
- raw materials
- factory labour
- factory overheads

In (8) you should have written three items:
- direct materials
- direct labour
- overhead absorbed

The three sets of terms in each symbol are similar, but there are important differences. Explain (briefly) the difference between the following two pairs of terms:

1. Raw materials (in (5)) and direct materials (in (8))

2. Factory labour (in (5)) and direct labour (in (8))

Budgeted absorption rates

The text and activities up to now will have given you the impression that overhead absorption rates are based on the actual overheads incurred in the period divided by the actual level of activity in that period. If you think of an accounting period as being (say) one month then a moment's thought will tell you that apart from being impractical, this approach will introduce distortions into the overheads per measurement of activity. Keep in mind that the basic idea of overhead absorption is to spread the total production overheads over all the units made, using a proxy such as direct labour hours to determine a cost per unit.

Activity 14

The cost of electricity (for a UK manufacturer) will be higher during the winter months than it is during the summer months. If the actual overheads incurred for each monthly accounting period are used as a basis for calculating an absorption rate, a distortion in the overhead cost per unit will occur. Try to describe the nature of the distortion for this situation.

The same problem occurs with other overheads such as maintenance. In one particular month the maintenance costs might be (say) £100,000, yet in the following month they might be only £100. If we used actual costs as the basis, the units made during the month when £100,000 was spent would appear to be costing more than those made during the month when a cost of £100 was incurred. Yet the benefits from a large maintenance cost (in terms of less frequent breakdowns) will be spread over a number of subsequent periods.

Apart from the cyclical nature of many costs, there is also the practical difficulty of using actual expenditure. The actual cost of many overheads (electricity is a good example) will not be known until some months after the cost has been incurred. In the meantime, the product made might have to be priced and sold – we cannot wait for the electricity bill to arrive before we work out the cost of that product.

In view of these difficulties, absorption rates are based on budgeted figures. These figures will usually be for a longer period than one month in order to ensure an even spread of the cyclical costs. The normal period used in the calculation is one year. The budgeted figures will take account of technical production facilities, expected overheads (using past periods as a guideline) and budgeted activity levels expressed in various ways, such as units to be produced, machine hours and direct labour hours. The result of the calculations is usually known as the budgeted overhead absorption rate (sometimes abbreviated to BOAR). The basic formula for BOAR is:

$$\frac{\text{Budgeted overheads for each production cost centre}}{\text{Budgeted activity (e.g. direct labour hours) for that cost centre}}$$

Activity 15

A manufacturing company has one production department. The total overheads to be allocated and apportioned to that department are budgeted at £120,000 for the next year. The total number of direct labour hours for that year are budgeted as 30,000 hours. Calculate the budgeted overhead absorption rate.

The use of budgeted overhead absorption rates introduces another factor into the way that production costs are processed in the accounting system. The amount of production overhead charged to finished goods is based on a budgeted rate multiplied by the actual level of activity achieved. As a formula it can be expressed as follows:

Overheads absorbed = BOAR × Actual level of activity

This means that the production overheads included in the cost of finished goods will be different to the actual overheads incurred. The difference between overheads incurred and the amount charged to the cost of finished goods (the amount absorbed) is known as the overhead 'under- or over-absorbed'. Sometimes the expression 'over- or under-recovered' is used to describe the same concept.

Activity 16

The following facts relate to the company in Activity 15: the actual production overheads in the period concerned were £122,000. The actual number of direct labour hours worked in that period were 29,000 hours.

1. Calculate the amount of overhead absorbed in the period

2. Calculate the amount of overhead under- or over-absorbed for that period.

At this stage in the recording process, the cost of finished goods will have been charged with a total amount of £116,000. The remaining £6,000 (i.e. £122,000 − £116,000) represents part of a production cost that has been incurred but has not (at this point) been treated as either an expense or an asset. The normal procedure is to treat it as an expense by transferring it to 'cost of sales'. In some cases there might be grounds for splitting it between cost of finished goods and cost of sales but this would only be done if the difference arose through some fundamental mistake in calculating the rate.

SSAP 9 and 'normal level of activity'

The process of treating overheads under-absorbed as an expense is in keeping with the financial accounting regulations mentioned in section 3.1. Although SSAP 9 requires the cost of manufactured stock to be on an absorbed cost basis, it does not regulate for any specific absorption basis. It merely states that the amount included in the cost of stock for fixed production overheads should be based on the normal level of activity (as opposed to actual activity).

This is quite an important rule in terms of profit measurement. It ensures that the effect of operating at less than normal capacity (through breakdowns or other inefficiencies) is not carried forward in the cost of closing stock. For example, if a company's fixed production overheads are budgeted at £10,000 and the normal capacity of the plant is to produce 10,000 units, the fixed overhead cost for financial accounting must be £1.00 per unit. If the company suffered production problems and actually produced 5,000 units it must still absorb only £5,000 (5,000 × £1) into the cost of finished goods. If the actual overheads were £10,000 (as per the budget) the remaining £5,000 under-absorbed must be treated as an expense.

This rule regarding absorption of fixed production overheads is an extension of a general principle in SSAP 9 that requires the cost of stock to be based on: 'expenditure incurred in the **normal course of business** in bringing the product to its present location and condition'. Using normal levels of activity for absorbing fixed production overheads is consistent with this requirement. The practice of calculating absorption rates based on budgeted figures for both overheads and activity ensures compliance with SSAP 9 because these budgets will have been based on the normal level of activity.

The bifurcated route

The practice of using budgeted overhead absorption rates means that the cost route emerging from (10) in Figure 3.2 is slightly naive. The actual

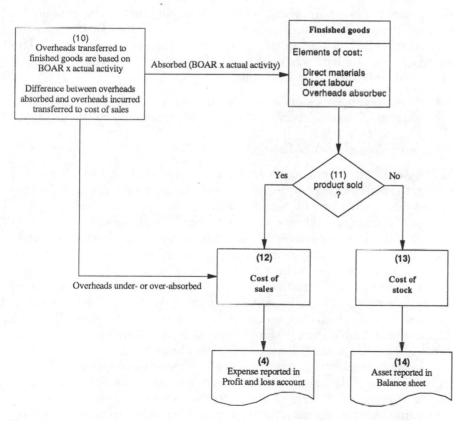

Fig. 3.3

expenditure on production overheads will take two separate paths after being accumulated on an account for each production cost centre. The amount absorbed goes to the cost of finished goods; the difference between the amount absorbed and the amount incurred is transferred to the cost of sales. This bifurcated route is shown in Figure 3.3. This deals with the bottom part of Figure 3.2 only, with the two financial statements in swopped positions for the sake of clarity in the new figure.

3.5 Confusion in terminology and accounting practices

A subject called 'manufacturing accounts' has existed in most financial accounting text books for very many years, even though developments in cost and financial accounting made the practice of preparing this account unnecessary except for small entities. Unfortunately, the preservation of manufacturing accounts as a subject in text books means that some examiners feel justified in setting questions requiring the preparation of manufacturing accounts, and in asking students to discuss some of the terminology and concepts on which it is based. In order to make sense out of the confusion that tends to surround this subject, we need to understand the purpose and basis of the manufacturing account.

A manufacturing account was a financial statement designed to ascertain the total cost of all finished goods manufactured in a period. Such a statement served no purpose other than to enable profits to be measured – it was of little value to management because a single figure showing the total cost of all goods made is virtually useless information. The manufacturing account was used for profit measurement because cost of sales could be based on the following:

- cost of opening stock of finished goods, plus
- total manufacturing costs for the period (determined by the manufacturing account), less
- cost of closing stock of finished goods.

Although the above approach was used at the start of this chapter to explain the financial accounting problem, it does contain a paradox. If cost of sales requires the cost of manufacturing for the period to be adjusted by the cost of opening and closing stock of finished goods, how do we ascertain the cost of these stocks without a cost accounting system? If we incorporate cost accounting into the system for this purpose, why do we need to produce a manufacturing account? The cost accounting system itself will produce a figure for cost of sales. The answer is that in the days before cost accounting became integrated with the financial accounting system, the cost of finished goods stock was calculated as a memorandum exercise (a clerical routine outside of the double entry). Manufacturing accounts are (as they stand in text books at the moment) a hangover from a bygone era.

But history has a habit of repeating itself. Some of the current suggestions being made for replacing the cost accounting system with one that is more suitable for managers seem to indicate that we might have to resort to something like the manufacturing account in order to measure profit. There is a discussion of this point in section 3.6.

The reason for mentioning the former type of manufacturing account here is because it causes a certain amount of confusion regarding terminology which is worth looking at while studying cost accounting. The chief culprit is a term known as **prime cost**, which was usually used when preparing the manufacturing account. By way of example, a manufacturing account might have looked something like the following:

	£	£
Cost of opening work in progress		10,000
Manufacturing costs for the period:		
Direct materials	40,000	
Direct labour	120,000	
Prime cost	160,000	
Factory overheads	60,000	
		220,000
		230,000
Deduct cost of closing work in progress		8,000
Total factory cost of finished goods manufactured		222,000

There is a slight difference between the above statement and the way that the cost of finished goods is produced by a cost accounting system. Notice that the manufacturing account includes a charge for actual overheads incurred, whereas a cost accounting system uses factory overheads absorbed (differences between incurred and absorbed are written off to cost of sales). However, this is unlikely to have any significant impact on the measurement of profit.

We need to look at the term 'prime cost' because it is often (incorrectly) used as a synonym for marginal cost. Prime cost and marginal cost are two separate concepts of cost. The difference between them can be explained by considering the official CIMA terminology. The two definitions can be stated as follows:

- Prime cost: The total cost of direct materials, direct labour and direct expenses. Direct expenses are costs other than direct materials and labour which can be identified in a separate product (*i.e. a discrete cost of the product such as a royalty paid to the holder of letters patent for each item produced*) (the words in italics are not part of the official definition).
- Marginal cost: The variable cost of one unit of product or service, i.e. a cost which would be avoided if the unit was not produced or provided.

Although these two concepts of cost look very similar, there are a number of important differences. For example, some of the direct labour cost included in prime cost might have to be regarded as a non-variable cost and, therefore, excluded from marginal cost. It could be argued that for certain types of short-term measurement the total cost of direct labour is fixed. Perhaps a more important difference relates to the overheads. Many of these overheads will be variable overheads but because they cannot be identified as a discrete cost of the product they are excluded from the definition of prime cost. These variable overheads will normally be treated as a part of the marginal cost, even though the methods used to attribute them to individual products might be somewhat arbitrary in conventional systems.

It is difficult to see what use can be made of the concept of 'prime cost' other than as a label for a particular sub-total in the old form of manufacturing account.

3.6 The recording system

Study signpost

Some students might be using this book on a general management course where the emphasis is on using management accounting information rather than recording it in the books. Others will be accustomed to thinking in terms of debit and credit, and might be attending a course where knowledge of the book-keeping is required. In order to accommodate both types of student, this section is divided between a general description, and the detailed double-entry.

Students who are not required to learn the underlying book-keeping should read through the general description (the technical terms 'debit' and 'credit' have not been used) in order to make sense of recent arguments for replacing existing systems. There is a short discussion on certain aspects of this in the section following the general description; this might be difficult to understand without some idea of how costs are routed through the ledger.

The actual details of how cost information is recorded will depend on the system of production. The general description given here is based on producing a batch of homogenous units for the finished goods store. You will learn more about how different production methods affect cost accounting in Chapter 6.

General description

An important point to remember is one that has been mentioned from time to time throughout this chapter: *none of the accounts used to record production costs are treated as expenses.* All expenditure on production finishes up as the cost of assets (overheads under-absorbed being the exception) and it is not until those assets are sold that their cost becomes an expense in the process of profit measurement. The cost accounting system is, therefore, a complex mechanism for keeping a track of stock costs in a way that is acceptable for financial accounting.

There are three asset accounts that are used as an accounting control over stocks, namely:

- raw materials control account
- work in progress control account
- finished goods control account

The raw materials control account keeps a record of both receipts and issues or raw materials. When raw materials are purchased, their cost is charged to this control account; when raw materials are issued to production, their cost is taken out of the control account. There is a running balance on the control account that represents the raw material stock.

Activity 17

For various reasons, the balance of cost on the raw materials control account will not be equal to the cost of raw materials in the stores department. Describe why this is likely to happen.

The work in progress control account is used for accumulating the various costs of producing each batch of finished goods. As each batch is processed in the production department, the work in progress control account is charged with the cost of direct materials, direct labour, and overhead absorbed. As each batch is finished, the total cost of that batch is taken out of the work in progress control account and charged to the finished goods control account.

Where production runs are completed over a relatively short time period, there is not likely to be any balance on the work in progress control account at the end of the accounting period. Where production takes several weeks (or months) to complete, it is conceivable that there will be products that are only partially completed at the accounting date. The cost of these uncompleted products is represented by the balance on the work in progress control account (the costs will have been charged to this account but will not have been transferred to finished goods control). The cost of work in progress is reported as one of the stock items in the balance sheet, along with the other stock items of raw materials and finished goods.

Production overheads (incurred and absorbed) are recorded in a production overhead control account. There will be one of these accounts for each production cost centre. The production overhead control account is charged with the various overheads incurred. As the production of each batch is completed, an appropriate amount of overhead (based on the BOAR) is taken out of the production overhead control account and charged to the work in progress control account. The overhead absorbed is included in the cost of the batch when transferring the total cost of that batch from work in progress to finished goods control. The balance on the production overhead control account represents overheads under- or over-absorbed. At the end of the accounting year, this balance is usually transferred to cost of sales.

Raw materials issued to production will be classed as either direct materials or indirect materials. The cost of all raw materials issued will be taken out of the raw materials control account, but the account to which they are charged will depend on whether they are direct materials or indirect materials. You can see if you have understood certain parts of this general description of the book-keeping by answering the question in Activity 18.

Activity 18

State the account to which the following costs will be charged:

1. Direct materials issued £18,000

2. Indirect materials (sprays and varnish) issued £1,000

A full explanation of how labour costs are dealt with in the books will be delayed until the next chapter. It is sufficient to understand for the time being that a **payroll control account** is usually kept which (through various adjustments) is eventually charged with the gross payroll cost, plus the employer's share of National Insurance. The gross total will consist of various types of labour cost (direct, indirect, administration and so on) and so the total cost is taken out of the payroll control account and charged to various accounts according to the class of cost. For example, the cost of direct labour will be charged to the work in progress control account, and the cost of indirect labour will be charged to the production overhead control account. The payroll control account should (in theory but not always in practice!) show a zero balance at the end of the accounting period.

From the foregoing description (and earlier text) it should be possible for you to see that (with the exception of overheads under- or over-absorbed) all production costs are eventually channelled into the cost of finished goods. When these goods are sold, the cost is taken out of the finished goods control account and charged to cost of sales. The balance on the finished goods control account represents the cost of finished goods in stock. As with raw materials, there is likely to be a difference between the cost of finished goods on the control account and the cost of finished goods in the store. These differences will arise for reasons similar to those mentioned for raw materials. In both cases (raw materials and finished goods) there will be an adjustment to the accounting records when the differences are discovered.

History returns

The system as described above has been used for very many years and the design is, to some extent, influenced by the need to keep a track of stock costs in a way that is acceptable for financial reporting. If you accept that it needs to be replaced by something more suitable for managers, we are left with the problem determining stock costs for profit measurement.

There might be a solution to this dilemma in the way that modern companies make use of what are called 'Just In Time' (JIT) techniques. This is discussed more fully in the next chapter, but the basic idea of JIT is to keep the stocks of raw materials and finished goods as low as possible in order to reduce unit costs (these economies result from lower stock holding costs). Companies who adopt JIT techniques will have a low level of stocks and the cost of these stocks could be determined by a separate valuation for the purposes of profit measurement.

When stocks are kept at such low levels through JIT techniques it seems unnecessary to use the existing complex systems for tracking production costs so that they can eventually be reported as cost of sales or cost of stock. We could calculate cost of sales by simply deducting the cost of closing stock (calculated separately) from the total production costs for the period. If this approach is eventually used, we will have turned full circle and be back to using something like the old manufacturing account in order to report profit.

Double-entry

This section is intended for those students who have some knowledge of double-entry book-keeping, and who might be required to demonstrate that knowledge in the context of recording cost information in the books. Readers to whom this applies will have noticed that in the above general description the terms debit and credit were represented by the following:

- charge to = debit
- taken out = credit

Details for the activities

Zambia Industrials Ltd manufactures a single type of product called a splogget. This product is made from a single type of raw material called coslag. The production process is set up on a batch basis, meaning that each production run is set up in order to produce a specified quantity of sploggets for the finished goods store. Each unit of coslag (the raw material) produces one unit of splogget (the finished product).

At the close of the previous accounting period, the balances in the books were as follows:

	£	£
Share capital		12,000
Profit and loss account		4,000
Creditors		2,000
Fixed assets	8,000	
Debtors	4,000	
Finished goods stock (100 units of splogget)	1,000	
Raw materials stock (20 units of coslag)	100	
Work in progress	nil	
Bank	4,900	
	18,000	18,000

The transactions during a period (in chronological sequence) were as follows:

1. Bought 10 units of the raw material coslag on credit terms at a price of £5 per unit.
2. Issued 12 units of raw material to production for the production of 12 units of splogget.
3. Paid wages and salaries by cheque. In this exercise we will ignore deductions and the employer's shares of National Insurance – instead we will assume that the amount paid out represents the gross wage cost (you will learn how to account for deductions etc. in the next chapter). The total amount paid was £66 and was analysed as follows:

Direct labour	£36
Indirect production labour	10
Administration salaries	20
	66

4. Paid overheads by cheque as follows:

Production overheads	£20
Administration expenses	30
	50

5. The overhead absorption rate is predetermined at £2 for each unit of splogget produced.
6. The 12 units of coslag issued to production were fully converted into 12 units of splogget during the period, and the 12 sploggets were transferred to the finished goods store.
7. Sold 15 units of splogget on credit for £300.
8. Received £500 from debtors and paid £200 to creditors.

There were no stock losses during the period. Depreciation of fixed assets and taxation are to be ignored.

Activity 19 requires you to identify the double entry for the transaction or event specified. Try to sort this out from the general description given earlier. For each transaction you must describe the name of the account debited and credited, and also state the amount. In the self-assessment questions at the end of this chapter you will be required to write up the relevant ledger accounts and produce the financial statements at the end of the period.

Financial transactions such as receipts from debtors, payments to creditors, purchase of fixed assets, etc. are all dealt with in exactly the same way as they would be in financial accounting. You should notice that when the recording system incorporates cost accounting, there is no account for 'purchases' as there is in simple financial accounting. Instead, there are three stock accounts representing assets, namely: raw materials control, work in progress control and finished goods control. In all three accounts, both types of stock movement (in and out) are recorded, thereby providing a running balance of what should be in stock.

You must also keep in mind that when goods are sold there are two double entries, one for the sales price (debit debtors or cash; credit sales) and one for the cost price (debit cost of sales; credit finished goods control). It is quite easy to forget the double entry for the cost price if you have become familiar with the book-keeping in financial accounting (where movements of the cost are not usually recorded).

Activity 19

Complete the table on page 81 by stating the account to be debited and the account to be credited for each transaction. In each case you should name the account concerned and also state the amount.

Now that you have had an opportunity of working with the book-keeping you might like to refer back to the manufacturing account set out on page 75. You should be able to see that the so-called manufacturing account is essentially a replica of the ledger account called 'work in progress control account'. The only difference is that the work in progress control account is debited with overheads absorbed rather than overheads incurred.

Transaction	Debit	Credit
Purchase of 10 units of coslag on credit		
Issue of 12 units of coslag to production		
Payment of wages		
Allocation of total payroll costs to the various cost centres		

Payment of overheads:
    Production overheads
    Administration		

Production overheads absorbed		
Production overheads over- or under-absorbed		
Transfer of batch of sploggets from work in progress to finished goods store (you will need to determine the total cost on a separate working paper)		
Sales of finished goods. In this case there will be two double entries – one for the sales price and one for the cost price. For the sales price: For the cost price (use the unit cost price of opening stock for this entry):		

Summary

The main learning points in this chapter can be summarized as follows:

- manufacturers need a cost accounting system in order to determine the cost of their manufactured products
- in most manufacturing companies, cost accounting and financial accounting are integrated as parts of one single recording system
- these single integrated systems tend to be designed in order to satisfy the legal requirements of reporting profits and financial position to shareholders rather than providing managers with useful cost information
- for financial accounting, all manufacturing costs (direct product costs and factory overheads) are treated as the cost of producing

assets, they are not treated as expenses (production costs are inventoriable costs, not period costs)

- in financial reports, production costs for an accounting period must be split between the cost of goods sold (to be matched with sales income) and the cost of closing stock (to be reported as an asset)
- measurement of profit is dependent upon the extent to which production costs for the period are carried forward in the closing stock of finished goods
- reported results differ according to whether the cost of closing stock is based on the principle of marginal cost or absorbed cost
- financial accounting regulations (SSAP 9) require the cost of closing stock to be on an absorbed cost basis with fixed production overheads absorbed according to the normal level of activity (which might differ from the actual production level)
- the effect of using absorbed cost for closing stock is to carry forward fixed production overheads from the period when they were incurred to the period when the stock is sold.
- it is acceptable in financial accounting to determine the absorbed cost of stock by using broad and somewhat arbitrary allocations of production overheads to the various products
- absorption methods that are acceptable in financial accounting are not suitable for managers who need cost information for planning, control and decision making
- conflicting demands for cost information suggest that a single system is unable to satisfy these demands – separate systems are needed for three separate functions, namely: control of departmental costs, product costs for managerial decisions and product costs for profit measurement
- conventional absorption costing systems rely on attributing all production overheads to production cost centres
- an absorption rate is determined by dividing the total overheads of each production cost centre by an activity measurement such as the number of direct labour hours for that cost centre
- absorption rates are based on budgeted figures (for cost and activity) in order to spread cyclical costs over a longer period and to avoid delay in processing cost information; budgeted figures also ensure compliance with financial accounting regulations
- overheads absorbed (charged to finished goods) in a period will differ from overheads incurred in that period; the difference is usually written off to cost of sales
- the cost book-keeping centres around three control accounts for different types of stock, namely: raw materials, work in progress, and finished goods
- all production costs (apart from overheads under- or over-absorbed) finish up being charged to a finished goods control account; when goods are sold their cost is transferred from finished goods control to a cost of sales account

Activity 1

	Marginal cost		Absorbed cost
Sales turnover		1,000,000		1,000,000
Manufacturing costs (total)	900,000		900,000	
Deduct cost of closing stock	100,000		200,000	
Cost of sales		800,000		700,000
Gross profit		200,000		300,000

Activity 2

	Marginal cost		Absorbed cost
Sales turnover		1,450,000		1,450,000
Cost of opening stock	100,000		200,000	
Manufacturing costs (total)	800,000		800,000	
Deduct cost of closing stock	nil		nil	
Cost of sales		900,000		1,000,000
Gross profit		550,000		450,000

Activity 3

Fixed production overheads amounting to £100,000 that were incurred in Year 1 have been carried forward (in the cost of stock) and treated as an expense in Year 2.

Activity 4

The answer is marginal cost. You can see an example of this by looking at the answer to Activity 2 again (where stock quantities fell to zero by the end of the period).

Activity 5

The cost of acquiring fixed assets (such as plant and machinery for use in the factory). The annual expense is called depreciation.

Activity 6

1. In the period when paid.
2. When the goods are sold.
3. Over the number of years that the van is used in the business.

Activity 7

1. Chargeable hour. Note that a chargeable hour means one person working on a job for a client for one hour (there will be different rates per hour for the different categories of staff).
2. A quantity such as one ream of A4 paper (of a particular quality).
3. Tonne mile (i.e. the cost of carrying one tonne for one mile).

Activity 8

1. Service cost centre.
2. Production cost centre.
3. Service cost centre.
4. Production cost centre.

Activity 9

The unit would have been processed in previous production cost centres before reaching the finishing department. Overheads for these cost centres must also be absorbed.

Activity 10

Three examples (described according to their functions) could be: selling and distribution, administration, finance.

Activity 11

The three classes of cost needed here are: raw materials, factory labour, factory overhead.

Activity 12

The three elements of cost needed here are: direct materials, direct labour, overhead absorbed.

Activity 13

1. The term raw materials includes both direct materials and indirect materials.
2. The term factory labour includes both direct labour and indirect labour.
You might need to refer back to Chapter 1 if you have forgotten how to distinguish between direct and indirect costs.

Activity 14

Products made during the winter months will have a higher unit cost than those made during the summer.

Activity 15

£120,000 ÷ 30,000 = £4.00 per direct hour.

Activity 16

1. 29,000 × £4.00 = £116,000.
2. £122,000 − £116,000 = £6,000 (in Chapter 5 you will learn how to analyse this amount between its two causes).

Activity 17

There are various reasons such as: losses through theft, pilferage and spoilage; book-keeping errors; incorrect quantities issued to production.

Activity 18

1. Work in progress control account.
2. Production overheads control account.

Activity 19

Transaction	Debit	Credit
Purchase of 10 units coslag on credit	Raw materials control £50	Creditors £50
Issue of 12 units coslag to production	Work in progress control £60	Raw materials control £60
Payment of wages	Payroll control £66	Bank £66
Allocation of payroll costs to the various cost centres	Work in progress £36 Production overheads £10 Administration expenses £20	Payroll control £66

Payment of overheads:
    Production overheads:
 	
    Administration:
	
	Production overheads £20
	
	Administration expenses £30
		Bank £50

Production overheads absorbed	Work in progress control £24 (12 × £2)	Production overheads £24
Production overheads over- or under-absorbed	Cost of sales £6 (total overheads are £30, overheads absorbed are £24)	Production overheads control £6
Transfer of batch of sploggets from work in progress to finished goods store	Finished goods control £120 (£60 + £36 + £24)	Work in progress control £120

Sales of finished goods.
    For the sales price:
 	
    For the cost price:
	
	Debtors £500
	
	Cost of sales £150 (15 × £10)
		
		Sales £500
		
		Finished goods control £150

Many past examination questions that could be answered from reading this chapter merely ask for certain terms (such as cost unit and cost centre) to be defined. Such questions are not reproduced here because they do not test anything other than memory. Question 3.2 is an exception, but this has been included because it does call for a wider discussion of certain terms. Questions on manufacturing accounts are not included – if this subject forms part of your syllabus you should refer to the relevant chapter in a financial accounting text book.

Questions for self assessment

Answers to self-assessment questions are given at the end of the book.

3.1 Rumbles Ltd manufactures a single product, with a variable manufacturing cost of £12 per unit and a selling price of £20 per unit. Fixed production overheads are £90,000 per period. The company's cost accounting system is designed to produce figures that comply with financial accounting regulations. Consequently, fixed production overheads are absorbed on the basis of normal activity which has been predetermined at 15,000 units per period, i.e. an absorption rate of £6 per unit. Overheads under- or over-absorbed are written off to cost of sales at the end of each period. It may be assumed that no other expenses are incurred.

Summarized below are the company's manufacturing and trading results showing quantities only, for Periods 2 and 3.

	Period 2 units	Period 3 units
Opening stock	5,000	11,000
Quantity produced	17,000	13,000
	22,000	24,000
Less closing stock	11,000	6,000
Quantity sold	11,000	18,000

The managing director of Rumbles Ltd, who has recently returned from a course on 'marginal costing', has calculated that since overheads are fixed, and sales have increased by 7,000 units in Period 3, the company's profits should have increased by £56,000.

However, the results produced by the accountant show that profits for Period 3 have dropped by £10,000. The figures produced by the accountant show profits for Period 2 as £34,000 and for Period 3 as £24,000. Not surprisingly, the managing director is confused by the accountant's figures.

Required
(a) Carefully explain:
  (i) how the managing director calculated the increase of £56,000 for Period 3
  (ii) how the accountant calculated the profits of £34,000 and £24,000
  (iii) what has caused the difference between reported results and the managing director's expectations.
(b) Produce a numerical statement that provides support for your explanation in (a) (iii).

(ACCA Level 1 Costing, adapted)

3.2 Terminology
(a) Briefly describe the following terms:
  (i) marginal cost
  (ii) prime cost

      (iii) period cost
      (iv) product cost.
  (b) How far is it true to state that:
      (i) the marginal cost of a product equates to its prime cost?
      (ii) absorption costing recognizes product costs in full, whereas marginal costing recognizes variable costs, but ignores period costs?

(ULSEB A Level, part)

3.3 Book-keeping. This question is intended for students whose syllabus requires them to be conversant with the book-keeping procedures.

Refer to the details for Zambia Industrials Ltd as used for Activity 19. You are required to write up a complete set of ledger accounts for the period. These should include balances brought forward from the previous period, transactions for the period and closing balances where appropriate. Remember that some financial transactions were not included in the list of double entries for Activity 19 (receipts from debtors and payments to creditors). After writing up the ledger accounts produce a profit and loss account for the period and a balance sheet at the end of the period.

Questions without answers

Answers to these questions are published separately in the *Teacher's Manual*.

3.4 Kapon Ltd commenced business on 1 January 1993 and is now in the process of preparing financial statements for year ending 31 December 1993. The company manufactures and sells three separate products. Products 1 and 2 are manufactured in two sequential processes and Product 3 is manufactured by a single process. Unfortunately, the company did not set up any cost accounting system and the managing director has asked for your advice on how to calculate the cost of closing stock of finished goods. The accounts assistant has been able to determine from technical estimates, and from some of the accounting records, that the direct costs could be estimated as follows:

	Product 1 per unit	Product 2 per unit	Product 3 per unit
Direct materials	£2	£4	£6
Direct labour	£4	£4	£2

When you enquire into the figure for total production overheads for the year you find that it amounts to £600,000. The accounts assistant has worked out that this represents 200% of the cost of raw materials consumed (£300,000) during the year. The managing director cannot understand why you are worrying over the production overheads and says: 'the money has been spent and so we should treat the £600,000 as an expense for the year'. He considers the above estimates for direct costs are sufficiently accurate and should be used as the basis for the stock valuation.

Required:
  (a) State how you would respond to the managing director's comments regarding the treatment of production overheads.
  (b) State the kind of information that you consider might be necessary in order to determine an overhead cost per unit.
  (c) The accounts assistant has suggested that since overheads represent 200% of the total cost of raw materials consumed, it would be reasonable to add on 200% of the cost of raw material for each unit in order to find an overhead cost per unit. Describe how you would respond to this suggestion.
  (d) The managing direct states that he is not really interested in the overhead cost per unit for the purposes of pricing decisions because he works on the basis of a contribution per unit. Suggest ways in which this approach might lead to bad decisions.

3.5 A new subsidiary of a group of companies was established for the manufacture and sale of Product X. During the first year of operations 90,000 units were sold at £20 per unit. At the end of the year, the closing stocks were 8,000 units in finished goods store and 4,000 units in work in progress. The work in progress was complete as regards material costs but only half complete in respect of labour and overheads (see author's note). You can assume that there were no opening stocks.

Total production costs for the year were as follows:

	£
Direct materials consumed	714,000
Direct labour	400,000
Variable overhead	100,000
Fixed overhead	350,000

Selling and administration costs for the year were:

	Variable cost per unit sold £	Fixed cost for year £
Selling	1.50	200,000
Administration	9.10	50,000

The cost of closing stocks has been determined as follows:

	Absorbed cost	Marginal cost
Finished goods	£124,000	£96,000
Work in progress	45,000	38,000

Author's note: The above information on stock values was not given in the original question and it had to be calculated from the data provided. The techniques required for doing this have not yet been covered – they are dealt with in Chapter 6.

The accountant of the subsidiary company had prepared a profit statement on the absorption costing principle which showed a profit of £11,000

The financial controller of the group, however, had prepared a profit statement on a marginal costing basis which showed a loss. Faced with these two profit statements, the director responsible for this particular subsidiary company is confused.

Required:
(a) Prepare a profit statement on the absorption costing principle which agrees with the company accountant's statement.
(b) Prepare a profit statement on the marginal costing basis.
(c) Explain the differences between the two statements given for (a) and (b) above to the director in such a way as to eliminate his confusion.
(d) It is often said that absorption costing favours production, while marginal costing favours sales. You are required to explain this statement, and also to explain the extent to which both profit statements (in (a) and (b) above) are acceptable.

(CIMA Stage 2 Cost accounting, adapted)

4 ▷ Stock control and labour costs

Objectives

After you have completed this chapter, you should be able to:

- evaluate the different methods for pricing materials issued or goods sold and illustrate how the choice of method affects the measurement of profits and assets
- calculate stock control levels and economic order quantities using conventional quantitative techniques
- evaluate the benefits of 'just-in-time' purchasing
- demonstrate the effect on unit costs of various remuneration schemes that include an incentive for production workers to increase output
- analyse production payroll costs between direct labour and indirect labour

Introduction

The procedures used for determining the cost of products (whether they be goods or services) are usually covered under the general heading of 'cost ascertainment'. Traditionally, cost ascertainment in text books is presented in the context of a manufacturer – probably because most of the techniques were developed in the manufacturing sector. There is nothing wrong with this approach because most of the techniques can form the basis of methods used in other industries. An interesting outcome of the work that has been done on improving cost accounting for overheads in manufacturing is that the new techniques are found to be equally suited to certain types of entity in the service sector.

The reason for mentioning this in a chapter entitled 'stock control and labour costs' is that cost ascertainment in manufacturing involves a study of the three key elements of cost, namely: raw materials, labour and overheads. These three elements cannot really be covered in one chapter because the subject of overheads has now become so important that it requires a chapter of its own (see Chapter 5). The remaining two elements, raw materials and labour costs, are covered in this chapter but the subject of accounting for raw material costs is included under the general heading of '**stock control**'. This allows the various techniques to be seen as relevant to many situations, not merely to raw material costs in manufacturing.

The largest part of the chapter deals with stock control. There are several aspects of stock control that you need to learn at a foundation level, such as the problems of keeping an accounting control over stocks (perpetual inventory), and calculating optimum stock levels. The subject of perpetual inventories is (to some extent) associated with the problems of profit measurement, whereas optimum stock levels is concerned with stock management and involves using quantitative techniques to help managers with this problem. You will also have to consider how recent stock management techniques (which originated in the Japanese car manufacturing industry) are causing most companies to reappraise their policy on stock holding levels. The small section on certain aspects of labour costs deals mainly with the issues that arise in the context of cost ascertainment in a manufacturing entity, but the same principles can be applied to other types of entity. This has been included here simply because the subject is too narrow to warrant a separate chapter.

4.1 Perpetual inventory: The accounting problem

In Chapter 3 you saw how the cost accounting system in a manufacturing entity maintains an accounting control over raw material stocks. This is done by treating raw materials in the accounting records as an asset which increases when materials are purchased and decreases when materials are issued to production. By keeping an accounting record of the cost of raw materials purchased and the cost of raw materials issued to production, the balance on the account represents the cost of raw materials that should be in stock at any particular date. For control purposes, this balance can be checked with the physical stock in the stores department and any differences investigated.

This idea of keeping an account with a running balance of the raw material stocks is known as a perpetual inventory. The accounting records usually keep a running balance in terms of both quantity and cost. The general idea of a perpetual inventory can be used by any type of entity that keeps a stock of products, whether these be raw materials, finished goods of a retailer or drugs in a hospital pharmacy. The procedures employed do require the organization to keep some kind of controllable record of goods received and goods issued, but the use of modern information technology has reduced the amount of clerical work involved.

In simple financial accounting there is no record of stock movements because the stock purchased is recorded at cost price and the stock sold is recorded at selling price. Since the two movements are recorded at different prices, it is impossible to use the figures to keep an accounting control over stocks. This is why small retailers have to count their stock at the end of the year and then calculate the cost price of this stock in order to work out the cost of the goods that were sold. Most of the larger supermarkets do keep a perpetual inventory of stocks by making use of modern information technology. In these cases, data on goods moving out of stock are collected at the point of sale through the use of bar codes.

Although information technology will solve most of the practical difficulties of recording stock movements, the main question that has to be addressed by profit orientated entities is how to determine the cost price of goods taken out of stock (by issue or sale). There would be no problem if cost prices were stable, but this is not usually the case. If we look at the purchase prices of a particular product over a period such as one year, we will find that those prices have been constantly changing. If there are several purchase prices, how do we determine the cost price of the goods that were issued or sold? There is no single answer to this problem; all we can do is adopt an accounting policy. The policy adopted for pricing the cost of goods issued or sold will have an effect on both the cost of sales and the cost of closing stock. The computer can do all the calculations, but it will have to be programmed to use the policy chosen by the company.

4.2 Pricing the issues

Although we will be looking at the problem of changing cost prices in the context of raw materials issued to production, you must keep in mind that the same problem (and its solution) relates to any kind of stock, such as bought in components, work in progress, finished goods and goods purchased for resale.

When the unit input prices to a perpetual inventory are constantly changing, the company must adopt an accounting policy in order to identify the cost price of the goods moving out of that inventory. In the case of raw materials, inputs are represented by purchases and outputs are represented by issues to the production department. From your study of Chapter 3 you will know that these issues are either charged to work in progress (if they are direct materials) or to production overheads (if they are indirect materials). The accounting policy adopted for pricing these issues could be one of several, although the following abbreviations and names identify those that you need to understand:

- **FIFO:** as an acronym it is pronounced as spelt (the letter 'I' pronounced as in 'eye'). The letters stand for first in, first out. As a pricing policy it uses the oldest price first, on the assumption that the first goods to come in are the first to go out.
- **LIFO:** as with FIFO, this is pronounced as spelt. The letters stand for last in, first out. It uses the last purchase price first, on the assumption that the last lot of goods to come in are the first to go out.
- **AVCO:** again, this is pronounced as spelt. The letters stand for average cost, and it is usually based on a weighted average price found by dividing the total cost of a particular material in stock at any time by the total quantity of that stock.

It is also possible to use a basis known as **standard cost** but you will have to postpone learning about this until Chapter 7. Interestingly enough, standard cost is acceptable under the regulations that govern financial accounting, even though standard cost is a predicted cost rather than a cost that was actually incurred.

Activity 1

Generally speaking, LIFO is considered unsuitable for determining the cost of closing stocks by the financial accounting regulation known as SSAP 9. This regulation does not prohibit the use of LIFO, it merely suggests that in most cases it would be inappropriate to determine the cost of closing stock on a LIFO basis. Notice how SSAP 9 addresses the problem by looking at the cost of closing stock rather than the cost of materials issued or cost of goods sold. These two aspects are different ways of looking at the same problem because one is a product of the other. Make a note here of why you think the accounting regulators came to their conclusion regarding LIFO.

A further problem arises where businesses (particularly small ones) do not keep a perpetual inventory showing all the movements in and out of stock. The problem does not arise in the case of FIFO, but if these businesses determine their closing stocks on a LIFO or AVCO basis at the end of the period (called a 'periodic' basis), the figures can differ from what they would have been if a perpetual inventory had been kept. We will look at this problem in Section 4.3.

An important point to keep in mind at this stage of your studies is that none of the three methods has any more merit than the others. There will be some cases where LIFO does represent the pattern of movement for goods. For example, in coal mining, new coal produced is constantly being added to an existing stock pile. When coal is removed for sale it might be taken from the latest lot of coal produced. There are also quite sound arguments for using LIFO as a means of correcting the distortions in profit measurement caused by inflation, but it requires a study of income theory in order to appreciate this point. Although LIFO is an acceptable basis under the 1985 Companies Act, you are unlikely to find it being used in practice; its condemnation stems from it being frowned upon by SSAP 9, and also that it is not acceptable by the tax authorities for measuring taxable profit.

The idea of AVCO might sound more scientific, but it can result in costs (cost of sales and cost of closing stock) that bear little relationship to the actual expenditure incurred. For financial accounting, SSAP 9 is concerned with the cost of closing stock, although you will know from your study of Chapter 3 that the cost carried forward in stock has a direct impact on the amount of profit reported. SSAP 9 treats the problem of identifying the cost price of stock (when those prices have been changing) as a practical problem rather than a matter of principle. Consequently, it merely requires management to select a method which provides the fairest possible approximation to the actual expenditure incurred on the stock; it does not stipulate that any particular method must be used.

Details for the activities

Although most companies use computers to maintain their perpetual inventory, you will have to use manual calculations for a series of simple transactions in order to evaluate the effect of the three different methods of pricing the issues. The details are as follows.

A computer manufacturer set up business on 1 January. Various components are bought in and assembled into a variety of products. One of these components is known as XYJ. A perpetual inventory is kept for all stock items. Purchases and issues of component XYJ for the three months to 31 March were as follows:

Purchases			Issues	
Date received	Quantity (units)	Cost per unit £	Date of issue	Quantity
13 January	200	36	10 February	500
8 February	400	40	25 March	600
11 March	600	44		

The stocks of XYJ were counted at 31 March and the quantity in stock was 100 units.

Activity 2

On the assumption that this company uses a FIFO basis for pricing issues to production, calculate (using your own paper) the following:

1. The total cost price of goods issued on:
   10 February
   25 March
   Total cost price of issues in the quarter.

2. The total cost price of closing stock on 31 March.

After checking with the Key, make a note of the amounts against each item above.

Activity 3

Now do the same thing again, except that this time assume that a LIFO basis is used for pricing the issues:

1. The total cost price of goods issued on:
   10 February
   25 March
   Total cost price of issues in the quarter.

2. The total cost price of closing stock on 31 March.

When an AVCO basis is used it will be necessary to calculate a new average price each time there is a purchase. The average price per unit is found by dividing the total purchase cost of all units in stock by the total quantity in stock. Because the average constantly changes, it is sometimes called a moving average.

Activity 4

Calculate the following on the assumption that an AVCO basis is used for pricing the issues:

1. The total cost price of goods issued on:
   10 February
   25 March
   Total cost price of issues in the quarter.

2. Total cost price of closing stock on 31 March.

A summary of the three methods is as follows:

	Costs charged to production £	Cost of stock £	Total cost of purchases £
FIFO basis (Activity 2)	45,200	4,400	49,600
LIFO basis (Activity 3)	46,000	3,600	49,600
AVCO basis (Activity 4)	45,276	4,324	49,600

It is not possible to identify specifically the effect this will have on reported profits because there are two other elements of cost (labour and overheads) that form part of the cost of finished goods and (when the goods are sold) the cost of sales.

Activity 5

On the assumption that all three elements of cost (materials, labour and overhead) are rising, and that the policy adopted for determining the cost of sales is the same as for pricing the issues of raw materials, which policy will produce the higher profits: FIFO or LIFO?

As you might have noticed, AVCO produces a compromise between the two policies.

4.3 Pricing, policy and profits

It is easier to see the effect of changing prices on profits if we forget about manufacturing and look at a simple model based on retailing. It is also possible to see how a perpetual basis (using a perpetual inventory) can produce different figures to a periodic basis (where the cost price of closing stocks is determined by a single calculation at the end of the period).

Details for the activities

Ima Sella started a retailing business for one particular product on 1 July. During July, Ima's transactions were as follows:

	£
1 July purchased initial stock, 40 items at £110 each	4,400
10 July purchased 50 items at £120 each	6,000
20 July purchased 20 items at £130 each	2,600
	13,000
15 July sold 50 items for £200 each	10,000
25 July sold 10 items for £250 each	2,500
	12,500

For Activities 6, 7, and 8 we will assume that Ima keeps a perpetual inventory to record all movements of stock items.

Activity 6

On a separate sheet of paper, work out the following figures for the month of July and make a note of the amount against each item:

1. Cost of sales for July.

2. Cost of stock at 31 July.

Check with the Key before going to the next activity.

Activity 7

Now do the same thing again except that this time use a LIFO basis. Remember that we are assuming a perpetual inventory is kept. Make a note here of the amounts:

1. Cost of sales for July.

2. Cost of stock at 31 July.

In order to save time, you are not going to be asked to work out the figures for AVCO. These would be as follows:

	Items in stock	Average price	Total cost	Cost of sales
at 15 July	90	£115.56	10,400	
sales on 15 July	50	£115.56	5,778	5,778
balance of stock	40		4,622	
purchase 20 July	20		2,600	
at 25 July	60	£120.37	7,222	
sales on 25 July	10	£120.37	1,204	1,204
stock at 31 July	50		6,018	
			Total cost of sales	6,982

Activity 8

In the outline format provided below, set out a calculation of Ima's gross profit for the month of July. Using the three bases for pricing goods sold:

	FIFO basis	LIFO basis	AVCO basis
Sales			
Less cost of sales			
Gross profit			

An interesting point to notice from Activity 8 is how LIFO charges the latest prices to cost of sales. It could be argued that this is more realistic in times of rising prices because it matches sales income with a purchase cost that is similar to the cost of replacing the stock sold. But financial accounts are prepared on what is known as the 'historical cost' convention, meaning (roughly) that sales income is matched with the original cost of assets consumed in the course of business, and not with the cost of replacing those assets. Consequently, although LIFO might go some way towards solving the problem of profit measurement when prices are rising, it violates the rules for historical cost accounting.

Using a periodic basis

If perpetual inventories are not kept, the application of the three pricing policies to closing stock valuations must still take account of price movements during the period. The way in which this could be done is as follows:

- **FIFO periodic:** work backwards from the accounting date until the number of units purchased equals the number in closing stock.
- **LIFO periodic:** work forwards from the opening stock until the number of units equals the number of units in closing stock.
- **AVCO periodic:** add the total cost of opening stock to the cost of purchases in the period, and divide this total by the total number of units in the opening stock and purchases.

The figures for FIFO will always be the same as when a perpetual inventory is kept. Stock valuations under LIFO and AVCO that are done on a periodic basis can differ from those produced by a perpetual inventory.

Activity 9

Calculate the cost of closing stock (50 items) for Ima Sella using the following bases:

FIFO periodic   LIFO periodic   AVCO periodic

A criticism of AVCO periodic as used above is that the cost of closing stock is influenced by purchase prices for goods that have long since been sold. A variation that might be more acceptable is to base the average on sufficient quantities of the latest purchases to cover the quantity in stock (e.g. in the case of Ima Sella, the average price could be based on the purchase of 50 items on 10 July and 20 items on 20 July).

4.4 Optimum stock levels

Just-in-time inventory management

The annual financial report of Marks and Spencer plc for 1993 includes a section entitled 'Review of activities'. The following text has been extracted from a section in that review called 'Operations' (on page 17 of the report):

> By applying information technology to our buying systems we have reduced the supply cycle for clothing and home furnishings from two weeks to five days. ... Similarly we have reduced the ten-day cycle for food to two or three days. Daily adjustment to orders allows precise control of stocks in stores ...

The expression 'supply cycle' refers to the length of time between two points: it starts when existing stocks reach a level at which they need to be replenished by a new order; it ends when the goods arrive and are available for sale (or use by the factory in the case of raw materials). In accounting jargon, the supply cycle is usually called the 'lead time'.

Activity 10

Identify and describe the main advantage for Marks and Spencer of being able to reduce the supply cycle, as described in the above quotation.

In an ideal (albeit make believe) world, businesses would prefer to have a situation whereby the stock arrives early in the morning, is placed on display before the shop opens, and by the end of the day there are no unsold goods left in the shelf. This would be 'just-in-time' (JIT) purchasing at its optimum, and the business could reduce its investment in stock to zero. But this state is virtually impossible to achieve. Even Marks and Spencer with its sophisticated information technology, recording sales data at the point of sale (POS) and with computer links to its main suppliers for placing orders, will have to carry sufficient stocks of clothing and home furnishing to cover the sales over a five-day cycle. It will probably carry a little more than this in order to be on the safe side.

The trend towards carrying the barest minimum of stocks is driven by the need to reduce costs. When thinking about these cost savings you should not think of the amount spent on buying the goods as a cost. Spending money on buying stock simply changes the form of an asset; the mere act of changing money into stocks does not create an expense. It is the fact that businesses must carry a quantity of stocks that creates an expense.

Activity 11

Identify and describe some of the costs associated with carrying stocks (apart from the cost of the stock itself).

You might find it interesting to learn that according to the financial statements included with Marks and Spencer's annual report, their 'net margin' (operating profit as a percentage of sales) was increased from 11.9% in 1992 to 12.5% in 1993. There will be several factors that contributed to this improvement, but reducing the supply cycle (and stock holding costs) must be one of them.

Manufacturers need to consider optimum stock levels for both raw materials and finished goods. Raw materials should not be ordered too far in advance of the time they will be used, and finished goods should not be produced too far in advance of expected demand. If it is possible for a manufacturer to take advantage of JIT management, these two aspects are called JIT purchasing and JIT production, respectively. The CIMA defines these two terms in the following way:

- **JIT purchasing**: a system that involves *'matching the receipt of material closely with usage so that raw material inventory is reduced to near-zero levels'*.
- **JIT production**: *'a system which is driven by demand for finished products whereby each component on a production line is produced only when needed for the next stage'*.

JIT purchasing often makes use of small but frequent deliveries against a bulk contract. The basic idea is to use suppliers as the warehouse for raw materials so that storage costs are pushed back to the supplier. Whether a business is able to take advantage of JIT will depend on several factors, such as its influence over suppliers, its ability to identify customer demand, and the stability of labour relations in those sectors of industry upon which the trade depends. As an inventory management technique, JIT was originated by Toyota, the Japanese car manufacturer. It was designed at a time when all of their operations were carried on within a 50 km radius of central office. Very few companies have the economic influence of Toyota, and in those cases where trading is spread over a wide geographic area (such as where raw materials must be imported) JIT will be almost impossible.

Activity 12

JIT is a useful inventory management technique but should not be seen as a panacea for all of the problems associated with manufacturing in Europe. Try to identify and describe further situations in which JIT might not be appropriate.

A number of companies that originally adopted JIT inventory management systems have abandoned them in favour of a more traditional approach despite the higher costs associated with such systems (e.g. see a report in the *Financial Times* on 4 October 1990 regarding Apple Computers, a company that was among the earliest to adopt JIT). Perhaps the most important lesson from JIT stock management is that it has made firms aware of the need to reappraise their ordering and production systems. There will undoubtedly be many cases where both JIT and traditional methods should be applied to different products in the same firm; there is no reason to assume that the total stock management system must be based entirely on one of the two approaches.

Quantitative methods in traditional stock control systems

The traditional quantitative methods for establishing optimum stock levels centre around a quantity known as the **economic order quantity** (EOQ). The EOQ is based on a financial model that takes the estimated demand for a product over a period and divides this up into a number of equal-sized batches for which purchase orders should be placed. Since each order is of equal size, the frequency of placing orders during the period is also established.

The EOQ model finds a balance between two opposing costs: the cost of placing orders (salaries, stationery, telephone, etc.) and the cost of holding stocks (cost of capital invested in stocks, insurance, handling, etc). You can see this by looking at two extremes. If the annual demand for a product is estimated at 10,000 units, ordering costs can be reduced to almost zero by placing one order each year. Yet this involves a high cost of holding stocks (if demand is constant, the average stock held for the period will be 5,000 units). If on the other hand we place orders for batches of 100 throughout the period, the cost of holding stock will be reduced but there will be a substantial increase in the cost of placing orders.

There are various ways of determining the EOQ, such as setting out a tabulation of costs for various order quantities until the minimum cost is found, or by using a graph. The most convenient way is to use the following formula:

$$EOQ = \sqrt{\frac{2 \times Cost\ per\ order \times Demand\ for\ period}{Cost\ of\ carrying\ one\ unit}}$$

There is little point in working through the mathematical derivation of this formula; you can accept it as producing the correct quantity for the EOQ model. The result can be proved by tabulating costs for order quantities either side of the quantity derived from the formula By doing this you will see some of the assumptions on which it is based. Some examiners expect you to remember the formula, others will provide it in the exam. A test of whether someone has remembered a formula is not really a test of skills and so examinations that require students to memorize formulae are on the decline. If you are required to remember the formula, you need to replace the words with some evocative symbols, such as:

$$EOQ = \sqrt{\frac{2\ Co\ D}{Cc}}$$

The symbols used above are different to those normally presented in a text book but they will help you to recall the formula (if you have to) by thinking about a take-away order at a fish-and-chip shop: '*two cod and two chips*'. Take care over what the symbols mean; they are as follows:

Co = Cost of ordering (i.e. the cost of placing an order)

D = Annual demand (measured in some quantity such as units or kilos)

Cc = Cost of carrying one unit in stock for the period

The cost of carrying one unit of stock is often given as a percentage of the cost of one unit. This is probably because the highest cost of carrying stock is related to the cost of capital that has been invested in stock. This is sometimes expressed as the return required from the investment in stock; a concept based on the idea of an opportunity cost. By investing money in stocks the firm is denied the opportunity of investing that capital elsewhere in order to earn a return.

Activity 13

A company is reviewing its stock control policy with regard to material X. The cost of placing an order (salaries, paperwork, telephone, etc.) is £100. Each kilo of product X costs £2.50. The opportunity cost of investing in stocks is 10% per annum (you can assume that there are no other carrying costs). The annual usage of material X is 80,000 kilos. Calculate the EOQ for material X (don't forget to display the result of the fraction by pressing the = key on your calculator before pressing the square root key).

The EOQ model assumes that demand for material X will be constant throughout the period and so the company will place (80,000 ÷ 8,000) 10 orders at intervals of (roughly) every five weeks throughout the year. The validity of the formula can be checked by working out total costs if the quantities ordered were (say) 5,000 kilos and 10,000 kilos (i.e. order quantities either side of the EOQ). In order to clarify the explanation, a few simple assumption will be made.

Assumptions:
1. There are no 'buffer' (or 'safety') stocks – in other words stocks are reduced to zero before a new order is placed.
2. There is no supply cycle (or lead time) – in other words as soon as stocks reach zero they are immediately replenished to a level equal to the new order.
3. Usage of material X is at a constant rate throughout the period.

The first two assumptions have been made for the sake of clarity in the explanation, they are not assumptions inherent in the EOQ model.

From these assumptions it should be clear that if orders are placed for 8,000 kilos, the quantities in stock at any one time must be somewhere between 8,000 kilos and zero kilos. If usage is at a constant rate, the average quantity in stock throughout the period will be 4,000 kilos (one-half of 8,000). The same concept applies to the other quantities ordered. The cost of holding stock can therefore be based on one-half of the quantity ordered. Costs of ordering will depend on the number of orders placed.

Data:

Order quantity (kilos)	5,000	8,000	10,000
Number of orders placed per annum	16	10	8
Average quantity in stock (kilos)	2,500	4,000	5,000
Cost of average stock (average quantity × £2.50)	£6,250	£10,000	£12,500

Costs:

Ordering costs (number of orders × £100)	£1,600	£1,000	£800
Holding costs (10% of cost of average stock)	625	1,000	1,250
Total costs	2,225	2,000	2,050

As can be seen, orders of 8,000 kilos result in the lowest cost. If you care to work out the total costs for any order quantity either side of 8,000 kilos you will find that they exceed £2,000.

Assumptions in the EOQ model

Although the EOQ model provides a useful way of approaching the problem of stock control, the figures must be interpreted with care. Some of the assumptions on which it is based are as follows:

1. There will be a constant rate of usage throughout each cycle.
2. If safety stocks (buffer stocks) are kept, they will remain the same irrespective of the size of the order.
3. Stock holding costs are constant per unit – this might be true for the cost of funds invested in stocks but other costs per unit (such as material handling) might vary according to the level of stocks maintained.
4. Ordering costs are variable and, therefore, the total amount spent on purchasing will depend on the number of orders placed.

Sensitivity of EOQ to changes in the relevant costs

It would be wrong to think of the EOQ model as something that simply provided a definitive answer to a decision problem (how many should we order each time?) The value of most financial models is that they allow mangers to explore the effect of making changes to the inputs of that model (the 'what if' approach). In some cases the model might be responsible for providing managers with information that they had previously ignored. A manager reviewing the EOQ model in Activity 13 might be surprised to learn that it costs £100 to place an order; experimenting with the effect of changing that input might lead to a better decision.

By examining the formula, we can see intuitively that a reduction in ordering costs will reduce the EOQ. We can also see that an increase in carrying costs (the denominator of the fraction) will also reduce the EOQ. If, for example, ordering costs can be reduced to £10 per order, the EOQ becomes 2,530 kilos if carrying costs per unit remain the same.

If order size is reduced from batches of 8,000 kilos (as in Activity 13) to 2,530 kilos (as in the above paragraph), it is quite likely that carrying costs per unit will increase. If there are no carrying costs other than the cost of capital invested in stocks, there is still likely to be an increase in the carrying costs per unit. Describe why this might be so.

If we assume that the purchase price increases to £2.60 per kilo, the carrying cost in our particular example will be £0.26. This will reduce the EOQ to 2,480 kilos. Now look at the costs associated with an EOQ of 2,480 units:

Data:

Order quantity (kilos)	2,480
Number of orders placed per annum	32
Average quantity in stock (kilos)	1,240
Cost of average stock (average quantity × £2.60)	£3,224

Costs:

Ordering costs (number of orders × £10)	£320
Holding costs (10% of cost of average stock)	322
Total costs:	642

As you would expect, the total cost of ordering and carrying a stock of material X is substantially reduced with these smaller and more frequent orders (compare the total costs to those for 8,000 kilos per order). This analysis goes some way towards justifying JIT purchasing, but it would be wrong to assume that a JIT policy will use the EOQ model as a guide. The EOQ model assumes a constant rate of usage and a constant amount per order whereas JIT needs to be flexible in terms of the timing and quantity for each order. JIT normally works by placing a bulk contract with one supplier and drawing on this as required. Such a policy can work only with the cooperation of the supplier.

Re-order level

Assuming that the EOQ has been determined, the next stage of the process (when traditional stock control methods are used) is to work out a point at which the order needs to be placed. In the explanation of the EOQ above it was assumed that if the stocks were run down to zero, a new order could be placed to replenish the stocks immediately. This is clearly unrealistic. As stated earlier, even Marks and Spencer (whose purchasing function is linked by computer to its major suppliers) must wait five days for a new order of clothing or home furnishing to arrive. The order will have to be placed when existing stocks are sufficient to cover sales over this five-day cycle (additional stocks will also be kept to be on the safe side). In cases where firms rely on manual procedures for making requisitions and posting orders, there could be internal and postal delays quite apart from the period of time that it takes for a supplier to deliver the goods.

If we use the details from Activity 13, and assume a year of 50 weeks, then the usage of material X will be at the rate of (80,000 ÷ 50) 1,600 kilos per week. We now need to establish a lead time for the period between when it is first recognized that a new order must be placed, and the time when that order is likely to be received. Suppose we establish (from past experience) that this lead time is likely to be between 2 and 3 weeks.

Activity 15

When calculating the re-order level, it is normal practice to assume that the lead time will be the longest. Consequently, firms must re-order when stocks have reached a level where there is a sufficient quantity in stock to satisfy production (or sales) during the longest lead time period. Calculate the re-order level for material X.

By taking the longest likely lead time, an element of safety is built into the procedure. On average, suppliers of material X will take $2\frac{1}{2}$ weeks to satisfy the order. The idea of an average lead time can be used to establish a minimum stock level.

Minimum stock level

If we assume that the suppliers of material X will take, on average, $2\frac{1}{2}$ weeks to deliver the order, then stocks will be run down to a level of 800 kilos before the new order arrives. The 800 kilos was calculated as follows:

re-order level	4,800 kilos
less usage during average lead time (1,600 × 2.5)	4,000 kilos
stock level after average lead time	800 kilos

This quantity can be established as a minimum stock level. It identifies a level at which the new order should normally have arrived. If stocks fall below this level, the company must chase its supplier since there is a danger of running out of stock. The minimum stock level is, therefore, seen as a warning point at which some action (chasing the order) is required. It is possible to introduce another factor into the calculation. In the example being discussed we have based the calculations on a constant usage of 1,600 kilos per week. It might be possible to establish a range of likely usage, for example, 1,400 to 1,600 kilos per week. The re-order level will still be based on the maximum usage and maximum lead time, but the minimum level (the warning level) could be based on the level that would be reached if the average quantity (1,500 kilos) had been used in the average lead time.

Maximum stock level

If a re-order level is established for each product, together with an order quantity (whether by way of the EOQ or otherwise) for that product, it should be possible to establish a maximum stock level. This is a level which we would not normally expect the stocks to exceed. In the case of material X, we have already established that an order for 8,000 kilos will be placed when stocks reach a level of 4,800 kilos. The maximum stock level is based on the level that will be reached if the supplier takes the shortest likely time (2 weeks) to deliver the goods and the new stock is added to the existing stocks at that point. It assumes that the usage of stock during the lead time will be at the minimum rate (1,400 kilos per week in our modified example).

Activity 16

Calculate the maximum stock level for material X based on the details discussed in the above text and assuming that the EOQ of 8,000 kilos (as in Activity 13) is used as the re-order quantity.

Maximum, minimum and re-order levels are recorded on the stock account for each type of stock. If a stock account shows that current quantities exceed the predetermined maximum for that type of stock, some kind of enquiry might be necessary to establish the cause.

Activity 17

Assume the stock records reveal that the quantities of material X have reached a level of 13,000 kilos and a physical count shows this to be the actual quantity in stock. Make a note of some of the factors that might have caused this to happen.

EOQ and production quantities

We have been using the EOQ model to determine the policy regarding purchasing of raw materials. The same model can be used to determine production quantities. In this case you can think of the finished goods department as placing an order for more goods. The main difference is that instead of using the cost per order (as with raw materials) we need to use the cost of setting up the production facilities to satisfy the order.

There are various costs associated with setting up the production facilities to produce a specific batch of finished units. These 'set-up' costs relate to the time taken, and resources used, in order to prepare the facilities for the production run. As with raw materials, we can see the problem by looking at two extremes. The total set-up costs for a period can be reduced to quite low levels if there is only one set-up for the period. On the other hand, one set-up per period means that we will be carrying quite high levels of finished goods stock of the type for which the set-up was made. The cost of carrying that type of stock will be quite high. If we produce in small batches, the cost of carrying finished goods stock will be reduced but the number of set-ups will increase. The EOQ model will find the right balance. The same formula is used, with set-up costs taking the place of ordering costs.

This section deals with two aspects of labour costs that should be studied at a foundation level. These are related to the classification of costs as between direct and indirect, and to the effect of incentive payments on unit costs. For students who are required to develop skills in the double-entry recording, there is a final section dealing with further aspects of the payroll control account.

Classification: Direct or indirect

It is quite important to establish whether the employment costs of a particular employee should be treated as direct or indirect. If the cost is classed as direct it will be treated as a specific cost of the job, batch or unit of service provided; if it is classed as indirect, it will be treated as an overhead and spread over all the units (goods or services) produced.

As a starting point, the type of work performed will affect the classification In some cases the distinction is quite clear, in others it will be somewhat hazy. In an accountancy practice, the cost of employing trainees and qualified staff to carry out professional work is quite clearly a direct cost of the various jobs they perform, whereas the costs of general office staff (secretaries, computer operators, etc.) are clearly indirect. Each person working specifically on a client's job will keep a record of the time spent on that job. The same kind of distinction is usually fairly clear in businesses such as car repairs and maintenance; the cost of an engineer working on a particular job is a direct cost of that job, whereas the cost of employees such as cleaners is indirect.

In manufacturing it is not always easy to make this distinction and the overriding aim should be to treat as many costs as possible (including labour costs) as direct. Failure to do this can produce distortions in product costs, a point that you will appreciate more fully after studying the next chapter on overheads. The difficulty of discussing this in a text book is that the factors taken into account when classifying employees as direct or indirect will depend on the production method. In traditional manufacturing, the cost of maintenance engineers will most likely be classed as indirect since their work affects the entire range of goods produced by the factory. In cellular manufacturing (sometimes referred to as 'a factory within a factory') the entire labour force of a particular cell can be classed as direct, even though some of them are carrying out work which would otherwise be thought of as indirect (such as moving materials and adjusting equipment).

Activity 18

Although the classification of labour costs (as direct or indirect) will vary from one manufacturer to the next, there will be a general pattern. Try to identify types of labour costs in the factory that are most likely to be classified as indirect, and make a note of them here.

Apart from the type of work that each employee does, there is a further classification problem for certain types of payment made to those employees who are classed as direct. Some employment costs of direct labour might have to be classed as indirect. These payments need not concern us if they relate to indirect labour because the total costs of such employees are classed as indirect in any case.

The clearest example of where part of the wage paid to a direct worker might be classified as an indirect cost is an overtime premium. The expression 'overtime premium' does not refer to the total wage paid to an employee for working in an overtime period, but to the extra pay for working in that period. An employee who is paid £6.00 an hour for work in normal contract time might be paid £7.50 for working overtime (in this case the overtime rate is said to be at 'time and a quarter'). The overtime premium in this example is (£7.50 – £6.00) £1.50 per hour. Except in cases where a customer requires a rush job and is prepared to pay a price that reimburses the supplier for the entire cost of overtime, an overtime premium is normally classed as an overhead. It will therefore be spread over all units produced according to the methods used for dealing with overheads.

Activity 19

See if you can identify the rationale behind treating the overtime premium of direct workers as an overhead and, after checking your ideas with those in the Key, make a note of any relevant points here.

This same kind of approach is usually taken in respect of pay for idle time. In this case the absence of work is likely to be related to scheduling problems or machine breakdowns and the cost of paying for idle time cannot be identified with any specific units of output.

Further troublesome areas relate to payroll fringe costs such as the employer's share of National Insurance contributions and holiday pay. For the sake of expediency, some companies treat these costs as indirect but this approach has very little conceptual merit. If you bear in mind that the cost of employing direct workers will be charged to the various 'jobs' on which they work, it should be possible to calculate an inflated charge rate that takes account of these additional costs. The basic approach is to divide the total employment costs of each direct worker for a period by the number of hours each employee is available for productive work. This gives an hourly charge rate for each employee that will be charged to the jobs on which they work.

Example

The total employment costs of an employee are estimated as follows:

Basic earnings for 52 weeks	£12,480
(at £6 per hour for a 40 hour week)	
Employer's share of National Insurance	2,000
Contributions to a retirement benefit scheme	1,840
Total for year	16,320

Hours available for productive work:
40 hours per week for 48 weeks   1,920 hours
(i.e. 4 weeks holiday per year)

Charge-out rate £16,320 ÷ 1,920 = £8.50 per hour

Note that although this employee is being paid at the rate of £6.00 per hour, the amount charged to each job on which he or she works will be £8.50 per hour. If the employee does record a total of 1,920 hours productive time by the end of the year, the total cost of £16,230 will have been treated as a direct cost.

Incentive schemes

Payroll incentive schemes are usually designed to encourage higher levels of output in order to reduce unit costs. They are less prevalent today than in the past because modern production methods tend to be highly automated and individual employees have little influence over quantities produced or the time taken to produce each unit. In these cases employees might be encouraged to add to the general efficiency of the firm by means of profit sharing schemes rather than pay incentives.

Payroll incentive schemes are still relevant when production is labour intensive. But even in these cases, unit costs are not the sole factor that has to be considered. As discussed earlier, there is a cost of holding finished goods stock and anything gained by way of reduced unit costs (through a pay incentive scheme) might be offset by an increase in stock holding costs if there is a fall in demand for the product.

Activity 20

See if you can identify any other factors that might result in additional costs when employees are encouraged (by means of pay incentives) to increase output.

In those cases where pay incentives are considered to be beneficial, the total payroll costs usually increase but, because of the increased output, the cost per unit is reduced. There are many different kinds of incentive scheme; some result in a reduction of both direct labour and fixed overhead cost per unit, others might result in an increase in the labour cost per unit which is more than offset by a reduction in the fixed overhead cost per unit. The reduction in fixed overhead costs per unit results from fixed production overheads being spread over a larger number of units.

A reduction in direct labour costs per unit is sometimes achieved by setting a standard production time for each unit. If an employee produces a unit in less than the standard time, the total pay of that employee will include a bonus. The total pay is usually calculated by adding a proportion of the time saved to the actual hours worked. For example, if the standard time for producing a unit is 2 hours and an employee completes it in 1 hour, the employee will be paid for $1^1/_2$ hours if the bonus is based on one half of the time saved.

Schemes that are akin to piecework might have a sliding scale whereby the amount paid per unit is increased for each increment in the quantity produced. This type of scheme will be beneficial where the reduction of fixed overhead costs per unit is greater than the increased labour cost per unit.

Payroll control account

This section is concerned with certain aspects of the double-entry recording and can be ignored by those students whose syllabus excludes the requirement to develop book-keeping skills.

As was mentioned in Chapter 3, a payroll control account is used to build up a total debit balance equal to the gross payroll cost, plus the employer's share of National Insurance (and the employer's contributions to a retirement scheme if there is one). This total debit balance is then charged out to various cost centres (according to an analysis of the total) by crediting the payroll control and debiting the relevant cost centres. For example, the amount for direct labour costs that has been allocated to jobs will be debited to work in progress control, indirect labour costs are debited to production overheads control, and administration salaries are debited to administration expense control. The entire process is usually carried out as a computer update routine and relies on the use of employee numbers, job numbers and time records showing time spent on each job.

In terms of double-entry, the main aspect that needs to be considered is how the total debit balance is built up on the payroll control account. The first double-entry can be thought of as originating from the total cash paid out. This will be credited to bank and debited to the payroll control account. But this amount represents only the net wages after deductions. The deductions for PAYE and National Insurance, together with the employer's contributions, could be debited to payroll control when they are paid to the tax office but this is bad bookkeeping. At the time the wages are paid, any deductions for PAYE and National Insurance represent a liability of the company that should be reflected in the books.

Activity 21

From the above explanation you should be able to see the double-entry required for PAYE and National Insurance deductions, and for the employer's contributions. Describe the double-entry here:

Debit:

Credit:

When the liability is paid, the double-entry will be debit Inland Revenue and credit bank.

The following details relate to Month 8 for a company:

	£
Net wages paid to all employees	62,800
PAYE and National Insurance deductions	4,600
Employer's share of National Insurance	2,600
Analysis of total employment costs:	
Direct costs of jobs	33,000
Indirect factory labour	10,000
Administration expenses	15,000
Distribution costs	12,000

Write up the payroll control account. Each entry in this account must name the account to which the other side of the double-entry is posted.

Payroll control account

Summary

A summary of the key points in this chapter is as follows:

- most entities can take advantage of modern information technology in order to keep an accounting control over stocks
- profit orientated entities have an added problem of identifying a price for determining the cost of units moving out of stock
- the cost price of units taken out of stock could be based on one of several policies such as FIFO, LIFO and AVCO
- the policy adopted will have an influence on the cost of closing stock, the cost of goods sold, and the profit reported
- financial accounting regulations (particularly SSAP 9) oppose the use of LIFO for historical cost accounting, even though this policy would compensate for some of the distortions in profit measurement that result from inflation

- optimum stock levels depend to a large extent on whether stock management can be based on JIT purchasing and JIT production
- JIT relies on contractual relationships with suppliers and the ability to identify customer demand
- traditional quantitative methods of stock control are based on the EOQ, which establishes the size of purchase orders and how often they should be placed
- the EOQ is a trade-off between the cost of ordering and the cost of carrying stocks; it determines a quantity where the total of these two costs will be at a minimum
- the EOQ can also be used to determine production quantities by using set-up costs in place of ordering costs
- re-order levels are based on maximum expected lead times and maximum usage during that lead time
- minimum stock levels represent a warning level and are usually based on a level that will be reached if the average quantity is used during the average lead time after placing the order
- maximum stock levels represent a level that will be reached if the new order arrives in the minimum lead time and the minimum quantities have been used since the order was placed
- labour costs must be classified between direct costs and indirect costs
- the classification between direct and indirect will be related to the type of work that each employee does, but in some cases certain payments to direct workers will be classed as indirect, such as overtime premiums
- certain types of fringe payroll costs for direct employees, such as employer's contributions to National Insurance, should be dealt with by establishing an inflated charge-out rate for each employee

Activity 1

LIFO results in stocks being stated in the balance sheet at amounts that **bear little relationship to recent cost levels**, thus giving a misleading presentation of current assets.

Activity 2

			£
1.	Issues on 10 February	200 at £36	7,200
		300 at £40	12,000
			19,200
	Issues on 25 March	100 at £40	4,000
		500 at £44	22,000
			26,000
	Total cost price of issues		45,200
2.	Closing stocks	100 at £44	4,400

Activity 3

			£
1.	Issues on 10 February	400 at £40	16,000
		100 at £36	3,600
			19,600
	Issues on 25 March	600 at £44	26,400
	Total cost price of issues		46,000
2.	Closing stocks	100 at £36	3,600

Activity 4

			£	
1.	Stocks at 10 February	200 at £36	7,200	
		400 at £40	16,000	
		600 at £38.67	23,200	
	Issue 10 February	500 at £38.67	19,333	19,333
	Balance at 10 February	100	3,867	
	Purchase 11 March	600 at £44	26,400	
	Balance at 25 March	700 at £43.24	30,267	
	Issue 25 March	600 at £43.24	25,943	25,943
	Total cost of issues			45,276
2.	Stocks at 31 March	100 at £43.24	4,324	

Activity 5
FIFO (because it will charge the oldest prices to cost of sales).

Activity 6
1. 40 at £110   4,400
    20 at £120   2,400
    ___   _____
    60   6,800
    ===   =====

2. 30 at £120   3,600
    20 at £130   2,600
    ___   _____
    50   6,200
    ===   =====

Activity 7
1. 50 at £120   6,000
    10 at £130   1,300
    ___   _____
    60   7,300
    ===   =====

2. 40 at £110   4,400
    10 at £130   1,300
    ___   _____
    50   5,700
    ===   =====

Activity 8

	FIFO basis	LIFO basis	AVCO basis
Sales	12,500	12,500	12,500
Cost of sales	6,800	7,300	6,982
Gross profit	5,700	5,200	5,518

Activity 9
FIFO periodic
    20 at £130   2,600
    30 at £120   3,600
    ___   _____
    50   6,200
    ===   =====

LIFO periodic
    40 at £110   4,400
    10 at £120   1,200
    ___   _____
    50   5,600
    ===   =====

AVCO periodic
£13,000 ÷ 110 = £118.18 per item
    50 × £118.18   5,909

Activity 10
Sales can be met from a reduced level of stocks. A reduction in stock levels reduces the amount of capital invested in stocks. Costs associated with holding stocks will be reduced.

Activity 11

Cost of capital invested in stock (often identified as an opportunity cost, i.e. the return that could be earned if the capital were invested elsewhere); insurance of stocks; stock handling costs; building costs (rent, light, heat, etc.); central services (e.g. cost accounting).

Activity 12

Where customer demand patterns are impossible to predict; where firms are vulnerable to disruptions in the supply chain (e.g. lack of stability in labour relations). You might have listed many other valid circumstances.

Activity 13

$$\sqrt{\frac{2 \times 100 \times 80,000}{0.25}} = 8,000 \; kilos$$

Activity 14

The purchase price per kilo might increase. (Note that we are talking about the carrying cost **per unit**, not total carrying costs. The total carrying costs will decrease with the lower stock levels – as demonstrated in the text following this activity.)

Activity 15

$3 \times 1,600 = 4,800$ kilos.

Activity 16

$4,800 - (2 \times 1,400) + 8,000 = 10,000$ kilos.

Activity 17

Usage was less than 1,400 kilos per week during the lead time. The lead time was less than 2 weeks. The wrong quantity (i.e. more than 8,000 kilos) was ordered and delivered.

Activity 18

Any list similar to the following will suffice: fork-lift truck operators, cleaners, security guards, supervisors and managers (except where they are specific to a production cell), maintenance engineers.

Activity 19

Overtime working is usually a **benefit to total production**. The premium should, therefore, be spread over total production and **not attributed to the specific units** made during the overtime period.

Activity 20

An increase in the number of defective units that have to be scrapped or re-worked; poorer standards, leading to customer complaints and/or after sales service costs.

Activity 21

Debit payroll control account, credit Inland Revenue. Note that companies will have several accounts with the Inland Revenue (including one for the corporation tax on profits) and so this account might be identified by an additional label such as PAYE and NI.

Activity 22

Payroll control account

Bank	62,800	Work in progress control	33,000
Inland Revenue (PAYE and NI)	7,200	Production overheads control	10,000
		Administration expense control	15,000
		Distribution costs control	12,000
	70,000		70,000

Questions

Questions for self assessment

Answers to self-assessment questions are given at the end of the book.

4.1 On 1 January Mr G started a small business buying and selling a special yarn. He invested his savings of £40,000 in the business and, during the next six months, the following transactions occurred:

Yarn purchases			Yarn sales		
Date of Receipt	*Quantity Boxes*	*Total Cost*	*Date of Despatch*	*Quantity Boxes*	*Total Value*
13 January	200	7,200	10 February	500	25,000
8 February	400	15,200			
11 March	600	24,000	20 April	600	27,000
12 April	400	14,000			
15 June	500	14,000	25 June	400	15,200

The yarn is stored in premises Mr G has rented and the closing stock of yarn, counted on 30 June, was 500 boxes.

Other expenses incurred, and paid in cash, during the six month period amounted to £2,300.

Required:
(a) Calculate the value of the material issues during the six month period, and the value of the closing stock at the end of June, using the following methods of pricing:
   (i) first in, first out,
   (ii) last in, first out, and
   (iii) weighted average (calculations to two decimal places only).
(b) Calculate and discuss the effect each of the three methods of material pricing will have on the reported profit of the business, and examine the performances of the business during the first six month period.

(ACCA Costing, 1.2)

4.2 Atlas Limited is having difficulty costing material X to the various jobs that it is used on. The material is bought in bulk and recent receipts and issues have bee;

1/6/93	Balance b/f	1,000 kilos at £4	per kilo
3/6/93	Receipts	2,000 kilos at £5	per kilo
6/6/93	Receipts	1,500 kilos at £5.5	per kilo
9/6/93	Issues	2,500 kilos	
12/6/93	Receipts	3,000 kilos at £4.5	per kilo
14/6/93	Issues	3,500 kilos	

Required:

(a) Cost the issue of material X for June and calculate the value of the closing stock on the following bases:
  (i) FIFO
  (ii) LIFO
  (iii) Weighted average.

(b) Atlas is reviewing its stock control policy with regard to material X. You are told that the cost of making one order is £100, the cost of holding one kilo for one year is 25p and the annual demand for material X is 80,000 kilos. There is no lead time or buffer stock.

Determine the following for material X:
  (i) The economic order quantity, briefly explaining what this figure represents.
  (ii) The average stock.
  (iii) The number of orders to be made per year.

(c) Explain what you understand by the terms 'buffer stock' and 'lead time' and briefly consider any stock policy that would minimize or eliminate such stock costs.

(AAT Cost accounting, Final)

4.3 Ordering schedule.

(a) Using the information stated below, you are required to prepare a schedule showing the associated costs if 1, 2, 3, 4, 5 or 6 orders were placed during a year for a single product.

From your schedule, state the number of orders to be placed each year and the economic order quantity.

- Annual usage of product 600 units
- Unit cost of product £2.40
- Cost of placing an order £6.00
- Stock holding cost as a percentage of average stock value 20%

(b) Comment briefly on three problems met in determining the economic order quantity.

(CIMA Cost Accounting 1, part)

4.4 The GT Company is considering introducing an incentive scheme to remunerate its employees. At present each employee receives £42 for an 8 hour day, and on average each employee produces 15 units of good output a day.

Production overhead costs are all fixed and are absorbed into unit costs at £4 per labour hour.

Under the proposed system each unit of good output will be paid for as follows:

Units of good output per day	Remuneration per unit
16	£2.92
17	£2.98
18	£3.04
19	£3.10
20	£3.16

Required:
A report detailing the economic advantages or disadvantages to the firm of adopting this scheme.

(AAT Cost accounting, Final, part)

Question without answer

The answer to this question is published separately in the *Teacher's Manual*. One question only has been set because the work required to produce a full answer to this question is quite demanding.

4.5 Incentive scheme – finishing shop

You have been approached for your advice on the proposed introduction of an incentive scheme for the direct operatives in the final production department of a factory producing one standard product. This department, the Finishing Shop, employs 30 direct operatives, all of whom are paid £3 per hour for a basic 40 hour week, with a guaranteed wage of £120 per week. When necessary, overtime is worked up to a maximum of 15 hours per week per operative and is paid at time rate plus one half. It is the opinion of the Personnel Manager that no more direct operatives could be recruited for this department.

An analysis of recent production returns from the Finishing Shop indicate that the current average output is approximately 6 units of the standard product per productive man hour. The Work Study Manager has conducted an appraisal of the working methods in the Finishing Shop and suggest that it would be reasonable to expect operatives to process 8 units of the product per man hour and that a piece work scheme be introduced in which the direct operatives are paid 55p for each unit processed. It is anticipated that, when necessary, operatives would continue to work overtime up to the previously specified limit, although as the operatives would be on piece work no premium would be paid.

Next year's budgeted production for the factory varies from a minimum of 7,000 units per week to a maximum of 12,000 units per week, with the most frequent budgeted weekly output being 9,600 units. The expected selling price of the product next year is £10 per unit and the budgeted variable production cost of the incomplete product passed into the Finishing Shop amounts to £8 per unit. Variable production overheads in the Finishing Shop, excluding the overtime premium of the direct operatives, are budgeted to be £0.48 per direct labour hour worked and it is considered that variable overheads do vary directly with productive hours worked. Direct material costs are not incurred by the Finishing Shop. The fixed overheads incurred by the factory amount in total to £9,000 per week.

Stocks of work in progress and finished goods are not carried.

Required:
(a) **Calculate the effect on the company's budgeted weekly profits of the proposed incentive scheme in the Finishing Shop.**
(b) **Explain the reasons for the changes in the weekly budgeted profits caused by the proposed incentive scheme.**

(ACCA Costing 1.2)

5 ▷ Overheads: Absorption costing and ABC

Objectives

After you have completed this chapter, you should be able to:
- identify appropriate cost centres in any organization and differentiate between cost centres that actually produce the goods or services and those that provide support services to the production cost centres
- carry out the basic calculations that cost accountants use to ascertain the overheads for each production cost centre, including the selection of appropriate bases for apportioning non-specific overheads to all cost centres
- select appropriate measurements of production activity and use these to calculate overhead absorption rates
- calculate the total amount of overhead absorbed during a period, compare this to the actual overhead incurred, and analyse the difference according to its cause
- discuss the defects of traditional overhead absorption and evaluate the benefits of providing management with cost information based 'activity-based costing' ABC
- compare traditional overhead absorption with ABC in a variety of situations including service industries and public institutions

Introduction

The conventional system of accounting for overhead costs was developed mainly in the manufacturing sector. There were (roughly) two needs that had to be satisfied by the system. In the first place, managers needed to identify product costs for pricing and/or cost control purposes. Secondly, it was necessary for manufacturers to ascertain the cost of closing stock in order to measure and report profits to the shareholders. Some companies avoided the profit measurement problem by valuing their closing stocks on a marginal cost basis, but financial accounting regulations were eventually introduced in the UK (by SSAP 9 in 1975) that required all companies to include manufacturing overheads in the cost of closing stock.

There seems little doubt that the design of conventional overhead recording systems was driven by the demands of financial accounting in manufacturing, particularly the need to determine the cost of products for closing stock valuations. Yet the same system has, for many years, been used to provide management with cost information. The approach developed for manufacturing has also been adopted in many other types of industry, including the service sector, where the problem of closing stock valuation does not usually arise. These conventional methods were probably suitable for management purposes when overheads formed a relatively small proportion of total costs, but cost patterns have changed over the years and in many cases overheads are now the largest element in the total cost of a product.

Conventional overhead absorption systems use a somewhat arbitrary method for charging overheads to product costs. Recent studies have shown that cost information derived from these conventional systems is not suitable for the needs of managers, and activity-based costing (ABC) was developed as a result of these criticisms. There have been quite a number of surveys in the UK to try to determine the extent to which ABC has been adopted by companies. The general picture seems to be (at the time of writing this edition) that something like 80% of the companies surveyed are still using conventional absorption systems There is clearly a robust interest in the subject because up to 90% of the companies surveyed have indicated that they are considering ABC. Students who are interested in keeping abreast of the latest developments are advised to read the *Management Accounting* magazine, where the results of these surveys are published from time to time.

In this chapter, both the conventional systems and ABC are covered. This will enable you to make a comparison between the two methods. Most of the basic explanations are given in the context of a manufactured product. This is considered to be the best way of learning the subject because it is easier to form a mental image of a physical product than an abstract idea such as a unit of service. Examples of how the approach used in manufacturing can be adapted to calculate unit costs in other sectors are dealt with after the basic explanation.

5.1 Conventional overhead absorption

Whatever method is used for allocating overheads to products, it will not be a simple process. If you look at any manufactured article, such as the book you are reading or the chair you are sitting on, you can imagine how it must be a relatively simple process to keep an accounting record of all the direct costs (such as the direct materials), but how can we attach an amount to that product for factory overheads? The cost of direct materials used can be measured from material issue notes, direct labour cost from time records, but overhead costs do not stem from a single source – they result from providing a whole network of resources without which the factory could not operate. The benefits from these resources is consumed by a variety of products, each type of product making different demands on facilities provided.

Blanket rates: A simple model

Some of the earlier attempts at finding an appropriate basis for calculating the overhead cost per unit provide us with an insight into this complex problem. The expression 'blanket rate' stems from the idea that a blanket covers everything. Sometimes the blanket rate was called a 'factory-wide' (or plant-wide) rate because the idea was to find an overhead cost per unit based on the total overheads of the factory. For example, if the total budgeted overheads of a factory were calculated as £100,000 and the budgeted direct labour hours were 50,000, the blanket rate was set at £2.00 per direct labour hour. If a product took a total of 6 direct labour hours to make, the overhead cost of that product was deemed to be £12.00.

An hourly rate was justified (and still is with conventional overhead absorption) on the grounds that many of the overheads were time related. Costs such as depreciation of the equipment and rent of the building result from the passage of time. But the blanket rate ignored the fact that a product might pass through a sequence of processes, such as machining, assembly and finishing. If we take a closer look at each of those processes we might find that overheads can be related to each process in such a way that the apportionment of the £100,000 will not be divided equally between the three departments. This would not be a problem if each product was processed for an equal amount of time in each department, but this is not likely to be the case.

Assume, for the example being discussed, that we find the total overheads and total direct labour hours can be split as follows:

	Total overheads	Direct labour hours
Machining	£30,000	10,000
Assembly	£49,000	25,000
Finishing	£21,000	15,000
	£100,000	50,000

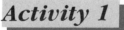

Activity 1

Calculate an overhead absorption rate for each department based on a rate per direct labour hour.

Machining:

Assembly:

Finishing:

Now assume that the production time of 6 hours for the unit previously mentioned is divided as follows:

- Machining: 3 hours
- Assembly: 2 hours
- Finishing: 1 hour

Activity 2

Calculate the total overhead cost for the unit based on the processing time in each production department.

This represents quite a significant difference to the overhead cost per unit (£12.00) that was derived from the blanket rate of £2.00 per hour.

Budgeted absorption rates

You will recall from Chapter 3 that absorption rates have to be based on budgeted figures for a period – usually one year. There are two components in the calculation, the budgeted overheads for each production cost centre and a measurement of production activity for each cost centre. In Activity 1 the measurement of production activity was direct labour hours for all three cost centres. Production activity can be measured in a variety of ways and these are discussed later in the chapter. The basic formula for calculating an absorption rate can be set out as follows:

$$\frac{\text{Budgeted overheads}}{\text{Budgeted production activity}}$$

As indicated by Activities 1 and 2, it is necessary to calculate a budgeted overhead absorption rate (BOAR) for each production cost centre. The first step is, therefore, to ascertain the total budgeted overheads for each production cost centre.

Ascertaining overheads for production cost centres

In Activities 1 and 2, the total overheads for each production cost centre were given. In practice, the task of attributing total factory overhead to production cost centres involves a significant amount of cost allocation, apportionment and re-apportionment. For cost control purposes, overheads are attributed initially to responsibility centres (such as a particular department in the factory). Cost control through responsibility accounting is normally based on requiring departmental managers to explain differences between budgeted expenditure and actual expenditure. But in this chapter we are not so much concerned with cost control as with ascertaining product costs, in particular the overhead element of that cost.

The aim of the process is to ensure that all factory overheads are attributed to production cost centres (those areas where the actual production process occurs). In some cases a production cost centre will be the same as a responsibility centre (such as the machining department) but it could be a subdivision of that department such as a particular machine. The total amount of factory overhead attributed to each production cost centre is derived from a series of allocations and apportionments. This procedure must take account of the following:

- There will be several cost centres in the factory and they will not all be classed as production cost centres – recall Chapter 3, where you identified the difference between a service cost centre and a production cost centre.
- Some overheads can be identified as direct costs of a particular cost centre, others represent indirect costs that will have to be apportioned over all cost centres, using some kind of proxy (such as floor area) to represent the benefits received.
- Production overheads attributed to service cost centres (such as a maintenance department) by the above process will have to be re-apportioned to production cost centres, also using some kind of proxy to represent the benefits received.

The expression 'direct costs' of a cost centre must not be confused with the direct costs of a product (such as direct materials and direct labour). Sometimes the expression 'specific cost' is used in order to avoid this confusion. But providing you keep in mind that we are thinking of the cost centre (not the product) as being the cost object, the idea of a direct cost of a cost centre should not cause any confusion. Similarly, overheads that are not specific to any particular cost centre can be described as the indirect costs of each cost centre. Note that we normally use the verb 'to allocate' when describing the process of charging overheads that can be identified as the direct costs of a cost centre, and 'to apportion' when spreading indirect costs over all cost centres. The term 'cost attribution' is used when referring to cost allocation and cost apportionment in a collective sense.

Before we work through a detailed example, we will complete two activities on the basic approach.

Activity 3

Some factory overheads can be allocated directly to cost centres, others relate to the entire factory and must be apportioned to cost centres. Make a note of some examples of these two types of overhead in the space below (remember we are thinking about factory overheads and cost centres – not direct costs of the product such as direct materials and direct labour).

1. Examples of overhead costs that might be allocated directly to cost centres:

2. Examples of indirect costs that will have to be apportioned to cost centres:

Activity 4

The cost attribution process will involve making apportionments of overheads that cannot be identified specifically with a particular cost centre. Various bases are used for making these apportionments, such as the floor area of a cost centre in relation to total floor area of the factory. Try to identify and describe the bases that could be used for apportioning the following types of overhead:

1. Rent, rates and lighting of the whole factory building.

2. Insurance of plant and machinery.

3. Employee related expenditure such as a staff canteen.

We can now work through a detailed problem in stages. The details given below are based on an examination question set by the Chartered Association of Certified Accountants in their (former) Level 1 Costing examination. It is typical of the details provided in many examination questions on this subject. There is a working sheet at the end of this chapter (on page 142) which should be completed in stages according to the guidelines provided by the various activities. Even if your syllabus does not require you to perform these calculations you will find it beneficial to work through the problem. The process is not complicated, and by working with the underlying figures you will develop a better understanding of why the conventional method of overhead absorption has been subjected to so much criticism.

Details for the activities

Bookdon plc manufactures three products in two production departments; a machine shop and a fitting section. It also has two service departments, a canteen and a machine maintenance section. Shown below are next year's budgeted production data and manufacturing costs for the company.

Product	X	Y	Z
Production	4,200 units	6,900 units	1,700 units
Direct costs:			
Direct materials	£11 per unit	£14 per unit	£17 per unit
Direct labour:			
Machine shop	£6 per unit	£4 per unit	£2 per unit
Fitting section	£12 per unit	£3 per unit	£21 per unit
Machine hours per unit	6 hours	3 hours	4 hours

Budgeted overheads:	Machine shop	Fitting section	Canteen	Main- tenance	Total
	£	£	£	£	£
Allocated overheads	27,660	19,470	16,600	26,650	90,380
Rent, rates, heating and lighting					17,000
Depreciation and insurance of equipment					25,000
Additional data:					
Gross book value of equipment	£150,000	£75,000	£30,000	£45,000	
Number of employees	18	14	4	4	
Floor space in square metres	3,600	1,400	1,000	800	

It is estimated that approximately 70% of the machine maintenance section's costs are incurred servicing the machine shop and 30% in servicing the fitting section.

The absorption bases adopted by the company are a machine hour rate for the machine shop and a rate expressed as a percentage of direct wages for the fitting section.

Activity 5

The first step is to tabulate the budgeted overhead costs for all four cost centres. The allocated overheads should be charged to each cost centre first – this merely requires you to write up the working sheet from the data supplied above. Then apportion the other two overheads (rent, etc. of £17,000; depreciation and insurance £25,000). Make a note of the apportionment basis used in the appropriate column of the working sheet. Do not total any of the figures at this point. Check your work with the Key before moving on to the following text and the next activity.

At this point, the total factory overheads have been attributed to four cost centres. But two of these (canteen and maintenance) are service cost centres and the objective is to attribute all overheads to production cost centres. It will, therefore, be necessary to apportion the total overheads of each service cost centre to the production cost centres. At this point we can hit a problem (but not in our example) because we might find that one service department not only provides services to another service department but also benefits from services provided by that department. This problem is known as 'reciprocal services' and some way has to be found of dealing with it, otherwise apportionments and re-apportionments will seem never ending.

In the main text of this chapter we will not be dealing with calculations that result from reciprocal services. There is an appendix for students whose syllabus requires them to perform these calculations and a reference to this is made at the end of the chapter. In the example we are working we can ignore the problem because although the maintenance section benefits from services provided by the canteen, the maintenance section does not provide services to the canteen.

Activity 6

Go back to the working sheet and deal with the apportionment of service cost centres in the following order:

1. Total the overheads for the canteen and apportion this total to the remaining three cost centres (state the basis used in the appropriate column). Indicate that the total canteen costs have been transferred out to other cost centres by showing a negative total (in brackets) underneath the original total.

2. Total the overheads for the maintenance section (which will now include the amount apportioned from the canteen) and then apportion this total to the two production cost centres on the 70/30 basis mentioned in the details. Show the transfer by including a negative total as you did for the canteen.

3. You can now total the overheads allocated and apportioned to the two production cost centres.

Check you work with the Key before moving on to the following text.

All factory overheads have now been attributed to production cost centres. You can easily check your arithmetic because total overheads were (£90,380 + £17,000 + £25,000) £132,380 and this should agree with the total overheads attributed to the two production cost centres.

Production activity and absorption rates

The next step is to calculate an overhead absorption rate for each production cost centre. In practice we would have to identify the total volume of work to be done in each cost centre for the same period as the budgeted costs. Measurements of this work can be expressed in different ways such as total machine hours or total direct labour hours. By dividing the total volume into the total overheads, a rate (per unit of measurement) is derived.

Activity 7

In a multi-product firm, the total number of finished goods units to be produced would not be suitable as a volume measurement for calculating an overhead absorption rate. Explain why you think this is so.

As stated earlier, time-related measurements of production (such as machine hours or direct labour hours) are often justified on the grounds that many of the overheads are time related. (In section 5.3 you will see how ABC challenges some of these assumptions.) On this basis, it seems sensible to use machine hours if production is machine-intensive and labour hours if it is labour-intensive. But if machine hours are used it will be necessary to keep a record of machine hours utilized during production, and for many companies this seems to be an added burden which they are reluctant to undertake at the moment. Recent surveys suggest that volume measurements based on direct labour (either direct labour hours or direct labour cost) are the most common.

This is probably a matter of expediency because there will be an existing accounting record of direct labour hours (and cost) that is used for recording the direct labour cost in the ledger. The overhead cost of each job or batch can, therefore, be based on the entries made when the ledger is updated for direct labour costs – the calculation of overheads absorbed is automatic when the computer is programmed to relate overheads to data on direct labour. This could change with advancements in information technology; it is quite easy to imagine computerized cost records being linked with information generated from computer aided production. The use of machine time might then be a more common factor in the calculation of overhead costs per unit.

In our example, we are told the basis to be used for each production cost centre. It is easier for beginners to make sense of an hourly rate and so we will start with the machine shop where the absorption rate is to be based on machine hours.

Activity 8

You will have to work out the total budgeted machine hours for the machine shop. This can be calculated from the following:

- there are three products,
- the number of machine hours per unit for each of these products
- the budgeted production quantities for each of those products.

Calculate the total number of machine hours, and a machine hour rate for the machine shop (budgeted overheads of machine shop divided by total machine hours). Make a note of your answers here.

1. Total machine hours.

2. Machine hour rate for the machine shop.

The absorption rate for the fitting section is described as 'a percentage of direct wages for the fitting section'. The volume of productive work does not have to be based on measurements of time, it could be represented by the amount to be spent on direct costs. If the total direct labour cost of a production cost centre is budgeted at £100,000 and the total production overheads for that cost centre are budgeted at £200,000, then we could work on the basis that overheads are 200% of the direct labour cost. If we use this basis for a job on which £100 had been charged as direct labour then we will add an overhead cost of £200.

Whether this represents a fair basis is open to argument, but it is certainly very convenient and this might account for its popularity. It is sometimes justified on the grounds that there is some kind of relationship between the amount spent on direct labour and the amount of time taken to produce a unit. This relationship is not always as close as might be imagined. For example, a skilled worker might be paid £10 per hour and a semi-skilled £5 per hour; if the skilled worker takes one hour to produce a unit and the semi-skilled takes 2 hours to produce a similar unit, the direct labour cost will be £10 in both cases.

Activity 9

You should now work out the total amount to be spent on direct labour in the fitting section. Use the same approach as when you worked out the total machine hours for the machine shop, but remember it is the total of direct labour cost in the fitting section that is needed – not the total direct labour cost for next year's production. When you have calculated the amount (and checked with the Key), express the total overheads of the fitting section as a percentage of the direct labour cost for that section. Make a note of your results in the spaces provided below.

1. Total direct labour cost of the fitting section.

2. Total overheads of fitting section (£48,060) expressed as a percentage of the direct labour cost in the fitting section.

We now have an overhead absorption rate for each production cost centre, as follows:

- machine shop, £1.60 per machine hour
- fitting section, 45% of the direct labour cost.

This information will be used to determine the total manufacturing cost of each unit made.

Activity 10

Calculate the total manufacturing cost of a unit of Product X. Remember that it passes through two production cost centres and absorbs overheads from each of these centres.

Activities 5 to 10 provide an insight into the basic procedures used in conventional overhead absorption. As was mentioned in Chapter 3, these procedures are certainly acceptable by the external auditors for the purposes of determining product costs for the closing stock valuation. Whether the product costs established by these procedures are suitable for managers is open to question. For instance, you will notice that overheads beyond the production stage are ignored. This is probably another example of where financial accounting has influenced the process because SSAP 9 requires any overheads that cannot be related to the production function to be excluded from product costs (there is one exception but it relates to a special case which is not very common). There are guidelines in SSAP 9 that allow costs of some central support services (such as accounting) to be allocated to production, but only to the extent that they are shown to be supporting the production function. The cost of providing cost accounting facilities could be allocated to the production function under this rule.

Generally speaking, absorption costing ignores overheads beyond the production stage. Yet overheads such as administration, marketing and distribution are usually quite substantial in most organizations. The demands made on the facilities provided by these functions could vary for different products. You will see in section 5.3 how ABC attempts to remedy some of the defects of conventional overhead absorption when providing managers with information on product costs.

Overheads under- or over-absorbed

Before leaving our detailed example, we should consider what happens when the actual expenditure and the actual volume of production is different to the budgeted figures. You will recall from Chapter 3 that overheads are absorbed into product costs at the budgeted rate. Any difference between overheads absorbed and overheads incurred is written off to cost of sales as an expense.

The amount of overhead absorbed will depend on whether or not standard costing is used. In standard costing (a subject covered by Chapter 7) there will be a standard overhead cost per unit. For example, in the problem we have been working there is a standard overhead cost for a unit of Product X of ($6 \times £1.60$) £9.60 in respect of work done in the machine shop. This amount will be absorbed each time a unit of Product X is processed in the machine shop, irrespective of the actual processing time. When standard costing is not used, overheads for the machine shop will be absorbed on the basis of the number of machine hours worked. In this case, the total amount of overhead absorbed for the machine shop is found by multiplying the predetermined rate of £1.60 per hour by the actual number of machine hours worked in the period.

Activity 11

Assume that the following facts are determined for the machine shop at the end of the budget period:

- Overheads actually incurred £86,000
- Machine hours actually worked 50,000

The company does not use standard costing. Calculate the amount of overhead under- or over-absorbed for the machine shop, and make a note of the amount here.

It is possible to analyse this amount under two headings, although the information is not very useful when standard costing is not used. This analysis recognizes that the amount under-absorbed arises from two causes, namely:

- the actual expenditure on overheads for the period was different to the budgeted amount (this is called an expenditure variance)
- the number of machine hours worked was different to budget (this could be called a volume variance)

In our example of the machine shop, the analysis of the £6,000 under-absorbed is as follows:

Expenditure variance (£86,000 – £84,320)	£1,680 adverse
Volume variance (52,700 – 50,000) × £1.60	£4,320 adverse
	£6,000 adverse

Although this information is slightly more useful than a single figure of £6,000, a number of contributory factors are still being disguised. In the first place no attempt has been made to separate variable overheads from the fixed ones. The amount spent on variable overheads will be dependent upon something, perhaps the number of machine hours worked or the number of units made. In order to make sense of an expenditure variance we would need to know the budgeted allowance for expenditure on variable overheads for the actual level of production achieved. Secondly, the volume variance is difficult to interpret since we have not been told how many units were produced in the 50,000 hours. All we can say at the moment is that there has been an under-recovery of overheads because 50,000 machine hours were worked instead of the budgeted level of 52,700 hours. When standard costing is used (see Chapter 7), it is possible to analyse this volume variance in a more meaningful way.

5.2 Traditional costing in service organizations

The cost of providing a unit of service includes both direct and indirect costs in much the same way as a manufactured article. In some cases the service process has characteristics similar to manufacturing in the sense that it results in tangible product, such as when:

- a car repair firm delivers a repaired car to the customer,
- an accounting practice delivers a set of financial statements to the client.

Strictly speaking the problem of ascertaining the cost of a unit of service is not confined to the problem of overheads but since many of the thought processes involved are developed during the study of overheads, you will find it quite helpful to consider the subject in this chapter.

Entities that provide services do not suffer the same stock valuation problem that imposes itself on the cost accounting systems used in manufacturing. Service companies that work on a jobbing basis, such as those who repair cars or who provide general engineering services, will carry stocks of spares and other materials but there is no finished product that has to be valued at cost for the purposes of measuring profit. Work is performed according to the customer's order; if there is a tangible product when the service is completed it will be handed over to the customer. (Companies involved in long-term contracts will have to determine the cost of any work in progress at the end of the period for financial accounting – but this is a financial accounting problem.)

Consequently, cost accounting systems in the service sector do not have to be dominated by the dictates of financial accounting. Cost accounting can be directed towards providing information for managers. This information might be needed for pricing or for cost control. The practice of calculating a selling price by adding a percentage to cost is more prevalent in the service sector than it is in manufacturing (where prices are often dictated by the market). The process of ascertaining the cost of a service is often an adaptation of the methods used in manufacturing. If the service is provided on a job basis the costing records usually consist of a job card (or job account) on which direct costs, such as labour and materials, are recorded. Overheads based on a predetermined rate are then added in much the same way as in manufacturing.

Some services are charged to customers at an hourly rate. In these cases the charge rate is calculated by a process similar to that used for calculating an overhead absorption rate in manufacturing. Cost centres are identified (which might be an individual or a department) and the total of the direct and indirect costs for each cost centre are accumulated. The total costs of each cost centre are divided by a unit of measurement, such as total chargeable hours, in order to find a cost per unit of measurement. If the service is being provided to an external customer, the charge rate can be based on adding a profit percentage to the cost.

In some cases, services are provided for internal purposes rather than for sale to an external customer. Computing services and reprographic services are but two examples where this might apply in a large organization. In these cases the costing system is used to determine what is known as a 'transfer price' that can be charged to the user departments. Internal transfer prices are discussed more fully in Chapter 8, but for the time being you can think of the objective of transfer prices as enabling central management to exercise control over the use of resources in the organization. For example, a garage might sell second-hand cars as well as provide car repair services. The car repair section will undoubtedly carry out some work for the car sales department. If this is done free (as a favour) then central management will have no idea how much of the costs associated with the car repair section are being used to subsidize the car sales department. One way of isolating this information is for the car repair section to make a charge to the car sales department for any work carried out.

In general terms, the process of ascertaining unit costs when traditional methods are used is similar to the way in which overhead absorption rates are calculated in manufacturing, for example:

- cost centres are identified
- costs are accumulated for each cost centre
- costs are attributed to the cost centres that provide the chargeable service
- these costs might consist of both direct and indirect costs of that cost centre
- some kind of work measurement for each cost centre is identified
- this measurement represents the cost unit and is used as a denominator in the calculation of unit costs.

We will look at the process in the context of providing 'in-house' computing services. There are several problems in the questions at the end of this chapter that relate to other services such as hotels and the health service. In all cases the basic approach outlined above can be applied.

Details for the activities

A company has established a centralized computer department that provides services to various user departments. The computer department has three main divisions of work, as follows:

1. systems development
2. data preparation
3. computer operations.

Budgeted costs for the forthcoming period have been allocated and apportioned to the computer department as follows:

	Total £	Systems development £	Data preparation £	Computer operations £
Direct costs:				
Salaries	200,000	69,000	31,000	100,000
Materials	10,000	1,000	2,000	7,000
Development costs	20,000	20,000		
Apportionment of general overheads:				
Maintenance	24,000		2,000	22,000
Electricity	10,000	2,000	2,000	6,000
Occupancy costs (rent etc.)	20,000	4,000	4,000	12,000
	284,000	96,000	41,000	147,000

Other data:
1. The systems development department carries out services for various user department This includes writing computer programs to accommodate the needs of users. The estimated number of development hours chargeable to user departments is 12,000.
2. The data preparation department accepts documented input from user departments and transcribes the data into transaction files for computer operations by means of keyboard terminals. The estimated number of key depressions on terminals in the data preparation department is 20,500,000
3. The total hours available for computer operations is 7,000 but because of downtime between computer runs, only 80% of this is available for charging to user departments.

You will notice from the above details that the three departments (software development, data preparation and computer operations) are the equivalent of production cost centres in a factory. They are the centres where some form of chargeable work is carried out. You will also notice how various indirect costs have been apportioned to these three centres.

Activity 12

In this case we need information to enable a price to be charged to user departments. The measures of work in each cost centre (the cost units) could be as follows:

Systems development: one development hour
Data preparation: 1,000 key depressions
Computer operations: one usable hour (i.e. based on 80% of available hours)

Calculate the cost of the cost units for each of the three departments and note them here.

1. One development hour.

2. 1,000 key depressions.

3. One usable operations hour.

Activity 13

A user department requires a job to be done by the computer department. The details for this job are estimated to be as follows:

Development work: 25 hours
Data preparation: 90,000 key depressions
Computer operations: 6 hours

Calculate the transfer price that should be charged for this job.

At this point it might be helpful to repeat a word of warning mentioned in Chapter 1. The price of the job in Activity 13 is used for charging the user department as part of a process of cost control. It is an internal accounting control that might be used where user departments have been allocated a budget allowance for central computer services. The information should not be used for decision making at a departmental level. If the user department finds that the job can be done more cheaply by an external agency, it might be tempted (in order to keep within its budget) to contract with that agency rather than use the internal services. This could be a bad decision as far as the company as a whole is concerned. The costs associated with running the centralized computer department include a number of costs that cannot be saved by not doing this particular job. If the external agency's fees exceed the costs that can be saved by not doing the job internally, there will be an incremental cost to the company as a whole. This problem is discussed more fully in Chapter 8.

5.3 Activity based costing

Traditional overhead absorption uses a single measure of volume for each production cost centre. This might be a time-related measure such as machine hours or direct labour hours, or a cost-related measure such as direct labour cost or direct materials cost. The idea of using direct material costs as an absorption basis was not discussed in Section 5.1 but the procedure is the same as when direct labour costs were used. For example if the direct material costs to be consumed by a production cost centre were budgeted at £100,000, and the overheads attributed to that centre were £10,000, the absorption rate would be 10% of the direct material cost of each product. If product X consumes £1.00 in materials an amount of £0.10 is added for overheads; if product Y consumes £100 in materials an amount of £10.00 is added for overheads.

This example of using material costs as an absorption basis opens our minds to some of the defects in traditional overhead absorption. It was one of the factors that caused the traditional approach to be questioned in the first place. What justification is there for assuming that product Y consumes 100 times the support resources used to manufacture product X? Time-related measures of volume might seem more logical but the traditional process of overhead absorption ignores the fact that different products make different demands on factory support services. It simply lumps all the overheads into one cost centre and uses a single time measurement for that cost centre. It is almost as if we were saying that 1 hour of production time causes a certain amount of overhead to be incurred, in much the same way as we would say that 1 hour of direct labour time has caused a certain amount of direct labour cost. This statement is only valid for short-term variable overheads such as machine running costs.

If we look more closely at the overheads for an individual production cost centre we might find various factors that are causing overheads to change in total apart from the number of hours that the plant is running. Some of these will be classed as 'long-term' variable costs because a variation of the total amount spent will be noticed over a much longer period of time than it is for machine running costs. The role of ABC is to identify the activities that cause total costs to change so that an appropriate rate of overhead can be applied to each product according to the demands made on the resources provided by those activities.

Cost drivers

Factors that cause costs to change in any activity area are known as 'cost drivers'. The basic mechanics of ABC are really very simple but the task of identifying cost drivers (and the associated costs) will require a company to make a detailed study of its various activities. This information is not likely to be available from the accounting records since traditional costing collects overheads according to individual production centres rather than individual activities.

According to the CIMA 'official terminology', a cost driver is '*An activity which generates costs*'. As a starting point, cost drivers can be identified under the two main headings, according to whether the overhead varies in the short-term or the long-term, as follows:

- short-term variable overheads (e.g. machine running costs) are driven by production volume and so the cost driver will be volume based such as machine hours or direct labour hours
- long-term variable overheads (such as materials handling costs) are probably driven by the number of transactions undertaken by the support department and so the cost driver will often be transaction based.

You have already studied volume based cost drivers in the section on conventional overhead absorption. There are no hard and fast rules regarding transaction based cost drivers and the examples in Table 5.1 are merely ideas of bases that could be used for the activities mentioned.

Table 5.1

Activity area (support services)	Cost driver (transaction)
Materials handling	Number of parts
Setting up production line (known as set-up costs)	Number of production runs
Quality control	Number of inspections (or hours of test time)

Cost pools

One of the tasks of cost accounting is to accumulate the costs of a cost object. Up to now we have been thinking of cost objects as being either a unit of product or a cost centre. In ABC there is another cost object – an activity. When individual costs are grouped under a single heading the result is known as a 'cost pool'. In traditional overhead absorption, cost pools are created for production cost centres; in ABC, cost pools are created for the activity areas (or support functions). The mechanics of applying activity based cost pools to individual products are similar to those used in traditional overhead absorption. An application rate is found by dividing each activity based cost pool by an appropriate quantity of the related cost driver.

Activity 14

The budgeted costs for materials handling (transferring goods from store to production) during the next period are £200,000. During this period it is budgeted that 100,000 parts will be moved. The company has adopted ABC and has identified material handling costs as being driven by the number of parts handled. Calculate the amount for materials handling overhead to be included in the costs of the following products:

1. Product A, which uses 4 parts

2. Product B, which uses 12 parts

This type of information would not have been available under conventional overhead absorption. The total cost of £200,000 would have been merged with other overheads for the cost centre and absorbed into product costs on some basis such as the number of direct labour hours taken to process each unit.

How can managers use ABC information?

Critics of the traditional volume-based absorption systems often claim that it under-allocates overhead costs to low volume products and over-allocates overheads to higher volume products. As a statement this could be true but as information it has no value. The reason why the information in Activity 14 is useful for managers is that it enables them to see the cost associated with using so many different parts. This might lead to a more cost-efficient product design. It is the 'attention directing' aspect of ABC that makes it useful rather than statements regarding its conceptual superiority. It enables mangers to see the activities that are causing overheads and provides an opportunity for exploring ways of reducing these costs.

A reasonable question to ask is whether product costs based on ABC will enable managers to make better pricing (and/or product mix) decisions. Several articles have been published revealing that when companies adopt ABC they find a very high proportion of their products are unprofitable. This does not necessarily mean that ABC will lead these companies to make a realignment of their prices or product mix immediately; they will be reluctant to do this if the market is highly competitive. But ABC will have provided them with a new focus of attention. They can now see where they are making money and where they are losing it and can use this information for evaluating future strategy, including matters such as product design. Most of the evidence available at the time of writing this edition, including exchanges between experts in the professional press, suggest that ABC is being used as an attention-focusing device rather than a decision making tool.

Exploring the theoretical model

We can experiment with our learning model to see if there is anything in the claim that volume based overhead absorption under-allocates overheads to low volume products and over-allocates overheads to higher volume products. Is this claim based on experience, or is it an inherent feature of the volume based model? If it is claimed that ABC redresses the problem, we should be able to test the truth of this by comparing the results of each method on a simple model.

We will use the details in Activity 14 and assume that there are no production overheads other than the materials handling cost of £200,000. We will also assume the following:

- a direct labour hour rate is used for volume based overhead absorption.
- the company is budgeting to make 4,000 units of Product A.

Activity 15

In order to involve yourself with the detail, work out from the data in Activity 14 how many units of product B the company was budgeting to make. You can assume that the number of parts (100,000) was based on making 4,000 units of Product A and the quantity of Product B which you are now being asked to calculate.

The product mix is, therefore:

- 4,000 units of Product A
- 7,000 units of Product B.

You will notice that the number of parts in Product B is three times that in Product A. If the amount of direct labour time taken on each product is in the same ratio (3 to 1), the overhead cost per unit will be the same under either method. You can see this for yourself by working on the following details:

	Number of units	Direct labour hours per unit	Total hours
Product A	4,000	1	4,000
Product B	7,000	3	21,000
			25,000

Activity 16

Work out the hourly absorption rate and then calculate the overhead cost per unit for each product:

Product A:

Product B:

As you can see, these are exactly the same as the figures produced by the ABC approach. Now look to see what happens if the production time for a unit of Product B is greater than 3 times that of Product A, by assuming the following:

	Number of units	Direct labour hours per unit	Total hours
Product A	4,000	1	4,000
Product B	7,000	4	28,000
			32,000

Activity 17

Work out the hourly absorption rate and then calculate the overhead cost per unit for each product using this new information:

Product A:

Product B:

In this case the argument is seen to be valid. The volume based approach produces a lower overhead cost for each unit of Product A (the low volume product) by comparison to what it was when we used ABC. Similarly, the high volume product (Product B) has a higher overhead cost per unit under the volume based approach. But if the production time of Product B is less than 3 times that of Product A, the result will be the reverse and in this case the argument seems to be invalid.

This does not disprove the argument, it merely shows that it does not necessarily apply with material handling costs when the number of parts is used as the cost driver. The model might be at fault since it deals with a single type of overhead. The following problem makes a comparison between the two methods when more detail is involved.

Practice problem

A company has one production department in which it manufactures two products. The total production overhead for the budget period is £15,500. A direct labour hour basis is used for the company's existing volume based overhead absorption. The budgeted quantities, and budgeted direct labour time per unit, for the next period are as follows:

	Quantity	Direct labour hours per unit
Product X	100 units	1
Product Y	1,000 units	3

Activity 18

Calculate the overhead absorption rate and the overhead cost per unit for each product.

1. Overhead absorption rate:

2. Overhead cost per unit for Product X:

3. Overhead cost per unit for Product Y:

For the purposes of experimenting with ABC, the company has identified the following activities and cost pools for the total overhead cost of £15,500:

	£
Short-term variable costs	3,100
Set-up costs	4,900
Materials handling	4,200
Quality control inspection	3,300
	15,500

The cost drivers for each of these activities have been identified as follows:

Short-term variable costs   direct labour hours
Set-up costs   number of production runs
Materials handling costs   number of parts
Quality control inspections   number of inspections

The data for each product are as follows:

	Units	Number of production runs	Number of parts per unit	Number of inspections
Product X	100	2	4	4
Product Y	1,000	5	8	7
		7		11

From this data the following application rates can be determined:

Short-term variable costs per hour (£3,100 ÷ 3,100)   £1 per hour
Set-up costs per run (£4,900 ÷ 7)   £700 per run
Materials handling cost per part (£4,200 ÷ 8,400)   £0.50 per part
Quality control cost per inspection (£3,300 ÷ 11)   £300 per inspection

---

Activity 19

From the above summary of application rates, you should be able to calculate the overhead cost per unit. For example, the set-up costs per unit for Product X can be found by working out the total set-up costs for 2 runs and dividing this by 100 to get a unit cost (2 × £700 ÷ 100 = £14 per unit). Calculate the overhead costs per unit and make a note of the amounts in the following summary:

	Product X (per unit)	Product Y (per unit)
Short-term variable costs		
Set-up costs		
Materials handling costs		
Quality inspection costs		
Total		

A summary of the overhead costs per unit under each method is as follows:

	Product X	Product Y
Using volume based absorption	£5.00	£15.00
Using ABC	£29.00	£12.60

The arithmetic can be proved by checking to see if the total amount of overhead applied to products is the same under each method, as in the following:

Volume based (100 × £5.00) + (1,000 × £15.00)   =   £15,500
ABC (100 × £29.00) + (1,000 × £12.60)   =   £15,500

A comparison of the two sets of figures reveals that ABC has resulted in a much higher overhead cost per unit for Product X (the low volume product), and a lower amount per unit for Product X (the high volume product). This lends support to the argument previously mentioned. But the real benefit to management will be the detailed analysis of overhead costs per unit, as produced in Activity 19. This information is not available under volume based absorption methods.

ABC and service organizations

If service organizations have quite low overhead costs by comparison to their direct costs, there seems little point in adopting ABC. There are, however, some service organizations that deal in a variety of products and incur quite significant overheads that are not easily related to individual products. Companies providing retail financial services (insurance, investment trust units, mortgages, etc.) are often cited as examples of where the application of ABC would be appropriate. The questions at the end of this chapter include one for an insurance company.

Overheads beyond the factory floor

We have looked at ABC purely from the viewpoint of factory overheads. The cost accounting systems used with conventional overhead absorption do not usually deal with overheads beyond the production stage because these overheads must be excluded from product costs under the financial accounting regulations. If managers require information on product profitability, the overheads beyond the factory floor (such as administration, selling and distribution) must also be allocated to the different products. A conventional approach to this problem is to allocate these overheads to products on some arbitrary basis such as the relative sales value for the quantities sold.

ABC is not restricted to production overheads, and companies that adopt ABC will have to examine their support services, where the overhead costs are normally accumulated under functional headings such as administration, selling and distribution. This involves identifying appropriate cost drivers within these functions so that an application rate can be calculated in order to trace the cost to individual products As with production overheads, many of the cost drivers will be transaction based. For example, distribution costs might be driven by the number of orders processed. It might be difficult to identify cost drivers in administration although sending invoices to customers is clearly an activity that drives the cost of invoicing.

It could be that many companies include the costs of providing factory support services under administration. Costs such as product design, production scheduling and cost accounting are often treated as central support services that are not traced to individual products. Costs such as these will form a significant part of total costs and they will increase in the long term as individual product life cycles become shorter and the diversity of products increases.

It is not yet clear how product costing under ABC will be viewed by the auditing profession. Under existing financial accounting regulations, any overheads that cannot be related to the production function must be excluded from the cost of closing stock whereas product costs under ABC will include non-production overheads. This aspect should be relatively simple to solve since there will be a detailed analysis of overhead costs for each type of product. But it does leave a problem of a change of accounting policy. If the cost of closing stock at the end of the previous year was determined by using conventional overhead absorption, and the company changes to ABC for the current year, it might be argued that the accounting policy for determining the cost of closing stock has been changed. This could have a significant impact on reported profits and, if it does, the effect of changing the policy will have to be disclosed in the annual report to shareholders.

The two charts set out in Appendix 1 illustrate how the approach taken in conventional overhead absorption differs to that taken by ABC.

If your syllabus requires you to deal with the problem of reciprocal services, you should refer to the example in Appendix 2.

Summary

The main learning points in this chapter can be summarized as follows:

- conventional overhead absorption is based on attributing production overheads to production cost centres and uses a volume based measurement for each cost centre in order to calculate an absorption rate
- the attribution of production overheads to production cost centres involves a number of steps in the allocation, apportionment and re-apportionment of the various costs
- apportionments often use arbitrary bases (such as floor area) as a proxy for measuring the benefits received by a particular cost centre
- overhead absorption is based on a budgeted rate and the amount of overheads under- or over-absorbed can be analysed by cause
- traditional costing in service organizations uses an approach similar to that adopted for manufacturing, except that the cost of closing stock is not a determinant in the design of accounting systems
- activity-based costing is based on attributing overheads to activity areas rather than to production cost centres
- a cost driver is an activity that causes total costs to vary over a period of time
- short-term variable overheads are usually driven by production volume
- long-term variable overheads are often driven by transactions
- the total cost of an activity area is applied to products under ABC by using the cost driver as a measuring device
- cost information under ABC is more useful to managers because it focuses attention on problem areas and provides a basis for evaluating strategy
- the application of overheads to individual products under ABC extends to those overheads beyond the production stage

Working sheet for Activities 5 to 10

	Basis	Machine shop	Fitting section	Canteen	Maintenance
1. Allocated costs					
2. Apportioned costs					
Rent, rates, heat, light					
Insurance					
3. Sub-total service centres					
4. Apportion service centres					
Canteen		____		(____)	
Maintenance					(____)
5. Total production centres		====	====		

Activity 1

The direct labour hour rate for each department is: Machining £3; Assembly £1.96; Finishing £1.40.

Activity 2

The total overhead cost is $(3 \times £3) + (2 \times £1.96) + (1 \times £1.40) = £14.32$.

Activity 3

1. Examples could include: any indirect labour costs relating to a specific centre, such as employees in the staff canteen or a cost centre supervisor; finishing materials of a finishing department; any consumable stores that are issued direct to a specific cost centre; depreciation of plant used in the cost centre.
2. Examples could include: occupancy costs (rent, business rates, insurance) for the whole building; electricity charges (unless they are separately metered for each cost centre); cost of managers or supervisors who are responsible for a number of cost centres.

Activity 4

1. Floor area. 2. Book value of the plant. 3. Number of employees.

Activity 5

The completed working sheet is on page xx. At this stage you should check your figures down to completion of step 2.

Activity 6

The completed working sheet is on page xx.

Activity 7

The products are not homogeneous. If a company produced (say) pocket calculators and personal computers, the same amount of overhead would be added to each product.

Activity 8

1. Total machine hours: 52,700.
2. The machine hour rate is $(£84,320 \div 52,700)$ £1.60 per machine hour.

Activity 9

1. The total direct labour cost in the fitting section is £106,800.
2. The percentage of direct labour cost in the fitting section is $(£48,060/£106,800)$ 45%.

Activity 10

One unit of Product X is budgeted to cost:

		£
Direct materials		11.00
Direct labour:		
Machine shop	6.00	
Fitting section	12.00	
		18.00

Production overheads:	
Machine shop (6 × £1.60)	9.60
Fitting section (.45 × £12)	5.40
Total	44.00

Activity 11
There is an amount under-absorbed of £6,000 (i.e. £86,000 – (50,000 × £1.60)).

Activity 12
1. £96,000 ÷ 12,000 = £8.00 per development hour.
2. £41,000 ÷ 20,500 = £2.00 per 1,000 key depressions.
3. £147,000 ÷ 5,600 = £26.25 per usable hour.

Activity 13
Cost of job:	£
Development work (25 × £8.00)	200.00
Data preparation (90 × £2.00)	180.00
Computer operations (6 × £26,25)	157.50
Total	537.50

Activity 14
Product A (4 × £2)	£8.00
Product B (12 × £2)	£24.00

Activity 15
The answer is 7,000 units. Note that 4,000 units of Product A will use (4,000 × 4) 16,000 parts, leaving (100,000 – 16,000) 84,000 that must relate to Product B. 84,000 ÷ 12 = 7,000.

Activity 16
The absorption rate is (£200,000 ÷ 25,000) £8.00 per direct labour hour. The amount absorbed by each product is Product A (1 × £8) £8.00 and Product B (3 × £8) £24.00.

Activity 17
The absorption rate is £200,000 ÷ 32,000) £6.25 per direct labour hour. The amount absorbed by each product will be Product A (1 × £6.25) £6.25 and Product B (4 × £6.25) £25.00.

Activity 18
1. Overhead absorption rate (£15,500 ÷ 3,100) £5.00 per direct labour hour.
2. Product X (1 × £5) £5.00.
3. Product Y (3 × £5) £15.00.

Activity 19

Overhead costs per unit	Product X £	Product Y £
Short-term variable costs	1.00	3.00
Set-up costs	14.00	3.50
Materials handling costs	2.00	4.00
Quality control inspection costs	12.00	2.10
Total	29.00	12.60

Completed working sheet for Activities 5 to 10

	Basis	Machine shop	Fitting section	Canteen	Main-tenance
1. Allocated costs		27,660	19,470	16,600	26,650
2. Apportioned costs:					
Rent, rates, heat and light	floor area	9,000	3,500	2,500	2,000
Depreciation and ins.	book value	12,500	6,250	2,500	3,750
3. Sub-total service centres				21,600	32,400
4. Apportion service centres					
Canteen	Employees	10,800	8,400	(21,600)	2,400
Maintenance	(70/30)	24,360	10,440		(34,800)
5. Total production centres		£84,320	£48,060		

Questions for self assessment

Answers to self-assessment questions are given at the end of the book.

5.1 You are the Cost Accountant of an industrial concern and have been given the following budgeted information regarding the four cost centres within your organization.

	Department 1	Department 2	Maintenance Department	Canteen	Total
	£	£	£	£	£
Indirect Labour	60,000	70,000	25,000	15,000	170,000
Consumables	12,000	16,000	3,000	10,000	41,000
Heating & Lighting					12,000
Rent & Rates					18,000
Depreciation					30,000
Supervision					24,000
Power					20,000
					315,000

You are also given the following information:

	Department 1	Department 2	Maintenance Department	Canteen	Total
Floor space in square metres	10,000	12,000	5,000	3,000	30,000
Book value of machinery in £	150,000	120,000	20,000	10,000	300,000
Number of employees	40	30	10		80
Kilowatt Hours	4,500	4,000	1,000	500	10,000

You are also told:
 i) The canteen staff are outside contractors.
 ii) Departments 1 and 2 are production cost centres and the maintenance department and canteen are service cost centres.
 iii) The maintenance department provides 4,000 service hours to Department 1 and 3,000 service hours to Department 2.
 iv) That Department 1 is machine intensive and Department 2 is labour intensive.
 v) That 6,320 machine hours and 7,850 labour hours are budgeted for Departments 1 and 2 respectively for 1991.

Required:
a) **An overhead cost statement showing the allocation and apportionment of overhead to the four cost centres for 1991, clearly showing the basis of apportionment.**
b) **Calculate the overhead absorption rates for Department 1 on the basis of the machine hours and Department 2 on the basis of labour hours.**
c) On the basis that for 1991 actual overheads for Department 1 turn out to be £155,000 and machine hours worked 6,000, whilst actual overheads for Department 2 turn out to be £156,000 and labour hours worked 7,900, **calculate the under or over recovery of overheads for each department.**
d) The Managing Director of your organization suggest to you that one blanket rate rather than separate overhead absorption rates for Departments 1 and 2 based on machine hours and labour hours respectively would be more beneficial for future years. **Draft a reply to this assertion.**

(AAT Final, Cost accounting and budgeting)

5.2 An organization has budgeted for the following production overheads for its production and service cost centres for the coming year:

Cost centre	£
Machining	180,000
Assembly	160,000
Paint shop	130,000
Engineering shop	84,000
Stores	52,000
Canteen	75,000

The product passes through the machining, assembly and paint shop cost centres and the following data relates to the cost centres:

	M/c	Ass	Paint shop	Eng shop	Stores
No. of employees	81	51	39	30	24
Eng shop – service hrs	18,000	12,000	10,000		
Stores (orders)	180	135	90	45	

The following budgeted data relates to the production cost centres:

	M/c	Assembly	Paint shop
M/c hours	9,200	8,100	6,600
Lab hours	8,300	11,250	9,000
Lab cost	£40,000	£88,000	£45,000

Required:

a) **Apportion the production overhead costs of the service cost centres to the production cost centres and determine predetermined overhead absorption rates for the 3 production cost centres on the following basis:**

> **Machining – machine hours**
> **Assembly – labour hours**
> **Paint shop – labour costs.**

b) Actual results for the production cost centres were:

	M/c	Assembly	Paint shop
M/c hours	10,000	8,200	6,600
Lab hours	4,500	7,850	6,900
Lab cost	£25,000	£42,000	£35,000
Actual O/h	£290,000	£167,000	£155,000

Prepare a statement showing the under/over-absorption per cost centre for the period under review.

c) **Explain why overheads need to be absorbed upon pre-determined bases such as the above. Consider whether these bases for absorption are appropriate in the light of changing technology, suggesting any alternative bases that you consider appropriate.**

(*AAT Final, Cost accounting and budgeting*)

5.3 An NHS hospital has several departments providing different kinds of treatment. The following budget information relates to two of these, the General Surgery and the Geriatric departments, for the year ending 31 December 1994

	General surgery	Geriatric
Patient information:		
Number of in-patients	5,000	100
Average stay per in-patient	10 days	200 days

Direct treatment costs:	£	£
Consultants	2,000,000	500,000
Junior doctors	500,000	1,000,000
Nurses	2,000,000	3,000,000
Medical supplies	500,000	1,500,000

Total overheads for the whole hospital:

	£
Administration	6,000,000
Catering	2,000,000
Cleaning	1,500,000
Maintenance	1,000,000
Sundry utilities and laundry	1,000,000

The total number of in-patients for the **whole hospital** has been budgeted at 10,000 for 1994 with an average length of stay in hospital of 25 days.

The hospital use a traditional absorption costing system for calculating total costs per in-patient day. The absorption rate is based on total in-patient days for the budget period.

Required:
(a) Calculate the hospital's overhead absorption rate (per in-patient day) for 1994.
(b) Calculate the budgeted total cost per in-patient day for the General Surgery and Geriatric departments.
(c) Discuss some of the limitations of the cost information produced in (b) and list some of the ways in which this information might be used.
(d) Suggest ways in which the hospital could adopt ABC instead of the traditional overhead absorption, and provide an example to support your suggestion.

(BABS, *University of Westminster*)

5.4 **ABC for insurance company.** Security Satisfiers are an insurance company selling two types of policy known as the Regular policy and the Super Security policy. In the past they have calculated the cost of their policies using a traditional volume-based overhead absorption rate. This rate used premium income as the measure of volume. All costs are treated as overheads, there are no direct costs.

The following data has been collected for the last financial year:

Type of policy	Quantity sold	Data on averages per policy			
		Premium income	Customer visits	Number of underwriting adjustments	Number of computer enquiries
Regular	70,000	£50	1	1	2
Super Security	10,000	£100	5	8	6

Overhead costs have been identified according to the following activities:

Selling	360,000
Underwriting	300,000
Computing	140,000
Premium collection	100,000
	900,000

The following information is given in order to clarify some of the above data:
1. *The underwriting department of an insurance company has the task of assessing the risks (and premium) for each policy. These risks vary according to characteristics of the applicant*

such as age, health, smoker/non-smoker. The average number of adjustments per policy relates to the number of adjustments made to the basic premium for these risk factors.

2. The insurance company holds details of all policies underwritten on a computer file for each applicant. These files are opened from time to time for various reasons, such as when a client wishes to change some details of the insurance cover. The average number of computer enquiries relates to the frequency of this kind of operation.

Required:
(a) Calculate unit overhead costs for the Regular and Super Security policies using the company's traditional method based on value of premium income.
(b) Use the activity-based costing method, and the data available, to recalculate unit costs on a basis that seems appropriate to you. Explain your choice of cost drivers.
(c) Indicate the advantages of activity-based costing for decision making when compared to traditional overhead absorption.

(University of Westminster)

5.5 Simultaneous equations
Author's note: The following question is included for the benefit of students preparing for A Level exams. The technique is explained in Appendix 2.

The Meldreth Manufacturing Company uses the algebraic (simultaneous equation) method to apportion the overheads of its service departments one to another.

		Service departments	
		A	**B**
Overheads (£)		4,200	2,400
Apportionment (%)	A	–	10%
	B	5%	–

Required:
(a) Calculate the overheads to be apportioned to each of the two service departments.
(b) Explain two other methods the company could have used.

(ULSEB A Level)

Questions without answers

Answers to these questions are published separately in the *Teacher's Manual*.

5.6 A large hotel has recently reorganized its costing system and split its activities into four cost centres:

1. Accommodation
2. Catering
3. Leisure
4. Outings

The hotel is moving towards standardizing its services and selling a hotel package to its customers which will include accommodation, meals, use of leisure facilities and a number of outings. There is to be a predetermined price per day for the use of each cost centre by the customer.

Labour and material can be identified and allocated to the cost centres in the budget but other overheads listed below cannot be so readily identifiable.

	Accommodation £	Catering £	Leisure £	Outings £	Total £
Labour	110,000	100,500	35,000	38,500	284,000
Materials	19,000	36,000	16,000	13,000	84,000
Power					84,000
Rent and Rates					72,000
Depreciation					60,000
Advertising					76,000
Office expenses					240,000

You are given the following information about the cost centres from the budget for the coming year.

	Accommodation	Catering	Leisure	Outings
Floor area (in sq. metres)	1,200	400	600	200
No of employees	32	16	24	8
Machinery value	£10,000	£20,000	£60,000	£30,000
Kilowatt hours	5,000	2,500	12,500	1,000
Expected customer usage in days	15,000	12,000	8,000	3,000

You are told that advertising is to be apportioned to the cost centres on the basis of customer usage and office expenses apportioned on the basis of total cost per cost centre before the apportionment of the office expenses.

The budget for the coming year has been based upon the strategy that customers will have the standard accommodation and catering package with the leisure facilities and outings package as optional. Hotel policy for the coming year is to operate a profit margin of 30% on price.

Required:

a) **Prepare a cost statement for the four cost centres showing the budgeted total cost and the budgeted cost per customer day per cost centre.**

b) **Calculate the price to be charged to a married couple who want to stay at the hotel for one week. They require accommodation and catering for seven days, use of the leisure facilities for three days and want to go on outings on three days.**

c) The actual results for the hotel for the year under review were as follows:

Cost centre	Total cost £	Customer days Usage
Accommodation	320,000	15,250
Catering	275,000	13,000
Leisure	200,000	6,800
Outings	125,000	3,200

Calculate the under/over-absorption of costs per cost centre.

(AAT Final)

5.7 **Mortgage product group.** The present product costing system of a small retail bank is based on a detailed work measurement system operating within the branch network. This system has proved to be accurate and reliable as far as direct costs are concerned. Branch support costs are, however, absorbed by using a traditional volume measure based on branch direct labour hours. The newly appointed chief executive has criticized this basis as 'distorting product profitability' and has asked you to investigate the introduction of a new activity based product costing system using the mortgage product group as a pilot study.

The results of your preliminary investigations of the mortgage product group are as follows:

1. **Budget data for 1994:**

Mortgage product type	Target sales (number of loans)	Branch direct labour hours per loan	Direct costs per loan £
Repayment	3,000	3	300
Endowment	6,000	4	400
Fixed rate	1,000	3	300

2. **Activity analysis:**

Mortgage product type	Forms processed per loan	Marketing publications per year	Credit status reports per loan	Entries in computer data base per loan
Repayment	1	20,000	1	10
Endowment	2	30,000	1	15
Fixed rate	3	50,000	2	30

3. **Budgeted support costs for the mortgage product group:**

	£
Mortgage publications section	2,000,000
Central mortgage processing	1,000,000
Mortgage credit status section	750,000
Mortgage computer input section	500,000
	4,250,000

Required:

(a) Calculate product costs for each type of mortgage using the current traditional absorption costing method. Under this method the total mortgage support costs are allocated to products on the basis of direct labour hours.

(b) Recalculate these product costs using activity-based costing.

(c) Describe the advantages to the bank of adopting activity-based costing and state any reservations that you might have regarding its implementation.

(BABS, University of Westminster, adapted)

5.8 Prime Pottery Ltd produces two types of vase, known as Blue and Green. It has traditionally costed its vases on a volume based overhead absorption basis. It is now considering using Activity Based Costing. The following budgeted data are available:

Vase type	Quantity	Direct costs	Machine hours	Material handling (number of moves)	Number of set-ups
Blue	100,000	£350,000	25,000	350,000	100
Green	25,000	£75,000	6,250	50,000	25

The total overhead costs are as follows:

Machine maintenance	£125,000
Materials handling	150,000
Set-up costs	225,000
	500,000

The existing absorption basis is to absorb total overheads on the basis of machine hours.

Required:

(a) Calculate total unit costs (direct costs plus overhead) using the existing absorption basis for overheads.

(b) Recalculate unit costs using activity-based costing based on the three cost drivers given.

(c) Proponents of activity-based costing argue that it has put the relevance back into management accounting. Do you agree with this statement?

(University of Westminster)

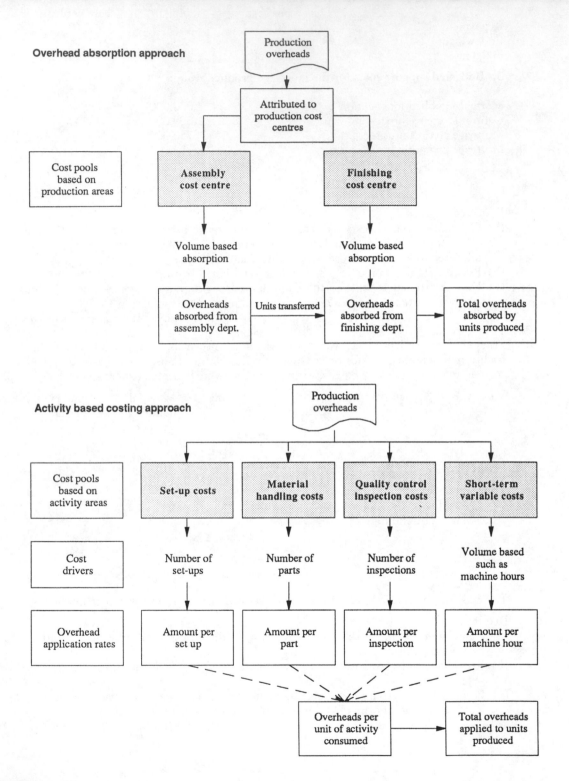

Fig. 5.1

Reciprocal services – example

A factory has two production cost centres. These are serviced by the maintenance section and a staff canteen. The overheads allocated and apportioned to the canteen are £12,000 and to the maintenance section they are £20,000.

The apportionment ratios for the overheads of these two service centres is as follows:

	Production centre 1	Production centre 2	Canteen	Main-tenance
Canteen	20%	70%	–	10%
Maintenance	30%	60%	10%	–

Notice that the canteen services the maintenance section and that the maintenance section services the canteen.

There are various ways of solving the problem, including the use of computer spreadsheets. In exams, there are two methods that lend themselves to manual calculations:

- repeated apportionment
- simultaneous equation

Repeated apportionment is best for students who do not like algebra. The idea is to repeatedly apportion the service department costs until the amount awaiting apportionment from one of the service centres becomes so small as to be insignificant. This is then shared between the production cost centres in the relevant ratios of those centres (e.g. 30/60 for maintenance costs in the above example). Consequently, no amount is apportioned to the other service centre and the repeated apportionment process can stop.

The simultaneous equation method will work as follows:

Let C = the total overheads of the canteen
Let M = the total overheads of the maintenance section

The term 'total overheads' means the totals already attributed to each service cost centre (£12,000 and £20,000 in the above example) plus the amounts apportioned from other service cost centres. These totals can be found from the following equations:

$$C = £12,000 + 0.1M$$
$$M = £20,000 + 0.1C$$

re-arranging:

$$C = £12,000 + 0.1(£20,000 + 0.1C)$$

therefore:

$$C = £12,000 + £2,000 + 0.01C$$

and so:

$$99C = £14,000$$

meaning that:

$$C = £14,000 \div 0.99 \text{ i.e. } £14,141$$

In this case:

$$M = £20,000 + (0.1 \times £14,141)$$

meaning that:

$$M = £21,414$$

These amounts are then apportioned to cost centres according to the percentages given, as follows:

	Production centre 1	Production centre 2	Canteen	Maint-enance
Overheads			12,000	20,000
Apportion canteen	(.2) 2,828	(.7) 9,899	(14,141)	(.1) 1,414
Apportion maintenance	(.3) 6,424	(.6) 12,849	(.1) 2,141	(21,414)
Apportionment of £32,000	9,252	22,748		

If you work out the figures using repeated apportionments, you will find that they are similar to the above.

Cost accumulation procedures

Objectives

After you have completed this chapter, you should be able to:
- distinguish between production methods that are established to satisfy specific orders and those that are established as a continuous process
- describe how production methods influence the cost accounting process and the determination of unit costs
- calculate unit costs where production consists of a continuous process
- evaluate how processes' losses affect unit costs according to whether the losses are classed as uncontrollable (normal losses) or controllable (abnormal losses)
- demonstrate the various accounting solutions for dealing with rejects, scrap sales, by-products and joint products, in a continuous process industry
- interpret decision making data that ignores past (or sunk) costs and focuses on the way in which future cash flows will change as a result of making a decision

Introduction

All economic entities produce goods and/or services, and need to know the cost of their products for various reasons. As discussed in earlier chapters, the process of accumulating unit costs in the manufacturing industry tends to be dominated by the need to determine product costs that will satisfy financial accounting regulations. You will also have discovered from earlier chapters that there are a number of difficulties, particularly with overheads, on establishing appropriate principles for calculating unit costs. In this chapter you will learn how another factor (the production method) has a bearing on the way that unit costs are accumulated.

The term 'production method' is slightly misleading because it suggests that the problem is confined to manufacturing activity. But an X-ray department of a hospital will produce services in different ways, such as providing a general service for the care of the hospital's own patients or carrying out a specific job for another (perhaps private) hospital. These are just as much different production methods as those that we find in manufacturing.

In order to explain how production methods affect the cost accumulation process in a general way it is helpful to identify the two ends of a fairly wide spectrum of economic activity. At one end there is a specific job, at the other there is a continuous process of mass production. The cost accumulation processes for each of these extremes are usually called job costing and process costing, respectively. The terminology varies according to the type of activity. In some businesses, such as car repairs, it is quite acceptable to refer to the work requested by a customer as a 'job', but in professions (such as medicine or law) the idea that the work for a client represents a job might seem undignified and so other labels, such as 'case', are used instead.

Although the system of accumulating costs for these two ends of the spectrum (jobs and continuous processing) are described separately in this chapter, production methods in practice (particularly in manufacturing) are often a combination of both. In car manufacturing, for example, there might be some processes for mass producing basic components and standard models, whereas other activities involve work on specific units (in the nature of a job) for customizing standard motor cars in order to produce luxury versions.

6.1 Differences in the cost accumulation process

The terms 'job costing' and 'process costing' are used mainly as labels for the different ways that the cost recording system identifies and accumulates costs for the units produced. These differences are related to the type of operation. Where the unit (or a batch of similar units) produced has characteristics that enable costs to be specifically identified with it, job costing is used. In this case, the accounting documents such as material issue notes and time records will identify the job (or batch) number to enable the costs of that job to be accumulated. Where there is continuous mass production of identical units, process costing will be used. In this case, the costs for a period (such as one month) are accumulated and then divided by the number of units produced in order to determine an average cost per unit.

Job costing

Job costing is sometimes called 'specific order costing' or 'job-order costing'. The word 'order' provides another signpost to when job costing is appropriate because the work is usually done according to the unique requirements of an order placed by a particular 'customer'. This customer might be external or internal. You can probably think of several examples of an internal order, such as where a second-hand car sales department requires the car repair section to carry out a specific job on a car before it is offered for sale, or where a user department requires the central computer department to redesign a system. In manufacturing, the internal customer might be the finished goods department requesting production of a small batch of customized basic products. In all cases it is the unique nature of each job that makes it necessary (and possible) to measure the varying inputs of direct materials, direct labour and production overheads associated with that job.

Activity 1

Consider whether job costing is likely to be suitable for the following types of operation.

		Delete as appropriate
1.	Installing central heating systems	yes/~~no~~
2.	Manufacture of light bulbs	~~yes~~/no
3	A printing company	yes/~~no~~
4.	Aircraft manufacture	yes/~~no~~
5.	Coal mining	~~yes~~/no
6.	Oil refining	~~yes~~/no
7.	Professional accounting practice	yes/~~no~~

The central document used to control the cost accounting entries is known as a job card (this might be known as a batch card in some cases). Job cards are pre-numbered so that each job has a unique number that can be quoted on all source documents, such as material issue notes and time records. The elements of cost (direct materials, direct labour and overhead) are accumulated on an account for each job. If (as is usual) there are several jobs in progress at any one time, the costs charged to individual job accounts will also be charged in total to a work-in-progress control account. As jobs are completed, the appropriate costs are taken out of the work-in-progress control account and charged either to cost of sales account (if the job was for an external customer) or to finished goods control if the job was to produce a batch of items for the finished goods store.

If the work takes place over several days or weeks there could be uncompleted jobs (work in progress) at the accounting date. The total cost of work in progress (reported under stocks in the balance sheet) is represented by the balance on the work-in-progress control account. This balance should be equal to a total that can be found by adding the balances on all the individual uncompleted job accounts. Notice that the cost of work in progress when job costing is used is derived from the accounting system itself because all input costs are associated specifically with either the completed or the uncompleted jobs. This does not happen with process costing.

Process costing

In some industries there is a continuous process of producing large quantities of like units. You can probably think of many examples, including those for which you answered 'no' in Activity 1. In these cases, the costing system can be simplified because there is no need to trace input costs to any specific job (or batch). Instead, input costs can be accumulated for a period (such as a month) and then divided by the number of units produced to find an average cost per unit.

Although process costing is usually associated with manufacturing (and mining), the idea can be used in many types of operation. For example, if a restaurant wanted to know the cost of providing a waiter service for each meal we could add up the total cost of employing waiters for a period and divide this by the number of meals served in that period. In these cases, however, the averaging process is probably being used to produce cost information to help managers with decisions (such as the price to charge for a meal), whereas process costing in a manufacturer forms the basis of a book-keeping system. As mentioned on a number of previous occasions, the accounting systems of manufacturers are also used to divide production costs between the cost of goods sold and the cost of closing stock for the purposes of financial accounting.

Activity 2

If process costing is used by a manufacturer as the basis of its book-keeping system, there could be a problem of determining the cost of work in progress (if any) at the end of the period. Try to describe why this problem arises. Keep in mind that input costs are accumulated for a period rather than for specific units as they are with job costing.

In process costing, the recording system itself is unable to divide total input costs for the period between the cost of finished goods produced in that period and the cost of work in progress at the end of that period. This allocation of costs relies on a separate external calculation which then forms the basis of entries in the ledger. The procedure for allocating costs between finished goods and work in progress is quite simple in principle. You will see how it works in a moment.

The two methods of cost accumulation (job costing and process costing) are illustrated by Figure 6.1. The diagram for job costing assumes that if the order was placed internally, it was for a batch of finished goods. The diagram for process costing is based on a pet food manufacturer and assumes three sequential processes. Since each production cycle for this type of product is relatively short, there is unlikely to be any work in progress at the accounting date.

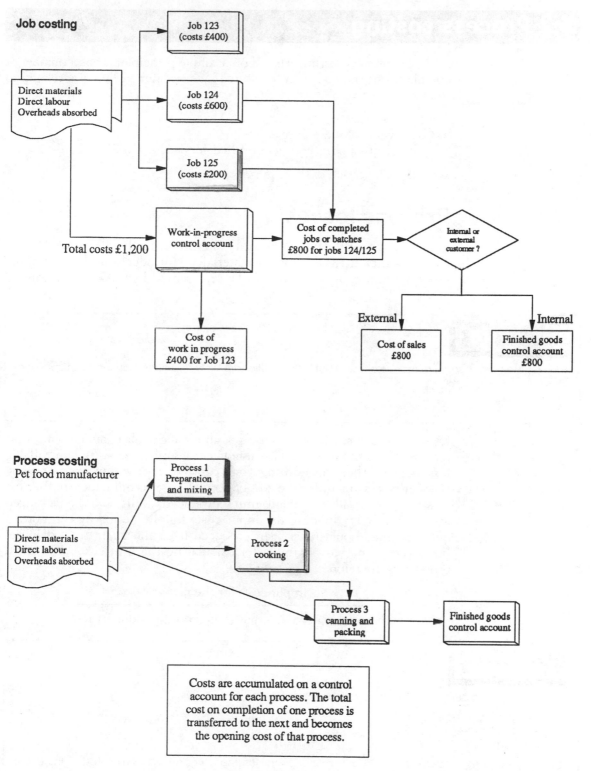

Job costing

Job 123
(costs £400)

Job 124
(costs £600)

Job 125
(costs £200)

Direct materials
Direct labour
Overheads absorbed

Total costs £1,200

Work-in-progress
control account

Cost of completed
jobs or batches
£800 for jobs 124/125

Internal or
external
customer ?

External

Internal

Cost of
work in progress
£400 for Job 123

Cost of sales
£800

Finished goods
control account
£800

Process costing
Pet food manufacturer

Process 1
Preparation
and mixing

Process 2
cooking

Process 3
canning and
packing

Finished goods
control account

Direct materials
Direct labour
Overheads absorbed

Costs are accumulated on a control
account for each process. The total
cost on completion of one process is
transferred to the next and becomes
the opening cost of that process.

Fig. 6.1

Although process costing is based on a simple principle, it has a number of complications that are often exploited by examiners. These are related to the following:

- process losses
- sales value of scrap or rejects
- allocation of costs between finished goods and work in progress

We will look at each of these in stages.

Process losses

It is unlikely that the output quantity of finished goods will be equal to the input quantity. If 1,000 kg of raw material are introduced at the start of the process, the output is unlikely to be represented by 1,000 kg of finished product.

Activity 3

Make a note here of some of the reasons why output quantities are likely to be less than the input quantities.

In many processes it should be possible to establish an amount that represents a 'normal loss'. This might be described as an uncontrollable loss because there is nothing that can be done to prevent it. The accounting treatment for the cost of normal losses is quite logical: the cost is spread over all the good units produced. This can be achieved arithmetically by dividing the input costs for the period by the normal quantity that should have been produced from the quantity of material introduced. The basic formula for calculating the unit costs of finished products is, therefore:

$$\frac{\text{Input costs for the period}}{\text{Normal expected output (based on input quantities)}}$$

Activity 4

The input costs of a process for Month 1 were as follows:

Raw materials 1,000 kg cost	£5,000
Direct labour	£1,000
Overheads	£3,000

Normal losses during processing are 10% of the input quantities. There was no work in progress at the end of Month 1 and 900 kg of finished goods were produced.

Calculate the cost per kilogram of finished product.

In Activity 4, the process losses were equal to the normal loss. This is not likely to occur in practice. If the output had been 850 kg there would have been an abnormal loss of 50 kg. This is sometimes called a 'controllable' loss and represents something for which the process manager is held accountable. The costs attributable to abnormal losses must be deducted from the input costs and charged to a separate account. There are two reasons why this is necessary:

1. **Responsibility accounting**: by removing the cost of abnormal losses from the process costs and charging them to an abnormal loss account, the cost is isolated for explanation by the process manager.
2. **Financial accounting regulations**: you might recall that SSAP 9 requires the cost of closing stock to be based on costs that arise in the **normal** course of business. The cost of **abnormal** losses should, therefore, be removed from the costs that are attributed to the cost of finished goods produced.

The costs attributed to abnormal losses will depend upon the processing stage reached at the time when the losses occurred. If they occurred at the start of the process (such as where some materials were accidentally wasted) the loss relates entirely to the cost of materials. If they occurred during the process, the loss will consist of material costs and a proportion of the conversion costs (direct labour and overheads). If they occurred at the end of the process (such as where more than the normal quantity of finished units were scrapped following a quality control inspection) their cost will be on the same basis as for the units transferred to the finished goods store.

In order to help with the learning process we will assume, for the time being, that all losses occur at the end of the process. You will learn how to calculate the cost of abnormal losses that occur during the process after studying the techniques used for calculating the cost of work in progress.

Activity 5

The inputs to a process for Month 1 were sufficient to make 1,000 units of a finished product. The input costs were as follows:

Raw materials	£5,000
Direct labour	£1,000
Overheads	£3,000

The company normally expects to reject 10% of the finished units produced. The rejected units have no scrap value. There was no work in progress at the end of the month. Out of the 1,000 units produced, 850 units passed the quality control inspection and were transferred to finished goods store. The 150 defective units were scrapped.

Allocate the total input costs of £9,000 between:

1. Finished units transferred to store.
2. Abnormal losses.

Note: This is not as difficult as it might seem. The cost of a finished unit (whether it be a good unit or a reject) is found by using the basic formula given above Activity 4.

In Activity 5, the defective units had no scrap value. In many cases, the rejects (if they cannot be re-worked) can be sold – either as scrap or as sub-standard products. In some cases, process losses might be represented by other types of scrap that can be sold such as wood chippings (which can be sold for making chipboard), metal filings and off-cuts in a textile company. In the case of rejects that can be sold as sub-standard, their retail value is likely to be in excess of cost. In these cases the rejects are merely treated as a different class of finished product and the costs related to them are transferred to a separate finished goods account.

Scrap sales are treated differently because the income is negligible by comparison to that earned on sales of the main product. In view of the incidental nature of this income, the usual procedure is to reduce the process costs by the sales value of scrap. Care is needed on this when the quantity of scrap is identified as being partly from normal losses and partly from abnormal losses. In these cases the process costs are reduced by the scrap value of the normal losses only; the scrap value of abnormal losses is treated as a reduction of the cost of abnormal losses. The introduction of scrap values means that the basic formula for calculating the unit cost of finished units produced (good or bad) must be revised to:

$$\frac{\text{Input costs for the period } less \text{ scrap value of normal losses}}{\text{Normal expected output (based on input quantities)}}$$

Notice that this refers to the 'scrap value' rather than to the actual income received from scrap sales. We will see what happens to the cash received from scrap sales after working through the next activity.

Activity 6

Use the same details as for Activity 5 but assume that the rejects can be sold as scrap for an amount of £4.50 per unit.

1. Calculate the total amount of process costs that will be attributed to the units passed to finished goods store.

2. Calculate the amount that will be reported as an abnormal loss.

Note: You will find this activity relatively easy to work if you use the revised formula given above. Remember that this formula relates to all units produced (whether they passed inspection or were rejected). The first thing to do is to use the formula for allocating the revised process costs between good units and abnormal losses, then deduct the scrap value of the abnormal losses from the costs allocated to abnormal losses.

The company in Activity 6 has spent £9,000 during the month. How has this expenditure been allocated in terms of stocks and expenses? If we assume that none of the stocks (neither good units nor rejects) were sold by the end of the month, the position is as follows:

Stocks:

Good units produced (850 × £9.50)	£8,075
Stock of scrap (150 × £4.50)	675
Total stock	8,750

Expenses:

Cost of abnormal losses	
(50 × £9.50) less (50 × £4.50)	250
Total expenditure	9,000

The cost of abnormal losses will be written off as an expense after appearing on a production report for the period. The £675 for scrap stocks will be held on a scrap control account. This account is treated as an asset which increases as more scrap is produced, and decreases as money is received on the sale of scrap. For example, if 20 units of the above scrap is sold for their scrap value of (20 × £4.50) £90, these proceeds will go to reduce the balance on the scrap control account by £90. The total amount of £675 is then changed into the following:

Stock of scrap (130 × £4.50)	£585
Cash in the bank	90
	675

So far we have been considering the cost of abnormal losses. The same set of principles are used where the production quantities of good units exceeds what is normally expected from the inputs. In this case there will be an abnormal gain. The next activity reproduces the details in Activity 5 but with the output changed so as to produce an abnormal gain.

Activity 7

The inputs to a process for Month 1 were sufficient to make 1,000 units of a finished product. The input costs were as follows:

Raw materials	£5,000
Direct labour	£1,000
Overheads	£3,000

The company normally expects to reject 10% of the finished units produced. The rejected units have no scrap value. There was no work in progress at the end of the month. Out of the 1,000 units produced, 950 units passed the quality control inspection and were transferred to finished goods store. The 50 defective units were scrapped.

Allocate the total input costs of £9,000 between:

1. Finished units transferred to store.

2. Abnormal gain.

Note: In this case the cost of abnormal gains will increase the total costs allocated to good units produced (although the unit cost remains the same as in Activity 4). Use the basic formula to produce a solution.

Isolating the costs associated with abnormal gains can be just as important as isolating the cost of abnormal losses. There could be several reasons why managers will be interested in abnormal gains, other than to provide an opportunity for congratulating the process manager.

Activity 8

Identify some of the reasons why managers will be interested in abnormal gains and make a note of them here.

Terminology

There is often some confusion in the use of terms such as: 'rejects', 'scrap' and 'waste'. Certain examiners (particularly those at A level) are quite keen on asking questions that are designed to see if candidates have a tidy and logical mind regarding the concepts behind these terms. The best approach to this type of problem is to use the definitions provided by the CIMA in their *Official Terminology* booklet. The CIMA definitions of the three terms mentioned above can be paraphrased as follows:

- **Rejects:** units of output that fail to reach the required standard of quality before despatch to customers. These units can either be rectified at further cost, or sold as sub-standard.
- **Scrap:** discarded material that has some recovery value and is either sold without further treatment or re-introduced into the production process in place of raw material.
- **Waste:** discarded substances that have no value.

You need to be careful over how you associate these terms with the concept of normal and abnormal losses as used in process costing. For example, although waste represents a normal loss in volume, the term 'normal losses' is not restricted to waste. Normal losses might relate to the normal quantity of rejects (as in Activities 5 and 6) or to the normal quantity of scrap produced. In certain types of chemical manufacturing, the waste might have to be subjected to a detoxification process. In these cases the cost of detoxification will be treated as a part of the cost of producing the main product (no cost can be attached to the waste because it has probably been flushed down the drain). Changes in production technology might result in a change of classification. For example, wood chippings and sawdust of a timber yard that were previously treated as waste (and perhaps used as fuel for the boilers) can now be sold as scrap and used as a raw material by a manufacturer of chipboard.

Work in progress

Process costing does not identify costs with any specific units, it merely averages the costs for a period over all the units produced in that period. The problem with calculating the cost of work in progress is that we need a common measure to divide into the input costs for the period. We cannot divide the input costs by a total number of units found from adding the finished units to the units in progress because this would mean that the finished goods had the same unit cost as those that were still being processed. This must be wrong; the cost of a completed unit must be higher than the cost of an uncompleted unit.

In order to express total production (finished goods and work in progress) in terms of a common denominator, a notional unit known as an 'equivalent unit' is used. An equivalent unit is a notional unit of finished product. For example, if there were 200 units in process at the end of the period and these units were considered to be half complete, they are the equivalent of 100 completed units. The notional quantity of 100 units can then be added to the actual number of completed units in order to determine a notional quantity known as the equivalent production. Unit costs are based on dividing input costs by the equivalent production.

Example

The process costs for a period were £9,000. There were no process losses. The quantity of finished goods produced was 800 and the units in process at the end of the period were 200. The units in process are considered to be 50% complete.

Commentary

In this case the notional quantity of completed units is (800 + (50% × 200)) 900 units. The unit cost is (£9,000 ÷ 900) £10.00 per equivalent unit. The allocation of the £9,000 costs for the period would be allocated as follows:

	Total	Per unit
Finished goods (800 × £10.00)	£8,000	£10.00
Work in progress (100 × £10,00)	1,000	£5.00
	9,000	

Notice that the cost of work in progress is found by multiplying the cost per equivalent unit by the number of equivalent units. Work in progress is actually 200 units (not 100) and so the actual cost of each unit of work in progress is (£1,000 ÷ 200) £5.00. This seems to be quite sensible when you consider that the unit cost of a completed unit is £10.00 (bearing in mind that a unit of work in progress is 50% complete).

Unfortunately, this is an oversimplification of the problem. In the above example, the process costs were given as one total of £9,000. This total will include direct materials, direct labour and overheads. In most processes, the materials are introduced at the start of the process. This means that work in progress is likely to be 100% complete as regards materials but only partially complete in respect of the conversion costs (direct labour and overheads). In order to allocate the input costs for the period between finished goods and work in progress, it will be necessary to look at each element of cost, and calculate a cost per equivalent unit for each element of cost.

It is not easy to learn how to do these computations without a demonstration and so the first stage of the process is illustrated below. This should enable you to complete the second stage where the costs are allocated between finished goods and work in progress.

Details for the activity

The input costs for processing 1,000 units in the period are as follows:

Direct material	£5,000
Conversion costs (direct labour and overhead)	£4,500

During the period 800 units were completed and transferred to finished goods store. There were 200 units in progress at the end of the period. These were 100% complete as regards materials but only 50% complete as regards conversion costs.

Stage 1

The first stage is to set out a table of equivalent units (EUs) and calculate the cost per equivalent unit (EU) for each category of cost. The computation is as follows:

		Materials		Conversion	
Total costs		£5,000		£4,500	
Equivalent production:	% complete	EUs	% complete	EUs
Finished goods (800 units)	100%	800	100%	800
Work in progress (200 units)	100%	200	50%	100
		1,000		900
Cost per equivalent unit		£5.00		£5.00

Stage 2

The costs per equivalent unit for each category of cost can now be used to allocate the total costs of £9,500 between the cost of finished goods and the cost of work in progress.

Activity 9

Complete the computation set out below. The multipliers used when calculating the cost of work in progress are different for each category of cost – there are 200 EUs for materials and 100 EUs for conversion costs.

Cost allocation:	Materials	Conversion	Total
Finished goods (EUs × cost per EU)			
Work in progress (EUs × cost per EU)			
			£9,500

When you become accustomed to this type of working, you should be able to see a short-cut in the calculation of the cost of finished goods. For example, in the above computation the multiplier for finished goods is 800 for both material and conversion costs. This means that the cost of finished goods could have been calculated as 800 × (£5 + £5) = £8,000. You cannot take this approach on work in progress because the multiplier (EUs) for material costs is 200 whereas it is 100 for conversion costs.

The same procedure must be used if some of the process costs are to be attributed to abnormal losses. If losses are assumed to occur at the end of the process, they will be 100% complete as regards both material and conversion costs. Consequently, they will be included in the EU table on the same basis as the finished units transferred to finished goods store.

Activity 10

The inputs to a process during Month 1 were sufficient to make 1,000 units of a finished product. The input costs were as follows:

Raw materials	£1,860
Conversion costs	£2,340

The company normally expects to reject 10% of the finished units produced. The rejected units have no scrap value. Total production for the month was as follows:

Completed	700 units
Work in progress	300 units

Out of the 700 completed units 100 were rejected and scrapped. The 300 units still being processed at the end of the month were half-way through the conversion process although they were 100% complete as regards material costs.

Complete the tables set out below. The aim is to allocate the total costs of £4,200 between: finished units accepted, abnormal losses and work in progress.

Stage 1. Table of equivalent units	Materials £1,860		Conversion £2,340	
	%	EUs	%	EUs
Finished units accepted (600 units)	100%		100%	
Abnormal losses (100 – 70) (30 units)	100%		100%	
Work in progress (300 units)	100%		50%	
Total number of EUs				
Cost per equivalent unit (costs ÷ number of EUs)				

Make sure that your figures agree with the Key before moving on to the second (cost allocation) stage.

Stage 2. Cost allocation table	Materials	Conversion	Total
Finished goods accepted (EUs × cost per EU)			
Abnormal losses (EUs × cost per EU)			
Work in progress (EUs × cost per EU)			
Total cost			£4,200

If abnormal losses are identified as having occurred during the process (rather than at the end) they will be included in the table as partly completed units in the same way as work in progress. In the case of abnormal gains, the procedure is exactly the same as the above except that the quantities will have to be shown as negative quantities in the EU table, and as a negative amount in the cost allocation table. This ensures that the costs attributed to abnormal gains inflate the costs attributable to the other units of production.

Equivalent units in a non-manufacturing context

Although we have been thinking of an equivalent unit as a measure to allocate production costs in a manufacturing process, there are many other situations where it is used. Equivalent units are a convenient way of expressing quantities in terms of a common denominator. For example, colleges and universities obtain central funding according to the number of full-time students enrolled. Yet these institutions usually run courses for both full-time and part-time students. In order to derive a number that represents full-time students, a formula is used whereby a certain number of part-time students are considered to be the equivalent of one full-time student. The concept is also used in farming. There is a question at the end of this chapter in which you will have to use equivalent units to allocate costs between fully reared chickens and those that die before they are fully grown.

Double-entry recording and opening work in progress

If your syllabus requires you to write up ledger accounts in process costing, you should refer to the Appendix at the end of this chapter. You will find this quite easy to follow after working through the above activities. This Appendix also explains how opening work in progress affects the calculation of unit costs in the current period.

6.3 Joint products and by-products

Some manufacturing processes result in more than one type of product emerging from a single process. The manufacturer of dairy products is a good example; a separation process will produce skimmed milk and cream, both of which can be sold as main products. Sometimes, one of the products emerging from the process is treated as a by-product rather than a main product.

By-products are defined by CIMA as products that are recovered incidentally from material used in the manufacture of recognized main products. Most firms will classify a product as a by-product where it has a very low sales value compared with the sales value of the main product (or products). Although by-products are similar to scrap they usually have a higher sales value than scrap and are often subject to further processing (such as packaging) before being sold.

Accounting for joint products is usually different to that for by-products. In the case of joint products it is a common (but not universal) practice to establish a basis for apportioning joint costs to the separate main products. There is usually no benefit to the company in attempting to isolate the costs of a by-product and so an expedient approach is often taken whereby the income from the by-product is treated as a reduction of joint costs. This income can be recognized as soon as the by-product is produced (as we did with the sales value of scrap) or when the by-product is sold. Recognizing the income when the by-product is produced has more conceptual merit and ensures that the company keeps a control account for by-product stocks as a part of the double-entry recording.

Allocating costs to joint products: Is it necessary?

In order to illustrate the problem of allocating joint costs to joint products we will use the example of a dairy product manufacturer as mentioned earlier. All costs up to the point where the two main products (skimmed milk and cream) emerge from the process are called 'joint costs'. The stage of processing reached when the products emerge as two separate products is known as the 'split-off' point. This can be illustrated as shown in Figure 6.2.

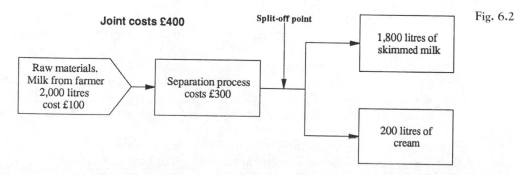

Fig. 6.2

Figure 6.2 suggests that we need to find a basis for allocating the joint costs of £400 between the two main products. But this invites the question: why do we need to apportion the joint costs?

You might have thought a little bit ahead of the suggestion made in the Key, but assuming that you thought along the lines suggested we now face a dilemma because there is no scientific way in which the joint costs can be traced to the individual products. There are several bases that could be used for the apportionment but they all have one thing in common; they are purely arbitrary. Information on individual product costs that is so ambiguous cannot possibly be used for pricing or cost control decisions. In many cases, prices are dictated by market forces and managers are more concerned to ensure that the total sales revenue from both products provides an adequate margin over the total processing costs. Nonetheless, we still sense that there must be a reason why it is necessary to apportion the joint costs to each product.

This is another example of where cost accounting procedures are designed to serve the needs of financial accounting. Some companies might need to allocate costs to joint products where the cost of one of the products forms the basis of a price received under a contract (such as with the government) but in most cases the procedure serves no purpose other than to allow the company to report the cost of goods sold (and closing stocks) to shareholders. In view of this, some companies do not bother to apportion joint costs in their management accounting reports. An apportionment is done at the end of a period (for closing stocks) merely to satisfy the financial accounting regulations.

There are several bases that can be used to apportion joint costs to individual products. The following are frequently used:

- a physical measure such as litres (this is possible only if the products at the split-off point have physical characteristics that can be measured in the same way – it cannot be used if one product is (say) liquid and another is solid)
- the sales value of production at the split-off point
- estimated net realizable value of production at the split-off point

Activity 13

Apportion the joint costs of £400 incurred by the dairy product company (as illustrated above) between skimmed milk and cream using the physical measure of litres as the apportionment basis. After allocating the total costs, calculate the cost per litre for each product and then make an observation.

	Allocation of total cost	Cost per litre
Skimmed milk		
Cream		
Observation		

When physical measures are used, the cost per unit of measure will always be the same for each product because all we are doing is dividing the joint costs by the total volume produced. If total volume produced in this example had been less than the input volume (for example, the cream produced was 180 litres) the cost per litre will still be the same for each product (roughly 20.2p). This has the effect of spreading process losses over both products according to their relative volume.

Apportionment of joint costs based on the sales value of production is often justified on the grounds that there will be some kind of relationship between cost and selling price. This can produce a circular argument in the case of joint products because joint costs cannot be uniquely traced to any individual product and we now seem to be suggesting the use of sales value as a basis for setting the sales price. But in many cases sales prices are determined by market forces and the apportionment of joint costs is not relevant for pricing decisions; it is done purely for purposes of profit measurement.

It is the sales value of production (quantity × price) for each product, not the sales price of a single unit, that is used for the apportionment. The total sales value for each product is then seen as a proportion of the total sales value for the entire production.

Activity 14

The dairy product manufacturer in Activity 13 is able to sell its products at the following prices:

Skimmed milk: £0.95 per litre
Cream: £0.25 per litre

Apportion joint costs of £400 between the two products using sales value of production as the apportionment basis. Then calculate the cost per litre for each product. Use the table set out below for your answer.

	Sales value of production (quantity × price)	Apportionment of costs	Cost per litre
Skimmed milk			
Cream			
Totals		£400.00	N/A

In Activity 14 we have assumed that the sales prices for each product were those that could be earned at the split-off point. This is unlikely to be realistic because each product emerging from the split-off point will usually require further processing before it can be sold. In the case of our dairy products manufacturer, both the skimmed milk and the cream will require packaging before they are sold, the skimmed milk might also be subjected to some kind of heat treatment. The costs of packaging and heat treatment are not a part of the joint costs of £400; they occur after the split-off point and are usually called 'post-separation' costs.

Post-separation costs are clearly traceable to individual products. And although we will take this into account when attributing costs to individual products, we also need to think about how it might affect the way we apportion the joint costs. If there is some relationship between sales price and cost (the argument behind our apportionment basis) then we need to recognize that the ultimate sales price of each product can be achieved only after the post-separation costs have been incurred. These post-separation costs are not likely to be equally divided between the different products.

We can think of the skimmed milk and cream as they pour out of the separation process as being 'intermediate' (bulk liquid) products. We could use the sales value of these intermediate products for the apportionment but this is often difficult to asses. Since we know the sales prices after further processing we can use a concept known as net realizable value at the split-off point. This is the first time we have used net realizable value in cost accounting although you may have encountered the idea in financial accounting. Roughly speaking, net realizable value means the ultimate sales value less the costs of completion.

For example, if the sales value of £450 for the skimmed milk in Activity 14 will be achieved after spending £50 on post-separation costs, the net realizable value of skimmed milk produced is (£450 − £50) £400. If the sales value of £190 for cream will be achieved after spending £10 on post-separation costs, the net realizable value of the cream is £180. The total net realizable value of production is (£400 + £180) £580. The cost apportionment would then be as follows:

	Joint costs apportioned	Joint costs per litre
Skimmed milk (400/580)	£276	15.33p
Cream (180/580)	124	62p
	400	

As you can see, these figures are similar to those that were used when post-separation costs were ignored. In order to work out the total unit costs, the post-separation costs can be included as follows:

	Joint costs apportioned	Post-separation costs	Total costs	Cost per litre
Skimmed milk (400/580)	£276	£50	£326	18.11p
Cream (180/580)	124	10	134	67p
	400	60	460	

What methods of apportionment do companies use in practice? A survey published by CIMA in 1984 (authors K. Slater and C. Wootton) gave the following as being the predominant methods for apportioning joint costs in the industries stated:

- Petrochemicals: sales value at split-off or net realizable value
- Coal processing: physical measure
- Coal chemicals: physical measure
- Oil refining: no apportionment

6.4 Joint products and relevant costs for decision making

The subject of relevant costs in decision making is covered by Chapter 11, but you will find it helpful to look at one aspect of this while the subject of joint products is fresh in your mind. You have already seen how the apportionment of joint costs is purely arbitrary and in view of this the cost of individual products produced by the apportionment cannot really be used for assessing the performance of individual product lines. The joint costs of a process (and their apportionment) should also be ignored in a certain type of decision problem.

Sell at split-off or process further

Many products can be sold at the split-off point for a certain price, or they can be subjected to further processing and sold at a higher price. The higher price will be achieved at the expense of the additional processing. A manager might be faced with having to make a decision on whether to sell at the split-off point or whether to process further in order to earn a higher sales price.

Business decisions all have one thing in common; they can only affect what will happen in the future, nothing can change what has happened in the past. Since the past cannot be changed by a decision, past costs are irrelevant in decision making. (Note that although past costs are irrelevant for decisions, they are relevant for measuring profits – but that is a different problem.) The relevant information for the problem being discussed can be based on how future cash flows will change if the manager decides to process further rather then sell at the split-off point. This information is usually presented to managers on an incremental basis and considers the following two factors:

1. How much extra income will be received if the product is sold after further processing rather than at the split-off point? This represents the incremental revenue.
2. What are the additional costs of processing further? This represents the incremental cost.

If the incremental revenue exceeds the incremental costs, the company will benefit financially from the decision to process the products further. We can see how it would work with our dairy food manufacturer. Imagine that instead of selling cream and skimmed milk, the following options are available:

> The skimmed milk could pass through a drying process in order to produce milk powder. The 1,800 litres of skimmed milk will be converted into 180 kg of dried milk powder. This product sells at a price of £4 per kg. The drying process will cost £210 for the 1,800 litres processed.

> The cream could be subjected to heat treatment so as to produce long-life cream. There will be no loss in volume as a result of this process. The long-life cream will sell at £1.20 per litre. The heat treatment process will cost £80 for the 200 litres.

Figure 6.3 helps to illustrate the options. Option 1 illustrates the position if neither product is processed further (apart from packaging as discussed

Fig. 6.3

Option 1. Sell after packaging at split-off

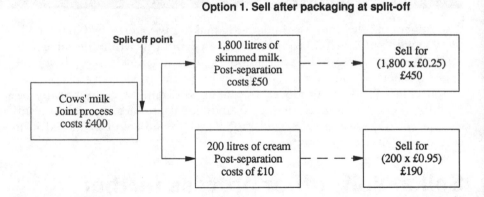

Option 2. Process further after split-off

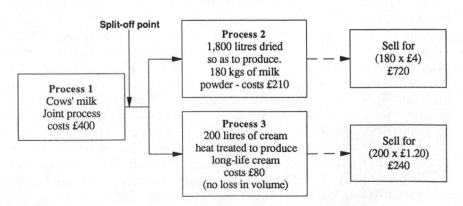

earlier). Option 2 illustrates the position if both products are processed further on the basis described above.

The following activity requires you to work out the incremental revenue and incremental costs of processing further. You will find this quite easy to do by completing the table provided.

Activity 15

Complete the table below in order to see whether it will be beneficial to process either (or both) of the dairy products further. The decision will be based on whether the additional income from the refined product exceeds the additional cost of producing that refined product.

	Skimmed milk or milk powder	Cream or long-life cream

Sale proceeds:
    If sold following the initial
        process
 	
    If sold after further processing
 	
    1. Incremental revenue		

Post-separation costs:
    If sold following the initial
        process
 	
    If subjected to further
        processing
 	
    2. Incremental costs		

Incremental profit or (loss) from processing further (1 minus 2)		

The above table shows that it will be beneficial to the company to process the skimmed milk into milk powder but not to process the cream into long-life cream. Whatever method is used to apportion the joint costs of £400, the same conclusion will be reached.

(Note that all of the figures used throughout the dairy food exercises were contrived purely for the purposes of study, they probably bear little relationship to real life figures.)

Summary

The main learning points in this chapter can be summarized as follows:

- cost accumulation procedures depend upon the method of production, in some cases costs can be identified with particular jobs or batches, others require costs to be averaged over a large number of units produced in the accounting period
- if costs can be identified with a particular unit (or batch), job costing is used; if there is continuous mass production of like units, process costing is used
- some production methods have characteristics that require a combination of both process costing and job costing
- job costing identifies costs with specific units that are either completed or uncompleted by the end of the period; process costing cannot do this, and the concept of an equivalent unit must be used to allocate costs to completed and uncompleted units
- equivalent units are notional quantities of finished units
- it is usually necessary to calculate equivalent units for each element of cost because in most cases the work in progress will be complete in respect of the material content but only partly complete in respect of the conversion costs
- joint products are main products emerging from a joint process, by-products are products that are recovered incidentally from material used in the manufacture of main products
- processing costs are not usually traced to by-products, their sales value is usually treated as a reduction of the processing costs
- the apportionment of joint costs (as reduced by the sales value of by-products) between the main products serves no purpose other than to facilitate financial accounting
- various apportionment bases are used, including: sales value at split-off, net realizable value at split-off, and physical measures
- in some cases, no apportionment of joint costs is done for management accounting since the information cannot be used for cost control or pricing decisions
- decisions regarding whether a product should be sold at the split-off point or processed further are based on information regarding incremental cash flows in the future; past costs (sunk costs) can be ignored

Activity 1
1. Yes
2. No (unless they are made in specific batches)
3. Yes
4. Yes
5. No
6. No
7. Yes

Activity 2
Some way has to be found of dividing the input costs between completed units and work in progress.

Activity 3
Wastage, spillage, evaporation, spoilt units.

Activity 4
£9,000 ÷ 900 = £10 per unit.

Activity 5
The unit cost for completed units is (£9,000 ÷ 900) £10 per unit.

1. Finished goods transferred to store (850 × £10)		£8,500
2. Abnormal losses (150 − 100) × £10		500
		9,000

Activity 6
Processing costs are reduced by the scrap value of normal losses and become £9,000 − (100 × £4.50) = £8,550. The unit cost of completed units is (£8,550 ÷ 900) £9.50 per unit.

1. Transferred to finished goods store (850 × £9.50)		£8,075
2. Abnormal losses (50 × £9.50)		250

Activity 7
The unit cost for completed units is (£9,000 ÷ 900) £10 per unit.

1. Transferred to finished goods store (950 × £10)		£9,500
2. Abnormal gain (100 − 50) × £10		(500)
		£9,000

Activity 8
They might represent something that can be exploited. It might mean that normal losses have been set at the wrong level and should be revised.

Activity 9

Finished goods: Materials (800 × £5.00) + (800 × £5.00)		£8,000
Work in progress (200 × £5.00) + (100 × £5.00)		1,500
		9,500

Activity 10

Stage 1. Table of equivalent units

Costs	Materials £1,860	Conversion £2,340
EUs:		
Finished units	600	600
Abnormal losses	30	3
Work in progress	300	150
Total	930	780
Cost per EU	£2.00	£3.00

Stage 2. Cost allocation

Finished goods accepted (600 × £2) + (600 × £3)	£3,000
Abnormal losses (30 × £2) + (30 × £3)	150
Work in progress (300 × £2) + (150 × £3)	1,050
	4,200

Activity 11

Perhaps you thought of reasons such as pricing or product profitability.

Activity 12

Stock valuation for financial accounting.

Activity 13

	Allocation of total cost	Cost per litre
Skimmed milk (1,800/2000)	£360	£0.20
Cream (200/2,000)	40	£0.20
	400	

Observation: we could have found the 'per litre' cost by simply dividing £400 by 2,000 litres.

Activity 14

	Sales value of production	Apportionment of costs	Cost per litre
Skimmed milk	450	£281.25	£0.15625
Cream	190	118.75	£0.59375
Totals	640	400.00	

Activity 15

	Skimmed milk or milk powder	Cream or long-life cream
Sales proceeds:		
If sold following the initial process	450	190
If sold after further processing	720	240
1. Incremental revenue	£270	£50

Post-separation costs:		
If sold following the initial process	50	10
If subjected to further processing	210	80
2. Incremental costs	£160	£70
Incremental profit/(loss)	£110	(£20)

Questions for self assessment

Answers to self-assessment questions are given at the end of the book.

6.1 A new subsidiary of a group of companies was established for the manufacture and sale of Product X. During the first year of operations 90,000 units were sold. At the end of the year the closing stocks were 8,000 units in finished goods store and 4,000 units in work-in-progress which were complete as regards material content but only half complete in respect of labour and overheads. There were no opening stocks and there were no abnormal losses during the period.

The work-in-progress account had been charged during the year with the following costs:

	£
Direct materials	714,000
Direct labour	400,000
Variable overhead	100,000
Fixed overhead	350,000

Required:
(a) On the assumption that absorption costing is used, prepare a working schedule showing how total production costs will be allocated to:
   (i)   cost of goods sold
   (ii) cost of closing stock
   (iii) cost of work in progress.
(b) Recalculate the three items in (a) on the assumption that marginal costing is used.

(CIMA *Cost accounting, adapted*)

6.2 ATM Chemicals produces product XY by putting it through a single process. You are given the following details for November 1991:

Input costs:
   • Material costs: 25,000 kilos at £2.48 per kilo
   • Labour costs: 8,000 hours at £5.50 per hour
   • Overhead costs: £63,000

You are also told the following:
   • Normal loss is 4% of input
   • Scrap value of normal loss is £2.00 per kilo
   • Finished output amounted to 15,000 units
   • Closing work-in-progress amounted to 6,000 units and was fully complete for material, 2/3 complete for labour and 1/2 for overheads
   • There was no opening work-in-progress

Required:

Prepare working schedules showing the following:
- Cost of finished goods produced
- Cost of abnormal losses
- Cost of work in progress
- Value of scrap stock (assuming none had been sold by the end of the period)

(AAT Final, requirement altered)

6.3 BI plc is in the food processing industry. A typical product range involves 3 joint products manufactured in fixed proportions by a common process which are subsequently refined by independent further processes.

The following table gives information for a typical month's activity:

	Product X	Product Y	Product Z
Output (tonnes)	100	60	80
Total further processing cost after separation	£30,000	£18,000	£12,000
Selling price (per tonne)			
(i) of the refined products	£750	£1,200	£900
(ii) of the products if sold before further processing	£450	£1,000	£700

Common costs incurred prior to separation are £144,000 in the month.

Required:

(a) **Assuming that common costs are apportioned on the basis of weight, determine the profit or loss which would be disclosed for each of the refined products in this month.**

(b) **Determine whether it would be beneficial to sell any product before the further process of refinement and briefly interpret your recommendations.**

(c) **Comment briefly on the relevance of common costs in decision-making situations.**

(ACCA Certified Diploma)

6.4 Poultry farmer

Note: The following question requires process costing principles to be used for a farmer. It also requires an incremental approach to be used to help with the decision in requirement (d). The whole problem can be solved by using exactly the same techniques and principles as used for a manufacturer.

Mr Boggin is a poultry farmer. He purchases day old chickens and, after rearing them for six months in his Chick Rearing Section, he transfers them as fully grown chickens (hens) to the Egg Laying Section. In the Egg Laying Section the hens are kept for a further six months and during this time the eggs are sold as they are laid. At the end of the period, the hens are slaughtered and sold.

The actual results of both sections, for the first six months of the year, are shown below:

Chick rearing section

	£
Purchased: 1000 chickens at 18p each	180
Rearing costs: Feed	1,044
Wages and overheads	968
	2,192

There were no chickens in this section at the beginning of the period. At the end of the period 850 fully grown chickens (hens) were transferred to the Egg Laying Section and there were no chickens remaining in the Chick Rearing Section. It is expected that, normally, 10% of the chickens purchased die at sometime during the rearing period. (It should be assumed that, on average, the chickens die at the end of three months, by which time 40% of feeding costs and 60% of wages and other costs have been incurred.)

Egg laying section

	£
Transferred from Chick Rearing Section: 900 hens	2,070
Other costs: Feed	2,340
Wages and overheads	2,475
	6,885
Sales: Eggs	5,750
Hens' carcases (700 @ £2.50)	1,750
	7,500

Normally no hens die in this section until they are slaughtered at the end of the period.

The eggs are sold at 50p for 12 and the hen's carcases at £2.50 each. At the end of the period there were in stock 2,400 fresh eggs and 200 fresh carcases.

Required:

(a) Assuming Mr Boggin operates a Process Costing System, prepare a statement to record the activities of the Chick Rearing Section for the above six months period. All workings should be clearly shown.

(b) Calculate the value of the closing stock in the Egg Laying Section assuming that the costs are to be apportioned to each joint product according to the market value of production.

(c) What explanation would you offer Mr Boggin who wishes to know which is more profitable: the sale of eggs, or the sale of hens' carcases?

(d) In future Mr Boggin is considering keeping the hens for an additional six month speriod in another Egg Laying Section. During this period it is expected that, on average, each hen would lay 120 eggs and the feeding and other variable operating costs would be £3.60 per hen. Additional equipment would be required which could be hired at a cost of £600 per annum. At the end of this second six months period the hens would be slaughtered and sold for £1.50 each.

Advise Mr Boggin whether it would be profitable to keep the hens for this additional six month period.

(ACCA Level 2 Pilot)

Questions without answers

Answers to these questions are published separately in the *Teacher's Manual*.

6.5 The following information relates to the PM Company, which uses a continuous process to produce its product:

Process 1 – April
Input of material: 10,000 kilos at £2.80 per kilo
Conversion costs: £31,200
Normal loss: 10% of input
Closing work in progress: 3,000 kilos 60% complete for conversion costs
Scrap value: £1 per kilo
Output: 6,000 kilos

The output from Process 1 is transferred to Process 2 where there was no opening work in progress at the beginning of April. The following information relates to Process 2:

Conversion costs: £27,000
Normal loss: 5% of input
Closing work in progress: 1,000 kilos 70% complete for conversion costs
Scrap value: £2.25 per kilo
Output: 4,900 kilos

Required:
A statement for both processes showing the allocation of costs between:
- completed output
- abnormal losses or gains
- work in progress

Author's guidance note: Take care with Process 2. There is an abnormal gain in this process and so you must remember to include this as a negative quantity in your table of equivalent units.

(*AAT Final, requirement modified*)

6.6 XY Ltd has a small processing operation from which two products X and Y jointly emerge. These joint products are produced in constant proportions and each require some further processing before being marketable. A proportion of product Y is of significantly poorer quality and consequently commands a lower market price. This is called Y2 and doubts have been expressed about its viability; the remainder is termed Y1.

The company enjoys a stable monthly demand pattern and plans its production accordingly. The products do not have a long storage life but occasionally the company may store them for a few days prior to a large delivery and this may occur at a month end.

The usual sales and production for the month is:

Product	Kilos
X	100,000
Y1	40,000
Y2	10,000

Current selling prices are:

Product	£ per kilo
X	1.50
Y1	1.00
Y2	0.30

Costs relating to a typical month's activities are:

Common processing costs:	£
Material	52,000
Labour and variable overhead	23,000
Apportioned fixed overhead	30,000
	105,000

Separate further processing costs:

	X £	Y1 £	Y2 £
Labour and variable overhead	40,000	6,200	800
Apportioned fixed overhead	4,800	2,000	200
	44,800	8,200	1,000

Required:
(a) Calculate for the month the profit attributable to each product if common costs are apportioned according to the weight of the three finished products and all production is sold. Comment briefly on the viability of product Y2.
(b) What profit would be reported if, in a month of typical production volume, only half the monthly output was sold (the remainder being held for delivery early next month) and closing finished stock was valued at:
  (i) full manufacturing cost?
  (ii) variable cost?
(c) Evaluate an enquiry from a new customer for 10,000 units of product X which is in excess of the normal monthly production and sales, all of which are fully committed. The price being offered for this product is £1.10 per kilo and this will not affect prices applicable to existing customers.

(ACCA Certified Diploma)

6.7 Expensive plant
Note: This question should be attempted only by students who have studied the material on opening work in progress in the Appendix.

A company operates expensive process plant to produce a single product from one process. At the beginning of October, 3,400 completed units were still in the processing plant, awaiting transfer to finished stock. They were valued as follows:

	£
Direct material	25,500
Direct wages	10,200
Production overhead	20,400 (200% of direct wages)

During October, 37,000 further units were put into process and the following costs charged to the process:

	£
Direct materials	276,340
Direct wages	112,000
Production overhead	224,000

36,000 units were transferred to finished stock and 3,200 units remained in work-in-progress at the end of October which were complete as to material and half-complete as to labour and production overhead. A loss of 1,200 units, being normal, occurred during the process.

The average method of pricing is used.

Your are required to:
(a) Prepare for the month of October, a statement (or statements) showing:
  (i) production cost per unit in total and by element of cost;
  (ii) the total cost of production transferred to finished stock;
  (iii) the valuation of closing work-in-progress in total and by element of cost.
(b) Describe **five** of the characteristics which distinguish process costing from job costing.

(CIMA Cost accounting)

6.8 Two processes
Note: This question should be attempted only by students who have studied all of the material in the Appendix.

A company manufactures a product that goes through two processes. You are given the following cost information about the process for the month of November:

	Process 1	Process 2
Unit input	15,000	–
Finished unit input from Process 1		10,000
Finished unit output to Process 2	10,000	
Finished unit output from Process 2		9,500
Opening WIP: units		2,000
cost		£26,200
Input: materials	£26,740	
labour	£36,150	£40,000
overhead	£40,635	£59,700
Closing WIP: units	4,400	1,800

You are also told:

(1) The closing WIP in Process 1 was 80% complete for material, 50% complete for labour, and 40% complete for overhead.

(2) The opening WIP in Process 2 was 40% complete for labour and 50% complete for overhead. The costs included in this opening WIP were £3,200 for labour and £6,000 for overhead.

(3) The closing WIP in Process 2 was two-thirds complete for labour and 75% complete for overhead.

(4) No further material needed to be added to the units transferred from Process 1.

(5) Normal loss is budgeted at 5% of the total input in Process 1 and Process 2. Total input is to be inclusive of any opening WIP.

(6) Normal loss has no scrap value in Process 1. In Process 2 it can be sold for the input value from Process 1.

(7) Abnormal losses have no sales value.

(8) The company uses the weighted average method of costing.

Required:

Prepare the accounts for:

Process 1
Process 2
Any abnormal loss/gain

Author's guidance note: Take care with the calculations for Process 1. This process produces an abnormal gain and you must remember to show this as a negative quantity in the table of equivalent units. You will find also that the question includes information that you do not need.

(AAT Final, modified)

Process costing: Double-entry book-keeping

If there are a series of processes (as illustrated in Figure 6.1) an account is kept for each process. A process account (sometimes called a 'work-in-process' control account) serves the same function as the work-in-progress control account which was introduced in Chapter 3. The process account is debited with all the processing costs for the period (direct materials, direct labour and overheads) and credited with the cost of goods transferred to finished goods store, and with the work in progress at the end of the period.

The closing work in progress is treated like any other closing debit balance; it is credited to the old period as a closing balance and debited to the new as an opening balance. Abnormal losses are credited to the process account (and debited to an abnormal loss account) and abnormal gains are debited. There are usually separate accounts for abnormal losses and abnormal gains.

A process account normally has two columns on each side of the account, one for quantities and one for money values. Since both columns (quantity and value) must be balanced at the end of the period, it will be necessary to include the normal losses on the credit side of the process account. The entry for normal losses has no monetary value (no cost is attached to normal losses) and is included merely to balance the quantity column. But if losses (normal and abnormal) have a scrap value, the scrap value of **normal losses** will be credited to the process account (the scrap value is included in the money column for the credit entry). This effectively reduces the process costs by the scrap value of normal losses.

The double entry for scrap value of normal losses is completed by a debit to the scrap stock control account. If there are also abnormal losses in this situation, there will be more scrap stock than the amount debited to the scrap stock control account for normal losses. The scrap value of abnormal losses is, therefore, debited to the scrap stock control account and credited to the abnormal loss account (thus reducing the loss reported as an abnormal loss). If there are abnormal gains, the amount debited to the scrap stock account for normal losses will exceed the amount of stock held. This is corrected by debiting abnormal gains and crediting the scrap stock control account with the scrap value of the units reported as abnormal gains.

The following 'T' account illustrates the process account that would have been written up for the situation described in Activity 10:

Process account (Activity 10)

	Units	£		Units	£
Direct materials	1,000	1,860	Normal losses	70	–
Conversion costs		2,340	Finished goods control	600	3,000
			Abnormal losses	30	150
			Work in progress	300	1,050
	1,000	4,200		1,000	4,200

In most examination questions on process costing you will have quite a lot of information to handle. You can get into a muddle with this unless you take a methodical approach to solving the problem. The best way of working is as follows:

1. Write up the process account as far as you can from the data provided. This includes entering details of all quantities even though the amounts are not known at this point for items such as finished goods, abnormal losses and work in progress. Also write in the details for normal losses (put a dash in the money column if there is no scrap value). Including all these details enables you to establish the quantity of abnormal losses.
2. Set up a working sheet to calculate equivalent production and the allocation of costs between finished goods, abnormal losses (or gains) and work in progress
3. Go back to your process account, write in the calculated figures and balance the account.

You could practise this based on some of the other activities in the chapter; there are also some problems in the question section that require the process account to be prepared.

Process costing: Opening work in progress

You might have noticed that the text ignored opening work in progress. This is because it can introduce a complication which is considered to be outside the skills required by the majority of students at a foundation level.

There is no complication providing the costing is done on an average basis. All that happens in this case is that the opening work in progress becomes one of the input costs for the current period. It will be necessary for the examiner to give you the analysis of this cost between materials and conversion costs (unless you prepared the account for the previous period, in which case you would know the analysis from your workings). The material and conversion costs included in opening work in progress are then simply added to the material and conversion costs for the current period when working out cost per equivalent unit.

Example

The work in progress at the end of the previous period consisted of 1,000 units that had been allocated with the following costs:

Materials	£12,000
Conversion	18,000
	30,000

During the current period a further 4,000 units were started and the input costs during the current period were as follows:

Materials	£40,000
Conversion	58,000

The throughput of 5,000 units was accounted for as follows:

Good units completed	3,000 units
Work in progress	2,000 units

There were no losses or rejects. The work in progress was 100% complete on material costs but only 40% on conversion costs.

The equivalent production and cost allocation would proceed as follows:

	Materials		Conversion	Total
Costs brought forward in WIP	12,000		18,000	
Costs in current period	40,000		58,000	
	£52,000		£76,000	£128,000
Equivalent production:	EUs		EUs	
Finished goods	3,000		3,000	
Work in progress	2,000	(40% × 2,000)	800	
	5,000		3,800	
Cost per equivalent unit	£10.40		£20.00	

The cost allocation would be as follows:		
Finished goods (3,000 × £30.40)		£91,200
Work in progress (2,000 × £10.40) + (800 × £20.00)		36,800
		128,000

The complication arises when a FIFO costing basis is used because a proportion of the costs for the current period must be allocated to finishing the opening work in progress. The units of opening work in progress will carry their costs from the previous period plus a proportion of the costs for the current period. This means that the costs for the current period will be allocated to the following:

- completing the units of opening work in progress
- the new units that were started and completed in the current period
- abnormal losses (or gains) if any
- the new units that were started but are still in progress at the end of the current period.

The total costs allocated to completed units for the period will comprise:

- cost of opening work in progress
- proportion of current period's costs needed to complete the opening work in progress
- proportion of current period's costs attributed to units started and completed in the period.

When calculating the amount of the current period's costs used to complete the opening work in progress, we can still use the concept of equivalent units but we need to think in the reverse of how we deal with closing work in progress. If the 1,000 units of opening work in progress in the above example were (say) 60% complete, the equivalent units produced out the current month's conversion costs will include 400 units (40% × 1,000) for completing the opening work in progress.

Working schedules for the previous example, assuming opening work in progress is complete on material costs and 60% complete on conversion costs, would be as follows:

	Materials		Conversion
Costs for current period	£40,000		£58,000
Equivalent production:	EUs		EUs
Opening WIP completed	0	(40% × 1,000)	400
Units started and completed			
(3,000 − 1,000)	2,000		2,000
Closing work in progress	2,000	(40% × 2,000)	800
	4,000		3,200
Cost per EU	£10.00		£18.125

The total cost to be allocated for the current period is £128,000 (cost of opening work in progress plus costs for the period) and this would allocated as follows:

Finished goods:			
1,000 units from opening work in progress			Per unit
costs brought forward	30,000		
conversion costs (400 × £18.125)	7,250		
		37,250	£37.25
2,000 units started and completed (2,000 × £28.125)		56,250	£28.125
		93,500	
Closing work in progress			
(2,000 × £10.00) + (800 × £18.125)		34,500	
		128,000	

Notice that the cost per unit of finished goods is significantly different to when the average basis was used. Under the average basis, all units produced in the period were allocated a cost of £30.40 per unit. This disguised the fact that production costs for the current month were substantially less per unit than in the previous month. Averages are misleading at the best of times; in this example the use of an average basis will hide information that could be useful to managers.

Abnormal losses were left out of the above explanation for the sake of clarity. In most cases, abnormal losses will relate to the current month's production. The quantities are, therefore, included in the equivalent production table, and the cost allocation table, in the normal way.

Control through use of standard costs

Objectives

After you have completed this chapter, you should be able to:
- discuss the concept of a standard unit cost for goods or services
- describe how standard costs can be used as a basis for control through variance accounting, and as a basis for stock valuation in manufacturing entities
- calculate cost variances for the main elements of cost in a manufactured product and analyse these variances according to their cause
- use the concept of a standard margin to analyse the effect on profits of differences between budgeted sales and actual sales
- produce a reconciliation report that uses the sales variances and cost variances to explain the difference between budgeted profit and actual profit
- discuss the interdependence of certain variances and how this affects the process of responsibility accounting
- describe some of the criticisms of standard as a control technique

Introduction

In all previous chapters we measured unit costs using the actual expenditure incurred, albeit that the cost per unit depended upon a number of factors, in particular:

- the **costing principle**, such as marginal cost or absorbed cost
- the **absorption method**, such as traditional absorption or ABC
- the **costing accumulation method**, such as job costing or process costing.

In this chapter we are not going to replace any of the above by suggesting an alternative approach, we are simply going to measure the elements of cost for each unit in a different way. Instead of using expenditure incurred we will be using what is known as the 'standard cost'. A standard cost is a cost worked out in advance of the accounting period and represents what each element should cost. We can then use this standard as a yardstick for comparison with actual expenditure. Variances between standard cost and actual expenditure can be analysed by cause, thus providing managers with a means of control.

The subject is usually called 'standard costing' but this is slightly misleading because it seems to imply an alternative to the costing methods previously discussed. This is not how you should view the subject, we are simply using a different cost measure. It does increase the number of permutations for calculating unit costs, as illustrated by Table 7.1.

Table 7.1

Costing principle/method	Measures for elements of cost
Marginal or absorbed cost	Costs incurred or standard cost
Traditional absorption or ABC	Costs incurred or standard cost
Job costing or process costing	Costs incurred or standard cost

There can be any number of combinations. For example, a manufacturer of toothpaste might use process costing on a marginal cost basis using standard costs, or it might adopt an absorption cost basis using ABC based on an actual expenditure. A moment's thought will tell you that there are a number of other combinations.

Adoption of standard costing can simplify some of the routine bookkeeping, but its main advantage lies in the ability to provide managers with a means of control through variance accounting. Standard costing has been used by some companies for very many years but in recent times it has been subjected to a number of criticisms because it can have the wrong motivational effect on departmental managers. We will look at some of these criticisms after learning how the system works.

As with most subjects in cost accounting, you will find it easier to learn the principles by using a manufacturer as the model. But there is unlikely to be any economic activity where standard costing cannot be used. You have already seen in previous chapters how various principles developed for manufacturing can be used in other economic activities such as farming, banking, insurance, hotels, education, transport and hospitals. You might find it even easier to see how standard costing can be used in non-manufacturing entities.

7.1 The basic system of standard costing

According to CIMA terminology, standard costing provides management with two, and sometimes three, facilities, namely:

- a basis of control through variance accounting
- a basis for the valuation of stocks and work in progress
- a basis, in some cases, for determining selling prices

Many students who have studied this subject previously seem to have the idea that it consists of arithmetical juggling in order to calculate variances. This is the wrong approach. Although a great deal of this chapter is concerned with calculating cost variances, it is important to keep in mind that standard costing is a feature of the book-keeping system. The variances that we will be calculating on a piece of paper are produced by the book-keeping system in real life. It is only necessary to look at the CIMA terminology again to see that the costs which are eventually routed through to closing stocks by the recording system of a manufacturer can be standard costs instead of actual expenditure.

Manufacturers who maintain their recording system on the basis of standard costs will finish up at the end of period with their stocks of raw materials, work in progress (if any) and finished goods all recorded in the books at standard cost. Any differences between standard costs and actual expenditure will be treated as expenses for the period.

Take raw materials as an example: a company might predict (when setting standard costs) that a particular type of material should cost £1.00 per unit. If there is a purchase of this material at £1.05 per unit, the raw materials account in the ledger is charged with £1.00 per unit (the standard price). But since the company will have to recognize a cost (and liability) of £1.05 per unit, the additional £0.05 per unit is charged to an expense account called the 'price variance account'. When this material is issued, the issue price is recorded as £1.00 per unit. The total price variance is included on a management report for the purposes of responsibility accounting; the balance on the price variance account is treated as an expense at the end of the period for the purposes of measuring profit.

Activity 1

The adoption of standard costs for the raw materials account will simplify some of the book-keeping problems. Make a note of why this is so. You might need to think about the work that you did in Chapter 4 on the pricing of raw materials issued to production.

For the benefit of students who need to understand how the book-keeping works, there is an appendix to this chapter setting out an explanation of the double-entry recording.

Standard cost is similar to normal cost

Before we look at how standard costing is used for cost control, you will find it interesting to think about its relationship to financial accounting. The accounting standard on stocks and work in progress (SSAP 9) allows closing stocks to be valued at standard cost. In previous chapters we have always thought of closing stock as being based on the 'actual cost' of past transactions; now we are suggesting that it can be based on a cost that has been thought up in advance of these transactions – a 'predicted cost'. This apparent contradiction is explained by a common misconception of the term 'actual cost' when used as label to identify the basis of product costs.

Financial accounting regulations require the cost of closing stocks to be based on the expenditure incurred in the normal course of business. This involves making prior judgements of what represents a normal cost, and treating some production costs as expenses rather than the cost of finished goods.

Activity 2

There is one element in the cost of a product that is actually based on predicted figures even when standard costing is not being used. Make a note here of the cost concerned.

If the amount included in the cost of production for overheads is different to the expenditure incurred, the difference is written off as an expense for the period. In the case of overheads it is quite clear that unit costs include a predicted amount rather than actual expenditure. But it is also necessary to make judgements in advance of the period to establish normal costs for both direct materials and direct labour. Judgements on these will enable the company to identify abnormal costs such as abnormal losses of materials and abnormal idle time. You will recall from the previous chapter how the cost of abnormal losses in a process are removed from the cost of production and treated as an expense. (Including these abnormal losses on a management report is a kind of variance accounting even if standard costing is not used.)

In any system of product costing the so-called 'actual cost' is to some extent influenced by judgements made in advance of the actual expenditure. In this respect the concepts of actual cost and standard cost are fairly similar. It can be argued that since the standard cost of a product is a prediction of what it should cost to make, it does represent a cost in the normal course of business. The extent to which standard costs differ from actual expenditure will be revealed by the accounts on which the cost variances are recorded. Where these show a significant difference, the company's auditors are likely to insist that the standard cost of closing stocks are adjusted so as to bring them in line with actual expenditure.

Setting standards

When setting the standard cost of a product, the company must take a realistic approach. There is little point in setting performance targets that are impossible to achieve. This aspect can be studied by considering the two terms used to identify standard performance: an ideal standard and an attainable standard. These are defined by the CIMA in the following way:

- **Ideal standard**: a standard which can be attained under the most favourable conditions. No provision is made for spoilage or machine breakdowns.
- **Attainable standard**: a standard which can be attained if a standard unit of work is carried out efficiently. Allowances are made for normal shrinkage, waste and machine breakdowns.

It is the comparison of actual performance against standard performance that forms the basis of cost control and accountability. The variances are analysed by cause (such as price or usage) and set out on a management report. Various departmental managers will then have the task of explaining the variances (both favourable and unfavourable) for their own area of responsibility.

If standard costs are based on an ideal standard there are almost bound to be constant reports of unfavourable cost variances. Proponents of the ideal standard claim that the unfavourable variances will be a constant reminder to managers of the need to improve performance. However, setting targets that are almost impossible to achieve is likely to result in frustration and very little will be gained from the process. Consequently, ideal standards are not used in practice.

Attainable standards represent a level of performance that is capable of achievement and, theoretically, any variance between actual performance and standard performance is capable of being controlled. Standard performance should, therefore, be based on attainable standards. As mentioned above, the variance report presented to central management will identify the different areas of accountability according to the factors that have caused actual performance to differ from standard.

Basic convention for measuring cost variances

When you start working on the detailed activities in this chapter, you must try to identify a central theme (and a convention) that runs throughout all variance analysis. This central theme can be labelled as 'price and quantity'. You will start to see this for raw material costs by working on a simple example based on the following details.

Example

A company manufactures a single product called Product X. For the next accounting period it is budgeting to make and sell 200 units of Product X.

Based on attainable standards, each unit of Product X should use 2 litres of Material A. The standard price of Material A is £3.00 per litre. The total standard material cost for each unit of Product X is, therefore, £6.00.

During the accounting period concerned, the company manufactured and sold 180 units of Product X. The total raw material cost was as follows:

390 litres of Material A costing £1,150

In this example, the standard material cost for producing 180 units of Product X is (180 × £6) £1,080, whereas the company has spent £1,150; an unfavourable variance of £70. If the company had not used standard costing this variance might be considered insignificant and no further enquiry conducted. Standard costing will isolate the causes of this variance and allocate a cost to each cause.

Activity 3

Look at the details again and identify the two basic factors that have caused actual material costs to differ from standard. Describe these two causes in your own words but do not attempt to attribute any cost measurements to them.

If you were now asked to allocate the total cost variance of £70.00 between these two causes, you will either finish up with a number of different answers, or a complete muddle. This would happen because you have not been told the convention that is used to allocate the total variance. We also need to establish some terminology. The difference between standard quantity of raw materials for 180 units of Product X and the actual quantity used is known as the **material usage variance**. The difference between the standard price of Material A and the actual price is known as the **material price variance**. Variances are identified as favourable if the actual cost is less than standard, and **adverse** when actual costs exceed the standard.

We need a convention for measuring the two variances in order to settle the following questions:

- Should the usage variance be measured using the actual price of the materials, or the standard price?
- Should the price variance relate to the standard quantity that should have been used, or to the entire quantity used?

The convention for raw material cost variances is as follows:

- **material price variances** are measured for the entire quantity used (in practice they are measured on the quantities purchased, but this introduces an unnecessary complication at this stage of learning), and
- **material usage variances** are measured at standard price.

You must keep in mind that this is merely a convention, it is not a statement of fact. For example, it could be argued that the true cost of using more materials than the standard quantity is the actual cost of those materials – not their standard cost. The convention on quantity variances is an arithmetic residue from the way that price variances are measured. Since the amount allocated to the price variance is for the entire quantity used, we are left only with the standard price as a means of measuring the quantity variance.

There are many different ways of learning how to calculate variances in standard costing; perhaps the least successful method is trying to memorize formulae. In this chapter we will not be using formulae; instead, you will be asked to try to make use of the basic convention as outlined above. You will discover that this convention is applied to all elements of cost, and is also relevant to the way that variances on sales income are measured.

Activity 4

You should now be able to calculate the price variance for the above example. If you keep in mind that it relates to the entire 390 litres used, your approach to the calculation can be as follows:

390 litres of Material A should have cost (at standard price)   £

390 litres of Material A actually cost   £

Difference equals the price variance

Having calculated the variance you must identify whether it is favourable or adverse.

With this type of approach there is little point in trying to work out a price variance per litre and then multiplying it by 390. In fact you will find the actual price per litre in this example (£1,150 ÷ 390) is a difficult number to use.

When it comes to working out the usage variance it is best to take two steps:

1. work out a quantity variance (in litres for the example), and
2. measure this quantity variance at the standard price.

You will find this makes more sense after working through Activity 5.

Activity 5

Calculate the usage variance and identify whether it is favourable or adverse. Use the following outline for your calculations:

1. 180 units of Product X should use   litres
    180 units of Product actually used   litres

    Difference (quantity variance)   litres

2. Quantity variance × standard price =   £

You have now allocated the total adverse cost variance of £70 as follows:

| Price variance | £20 | favourable |
| Usage variance | (£90) | adverse |

This information is clearly more valuable for cost control purposes than a single figure of £70 adverse. In terms of accountability, the purchasing manager will be responsible for explaining the price variance, the production manager must explain the usage variance. It is wrong to think of this part of the control process as something that leads to blame or praise, it is done to enable central management to make relevant enquiries when actual results differ from standard. In the above example, it might be discovered that the cheaper materials contributed to the adverse usage variance because of their inferior quality (perhaps resulting in more wastage than standard). This kind of information gives central management the opportunity of making appropriate decisions on what should be done to reduce costs in the future.

7.2 Standard costs and budgeting

Budgeting is much more than a control system, as you will discover when studying the next chapter. As a control system, budgeting involves setting targets for each department. These targets will be for expenditure in respect of departments that incur costs, and for income in respect of departments that are responsible for sales. Control takes the form of comparing actual results with targets and reporting variances to central management. This provides managers with an opportunity to take remedial action if they consider it necessary.

Standard costing is normally a part of budgeting. In the case of a manu-facturer, standard costs can be thought of as budgets at the individual product level (in contrast to budgets at a departmental level). This does not mean that budgeting involves the use of standard costing, but the two techniques are so closely linked that they are often used together.

Profit reconciliation

A variance report normally takes the form of a statement that reconciles budgeted profit with actual profit. There are three basic reasons why actual profit differs from budgeted profit:

- sales are different to budget
- production costs are different to budget
- overheads beyond the production stage are different to budget

In this chapter we will ignore overheads beyond the production stage and concentrate on profit at the gross profit level (the difference between sales income and the cost of sales). In order to measure how actual sales have caused actual profit to differ from budget, the normal practice is to measure sales variances on the assumption that each unit sold has a cost equal to its standard cost. This approach recognizes that cost variances are not the responsibility of the sales department, and ensures that cost variances in the reconciliation report relate to the entire quantity produced and sold.

This reconciliation statement holds the key to how you must approach solving a detailed problem and it is essential to have a general idea of how it works before embarking on the detailed calculations of cost variances. It can be quite difficult to see how it works without an example and so we will work on the following simplified problem.

Example

The following data relate to a single product company:

	Budget/standard			Actual		
	Qty	Per unit	£	Qty	Per unit	£
Sales	100	£10.00	1,000	110	£9.50	1,045
Production cost	100	£6.00	600	110	£6.10	671
Gross profit			400			374

Notice how actual sales activity differs from budget for both quantity and price (remember that quantity and price are the key factors in all variance analysis). In this example we are not given details of production costs and so the cost variance will have to be calculated as a single (total) amount. This will enable us to concentrate on the top part of the reconciliation statement that deals with the sales variances.

The reconciliation statement

A reconciliation statement starts with budgeted profit; the favourable variances are then added and the adverse variances deducted in order to arrive at actual profit. If (as stated earlier) the reconciliation statement assumes that all goods actually sold have a cost equal to their standard cost, it means that sales variances will have to be measured according to their effect on the budgeted margin of £4.00 per unit. If a unit is sold for less than the standard price, there is an adverse effect on budgeted margin equal to the difference in price on each unit actually sold. If more units than budget are sold, there is a favourable effect on budgeted margin equal to the budgeted margin on each extra unit sold.

Notice how the basic convention is applied to sales variances: price variances are measured on all units sold, quantity variances are measured at a standard amount (in this case the standard, or budgeted, margin).

Activity 6

Try to measure the sales variances based on the above explanation. You might not find this as easy as the material cost variances, but make an attempt before referring to the Key. Make sure that the correct workings and figures are recorded here before moving on to the following text.

1. Sales price variance:

2. Sales volume (quantity) variance:

The reconciliation statement (with adverse variances in brackets) will be set out as follows:

Budgeted gross profit		£400
Sales variances:		
Sales price	(55)	
Sales quantity	40	
		(15)
		385
Cost variances (in total)		
$110 \times (£6.10 - £6.00)$		(11)
Actual gross profit		374

There is an important learning point in the above example. Notice how the cost variances are related to the quantity of goods actually produced – not the budgeted quantity. Beginners often make a mistake on this when asked to calculate cost variances for a reconciliation statement. It is important that you focus on the quantity produced; the budgeted quantity is not relevant when calculating cost variances. You might have noticed that in the example used to calculate material cost variances (in section 7.2) the budgeted quantity of finished goods for the period was not used in any of the calculations.

7.3 Variance calculations: Detailed example

The text and activities in this section will be based on the following data. The details have been taken from a question set by the Association of Accounting Technicians. It covers all the basic variances and requires a reconciliation statement.

Details for the activities

A company produces a single product and uses a standard costing system for which the following standard costs apply:

	£
Direct material: 4 kilos at £2 per kilo	8
Direct wages: 2 hours at £5 per hour	10
Variable overhead: 2 hours at £1 per hour	2
Fixed overhead: 2 hours at £2 per hour	4
	24
Standard margin	16
Standard selling price	40

Budgeted production and sales for December are 10,000 units.

The actual results for December were as follows:

Production and sales: 10,200 units
Actual sales price: £42 per unit
Actual materials consumed: 39,000 kilos costing £84,180
Actual direct wages cost: 21,500 hours costing £107,190
Actual variable overhead cost: £23,650
Actual fixed overhead cost £38,000

We can start by calculating the budgeted profit and actual profit. This will give us the starting and closing figures for the reconciliation statement.

Activity 7

Calculate budgeted profit and actual profit, and make a note of the amounts here:

1. Budgeted profit:

2. Actual profit:

Materials and labour

The cost variances for materials and labour are the easiest to calculate and so we will start with these. You have already seen how to calculate the material price in Section 7.1, and you should use the same approach here. Remember the following points:

- cost variances relate to the actual production of 10,200 units
- the total material cost variance is the difference between the standard material cost of 10,200 units and the actual material cost of those units
- the material price variance relates to the entire quantity used
- the usage variance is measured at standard price

Activity 8

Calculate the following variances for material costs:

1. Total cost variance:

2. Material price variance:

3. Material usage variance:

The labour cost variances are worked out in exactly the same way as those for materials, except that the terminology changes. Instead of having a price variance we have a **labour rate variance** and instead of having a usage variance we have a **labour efficiency variance**. The same basic convention is used. In the case of wages, the various points can be described as follows:

- cost variances relate to the actual production of 10,200 units
- the total wages cost variance is the difference between the standard wages cost for 10,200 units and the actual wages cost of those units
- the labour rate variance relates to the entire number of hours worked
- the labour efficiency variance is measured at the standard rate.

Activity 9

Calculate the variances for labour cost. Since this is the first time you have been asked to calculate variances for wages costs, an outline format is provided for the rate and efficiency variances. Notice how these take the same form as for material costs.

1. Total labour cost variance:

2. Labour rate variance:
   The 21,500 hours worked should have cost (at standard rate)   £
   The 21,500 hours actually cost   £
                                                                        _____
                Difference = labour rate variance
                                                                        ======

3. Labour efficiency variance:
   The standard time allowed to produce 10,200 units is   hours
   The actual time taken to produce 10,200 units was   hours
                                                                        _____
                Difference = time variance
                                                                        ======

   Labour efficiency variance: time variance × standard rate =

The variances calculated in Activities 8 and 9 will eventually be included in the reconciliation statement and so it is important to make sure that you have labelled them as either favourable or adverse. It is also a good idea to calculate a total cost variance for each type of expenditure (as you did in Activities 8 and 9) so that you have control figures against which to agree the net result of the individual variances for that type of expenditure.

Overhead variances

There is a significant difference between variable overheads and fixed overheads when it comes to calculating cost variances. Variable overheads are the easiest and so we will deal with these first.

Variable overheads

The analysis of cost variances for variable overheads is similar to that for wages, except that the rate variance is usually called an **expenditure variance**. A description of the basic convention as applied to variable overheads is as follows:

- cost variances relate to the actual production of 10,200 units
- the total variable overhead cost variance is the difference between the standard variable overhead cost for 10,200 units and the amount actually spent on variable overheads for those units
- the variable overhead expenditure variance relates to the entire number of hours worked
- the efficiency variance is measured at the standard variable overhead absorption rate.

Activity 10

Calculate the variances for variable overheads, using the outline formats provided for the expenditure and efficiency variances. Notice how these are similar to those used for labour costs.

1. Total variable overhead cost variance:

2. Variable overhead expenditure variance:
   The 21,500 hours taken should have cost (at standard rate)   £
   The 21,500 hours actually cost   £

   Difference = variable overhead expenditure variance

3. Variable overhead efficiency variance:
   The standard time allowed to produce 10,200 units is   hours
   The actual time taken to produce 10,200 units was   hours

   Difference = time variance

   Variable overhead efficiency variance: time variance × standard rate =

Fixed overheads

It takes a little longer to learn how the fixed overhead variances are calculated. There are still the two basic variances; one relates to spending and the other to volume in much the same way as the other variances. But the volume variance by itself has very little meaning and has to be analysed further before the information has any value to managers. It is important to study the calculation of fixed overhead variances by taking one step at a time. The following text and activities break the subject into a series of small steps; you will find it helpful to take this approach when calculating variances without tutorial guidance.

Total fixed overhead cost variance

The total fixed overhead variance is the same as what we called overheads under- or over-absorbed in Chapter 5. In other words it is the difference between the fixed overheads incurred and the amount absorbed. If fixed overheads are over-absorbed the variance is favourable; if they are under-absorbed, the variance is adverse. There is, however, one slight difference when standard costing is used; overheads are absorbed on the basis of a standard amount (in £s) per unit. Absorption is not based on the actual time taken.

Activity 11

Calculate the total fixed overhead cost variance and indicate whether it is adverse or favourable:

The actual expenditure on fixed overheads was   £

The amount absorbed on making 10,200 units was   £

Total fixed overhead cost variance   £

This provides a total against which we can eventually reconcile the individual variances.

Fixed overhead expenditure variance

This is the easiest of the fixed overhead variances to calculate. It is not calculated in the same ways as the variable overhead expenditure variance, because we are now dealing with a fixed period cost; the total amount spent does not vary with the level of activity. Consequently, the expenditure variance is simply the difference between the budgeted expenditure for the period and the actual expenditure in that period.

Activity 12

Calculate the fixed overhead expenditure allowance. You will notice that the details do not state (directly) how much was budgeted for fixed overheads in the period. This information has to be determined from the budgeted production quantities and the fixed overhead cost per unit (examination questions are often set like this).

The actual expenditure on fixed overheads was   £

The budgeted fixed overhead for the period was   £

Difference = fixed overhead expenditure variance

There are two basic reasons why fixed overheads have been over-absorbed: (1) the amount spent on fixed overheads was different to budget and (2) the production volume was different to budget. You have calculated the expenditure variance in Activity 12; this leaves us with the volume variances.

Fixed overhead volume (or activity) variances

The total fixed overhead variance was £2,800 favourable and the expenditure variance was £2,000 favourable. The balance (£800 favourable) represents a volume variance. This variance will have to be analysed further in order to produce information that might be useful to managers. Before we do this analysis, however, you need to understand a concept known as a **standard hour**. A standard hour is not a measurement of time, it is a measurement of work. In our example, the 10,200 units produced represents 20,400 standard hours of work because each unit should (according to the standard) take 2 hours to make.

In Activity 11 you calculated the amount absorbed as 10,200 units at £4.00 per unit. You could have calculated this using the concept of a standard hour. The 10,200 units produced represent 20,400 standard hours and since the fixed overhead absorption rate is £2.00 per hour the amount absorbed could have been calculated as 20.400 × £2.00.

We can use the concept of a standard hour to make sense of the £800 favourable volume variance. This has arisen because the fixed overhead absorption rate (FOAR) was based on (10,000 × 2) 20,000 standard hours whereas the work produced represents 20,400 standard hours. The difference of 400 standard hours at £2.00 per hour is £800. As a computation, it can be set out in the same (two-step) form as all quantity variances, as follows:

Budgeted standard hours for the period	20,000 hours
Standard hours in the work produced	20,400 hours
Difference	400 hours

400 standard hours at £2.00 per hour = £800 favourable

But this single volume variance is ambiguous because it hides a combination of two factors:

- the effect of working at a higher capacity level to that budgeted (21,500 hours against 20,000)
- the effect of working at a lower efficiency level to that budgeted (10,200 units should take 20,400 hours, not 21,500)

The single volume variance is, therefore, analysed under these two headings. They are usually called the **capacity variance** and the **efficiency variance**, respectively. In both cases the difference in hours is measured at the standard FOAR of £2.00 per hour. In the example we are working, the capacity variance (21,500 hours instead of 20,000) is favourable. Beginners often find this confusing because they tend to relate it to the efficiency variance. The best way of looking at this is to say that if the company was budgeting to work for 20,000 hours, and it actually worked for 21,500 hours, it had additional capacity of 1,500 hours and could have produced more units. The fact that this additional capacity was wasted will be revealed by the efficiency variance.

Activity 13

Calculate the capacity variance and the efficiency variance on your own paper and summarize your calculations here:

1. Fixed overhead capacity variance:

2. Fixed overhead efficiency variance:

Sales variances and the reconciliation statement

You practised calculating sales variance in Activity 6. Here is a reminder of the key points:

- the sales price variance is calculated for the entire quantify sold and is based on the difference between the standard selling price and actual selling price
- the sales quantity variance is measured by using the standard margin

Activity 14

Calculate the sales variances for our current example and make a note of them here:

1. Sales price variance:

2. Sales quantity variance:

You are now in a position to complete the reconciliation statement.

Activity 15

Complete the reconciliation statement set out below.

Reconciliation statement

Budgeted profit (10,000 × £16)			£160,000

Sales variances:
   Sales price
   Sales quantity

	Favourable	Adverse	
Cost variances:			
Material price			
Material usage			
Labour rate			
Labour efficiency			
Variable overhead expenditure			
Variable overhead efficiency			
Fixed overhead expenditure			
Fixed overhead capacity			
Fixed overhead efficiency			

Actual profit			£175,380

7.4 Some criticisms of standard costing

The JIT environment

A number of arguments have been put forward in recent times to show that traditional variance analysis is unhelpful and can be misleading. Most of these arguments are connected to the JIT techniques discussed in Chapter 4. A further argument is that standards are set too late; we tend to establish a standard cost for a product after it has been designed, whereas cost factors should be considered during the design stage.

Two of the arguments that show a contradiction between variance analysis and JIT techniques can be summarized as follows:

- **Material price variance**: this will encourage purchasing managers to buy in greater bulk in order to take advantage of higher discounts. This can result in holding excessive stocks and higher stock holding costs.
- **Labour efficiency variance**: this will encourage greater output resulting in excessive stocks of finished goods, perhaps of the wrong type.

The same kind of argument regarding greater output can be made for any of the efficiency variances.

It could well be that some of these arguments are misdirected. It is not so much standard costing itself that is at fault, but failure to use it alongside some of the more modern methods of stock management. There is no one fallible system. We cannot say that if we are using JIT techniques we must scrap standard costing. In fact it would be easier to establish standard material prices if JIT purchasing is being used. JIT purchasing tends to rely on placing a bulk contract with one supplier against which small quantities are drawn as needed.

Traditional criticisms

In addition to these recent arguments, traditional variance analysis has been criticized over many years because some of the information can be misleading when used for performance evaluation. The more important of these (traditional) criticisms can be identified as follows:

- **planning variances**: some variances might be caused by poor planning information
- **joint variances**: problems can arise from the convention used for measuring price and quantity variances
- **fixed overheads**: these variances can be deceptive because of the way they tend to treat a fixed cost as if it were variable
- **sales mix variances**: a single sales volume variance for each product is misleading when there are a mixture of different products.

Since these conflicts stem from the way that standard costing is used for evaluating the performance of departmental managers, they are dealt with in the next chapter. It is important at this stage of your studies to develop some competence in the traditional variance analysis before studying these additional points. The questions at the end of this chapter are, therefore, all related to the traditional variance analysis as described in the text.

Summary

The key learning points in this chapter can be summarized as follows:
- a standard cost is a predicted cost based on attainable standards for each element of cost
- financial accounting regulations permit closing stocks to be valued on the basis of their standard cost providing the cost variances are not excessive
- in manufacturing, standard costing forms a part of the double-entry recording
- the subject is usually seen as a method of control through variance accounting
- standard costing is usually part of a budgeting process, with standard costs being seen as budgets at the individual product level
- variance analysis is based on a common convention that identifies factors relating to price and quantity
- this convention applies to both costs and sales
- in the case of costs, price variances are manifest in material prices, wage rates and variable overhead rates: quantity variances are manifest in material usage, and the hours worked for both labour and variable overheads
- in the case of sales, price variances relate to sales price and quantity variances to sales quantity

- the basic convention requires price variances to be based on the entire quantity (of resources used or goods sold) and all quantity variances are measured at a standard rate
- the standard rate in the case of sales volume variances is measured at the standard margin
- the total fixed overhead variance is represented by the amount of overhead under- or over-absorbed
- this total results from two causes, expenditure and activity
- the expenditure variance is the difference between the budgeted expenditure for the period and the actual expenditure incurred
- the activity variance must be analysed between capacity (working more hours in the period than budget) and efficiency (producing the goods in more, or less, time than the standard)
- an analysis of the activity variance between capacity and efficiency makes use of a concept known as a standard hour
- a standard hour is a measurement of work, it is not a measurement of time; it is represented by the number of standard hours in the goods produced

Activity 1
The will be no need to price issues on a FIFO, AVCO or LIFO basis.

Activity 2
Overheads, where the rate per unit is based on budgeted expenditure ÷ budgeted activity.

Activity 3
Material usage and material price. The quantity of materials used for the 180 units was different to the standard quantity, and the price per litre was different.

Activity 4

390 litres of material A should have cost (390 × £3)	£1,170	
390 litres of material A actually cost	1,150	
Price variance	20	favourable

Activity 5
1. The quantity variance is (390 – 360) 30 litres adverse.
2. The material usage variance is 30 × £3 = £90 adverse.

Activity 6
1. Sales price variance: 110 × £0.50 = £55 adverse.
2. Sales quantity variance (110 – 100) × £4.00 = £40 favourable.

Activity 7
1. Budgeted profit: 10,000 × £16 = £160,000.
2. Actual profit: Sales (10,200 × £42) = £428,400. Total costs are (£84,180 + £107,190 + £23,650 + £38,000) £253,020. Profit: (£428,400 – £253,020) £175,380.

Activity 8
1. Total variance:

Standard material cost of 10,200 units is	£81,600	
Actual material cost was	84,180	
Total adverse variance	2,580	

2. Material price variance:

The 39,000 kilos used should have cost	£78,000	
The 39,000 kilos actually cost	£84,180	
Adverse price variance	6,180	

3. Material usage variance

10,200 units should consume	40,800	kilos
10,200 units actually consumed	39,000	kilos
Favourable usage variance	1,800	kilos

1,800 kilos at £2.00 per kilo = £3,600 favourable

Activity 9

1. Total labour cost variance: (£107,190 – £102,000) = £5,190 adverse.

2. Labour rate variance:

21,500 hours should have cost	£107,500
21,500 hours actually cost	107,190
Favourable rate variance	£ 310

3. Labour efficiency variance:

10,200 units should take	20,400	hours
10,200 units actually took	21,500	hours
Adverse time variance	1,100	hours

1,100 hours at £5 = £5,500 adverse

Activity 10

1. Total variable overhead cost variance

10,200 units should cost	£20,400
10,200 units actual cost	£23,650
Adverse variance	£3,250

2. Variable overhead expenditure variance

21,500 hours should cost	£21.500
21,500 hours actually cost	£23,650
Adverse expenditure variance	£2,150

3. Variable overhead efficiency variance

10,200 units should take	20,400	hours
10,200 units actually took	21,500	hours
Adverse time variance	1,100	hours

1,100 hours at £1 = £1,100 adverse

Activity 11

Actual expenditure	£38,000
Overheads absorbed (10,200 × £4)	40,800
Total favourable variance	£2,800

Activity 12

Actual expenditure	£38,000
Budgeted expenditure (10,000 × £4)	£40,000
Favourable expenditure variance	£2,000

Activity 13

1. Capacity variance (21,500 – 20,000) × £2.00 = £3,000 favourable
2. Efficiency variance (21,500 – 20,400) × £2.00 = £2,200 adverse

Activity 14

1. Sales price variance 10,200 × £2.00 = £20,400 favourable
2. Sales quantity 200 × £16 = £3,200 favourable

Activity 15

Reconciliation statement

Budgeted profit (10,000 × £16)			£160,000
Sales variances:			
Sales price		Favourable	20,400
Sales quantity		Favourable	3,200
			183,600

	Favourable	Adverse	
Cost variances:			
Material price		6,180	
Material usage	3,600		
Labour rate	310		
Labour efficiency		5,500	
Variable overhead expenditure		2,150	
Variable overhead efficiency		1,100	
Fixed overhead expenditure	2,000		
Fixed overhead capacity	3,000		
Fixed overhead efficiency		2,200	
	8,910	17,130	Adverse (8,220)

Actual profit			£175,380

Questions for self assessment

Answers to self-assessment questions can be found at the end of the book.

7.1 On the basis of a production and sales level of 10,000 units a month, the standard unit cost of a carton of Gimmet which sells for £12 is:

Material 12 kg at 50p	£6.00
Labour 1¹/₂ hours at £1.60	2.40
Fixed overhead	0.60

The profit reconciliation statement for November was as follows:

		£
Budgeted profit		30,000
Add favourable variances:		
Sales volume	1,500	
Material price	1,268	
Labour efficiency	240	
Fixed overhead volume	300	
		3,308 12
Less adverse variances:		
Sales price	1,000	
Material usage	400	
Labour rate	780	
Fixed overhead expenditure	200	
		(2,380)
Actual profit		30,928

There were no opening or closing stocks.

Required:
(a) Prepare a profit statement in conventional accounting form (actual sales and actual costs) showing how the profit of £30,928 was determined.
(b) Explain what is meant by 'interdependence' of variances, illustrating your answer by references to the above statement.

Author's guidance note: A clue to getting started is to work out the quantity sold, which you should be able to do from the sales volume margin variance.

(ACCA Costing)

7.2 The graph shown below depicts labour costs within a standard costing system. All of the variances shown are unfavourable.

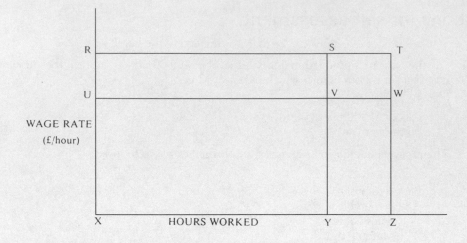

(a) State with reasons which areas represent:
   (i)   the standard costs
   (ii) the actual cost
   (iii) the wage rate variance
   (iv) the labour efficiency variance
   (v)   the total labour cost variance.
(b) Give two reasons why it is as important to examine favourable variances as to examine unfavourable (adverse) variances within a standard costing system.

(ULSEB A Level)

7.3 B Limited started trading on 1 November 1993, manufacturing and selling one product. The standard cost per unit was:

Direct material: standard price £10 per kg
                  standard quantity 20 kg per unit
Direct labour   standard rate of pay £5.50 per hour
                  standard time allowance 12 hours per unit

Production overhead costs, all classified as fixed, were budgeted at £900,000 per annum. The standard time for producing one unit is 12 machine hours and normal capacity is 60,000 machine hours per annum. Production overhead is absorbed on machine hours.

For the year ended 31 October 1994, the costs incurred and other relevant information is given below:

Direct material used – 100,000 kilogrammes at a cost of £1,050,000
Direct wages paid – £310,000 for 62,000 hours
Production overhead – £926,000
Machine capacity used – 60,000 hours
Actual output – 4,800 units
Assume no stocks of work-in-progress or finished goods at year end.

You are required to
(a) show the standard product cost for one unit;
(b) calculate the appropriate variances for material, labour and overhead including the total variances;
(c) present a statement for management reconciling the standard cost with the actual cost of production.

(d) suggest **two** possible reasons for **each** of the sub-variances you have calculated for direct material and direct labour.

(CIMA Cost accounting)

7.4 *Note*: This question has been altered from the original in order to make it more satisfying. The original question did not require an analysis of sales variances or a reconciliation statement.

Dour Ltd manufactures moulded furniture including chairs for general purpose use. These chairs are manufactured from a chemical mixture purchased in a prepared state. Details of the contribution made by these chairs to the overall company results for the year ended 31 October 1993 were:

Contribution statement for chairs for the year ended 31 October 1993

	£	£
Sales		112,500
less variable costs:		
Raw materials	55,000	
Direct labour	26,000	81,000
Contribution		31,500

Additional information:
1) There were no opening or closing stocks of chairs.
2) The budget and standard cost details prepared prior to 1 November 1992 revealed:
   i) budgeted sales of chairs 18,000 at £8.00 each.
   ii) each chair should take 3 kg of chemical mixture at £1.00 per kg.
   iii) each chair should take 20 minutes of direct labour time.
   iv) the direct labour rate was £6.00.
3) In investigating the actual results for the year ended 31 October 1989 the following information came to light:
   i) 15,000 chairs were sold.
   ii) 44,000 kg of raw material was used;
   iii) 4000 hours of direct labour time was clocked.

Required:
(a) Calculate sales variances for the year ended 31 October 1989.
(b) Calculate the overall labour variance for the year ended 31 October 1989 analysing it into:
   i) rate variance;
   ii) efficiency variance.
(c) Calculate the overall material variance for the year ended 31 October 1993 analysing it into:
   i) price variance;
   ii) efficiency variance.
(d) Prepare a statement reconciling budgeted contribution with actual contribution for the year ended 31 October 1989.
(e) Examine the variances calculated in (a), (b) and (c) above and give possible reasons for each.

(AEB A level)

Questions without answers

Answers to these questions are published separately in the *Teacher's Manual*.

7.5 The Direct Cost Company makes a single product and has forecast in financial year 1993/94 that it will sell 400,000 units at a price of £40 each.

Below is an extract from the annual budget:

Material	Total usage	Total £000s
	000s kg	
A	2,000	8,000
	000s metres	
B	1,200	2,400
Labour		
	000s hours	
Assembly	400	1,200

For the first month of the financial year you are informed: Planned production and sales were 40,000 units. In fact, only 36,000 units were produced and sold for £1,496,000. The company holds no stocks.

Total spending on materials used was £886,000 of which material A accounted for £690,000. 180,000 kg of material A were used; material B cost £1.75 per metre.

46,000 hours were worked for total wages of £138,000.

For the purpose of variance reporting to production and sales management the company ignores overhead costs.

Required:
(a) Determine the standard cost and standard gross profit per unit for 1993/94, showing separately the individual elements of cost.
(b) You are provided with the variances for material cost, which are:

Material A	Usage variance	Nil
Material A	Price variance	£30,000 F
Material B	Usage variance	£8,000 A
Material B	Price variance	£28,000 F

Compute the labour and sales variances and incorporate these with the material variances in order to reconcile the forecast profit for the month with the actual.

(c) Interpret the variances and comment on any possible interrelationships between them.

(ACCA Certified Diploma)

7.6 A private bus operator runs a bus service in a rural district. One route, number 66, is served exclusively by a single bus from a thriving village to the nearest main town. The bus operator works closely with the local community and carefully prepares a timetable to cover all peak journeys – for schools, train connections, market days and the normal working day.

It is this close collaboration which has resulted in a fare of 50p for all journeys into the town for the current financial year, 1988, just ended. The fare is a standard rate applied to all passengers over 10 years old (others travel free) and has been applied all the year.

Statistics for the year show that on average 35 passengers were carried on each journey into the town compared with 25 passengers per journey in the budget.

It is possible to collect revenues and costs in relation to the bus which serves route 66 and this has been provided to the owner in the form of a computer print out of budget and actual results for the year 1993 shown below:

Route 66
Revenue and Cost Summary, 1988

| | Budget | | Actual | |
	£	£	£	£
Sales revenue		30,000		35,000
Cost:				
Fuel	10,000		12,000	
Fixed overhead	15,000		18,000	
		25,000		30,000
Profit		5,000		5,000

The costs do not include any general overheads of the company.

The budget for 1998 was prepared on the basis of a fare of 60p per journey.

The operator is to meet with his accountant to examine all his financial results but, in the meantime, has asked you to help in interpreting this information.

Required:
(a) **Determine the budgeted and actual number of passenger/journeys undertaken and so determine the effect of price and volume on total sales revenue. Briefly interpret your results.**
(b) **State the likely composition of fixed overhead.**
Speculate as to the possible causes of changes in fuel and fixed overhead costs. State what the operator can do to 'manage' costs.

(ACCA Certified Diploma)

7.7 (a) **Explain fully how the variances between actual and standard production overhead costs may be analysed, where overhead absorption is based upon separate direct labour hour rates for variable and fixed overheads.**
(b) **Calculate fixed production overhead variances in as much detail as possible, in the following situation:**

	Budget	Actual
Fixed overhead (£)	246,000	259,000
Direct labour (hours)	123,000	141,000
Output (units)	615,000	(see below)

The company operates a process costing system. At the beginning of the period 42,000 half completed units were in stock. During the period 680,000 units were completed and 50,000 half completed units remained in stock at the end of the period.

(ACCA Costing)

7.8 (a) Discuss in general the ways in which variance analysis helps management to control a business.
(NOTE – there is no need to refer to specific variances.)
(b) NC Limited uses flexible budgets and standard costing for its single product P which it makes and sells.

Three kilogrammes of material, having a standard cost of £4.40 per kilogrammes, are required for each unit of P. Actual material purchased and used in April cost £336,000 with the actual purchase price being £4.20 per kilogramme. Each unit of P requires 30 minutes of direct labour time and the standard wages rate per hour is £5. The actual wages rate in April was £5.40 per hour. Sufficient direct labour time was utilized to produce 28,000 units of P although actual production in April was 25,000 units.

The company has a normal operating capacity of 15,000 hours per month and flexible overhead budgets are:

Hours of operation	12,500	14,000	15,000
	£	£	£
Variable production overhead	150,000	168,000	180,000
Fixed production overhead	270,000	270,000	270,000
	420,000	438,000	450,000

Actual overhead incurred in April was £430,000, of which £270,000 was fixed.

You are required to
(i)   calculate the appropriate variances for material, labour and overhead.
(ii) show the variances in a statement suitable for presentation to management, reconciling the standard cost with the actual cost of production.

(CIMA Costing)

Appendix 1

This appendix is intended for students whose syllabus requires them to develop competence in the double entry recording aspect of a standard costing system. The principles are explained by means of examples.

Example 1

A newly formed company has set up its cost accounting system on a standard costing basis. Its first transaction was to buy 100 units of raw material on credit. The standard price for this material had been predetermined as £2.00 per unit but when the invoice arrived from the supplier, the price charged was £2.10 per unit.

Price variances can either be separated when the goods are purchased or when they are issued to production. The normal practice is to separate the price variance on purchase. This enables all entries in the stores account to be recorded at standard price. If this basis is adopted for the above transaction, it will be recorded as follows:

Double entry

Debit raw materials control account	£200	
Debit price variance account	£10	
Credit trade creditors control account		£210

When these materials are issued to production they will be charged to work in progress control account at the price of £2.00 per unit. Various procedures are used to keep a track of usage by the production department. A fairly typical approach is to issue sufficient materials to enable the batch of products to be completed according to the standard specification. If these quantities turn out to be insufficient, the production department will have to originate an excess materials requisition. This is often printed in a different colour to the standard requisition so that it can easily be recognised by the cost accounting department. If there were some materials left over from the original quantity issued, they will be returned to store and recorded on a materials return note.

These excess materials requisitions, and materials return notes, are used as source documents for recording the quantity variances.

Example 2

The next transaction for the company in Example 1 was to issue 50 units of the raw material to production. These 50 units were the standard quantity required by production for a batch of finished goods ordered by the finished goods department. On completion of the batch, the production department had used all but 4 units of the raw material. These four units were recorded on a materials return note and then sent back to the stores department.

The double entry for these transactions will be as follows:

Double entry

On issue

Debit work in progress control account		
$(50 \times £2.00)$	£100	
Credit stores control account		£100

On return

Debit stores control account $(4 \times £2)$	£8	
Credit material usage variance account		£8

Notice that entries in the usage variance account are recorded at the standard price (in keeping with the basic convention on usage variances). Notice also that debit balances on variance accounts represent adverse variances and credit balances represent favourable variances.

If the production department had required materials in excess of standard, the double entry would have been to debit raw material usage account and credit stores control account. The amount would have been recorded at standard price.

From the foregoing explanation it should be possible for you to see how the other elements of cost will be recorded.

In this example, the price variance account of £10.00 relates to the entire quantity purchased. This enabled the raw materials control account to be kept at standard price. The raw materials control account does show a balance of (54 × £2.00) £108, whereas the actual cost of these materials was (54 × £2.10) £113.40. Although the amounts in this example are trivial, it can be used to show what happens if the auditors insist on raw material stocks being shown in the annual financial statements at their actual cost. The procedure involves splitting the adverse price variance account at the end of the period; part of it is carried forward as stock, and part written off to cost of sales. If this approach is taken, the price variance account will be split as follows:

Carried forward as a part of raw material stock (54 × £0.10)	£5.40
Written off as cost of sales (46 × £0.10)	4.60
	£10.00

The raw material stock will then be shown in the annual financial statements at the actual cost of (£108.00 + £5.40) £113.40.

8 ▷ Assessing performance

Objectives

After you have completed this chapter, you should be able to:

- evaluate situations where traditional variance analysis might be misleading and provide additional analysis to help resolve the conflicts
- assess the performance of a business entity by using financial accounting information
- discuss the objectives and problems of monitoring divisional performance in a decentralized organization
- explain what is meant by cost centres, profit centres and investment centres
- illustrate the likely motivational effect of the various methods used for monitoring divisional performance
- explain why internal transfers (of goods or services) between departments and divisions should be priced and charged to the receiving department
- discuss some of the difficulties in establishing a transfer price in decentralized organizations where the objective is to ensure that decisions taken at a local level will coincide with the aims of central management
- identify alternative measures of performance using non-financial information available to management

Introduction

A study published in 1954 (by H. A. Simon and others) identified three uses of accounting information that managers considered important. These uses were labelled as:

- scorekeeping
- attention directing
- problem solving

These three functions can be seen as providing answers to managers' questions such as:

- how well am I doing? (scorekeeping)
- what problems do I need to investigate? (attention directing)
- out of the various ways of doing something, which option provides us with the best economic advantage? (problem solving)

This chapter is concerned mainly with the scorekeeping function. It also deals with the way that performance reports can influence the behaviour of those being assessed. Although accounting information is not the only source of information available for assessing the performance of departmental managers, it does have a strong tradition of being used for this purpose. Recent developments in the use of non-financial indicators are outlined in section 8.7, although these are usually part of a subject known as 'total quality management'.

8.1 Problems with traditional variance analysis

In the previous chapter we discussed standard costing in the context of a tool for planning and cost control. The comparison of actual performance with standards is, however, often seen as a procedure for assessing the performance of individual departments. In view of this we need to consider some of the defects in traditional variance analysis and how these might mislead those whose actions are motivated by the variance reports.

Planning variances

Standards are based on conditions that are expected to prevail during the budget period. If these conditions turn out to be significantly different to those expected, traditional variance analysis does not recognize that managers were operating in an environment that was different from the one expected when the plans were made. The argument in this situation is that actual performance should be compared to standards that reflect the changed conditions. This can be achieved by applying planning variances to the original budgeted profit and then measuring the sales and cost variances based on the revised standards. You can see how this is usually done by working through a simple example.

Details for the example

The idea for this example was provided by a question set in the management accounting examination for the Certified Diploma in Accounting and Finance.

Arthur has decided to undertake a business venture that involves buying a recently developed edible product (code name 'choeuf') and selling them in cartons of six. His budget for March was as follows:

Sales	1,000 cartons (of 6 choeufs each) at £1	1,000
Costs	6,000 choeufs at 10p	600
Budgeted profit		400

Note: In order to keep the example simple, we will assume that Arthur has already obtained the cartons free of charge and that they cannot be used for any other purpose.

Arthur is pleased to find that sales go well in March and he was able to charge more than £1 per carton due to heavy demand. Unfortunately, the supplier of choeufs had sensed this and increased the price of bulk supplies. Arthur's actual results for March were as follows:

Sales	1,200 cartons (of 6 choeufs each) at £1.30	1,560
Costs	7,200 choeufs at 12p	864
Actual profit		696

Activity 1

Although Arthur is pleased with his results he asks you to analyse the difference between budgeted profit and actual profit. You decided to do this by traditional variance analysis. Set out your figures in the outline computation shown below.

Budgeted profit	£400
Sales margin price variance	
Sales margin quantity variance	
Material price variance	
Actual profit	£696

If you were asked to comment on this report, it might not be wise to do so straight away if you suspected that the original budget was inappropriate in the market conditions that actually prevailed during the period. Imagine that you get in touch with another person in the same line of business and obtain the following information:

1. Sales of this product were up countrywide. A 50% increase in budgeted quantities should have been expected because market size had risen by that amount.
2. An average price for this product during March was £1.35 even after taking account of the increased demand.
3. The cost of bulk supplies of 'choeufs' (unpacked) tended to be about 11p each.

We will now consider how this new information might affect the way we calculate variances for reconciling budgeted profit with actual. The gist of our approach is to use the benefit of hindsight for revising standards to a best estimate of what could have been achieved under the market conditions that actually existed. Differences between the original standards and these best estimates are called planning variances. The performance variances are then measured by using the revised standards. Planning variances are inserted in the reconciliation statement between budgeted profit and the performance variances as follows:

Budgeted profit	X
Planning variances	X
Revised budgeted profit	X
Performance variances	
(sales and costs based on revised standards)	X
Actual profit	X

In this example we will assume that planning variances are based on the following adjustments to the original budget:

1. Budgeted sales price should have been £1.35 (planning variance = 35p per unit).
2. Budgeted quantity should have been (1.5 × 1,000) 1,500 (planning variance = 500 units).
3. Budgeted material price should have been 11p per unit (planning variance = 1p per unit).

The planning variance for sales prices is based on quantities sold. The planning variance for sales quantity is measured at the original budgeted margin (as is the performance variance for sales quantities). The planning variance for material prices is based on the quantity purchased. The new reconciliation statement, with the top part completed for the planning variances, will be as follows:

Budgeted profit			£400
Planning variances:			
Sales price (1,200 × 35p)	420	Favourable	
Sales quantity (500 × 40p)	200	Favourable	
Material price (7,200 × 1p)	(72)	Adverse	
			548
Revised budgeted profit			948
Performance variances:			
Sales price			
Sales quantity			
Material price			
Actual profit			£696

> **Activity 2**

Calculate the performance variances and insert them into the above reconciliation statement. These are calculated by comparing actual performance with the adjusted standards.

Some students have problems in identifying whether planning variances are favourable or adverse. If you keep in mind that the objective is to arrive at a budgeted profit that the company could have achieved (taking account of market potential) you should be able to see whether the variance needs to be added or deducted from the original profit.

The arguments in favour of identifying planning variances can be stated as:

- it enables managers to focus on both planning and performance factors
- the information provided for assessing performance is more meaningful because it represents controllable factors

In our example, the revised analysis might prompt Arthur to examine the procedures used for gathering market information. This might lead to improved forecasting. The performance variances should prompt Arthur into asking himself why he failed to sell at a price that other firms were able to achieve and why he failed to capture his share of the increased market.

The arguments against this approach can be stated as:

- the use of general market values is subjective and approximate
- managers are being asked to perform against targets that might be changed

Joint price and usage variances

You will recall from the previous chapter how variance analysis uses a basic convention. For example, in the case of raw materials the convention measures price variances on the entire quantity purchased and measures usage variances at the standard price. This could create a conflict between the two managers responsible for explaining these variances, although the amounts involved are often quite small. It is easier to see how the argument would run if both price and usage variances are adverse. Consider the following example.

Example

Production requires 20,000 kilos of Material A with a standard price of £3.00 per kilo. The production department used 22,000 kilos of Material A which cost £3.20 per kilo.

Activity 3

The total cost variance is £10,400 adverse. Analyse this as a price variance and usage variance by using the basic convention.

1. Material price variance:

2. Material usage variance:

Now consider these variances from the viewpoint of the two managers involved. The purchasing manager could argue that he (or she) should only be held responsible for the price variance on the standard quantity of 20,000 kilos. If the production department had not wasted so much material, it would not have been necessary to buy an extra 2,000 kilos. In any event the extra 2,000 kilos did cost £3.20 (not £3.00). The production manager might counter this argument by accepting responsibility for using the extra 2,000 kilos but then claim that he (or she) had no control over the price paid and should not be held accountable for price variances.

This type of conflict could be resolved by isolating the price variance for the additional usage and describing it as a joint price/usage variance. The analysis will then be as follows:

Usage variance (2,000 kilos at £3.00)	£6,000
Price variance (20,000 kilos at £0.20)	4,000
Joint price/usage variance (2,000 × £0.20)	400
Total cost variance	10,400

This resolves the conflict, but the argument should not have arisen in the first place. Although performance variances are often seen in a blame or praise context, their primary aim is to provide central management with a means of control when actual performance differs from the plan. (This is sometimes described as management by exception because no action is needed from central managers where actual performance is similar to the plan.) Central managers can usually do something to remedy usage variances but price variances are largely influenced by external factors. The purchasing manager is unlikely to be rebuked for a price variance, although he (or she) will be responsible for explaining it. For this reason, fewer internal conflicts are likely to arise if the joint price/usage variance is included in the price variance (as it is in the conventional approach).

Fixed overheads

Assessing performance from the fixed overhead variances produced by traditional variance analysis can be misleading. The standard fixed overhead per unit is found by dividing a standard fixed cost for the period by a standard number of units to be produced in that period. We then proceed to treat the fixed cost as if it were variable with production because each time a unit is made we assert that its total cost includes an amount for fixed overheads. The total amount of fixed overheads imputed to finished goods will, therefore, depend on the number of units made.

There will be a volume variance if actual production levels are different from the levels that were used when the standard amount per unit was set. Yet if production overheads are fixed, these overheads will not vary with the level of production achieved. So how are managers meant to interpret the accounting values that are assigned to the volume variances of capacity and efficiency? In any event, what activity was responsible for these volume variances: was it sales activity or production activity?

A more meaningful approach might be to report volume variances in non-monetary terms such as physical units or as productivity ratios (see below). The variance report would then direct managers' attention to the accounting values placed on the expenditure variance (the difference between budgeted fixed overheads and actual fixed overheads). But even the expenditure variance cannot be used for evaluating performance if it is presented as a single figure. It needs to be analysed under appropriate headings of responsibility and some attempt made to distinguish between controllable and uncontrollable costs.

Productivity ratios as an alternative to volume variances

Fixed overhead volume variances produced by traditional variance analysis are given in *absolute* monetary terms. The productivity ratios mentioned above are simply a way of replacing these absolute measures with a *relative* measure. In the standard costing activities for Chapter 7 you calculated fixed overhead volume variances and included them in the variance report as a monetary value. We will now consider how the same information can be presented in the form of ratios.

These ratios use the concept of a standard hour as described in Chapter 7. Remember that a standard hour is a measurement of work, not a measurement of time. If a unit should take 1 hour to make (at the standard time) and 75 units were produced, we would say that the standard hours produced was 75. If it actually took 100 hours to produce this work we would say that the efficiency ratio was (75/100) 75%. A similar idea can be used to measure a capacity usage ratio.

In the standard costing exercise, the fixed overhead variances were initially identified under two main headings: expenditure variance and volume (or activity) variance. We can ignore the expenditure variance in this section because productivity ratios are an alternative way of expressing the volume variance. The volume variance arose because the standard hours of work produced was different to the budgeted hours on which the standard overhead absorption rate was based. This total variance was subdivided under two headings.

- **efficiency variance**, which arose because the time taken to produce the goods differed from the standard hours allowed to produce those goods
- **capacity variance**, which arose because the total number of hours worked in the period differed from the number of hours budgeted to be worked

The same idea is used in calculating productivity ratios. The three ratios used are expressed as percentages and are based on the following fractions:

$$\text{Activity ratio:} \quad \frac{\text{Standard hours produced}}{\text{Budgeted hours for the period}}$$

$$\text{Efficiency ratio:} \quad \frac{\text{Standard hours produced}}{\text{Actual hours worked}}$$

$$\text{Capacity usage ratio:} \quad \frac{\text{Actual hours worked in period}}{\text{Budgeted labour hours for that period}}$$

In the same way as the volume variance was the total of the efficiency and capacity variance, the activity ratio is the product of the efficiency and capacity usage ratios. This is easier to see when you set the three fractions out alongside each other, as follows:

Activity		Efficiency		Capacity
$\dfrac{\text{Standard hours produced}}{\text{Budgeted hours for period}}$	$=$	$\dfrac{\text{Standard, hours produced}}{\text{Actual hours worked}}$	$\times$	$\dfrac{\text{Actual hours worked}}{\text{Budgeted hours for period}}$

Notice how 'actual hours worked' can be cancelled to give the product for the activity ratio.

We can use the details from the standard costing exercise to practise calculating these ratios. The details are repeated here as follows:

Budgeted hours for the period (10,000 × 2)	20,000
Standard hours produced (10,200 × 2)	20,400
Actual hours worked	21,500

Activity 4

Calculate the three productivity ratios, and ensure that the product of the efficiency and capacity ratios is equal to the activity ratio.

Activity ratio   Efficiency ratio   Capacity usage ratio

Productivity ratios can be used for assessing performance even if standard costing is not being used. You will discover this by working through some of the questions at the end of this chapter.

Problems with sales variances

Although we have been including the sales margin variances (for both quantity and price) in our variance reports, these variances do not necessarily provide useful information for assessing performance. Sales price and sales quantity are usually interrelated; reduce the price and quantity is likely to increase, raise the price and quantity is likely to decrease. The analysis of the total sales margin variance between price and quantity enables managers to see the effect on budgeted profit of price adjustments. A price reduction will have an adverse effect on budgeted profit but if this was more than compensated by a favourable quantity variance, the price reduction will be seen as beneficial.

But the problem with sales performance is that it is largely influenced by external factors. For this reason, central management might find it more appropriate to assess performance of the sales department by using a non-accounting measure such as market share. This type of performance indicator is discussed in section 8.7.

Sales mix variances

The standard costing examples and exercises used up to now have been somewhat unrealistic in the sense that they were based on a single product company. There is nothing wrong with this for learning purposes because if we used anything other than a single product company the principles would become obscured by a mass of detail. In a multi-product concern, the sales margin variances will be based on a combined total for each type of product. Consider the following example.

Example

The standard cost and budget information for a two-product company in respect of the next period is as follows:

	Product A	Product B
Standard selling price	£10	£20
Standard cost	6	12
Standard margin	4	8
Budgeted sales quantities	1,000	2,000

The actual sales results were as follows:

Quantity sold	1,400	2,200
Selling price	£9	£22

If we assume (for the exercise) that actual costs were the same as standard costs, the budgeted profit, and actual profit earned would be as follows:

Budgeted profit:
Budgeted margin (1,000 × £4) + (2,000 × £8)   £20,000

Actual profit:
Actual margin (1,400 × £3) + (2,200 × £10)   £26,200

Total sales margin variance (favourable)   £6,200

Activity 5

Work out the sales price and sales quantity variance for each product using the traditional basis. Combine these variances so as to produce a single total for the variance report. Make sure that your total agrees with the above total variance, and summarize the results of your calculations below:

	Product A	Product B	Total
Sales margin price variance			
Sales margin quantity variance			

The total quantity variance is £3,200 favourable and this arises because the quantity actually sold (3,600 units) exceeded the budgeted quantity of 3,000 units. But this single volume measure hides the impact on budgeted profit of actual sales mix (14 of A to 22 of B) not being in the same ratio as the budgeted sales mix (1 of A to 2 of B). This would not matter if all products had the same profit margin; if this is not so it might be quite useful for managers to see the impact on budgeted profit of selling in different proportions to the budget.

The sales mix variance is a subdivision of the sales quantity variance. It is calculated by comparing the margin earned on actual sales with the margin that would have been earned if actual sales quantities had been in the same mix as budget. The calculations can proceed as follows:

	Product A	Product B	
If actual sales quantities (3,600) had been in the same proportion as budgeted mix (1:2)	1,200	2,400	
The actual sales quantities were	1,400	2,200	
Variance in units	200 Fav	(200) Adv	
Standard margin per unit	£4	£8	
Variance in units at standard margin	£800	(£1,600)	(£800)

The sales mix variance is £800 adverse. This has arisen because the company sold less of the high margin product (Product B) than it would have done if sales quantities had been in the same proportions as the budgeted mix. This means that the sales volume variance would have been £4,000 favourable (instead of £3,200 favourable) if actual sales had been in the budgeted mix.

This £4,000 can be calculated separately but it is difficult to give it a meaningful label (other than to say it is the sales margin quantity variance that would have arisen if sales mix had been the same as budget). For this reason, the usual practice is to report the sales quantity variance in the normal way (£3,200 favourable in this example) and to report the sales mix variance in a subsidiary schedule.

8.2 Accounting ratios as measures of performance

Prior learning

Some of the performance indicators used in management accounting are based on techniques that were really developed in financial accounting. They are normally used by external investors who wish to assess the performance of the company in which they have invested. In financial accounting the subject is usually called 'ratio analysis'. You might have studied this previously, in which case you will be familiar with a lot of the material in this section.

You will not be learning (or re-learning) all the ratios used in financial accounting because we need only consider those which might be useful in the context of management accounting. The accounting ratios that we need to consider fall under two broad headings:

1. **Performance ratios:** external analysts use these ratios to measure the performance of the whole company: managers might use these ratios for assessing the performance of individual divisions within the company.
2. **Working capital activity ratios:** these ratios can be used by managers for control over working capital items such as stocks, debtors and creditors. They are also used in the context of budgeting, particularly for cash budgeting and for calculating the funds required to support the investment in working capital.

   Although you will be learning about the working capital activity ratios in this chapter, their application to management accounting is dealt with in Chapters 9 and 10.

8.3 Business performance ratios

The primary ratio

The amount of profit earned by a company is often thought of as a measure of performance. But if we isolate the amount of profit from the resources that created it we have no way of judging how successful management have been in using those resources. To take a simple example, if profit for the current year is £20,000 and it was £10,000 in the previous year, we could say that profits are up by 100% and might conclude that all was well. But if the amount of capital invested in the business during the current year was more than twice the amount invested in the previous year then we would conclude that the company had been less profitable in the current year.

Profit is an absolute figure: in order to assess performance we need to relate profit to the factors that created it. The primary ratio does this by relating profit to net assets invested in the business. Profit is then expressed as a percentage of those net assets. The primary ratio is sometimes called the 'return on capital employed' and this is usually abbreviated to ROCE.

In financial accounting, this ratio suffers from a problem of definition and various formulae are used in practice. There are different interpretations of what is meant by profit and what is meant by capital. We will not be considering these problems here (you can read about them in a financial accounting text book) and will use the most common basis, which is as follows:

$$\frac{\text{Operating profit (i.e. profit before tax and interest)}}{\text{Total assets less current liabilities}}$$

The fraction is then expressed as a percentage.

The calculation of ratios in this section will be based on the set of financial statements set out in the Appendix. It is assumed that you are reasonably familiar with the form of published financial statements at this stage of your studies. If not, you should not experience too many problems because the relevant figures are clearly labelled in the accounts.

If you turn to the Appendix now you will note that the denominator in the above fraction is labelled in the net asset side of the balance sheet. It is sometimes called total capital employed but if you wish to find the figure from the financing side of the balance sheet it will be necessary to add the long-term loan to the total of share capital and reserves. In other words total capital employed includes long-term loans. The numerator is the amount described as 'operating profit' in a company's profit and loss account.

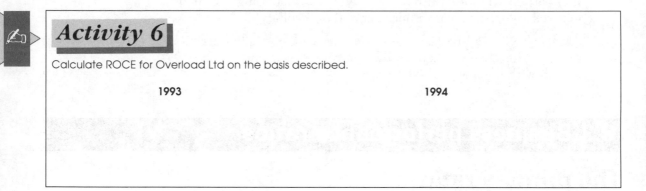

Activity 6

Calculate ROCE for Overload Ltd on the basis described.

1993   **1994**

The only comment we could make at this point is that the return is down by 5.5%.

The secondary ratios

The purpose of the secondary ratios is to isolate causes of the variation in ROCE. In the case of Overload Ltd, we know that ROCE has fallen during 1994 and we must now look for possible explanations. These secondary ratios attempt to find out if the change in ROCE has been caused by earning less sales with the assets, or earning less profit on the sales. Notice how 'sales' is used as a constant in these secondary ratios and so before we look the formulae, deal with Activity 7.

Activity 7

When we write down the primary ratio and the two secondary ratios alongside each other, we find something interesting. What do you notice about the following?

Primary ratio   **Secondary ratios**

$$\frac{\text{Profit}}{\text{Net assets}} \qquad \frac{\text{Profit}}{\text{Sales}} \qquad \frac{\text{Sales}}{\text{Net assets}}$$

Comment:

The net profit to sales ratio is usually called the profitability ratio; the sales to net assets ratio is called the asset turnover ratio. The profitability ratio is expressed as a percentage, the asset turnover as so many 'times' (how many times the net assets divide into the sales). You will see how to make use of this information in a moment.

Activity 8

Calculate the two secondary ratios for Overload Ltd. Make sure that you use the same figures for profit and net assets as used in Activity 6. Summarize the results of your calculations here.

Primary ratio		**Secondary ratios**			
		Profitability		Asset turnover	
1993	1994	1993	1994	1993	1994
29.5%	24%				

Activity 9

After checking Activity 8 with the Key, check that the product of the two secondary ratios does agree with the primary ratio. Set out your calculations here.

1993   **1994**

The relevance of the asset turnover ratio is difficult to see when expressed as so many times. A more informative interpretation of this ratio is to say that in 1993 each £1 of net assets produced £3.57 in sales, whereas in 1994 each £1 of net assets produced £4 in sales. This kind of interpretation gives an indication of how efficiently the assets have been utilized. The asset turnover ratio is sometimes called the asset utilization ratio.

If you use this approach, the correlation between the primary and secondary ratios can be explained in a way that is easy to understand. If we take the figures of Overload Ltd for 1994 as an example, the explanation could take the following form:

> Each £1 of net assets produced £4 in sales; the profit earned on these sales is 24p (i.e. 6% × £4). This 24p represents 24% of the £1 of net assets used to generate the sales.

Having dissected the primary ratio into two secondary ratios we can continue the analysis by breaking down each secondary ratio into its constituent parts. The profitability ratio can be analysed further by expressing each key figure in the profit and loss account (gross profit and operating expenses) as a percentage of sales; the asset to turnover ratio can be calculated for individual classes of asset. We will not be carrying out such a detailed analysis in this text book since we are mainly concerned with forming a bridge between the performance indicators used in financial accounting with those used in management accounting. If you have not studied this subject previously, and wish to pursue it further, you will find adequate explanations in most financial accounting text books. This particular example (Overload Ltd) is used in Chapter 13 of *Foundations of Business Accounting*, Roy Dodge, Chapman & Hall, London, 1993.

In management accounting, the ROCE is sometimes used for assessing the performance of separate business units within the company. These business units usually operate as semi-autonomous divisions, and the use of ROCE for measuring their performance can cause a number of problems. These matters are dealt with in section 8.5.

8.4 Working capital activity analysis

The ratios used by external analysts to see how well the company has controlled stocks and debtors are also useful to managers. Apart from being used for control purposes they also play a part in the planning process (as discussed in Chapters 9 and 10).

Debtors collection period

By relating debtors in the balance sheet with sales reported in the profit and loss account, it is possible to calculate how long (on average) debtors are taking to pay their debts. For example, if credit sales for the year were £365,000 and debtors in the balance sheet were £30,000 we could conclude that, on average, debtors are taking 30 days to pay. The 30 days in this example can be seen almost by intuition. If sales are £365,000 for 365 days it means that sales averaged £1,000 per day and, since debtors are

£30,000, they represent sales for 30 days. In mathematical form the computation was as follows:

$$\frac{\text{Debtors}}{\text{Sales} \div 365}$$

This resolves into a formula that is easier to handle, as follows:

$$\frac{\text{Debtors}}{\text{Sales}} \times \frac{365}{1}$$

The same kind of approach is taken for the other two components of working capital, stocks and creditors.

Stock turnover period

This ratio links closing stocks to cost of sales for the year. It gives an indication of the length of time that stocks will remain on hand before they are sold. Although the formula gives a measure in days (weeks or months) the result of the calculation should not be interpreted too literally. The amount invested in stock can be quite substantial and management of this requires something more sophisticated than merely keeping a watchful eye on trends in the stock holding period.

As a formula, the stock turnover ratio can be set out as follows:

$$\frac{\text{Closing stock}}{\text{Cost of sales}} \times \frac{365}{1}$$

Creditors payment period

This ratio is similar to the collection period for debtors. Creditors in the balance sheet are related to credit purchases for the year. An amount for 'purchases' is not usually given in a published profit and loss account, although it can be derived from cost of sales. The amount shown as cost of sales is based on: opening stock, plus purchases, less closing stock. The opening and closing stocks can be found from successive balance sheets and these should enable you to work out a figure for purchases. The formula for the ratio is as follows:

$$\frac{\text{Trade creditors}}{\text{Purchases}} \times \frac{365}{1}$$

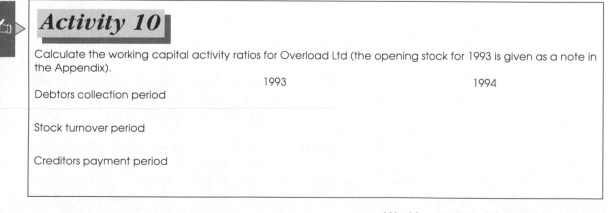

Activity 10

Calculate the working capital activity ratios for Overload Ltd (the opening stock for 1993 is given as a note in the Appendix).

	1993	1994
Debtors collection period		
Stock turnover period		
Creditors payment period		

The net operating cycle

The three operating cycles identified in Activity 10 can be put together in order to find what is known as the net operating cycle (sometimes called the net cash cycle). For Overload Ltd, the net operating cycle would be calculated as follows:

	1993 Days	1994 Days
Stock	30	45
Debtors	34	42
	64	87
Less creditors	26	42
Net operating cycle	38	45

The significance of the net operating cycle is that it enables the firm to forecast the amount of funding needed to finance the trading cycle. This cycle relates to the time period between arrival of stock and when cash for the sale of that stock is received. The firm needs sufficient cash to enable it to meet all payments during this cycle.

Using the 1994 figures of Overload as an example, the stock comes in and remains on the shelf for 45 days, then it is sold, but the firm has to wait another 42 days before any money is received from the customers. In the meantime it will have to pay for the stock (three days before it is sold) and pay all operating expenses for the 87 days. Firms aim to keep this cycle as short as possible in order to reduce the amount of money invested in working capital. You will see how the net operating cycle is used for working capital management in Chapter 10.

8.5 Divisional performance appraisal

This subject is usually associated with the problems of decentralization in complex (often diversified) organizations. In the context of performance appraisal, decentralization refers to situations where a high degree of managerial decision making is delegated to divisional managers. This leaves central management with the task of monitoring and controlling the entire group of divisional units.

The information system in a decentralized organization aims to achieve a number of things but the following three objectives indicate the key points:

1. **To provide feedback for central management:** this will enable central management to assess the performance of divisional managers and consider the economic worth of the division as an operating unit.
2. **To encourage initiative and provide motivation:** the appraisal system must be such that local managers are allowed to operate with a reasonable degree of autonomy, and with the assurance that their performance is being measured in a way that is perceived to be fair.

3. **To promote goal congruence:** in an ideal world, the goals of local management will coincide with the overall goals of the company (known as perfect goal congruence). This is not always the case and so the appraisal system must help local management to direct operations in a way that fulfils the company's objectives.

In some (usually small) organizations, the financial responsibility of departmental managers is limited to the costs of their departments. In the context of responsibility accounting we usually refer to these departments as **cost centres**.

Control by central management in the case of a cost centre is usually achieved through the budgeting process. Budgets are set and actual performance is compared to the budgeted figures. Departmental managers are responsible for explaining variances from budget. In the case of production costs for a manufacturing concern, budgeting is usually linked to standard costing, as discussed in Chapter 7. Cost centres do not provide a means of motivating the performance of departmental managers, other than through the process of requiring them to operate within the budgeted figures.

In divisional organizations, financial responsibility (and hence performance appraisal) extends beyond costs. Two types of financial responsibility centres (other than standard cost centres) that are frequently found in practice are **profit centres** and **investment centres**.

Profit centres relate to divisions where managers are responsible for a combination of costs and revenues. Investment centres are divisions where managers are responsible for the best combination of costs and revenues in relation to the capital employed in their division. In practice, the term 'profit centre' is often used to refer to both profit centres and investment centres. Both types of responsibility centre involve a measurement of divisional profit and so some of the problems are common to both.

You will already be aware that accounting profit is a highly subjective measure. The amount reported as accounting profit depends on various judgements, particularly in relation to the costs allocated to each accounting period. If divisional profit is to be used for performance appraisal, a further difficulty arises with costs over which the divisional manager has no control. This has led to a concept of 'controllable profit', which is often used a starting point for performance appraisal in both profit centres and investment centres.

Activity 11

See if you can identify some costs over which a divisional manager would have no control and which should, therefore, be left out of account when calculating controllable profit.

Roughly speaking, controllable profit for each division results from the following:

Divisional revenue		X
Less divisional variable costs		X
Divisional contribution		X
Less: fixed overheads controllable by the division	X	
depreciation on assets controllable by the division	X	
		X
Controllable profit		X

In the case of an investment centre, there are usually other deductions from controllable profit when profit is related to the capital invested. You will recall that because profit is an absolute figure it is often more appropriate to consider profit in relation to the assets that have generated that profit. But if divisionalized companies simply use the return on capital employed (ROCE) as an indicator of divisional performance it might lead to local managers making decisions that are not in the best interest of the company as a whole.

There are several problems associated with using ROCE as an indicator of divisional performance. We will look at two of them here.

Details for the activity

Division A's fixed assets were purchased ten years ago and are being written off over 15 years. Division B's fixed assets were purchased during the current year and are also being written off over 15 years. The rate of inflation on the type of fixed asset used has averaged 10% over the last 10 years. The following is a summary of each division's financial reports:

Balance sheets

	Division A	Division B
Fixed assets at cost	30,000	75,000
Aggregate depreciation	20,000	5,000
Net book value	10,000	70,000
Net current assets	5,000	5,000
	15,000	75,000

	Division A	Division B
Profit and loss accounts		
Profit before depreciation	8,000	8,000
Depreciation	2,000	5,000
Net profit	6,000	3,000
Return on capital employed	40%	4%

Notice how the profit before depreciation is the same in both divisions. If we were considering this in financial accounting we might be trying to makes sense of a comparison between two companies. The problem is somewhat different when measuring divisional performance because we need to think about the motivational aspects of the performance indicators used. If we use the wrong indicator, we might motivate a divisional manager to make decisions that are simply aimed at maximizing that indicator.

The above example is highly contrived in order to demonstrate a point. In reality, it is likely that the new fixed assets in Division B will be more efficient than those in Division A and should produce higher profits. But it would require a considerable increase in profitability in order to bring the ROCE of each division into line with each other. You can see this by doing Activity 12.

Activity 12

Imagine that you are the divisional manager of A and that you are considering whether or not to renew the fixed assets of your division. You realize that at the end of the first year with the new assets, the balance sheet of your division will be the same as that in Division B, but the profits before depreciation will be £20,000 instead of £8,000. Your performance is being monitored on the basis of ROCE. Consider whether you would decide to go ahead with the renewal and make a note of your calculations and observations here.

Note that if you had decided to go ahead with the replacement, there would have been an increase in the company's overall profits by £12,000. This opportunity has been lost simply because of the way in which the performance of your division was appraised.

Details for the activity

A large, divisionalized, company has an overall target rate of return of 25% on capital invested. The details of Division A are as follows:

Capital employed	£1,000,000
Current earnings per annum	£400,000

Division A's manager identifies a new project requiring an investment of £250,000, which will yield an annual average profit of £75,000. The divisional manager's performance is measured on the basis of ROCE.

Activity 13

Consider whether the manager of Division A is likely to decide in favour of undertaking this project. Set out your figures below, and state any problems of goal congruence revealed by your analysis.

In order to solve this type of problem, assessment of divisional performance is often based on a measure known as **residual income**. Residual income is usually calculated by taking controllable profit and deducting an amount of interest imputed to the division at a rate specified by central management. This rate is usually based on cost of capital (or the company's agreed target rate of return). Cost of capital is dealt with in Chapter 12; for the time being you can think of the cost of capital as the rate of return paid to those who have invested in the business.

Residual income is an absolute amount, not a relative amount. The underlying idea is that divisional managers will decide in favour of any project that produces income in excess of the rate of imputed interest because the excess will go to swell the residual income of their division.

Activity 14

Assume that the manager in Activity 13 is to be rewarded on the basis of residual income. Calculate the residual income in two ways, (1) without the new project, and (2) including the new project. Comment on your figures.

Activity 15

Can you think of some problems associated with using residual income as a measure of performance appraisal?

8.6 Transfer prices

Traditionally, the subject of transfer prices has been associated with the problem of measuring performance in divisionalized organizations. These are often vertically integrated groups of companies, such as where a manufacturing division transfers goods to a trading division. But its application to performance appraisal is much wider, and transfer prices become necessary in most organizations where there is an internal transfer of goods or services between departments. Examples of these transfers include the provision of computer services to the user departments, the provision of photocopying services by a central reprographic department, and provision of vehicle maintenance services. You will probably find many other examples in your own organization.

The provision of these services could be made 'free' or as a 'favour' to the department receiving the benefit but this will not enable central management to assess the financial performance of the supplying and receiving departments. For example, a garage that has a car repair section and a car sales section is likely to make use of the car repair section to service cars being held for sale. If no accounting record is made for this service, management have no way of checking on the resources used in running the car sales department, and an inaccurate record of profitability in the car repair section.

One way of keeping a record of the internal transfer is to give it a price and to charge this to the department receiving the benefit. In general terms, a system of transfer pricing is an internal book-keeping procedure and does not affect the total profit of the firm. If goods are transferred from one division to another at a price in excess of cost, the total profit (assuming the goods have been sold by the receiving division) is merely split between the two divisions.

In some cases, however, a system of transfer pricing can affect profitability by influencing decisions at a local level. For example, a divisional manager might decide to purchase externally rather than accept an internal transfer, even when this reduces the overall profit of the company. Internal transfer prices can also lead managers in non-profit organizations to act in a manner that is detrimental to the organization as a whole. Consider the following case.

Details of the case

A university established a central reprographics department two years ago. This department is equipped with sophisticated machines and is capable of servicing the reprographic needs of all departments in the university. The teaching departments use these services for producing hand-out notes and exercises for their students. For internal budgeting purposes, the rate charged to each department is 8p per copy.

The head of the business and management department has recently been rebuked by the financial controller for exceeding his budget allowance for photocopying services in the previous period. There is a photocopying machine in this manager's department that was intended to be used for administration purposes and also by lecturers when they needed a small number of photocopies in a hurry. The cost of using this machine is 6p per copy. In order to save on costs, the head of this department has instructed all lecturers to use the department's photocopier rather than the services of the central reprographics department.

Activity 16

Identify some of the problems that might ensue from this decision.

A full study of transfer pricing involves certain aspects of economic analysis in order to determine a theoretical optimum price. In practice, this analysis is not always feasible and management will take a pragmatic approach by choosing a method that meets most of their objectives in terms of performance appraisal and goal congruence. The methods that are used fall into three classes:

- cost-based prices
- market-based prices
- negotiated prices.

Cost-based prices are based on a particular variant of cost such as marginal cost, full cost (marginal cost plus absorbed fixed overheads) or standard cost. If the transferrer is a profit (or investment) centre, cost-based transfer prices are based on any of these variants of cost plus a profit 'mark-up'.

Details for the next activity

Division A manufactures goods and transfers them to the trading division, Division B. Transfer prices are based on full cost, plus a mark-up of 1/3, and Division B uses the same basis for arriving at external sales prices. The cost/pricing structure for one unit is as follows:

Division A		Division B	
Marginal cost per unit	£300	Price charged	560
Fixed cost per unit	120	Own marginal costs	100
		Fixed costs per unit	150
Total (full) cost per unit	420		
			810
Mark-up	140	Mark-up	270
Transfer price	560	Selling price	1,080

Activity 17

Division B is having difficulty in moving this product and is negotiating a special price with a large customer. The manager of this division intends to base the price on an amount that exceeds marginal cost. Describe how a sub-optimal decision (for the company as a whole) might arise because of the transfer price structure. You can make any assumptions that seem appropriate (such as the price acceptable to the customer) when presenting your answer.

Activity 18

Think about some of the problems associated with using a cost-based transfer price and make a note here of any points that occur to you.

Market-based prices can only be used if a market exists for the products concerned. This is not always the case with certain types of intermediate product. If a market does exist then market-based prices usually meet most of the objectives of a transfer pricing system because they create a truly competitive environment and encourage operational efficiency. They are not, however, entirely free of problems.

Activity 19

Identify two problems associated with using market-based transfer prices. Keep in mind that in divisionalized companies, local managers are given a reasonable degree of freedom to operate in the best interest of their division.

Negotiated prices require the intervention of central management. They are used when either of the other two bases causes a conflict or is inappropriate for performance appraisal. A good example is an adjusted market price which recognizes that the transferring division does not incur any marketing costs. In these circumstances a market price that made no adjustment for the fact that the transferring division is relieved from the need to advertise its products might not be a perfect indicator of the value of goods transferred.

8.7 Non-financial measures of performance

In a book on management accounting, it is only appropriate that the subject of performance assessment should concentrate on measurements that are derived from the accounting information system. After all, the subject is called 'management accounting'; it is not called 'information for management'. However, it would be wrong for students of management accounting to ignore the fact that a number of respected academics have recently suggested that accounting information is irrelevant for making management decisions in a globally competitive economy.

Perhaps the most notable work in this area is by H.T. Johnson in his book *Relevance Regained*. Johnson suggests (and many management accountants will have a sneaking regard for the points that he makes) that accounting has no place in controlling how people work in a globally competitive business environment. Johnson states:

> *Accounting goals should not be used to direct and control workers or managers. Accounting information is necessary to track financial results and to plan the extent and financing of a company. But companies that control their people and processes with accounting information will not survive in the global economy.*

The thrust of Johnson's argument is based on the notion that traditional systems work in the wrong direction. Accounting information is used to empower top management to control the workforce, who will then manipulate processes and cajole customers in order to achieve accounting results to be fed back into the accounting information system. Johnson calls this 'the top-down control cycle'. This is contrasted with management information that flows through what Johnson calls 'the bottom-up empowerment cycle'. Such a system is aimed at satisfying customers and the information *'must come from customers and from processes and it must be gathered and used primarily by people in the work force who face the customers and who run the processes'*.

Ideas such as these are usually considered as part of a separate subject known as 'total quality management' (TQM). This is an extensive subject and cannot be included in a book that is aimed at providing a foundation in cost and management accounting. Some of the texts on TQM include lists of what are known as 'non-financial indicators' (NFIs) for measuring performance. NFIs compare two items of information, both of which are non-financial, such as comparing the number of defects with the number of returns by customers, or the number of customer complaints with the number of customers. Measures such as these are aimed at assessing performance on customer satisfaction.

It is possible to compare anything with anything. NFIs tend to use data on 'failures' such as defects, returns, machine breakdowns, stockouts, complaints and warranty claims, and compare them to appropriate non-financial measurements such as time, physical quantities, and numbers of people (such as customers, suppliers and employees).

These are relatively new ideas. For many years, companies have combined financial and non-financial information in order to produce performance indicators which they consider useful. The two most popular measures in this respect are:

- sales per square meter of shop space
- sales per employee

It is also possible to combine financial information with statistical information produced by external agencies such as the Central Statistical Office (CSO). For example, the CSO publishes index numbers (in a monthly digest) showing growth in retail sales. A comparison of the company's own growth with national growth will indicate whether its 'market share' is increasing or decreasing.

Summary

The key points in this chapter can be summarized as follows:
- performance variances in standard costing are sometimes more meaningful if the original standards are revised when they were based on a false assumption regarding economic conditions in the budget period
- revision of the original standards is achieved by calculating planning variances
- the standard convention for measuring price and quantity variances can sometimes cause arguments that might be resolved by measuring joint price/quantity variances

- the monetary values placed on fixed overhead volume variances are difficult to interpret, and information in the form of productivity ratios can be more meaningful
- sales margin variances help management to evaluate the effect of price adjustments on budgeted profit but are difficult to use for performance assessment
- sales quantity margin variances in a multi-product firm are likely to include a variance known as the sales mix variance
- performance of internal divisions is sometimes assessed by using ratios that were originally developed by external users for assessing performance of the entire company
- the primary ratio measures profit as a percentage of the net assets that were used to earn that profit
- measures of divisional performance should be designed to give appropriate feedback to central management, provide motivation for the divisional managers, and promote goal congruent actions by the division
- divisions can be established as either cost centres, profit centres or investment centres
- profits used to assess the performance of profit centres and investment centres should be based on controllable profit
- measurements of divisional performance based on ROCE can cause divisional managers to act in a way that is not goal congruent, and a measure known as residual income is preferable
- residual income represents controllable profit less interest (at a rate specified by central management) on the capital employed in the division
- the objective of residual income is that divisional managers will always undertake a project where the return is greater than the rate specified by central management because the excess goes to swell residual income
- transfer prices can be used in any organization and are a way of keeping an accounting record of goods or services provided by one department to another
- transfer prices can be based on cost (including cost plus profit), market price or a negotiated price
- transfer prices based on cost are the least acceptable because they transfer operating inefficiencies from one department to another
- market-based prices meet most of the objectives of a transfer pricing system
- performance assessment does not have to be based on financial factors; there are many non-financial indicators of performance, and firms sometimes use ratios based on financial and non-financial information

Activity 1

Budgeted profit	400
Sales margin price variance (1,200 × £0,30)	360 Favourable
Sales margin quantity variance (200 × £0.40)	80 Favourable
Material price variance (7,200 × £0.02)	(144) Adverse
Actual profit	696

Activity 2

Revised budgeted profit (after planning variances)	948
Performance variances:	
Sales price (1,200 × £.05)	(60) Adverse
Sales quantity (300 × £0.40)	(120) Adverse
Material price (7,200 × £0.01)	(72) Adverse
Actual profit	696

Activity 3

1.	Material price variance (22,000 × £0.20)	4,400	Adverse
2.	Material usage variance (2,000 × £3.00)	6,000	Adverse

Activity 4

Activity ratio (20,400/20,000) = 102%
Efficiency ratio (20,400/21,400) = 95.32%
Capacity ratio (21,500/20,000) = 107.5%

Activity 5

Sales margin price variance		
Product A (1,400 × £1)	1,400 Adverse	
Product B (2,200 × £2)	4,400 Favourable	
		3,000 Favourable
Sales margin quantity variance		
Product A (400 × £4)	1,600 Favourable	
Product B (200 × £8)	1,600 Favourable	
		3,200 Favourable
Total		6,200 Favourable

Activity 6

1993 (33,000/112,000) = 29.5%
1994 (34,835/145,000) = 24%

Activity 7

The primary ratio is an arithmetic product of the two secondary ratios (this can be seen by cancelling 'sales' in the fractions for the two secondary ratios). You can indicate this in the activity box by placing arithmetic signs between the fractions, as follows:

$$\frac{\text{Profit}}{\text{Net assets}} = \frac{\text{Profit}}{\text{Sales}} \times \frac{\text{Sales}}{\text{Net assets}}$$

Activity 8
Profitability
1993 (33,000/400,000) = 8.25%
1994 (34,835/580,000) = 6%

Asset turnover
1993 (400,000/112,000) = 3.57 times
1994 (580,000/145,000) = 4 times

Activity 9
1993 3.57 × 8.25% = 29.5% (allowing for rounding)
1994 4 × 6% = 24%

Activity 10
Debtors collection period: 1993 = 34 days; 1994 = 42 days.
Stock turnover period: 1993 = 30 days; 1994 = 45 days.
Creditors payment period: Purchases can be found either by adding the stock increase to cost of sales, or by setting out a computation for cost of sales with the known information and then inserting purchases as a balancing figure. Purchases are: 1993 £302,000; 1994 £483,950. This makes the creditors payment period: 1993 = 26 days; 1994 = 42 days.

Activity 11
Apportioned items such as apportionments of central administration costs, depreciation of fixed assets where the divisional manager is not responsible for investment and disinvestment decisions, apportionment of interest charges on long-term (strategic) financing for the whole company.

Activity 12
The profits of (20,000 − 5,000) £15,000 represent 20% on the capital invested. This is less than the 40% currently earned. This might lead to a decision not to renew the fixed assets.

Activity 13
Without the new project, ROCE is 40%. If the project is included, ROCE will become (475,000/1,250,000) 38% and is likely to be declined. Yet the new project does provide a return of 30% which is well in excess of the target ROCE of 25% set by central management.

Activity 14

	With project	Without project
Profit	475,000	400,000
Less imputed interest (25% of capital invested)	(312,500)	(250,000)
Residual income	162,500	150,000

Since residual income is higher with the project, it will be accepted.

Activity 15
Difficulties in establishing an interest rate. Assets might be sold where they do not meet the required return (yet this might not be in the interest of the company as a whole). The amount is an absolute figure and therefore difficult to use.

Activity 16

The sophisticated equipment in central reprographics might be underutilized. Lecturers' time is badly used. Machine breakdowns in the department due to heavy use of a smaller machine. Frustrated lecturers and poorly served students, leading to customer dissatisfaction and loss of students in the future.

Activity 17

The manager of Division B might consider marginal cost to be (£560 + £100) £660 and try to base a price on this. Yet the marginal cost to the firm as a whole is (£300 + £100) £400. If the manager in Division B attempted to negotiate a price by adding 1/3 to his (perceived) marginal cost, the price would be £880. If the customer was prepared to pay (say) £600 the manager would refuse this, yet it does exceed a price that could be determined by adding 1/3 to the true marginal cost for the company as a whole (£400 + £133 = £533).

Activity 18

There is no incentive for the transferrer to be efficient. The whole cost of being inefficient is passed on to the transferee. If there is a profit mark-up, there is an incentive to be inefficient because the higher the cost, the higher the plus. Costs are based on accounting measurements that include a number of subjective allocations.

Activity 19

Managers might purchase externally rather than accept an internal transfer at a higher price. Market prices might require some adjustment to reflect the fact that the transferring division does not incur any marketing costs. Transferee division might misunderstand marginal cost when making decisions (as in Activity 17). There might be more than one market price.

Questions for self assessment

Answers to self-assessment questions are given at the end of the book.

8.1 Torpid PLC set the following budget for a new product that it was adding to its product range at the beginning of the fourth quarter of 1993/94:

Sales 10,000 units at £10.00		100,000
Production 12,000 units		
Cost of production		
Direct material 37,200 square metres at £0.65	24,180	
Direct labour 8,000 hours at £3.00	24,000	
Variable overhead 8,000 hours at £2.40	19,200	
	67,380	
Less: Stock of finished goods		
2,000 units at £5.615	11,230	
		56,150
		43,850
Less:		
Fixed overhead	16,800	
Promotional expenses	17,050	
		33,850
Budgeted profit		£10,000

During the quarter it became obvious that:
(a) the standard usage of direct material had been set at too low a level; a more realistic standard would be 3.55 square metres per unit of output
(b) the standard ware rate had become outdated; from the beginning of the period a new rate of £3.30 per hour had come into operation
(c) the company had been over-optimistic in setting the standard selling price at £10; the price was reduced to £9.50 from the beginning of the period.

The actual data recorded for the quarter were as follows:

Units produced	10,500
Units sold	8,500
Hours worked	8,500
Wages paid	£26,500
Direct material used	40,240 sq metres
Cost of direct material used	£27,000
Variable overheads	£20,150
Fixed overheads	£17,100
Promotional expense	£15,000

Required:
A statement reconciling the actual profit with the original budgeted figures. Show deviations from budget in a way which attempts to distinguish planning variances from performance variances. Assume that finished goods stock is to be valued at standard marginal cost after incorporating the revised material usage and wage rates into the standard.

Author's note: The original question included much more detail (including details for calculating learning variances for the first half of the period). These details have been excluded in order to present a problem that is capable of being solved at a foundation level. Note that when closing stocks are valued at standard cost, the cost variances in the reconciliation report relate to the total quantity of finished goods produced.

(ACCA Management Accounting, adapted)

8.2 **Garden equipment**. A company manufactures three types of garden equipment, for which the standard times and budgeted production quantities were as follows:

Product	Standard hours per unit	Number of units budgeted
Lawn mower	10	2,000
Hedge trimmer	1	8,000
Garden rake	2	8,000

During the period 43,000 hours were actually worked, and the following production was achieved:

Lawn mower	1,800 units
Hedge trimmer	8,000 units
Garden rake	12,000 units

Required:
Explain what is meant by a standard hour and illustrate how it can be used to calculate performance (productivity) ratios based on the above data.

(Based on ACCA Costing)

8.3 The following data relate to two divisions:

	Division A	Division B
Operating profit	£120,000	£20,000
Operating assets	£800,000	£100,000
Sales	£400,000	£400,000

Required:
(a) Compute the Return on Investment (ROI) and its constituent elements for each division.
(b) The present cost of capital is now 12% and will increase to 18%. Using the above information comment on the problems in assessing performance of Divisions A and B.

(ACCA Certified Diploma)

8.4 A privately owned retail business operating from one location has been going through a period of adverse trading conditions. Its sales turnover, excluding sales taxes, and the operating profit were £84 million and £200,000 respectively during the latest financial year ended 30 April 1994. An analysis of sales and direct and indirect expenses for 1993–94 is shown below. At a recent board meeting several issues arose for discussion:
(i) Director 1, John Smith: 'All departments should bear their share of indirect costs and for simplicity these should be shared out pro rata to sales turnover. I don't like the current accounting policy.'
(ii) Director 2, Helen Davies: 'All departments should earn the same operating profit per £ of sales, so those departments with low figures should put up their prices.'
(iii) Managing Director: 'We've just had an offer from a cosmetics retailer to take over 10% of our floor space for a fee of £270,000 in total per annum. We certainly won't give up retailing this year, but I don't mind renting out up to 15% of our floor space.'

Exhibit A

	Foods	*Clothing*	*Electric*
Year ended 30 April 1994			
	£ million	*£ million*	*£ million*
Turnover	37.5	24	22.5
Cost of sales	30.6	16.5	15.2
Direct staff and advertising	2.4	2.7	6.4
Indirect costs*	2.1	3.6	4.3

*Including rent, rates, administration, directors' fees etc. apportioned on the basis of floor space.

You are required to:
(a) prepare an operating report of the departmental profitability for the directors based on John Smith's ideas,
(b) comment on the validity of the existing basis of apportionment,
(c) state if you agree with Helen Davies' comment. Why?
(d) discuss whether the cosmetics retailer's offer is worth considering.

(ACCA Certified Diploma)

8.5 Information has been summarized from the returns of two divisions in the Citadel Group and is shown in the table below. Division 1's major activity is the retailing of food products. Division 2 has two major activities: these are the manufacture of electrical components, and the sale of computer services (hardware, software and consultancy).

Summarized Profit and Return on Capital Employed for previous year

	Division 1	Division 2	
		Electrical components	Computer services
Profit (before tax and interest) £m	14.4	1.6	6.2
Return on capital employed	18%	16%	31%
Sales turnover £m	148.6	5.6	95.2

Citadel Group considers that its cost of capital (pre-tax) is 15%.

You are required to:
(a) calculate the residual income for each division;
(b) state with reasons which division you consider to be more profitable;
(c) should the manager of Division 2 consider abandoning either activity? Briefly give your reasons.

(ACCA Certified Diploma)

Questions without answers

Answers to these questions are published separately in the *Teacher's Manual*.

8.6 ABC plc is a large public company which is organized into autonomous divisions. For the purposes of managerial performance measurement a return on capital employed (ROCE) is calculated by relating net profit to gross capital employed. This company interprets gross capital employed as current assets plus fixed assets at original cost.

Extracts from the budgeted results of Division A and Division B for 1994 are shown below:

	Division A	Division B
	£000s	£000s
Net profit	200	64
Current assets	200	150
Fixed assets	800	650

There are two projects which are being considered by the division managers. Neither of them is included in the figures given above. They are:

(i) Project Alpha – in which Division A has the opportunity to increase annual sales by £200,000 by undertaking an annual advertising campaign which will have a fixed cost of £15,000. The sales increase will improve the division's contribution by £30,000 but will require stock levels to be increased by £100,000 per annum on average.

(ii) Project Beta in which Division B can invest in some new equipment costing £200,000 which will improve annual profits by £20,000 due to increased efficiency.

Required:

(a) Determine the budgeted return on capital employed (ROCE) for each division
   (i) before the two projects are incorporated;
   (ii) assuming the managers adopt the projects available to their division and incorporate them in their budgets.

(b) Determine the budgeted residual income (RI) for each division before and after the incorporation of the respective projects. The company has a cost of capital of 12% per annum.

(c) Contrast the results under (a) and (b) and consider to what extent they encourage the division managers to pursue corporate profit objectives whilst acting in their own best interests.

(ACCA Certified Diploma)

8.7 (a) What are the main objectives of a transfer pricing system? Briefly state why there might be problems in attaining these objectives.

(b) Griznez Company has several divisions which include a computer services division (CSD) and an office equipment division (OED). CSD wishes to purchase some office equipment. This can be acquired either from OED or from other suppliers. OED supplies direct to independent retailers. The price which a retailer would normally charge to its customers for the equipment needed by CSD would be £80,000, and the retailer normally marks up office equipment supplied by OED by 60%. The sales management of OED has offered to sell the equipment to CSD for £75,000. This reduction of £5,000 represents savings which OED makes on costs of marketing, selling and credit management as a result of a sale inside the company. It is company policy to pass on these savings to the purchaser within the company.

OED itself sub-contracts all manufacturing. OED's purchasing manager indicates that OED has a backlog of orders from the independent retailers which cannot currently be met due to a shortage of reliable supplies. She also indicates that the office equipment of the type required by CSD would cost OED £20,000 if it were delivered by sub-contractors to OED's warehouse ready for despatch to the independent retailers.

You are required to write a short memo to the general manager of CSD, giving the following:
(i) a recommended transfer price for the office equipment;
(ii) the reasons why you have chosen this price.

(ACCA Certified Diploma)

8.8 The following information applies to the planned operations of Division A of ABC Corporation for 1994

	£
Sales – 100,000 units at £12	1,200,000
Variable costs at £8 each	800,000
Fixed costs (including depreciation)	250,000
Division A investment (at original cost)	500,000

The minimum desired rate of return on investment is the cost of capital of 20%.

The company is highly profit conscious and delegates a considerable level of autonomy to divisional managers. As part of a procedure to review planned operations of Division A a meeting has been convened to consider two options (shown below):

Option I

Division A may sell a further 20,000 units at £11 to customers outside ABC Corporation. Variable costs per unit will be the same as budgeted but to enable capacity to increase by 20,000 units one extra piece of equipment will be required costing £80,000. The equipment will have a four year life and the company depreciates assets on a straight-line basis. No extra cash fixed costs will occur.

Option II

Included in the current plan of operations of Division A is the sale of 20,000 units to Division B also within ABC Corporation. A competitor of Division A, from outside the group, has offered to supply Division B at £10 per unit. Division A intends to adopt a strategy of matching the price quoted from outside the company to retain the order.

Required:

(a) Calculate for 1994 for Division A the residual income of:
   (i)   the original planned operation,
   (ii) Option I only added to the original plan,
   (iii) Option II only added to the original plan, and briefly interpret the results of the options as they affect Division A.

(b) Assess the implications for Division A, Division B and the corporation as a whole of Option II, bearing in mind that if Division A does not compete on price it will lose the 20,000 units order from Division B. Make any recommendations you consider appropriate.

(ACCA Certified Diploma)

Financial statements for Overload Ltd

Profit and loss accounts year to	31 Dec 1993	31 Dec 1994
Turnover	400,000	580,000
Cost of sales	300,000	452,400
Gross profit	100,000	127,600
Selling and administration	67,000	92,765
Operating profit	33,000	34,835
Interest paid and similar charges	5,000	5,835
Profit before tax	28,000	29,000
Taxation	4,200	4,350
Profit after tax	23,800	24,650
Dividends	nil	nil
Profit retained	23,800	24,650

Balance sheets at	31 Dec 1993		31 Dec 1994	
Fixed assets		69,310		81,335
Current assets:				
Stock	25,000		56,550	
Debtors	37,260		66,740	
Bank	6,000		500	
	68,260		123,790	
Creditors due within one year				
Creditors	21,370		55,775	
Taxation	4,200		4,350	
	25,570		60,125	
Net current assets		42,690		63,665
Total assets less current liabilities		112,000		145,000
Creditors falling due after one year				
10% Debenture 1998		50,000		58,350
		62,000		86,650
Capital and reserves				
Ordinary shares of £1 each		10,000		10,000
Profit and loss account		52,000		76,650
		62,000		86,650

Note: Stock in the balance sheet at 31 December 1992 was £23,000

Activity 6
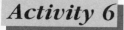

Go back to the material purchases budget (box number 7). This is linked to the cash budget through box number 9. This box represents a budget that will be taken into account when calculating the amount of cash that the company expects to pay to its suppliers during the period. Identify the name of this budget, check your idea with the Key and write the name of the budget in the empty box.

You will notice that there is one more empty box, box number 12, to represent other planning matters that will affect the cash budget. The cash receipts and payments resulting from the budgets identified by boxes 1 to 11 are all related to trading items such as selling goods, making them and incurring various overheads. There will be transactions apart from trading items that result in cash movements.

Activity 7

Make a list of the types of cash transaction that could be included in box number 12.

In view of the limited space in the diagram, you could write 'see Activity 7' in box 12.

The overview provided by this diagram will help you to deal with the computations required by the next series of activities.

Details for the activities

1. The company manufactures a single product (known as XYZ) from a raw material component called CDS.
2. The company uses a standard marginal costing system. For internal accounting purposes, stocks are valued on the basis of standard marginal cost.
3. The company's balance sheet at 31 December 1993 was as follows:

Fixed assets		71,000
Current assets:		
Stocks: Raw materials (2,000 units of CDS)	10,000	
Finished goods (1,500 units of XYZ)	45,000	
	55,000	
Debtors	120,000	
	175,000	

Creditors falling due within one year

Trade creditors	20,000	
Bank overdraft	66,000	
		86,000

Net current assets	89,000
Total assets less current liabilities	160,000
Long-term loans	60,000
	100,000

Capital and reserves

Share capital	70,000
Profit and loss account	30,000
	100,000

4. Standard manufacturing costs per unit, and standard selling price per unit have been set for 1994 as follows:

	per unit £
Raw materials – 2 units of CDS	10
Direct labour	20
Variable (marginal) cost	30
Selling price	50
Contribution	20

5. Other budgeting costs for 1994 are as follows:

	£
Fixed production overheads (including £4,000 depreciation)	60,000
Selling and administration costs (all fixed – including £1,000 depreciation)	160,000

Note that loan interest has been included in selling and administration costs.

6. Other matters relating to 1994 are as follows:
   By the end of 1994, the company plans to:

Increase the stock of finished goods to	2,000 units
Reduce the stocks of raw materials to	1,000 units

Debtors currently stand at (roughly) 3 months' sales; the company plans (through the introduction of tougher credit control procedures) to reduce this to 1 month's sales by the end of 1994.

Trade creditors relate entirely to raw materials. The company plans to push creditors to the limit so that by the end of 1994 creditors will represent 3 months' purchases.

Cash budget

Cash balance at 1 January 1994
Cash receipts:
   Received from customers
     (opening debtors + sales – closing debtors)

Cash payments:
   Paid to suppliers
     (opening creditors + purchases – closing creditors)
   Paid for direct labour
   Paid for overheads (depreciation is not a cash payment)
     Production overheads
     Selling and administration
   Other payments (you will find one in the details)

Cash balance at 31 December 1994

If your cash budget agrees with the Key we can proceed to the final stage of preparing the budgeted financial statements. In order to help students who are not accustomed to producing financial statements, outline formats are provided. You should note that since the company is valuing closing stocks on the basis of standard marginal cost, there is no need to present 'cost of sales' in detailed form (manufacturing costs adjusted for opening and closing stocks). The standard marginal cost of sales is simply the quantity sold multiplied by the standard marginal cost per unit.

Activity 15

Prepare the budgeted profit and loss account for year ending 31 December 1994, and the budgeted balance sheet at 31 December 1994, by completing the outline formats shown below. Remember to deduct annual depreciation when calculating the carrying value for fixed assets in the balance sheet.

Budgeted profit and loss account for year ended 31 December 1994

Sales

Standard marginal cost of sales

                Budgeted contribution

Fixed overheads:
   Production

   Selling and administration

Budgeted profit

In this series of exercises we have looked at a complete year. There will be many students for whom this book is intended who are required to prepare budget statements as part of their course work where the cash budget must be presented on a monthly basis. The principles involved are exactly the same as those used in this exercise, any differences between a monthly cash budget and one for the whole year are simply a matter of detail. For example, in this exercise debtors were to be reduced from three months' sales at the beginning of the period to one month's sales at the end – no information was given on the pattern of this reduction over the year. If we were asked to produce a monthly cash budget, we would need more detail on this in order to work out the timing of cash flows from customers.

In this book, the subject of cash budgets forms part of Chapter 10, Management of working capital. There are, however, questions at the end of this chapter that include a requirement to produce a monthly cash budget. This is not really a topic that requires a separate study text because it is merely an application of general principles; what is needed is practise.

9.4 Sundry budgeting topics

Flexible budgeting

Budgets are produced as part of a system for planning and control. Control takes the form of comparing actual results with the budget and taking appropriate action where there are significant variances. If a budget is prepared for a particular level of activity, the variances between budgeted and actual results will be meaningless if the actual level of activity was significantly different to the budgeted level. You can see this from the following simplified example.

Example

The budgeted and actual results of a company were as follows:

	Budget £	Actual £
Sales	10,000	12,000
Cost of sales	6,000	7,750
Gross profit	4,000	4,250
Overheads	2,000	2,200
Profit	2,000	2,050

As you can see, there is very little difference between budgeted profit and actual profit. In a situation like this the managers might not feel that any action was needed. Even if variances between budget and actual were listed in an additional column, the figures would be almost meaningless for control purposes if the actual level of activity differed from the budgeted level. Such variance would be a combination of volume and price variances. What we need to know are the budgeted figures for the actual level of activity achieved.

Suppose you were informed of the following:

1. This is a single product company.
2. The budgeted level of activity was 10,000 units, the actual level was 12,500 units.
3. In a previous period when sales were 8,000 units, the overheads were £1,800.
4. Planning variances can be ignored.

In order to make a useful comparison between budget and actual, we must 'flex' the original budget to reflect what the budgeted figures would be for 12,500 units. In the context of flexible budgeting this would be called an activity level of 125%. The original budget (which in this case had been set for 10,000 units) is always identified as the 100% level.

Activity 16

Complete the table below as far as sales and cost of sales are concerned. This requires you to work out the budgeted figures for 12,500 units, write in the figures for the actual results and calculate the variances. Leave the row for overheads blank at this stage.

	Budgeted figures		Actual	Variance
	100%	125%		
Units	10,000	12,500	12,500	
	£	£	£	£
Sales	10,000			
Cost of sales	6,000			
Gross profit	4,000			
Overheads	2,000			
Profit	2,000			

We now need to think about the overheads. If these were all fixed overheads the budget allowance for the 125% level of activity would be the same as for the 100% level. However, the information given in point 3 above, in conjunction with the budgeted overhead cost, suggests that overheads are a mixture of fixed and variable costs. You might recall how we used the 'high/low' technique in Chapter 2 in order to split mixed costs between their fixed and variable elements. You can do the same here by using the number of units as the cost driver.

Activity 17

Identify the fixed element of overheads, and the variable overhead cost per unit, by using the high/low technique. You can use the following outline format. After having worked out the figures, include the budget allowance for overheads in the above table and work out the variance

	Low	High	Increase
Cost driver (units)			
Total costs			
Less variable costs			
Fixed costs (balance)			

The kind of problem dealt with in Activities 16 and 17 does not arise with production costs in a manufacturing entity if standard costing is used. This is because the variances are related to the actual level of activity achieved. The variance report that you have now completed is more meaningful than it would have been if actual results had been compared to the original budget. However, the format used above does not show clearly the effect of sales quantity and sales price variances; the sales variance relates entirely to price. Since this is a single product model we could present the figures in the same kind of format as we did when producing variance reports in standard costing. This will enable managers to evaluate the effect on budgeted gross profit of reducing prices in order to increase volume.

Complete the variance report shown below. Use the same principles as you did for standard costing. The report deals with profit at the gross profit level. In view of the lack of detail, we will assume that the cost of sales variance relates entirely to price.

Variance report

Budgeted gross profit for 10,000 units	£4,000
Variances:	
Sales margin price variance	
Sales margin quantity variance	
Material price variance	
Actual gross profit for 12,500 units	£4,250

Flexible budgeting can be used in any organization. A flexed budget normally shows the budgeted figures for different levels of activity based on stepped percentage points either side of the planned (100%) level. For example, the flexed budget might show figures for 80%, 90%, 100%, 110% (and so on) activity levels. Budgeted figures are based on known patterns of cost behaviour and on predictions of how costs will respond to changes in activity. This will include recognizing that some costs will be fixed for a particular range of activity but will show a stepped increase for activity levels beyond that range. When the actual level of activity does not coincide with any of the percentage levels shown in the flexed budget, the budgeted figures can be found by interpolating between two percentage points.

Rolling budgets

Rolling budgets are sometimes used when future costs and activities are difficult to forecast with any degree of conviction. They are set for short periods and continually updated by adding a further period, such as one month or one quarter, and deducting the earliest month or quarter. The rolling budget attempts to reflect current conditions.

Zero base budgeting (or activity base budgeting)

The way in which figures for budgets are gathered is quite important. If the manager of a department was given a budget spending allowance of £50,000 for last year, that manager is likely to use this as a starting point when negotiating a budget allowance for the new budget year. This approach is sometimes called 'incremental budgeting'. The manager uses £50,000 as a starting point, adds on an amount for inflation, and perhaps an amount for any increase in planned activity. The problem with this approach is that it ignores making any attempt to establish whether the £50,000 spent last year was an appropriate amount for that department.

Zero base budgeting evaluates all activity areas from a starting point of zero cost. In other words, it assumes that each activity does not exist. Any increment of cost above zero must be justified on the grounds of the incremental benefits to the organization if that cost is incurred. These benefits can often be evaluated in terms of what would happen if the budget allowance was not granted.

This approach to establishing budgeted figures is probably more common than is often supposed, but it might not always be called zero base budgeting. The number of companies using activity based costing is increasing and these companies use information on cost drivers for budgeting. If a service organization establishes its planned income activity for the next year, the process of establishing budgeted costs can start by considering what support activities are needed in order to sustain this level of income. Information on cost drivers for each activity area can then be used to establish a budgeted cost for that activity. In some ways this is like zero based budgeting because it ignores the total cost of a department for the current year, and considers the costs that will have to be incurred in order to support the planned level of income. This type of approach is usually called 'activity base budgeting'.

Summary

The key learning points in this chapter can be summarized as follows:
- producing forecast statements is not the same as budgeting
- a budget is a plan for a future period quantified in financial terms
- budgets are used for control purposes; actual results are compared to the budget and action is taken when there are significant variances
- a master budget is a budgeted profit statement, a budgeted balance sheet and a budgeted cash flow statement
- the master budget is prepared from budgeted information for each activity area
- the sequence of preparing budgets is usually: sales, finished goods stock, material usage, raw materials stock, purchases, direct labour, overheads
- cash budgets identify the timing of cash flows and use information on the budgets for debtors and creditors
- budget administration is assisted by budget manuals and the work is coordinated through a budget committee
- flexible budgeting shows budgeted income and budgeted costs for various levels of activity, actual results are compared to the budgeted figures for the level of activity achieved
- zero base budgeting forces managers to justify the costs of their department by assuming that the department does not exist
- activity base budgeting considers the support activities needed to sustain the planned level of sales activity and determines the budgeted costs for these activities by using information on cost drivers

Key to activities

Activity 1
Item 3 (cash to be received) and Item 6 (operating profit) do not feature in any of the functional budgets.

Activity 2
The most appropriate headings are:
Situation 1: coordination
Situation 2: communication
Situation 3: performance evaluation
Situation 4: control (no action was taken on the variance)
Situation 5: planning (this situation is more common than you might imagine)

Activity 3
Finished goods budget.

Activity 4
Debtors budget (the company will plan for the level of debtors).

Activity 5
Raw materials stock budget.

Activity 6
Creditors budget.

Activity 7
1. Capital transactions such as purchase of fixed assets, sale of fixed assets, new share issues, loans received or repaid.
2. Taxation payments.
3. Dividend payments.

Activity 8
Target profit: 20% of £100,000 = £20,000.
Sales quantity (£20,000 + £60,000 + £160,000) ÷ £20 = 12,000 units.
Sales value 12,000 × £50 = £600,000.

Activity 9
12,000 (for sales) + 500 (stock increase) = 12,500 units.

Activity 10
12,500 × 2 = 25,000 units of CDS.

Activity 11
Quantity: 25,000 units (usage) − 1,000 (stock reduction) = 24,000 units.
Cost: 24,000 × £5 = £120,000.

Activity 12
12,500 × £20 = £250,000.

Activity 13
Debtors: 1/12 × £600,000 = £50,000.
Creditors 3/12 × £120,000 = £30,000.

Activity 14

Cash at 1 January 1994	(66,000)
Receipts from customers	670,000
	604,000
Payments:	
To suppliers	(110,000)
To direct labour	(250,000)
For production overheads	(56,000)
For selling and administration	(159,000)
Other payments:	
Loan repayment	(10,000)
Cash at 31 December 1994	19,000

Activity 15

Budgeted profit and loss account for year ended 31 December 1994

Sales		600,000
Standard marginal cost of sales		360,000
Budgeted contribution		240,000
Fixed overheads:		
Production	60,000	
Selling and administration	160,000	
		220,000
Budgeted profit		20,000

Budgeted balance sheet at 31 December 1994

Fixed assets			66,000
Current assets:			
Stock: Raw materials		5,000	
Finished goods		60,000	
		65,000	
Debtors		50,000	
Bank		19,000	
		134,000	
Current liabilities:			
Trade creditors		30,000	
			104,000
Total assets less current liabilities			170,000
Long-term loans			50,000
			120,000
Capital and reserves			
Share capital			70,000
Profit and loss account:			
Balance at 1 January 1994		30,000	
Profit for the year		20,000	
			50,000
			120,000

Activity 16

At this stage your figures should be:

	Budgeted figures		Actual	Variance
	100%	125%		
Units	10,000	12,500	12,500	
	£	£	£	£
Sales	10,000	12,500	12,000	(500)
Cost of sales	6,000	7,500	7,750	(250)
Gross profit	4,000	5,000	4,250	(750)
Overheads	2,000			
Profit	2,000			

Activity 17

	Low	High	Increase	
Cost driver (units)	8,000	10,000	2,000	
Total cost	£1,800	£2,000	£200	Variable cost = £0.10 per unit
Less variable cost	800	1,000		
Fixed cost (balance)	£1,000	£1,000		

Budget allowance for 12,500 units (12,500 × £0.10) + £1,000 = £2,250

Inserting this in the table for Activity 16 produces the following:

	Budgeted figures		Actual	Variance
	100%	125%		
Units	10,000	12,500	12,500	
	£	£	£	£
Sales	10,000	12,500	12,000	(500)
Cost of sales	6,000	7,500	7,750	(250)
Gross profit	4,000	5,000	4,250	(750)
Overheads	2,000	2,250	2,200	50
Profit	2,000	2,750	2,050	700

Activity 18

Budgeted gross profit for 10,000 units	4,000	
Variances:		
Sales margin price variance	(500)	Adverse
Sales margin quantity variance	1,000	Favourable
Materials price variance	(250)	Adverse
Actual gross profit for 12,500 units	£4,250	

Questions for self assessment

Answers to self-assessment questions are given at the end of the book.

9.1 *Author's guidance notes:* The following question includes a requirement to prepare a six-monthly cash budget. If you are not accustomed to doing these and you are preparing the statement manually (rather than with the help of a computer spreadsheet), I suggest you take the following approach:

1. Set up a tabulation with a column for each month and an additional left-hand column where you can describe the various receipts and payments.
2. You will need two sets of rows: the first set should be for the receipts and the second for the payments. It is usually possible to find a description for each type of receipt and payment from the details. There is often one type of receipts only – cash from customers.
3. Write in all the easy figures in their appropriate month. By easy figures, I mean those where the timing of the cash flow is given such as the month when taxation is paid or fixed assets are purchased. You quite often find that overheads are also easy because they tend to be paid in the same month as when they were incurred.
4. Write in all the figures where the timing is more complex, such as cash received from customers and cash paid to suppliers. You might find it easier to set out the receipts from customers on two rows, one for those received within the month and one for those received from credit customers.
5. Find the cash balance at the end of each month and carry this forward as the opening balance for the start of the next month.

If the above description of the format is not very clear, you could look at the answer to this question for guidance on how to set out the tabulation.

Freewheel is in the process of preparing its master budget for the 6 months ending December 1992. The balance sheet for the year ended 30 June 1992 is estimated to be as follows:

	Cost £	Deprec. Prov. £	Net book value £
Fixed assets	140,000	14,000	126,000
Current assets:			
Stock	25,000		
Trade debtors	24,000		
Bank	3,000		
Net current liabilities		52,600	
Creditors:			
Amounts falling due within 1 year			
Trade creditors	25,000		
Other creditors	9,000		
		34,000	
Net current assets			18,600
Total assets *less* current liabilities			144,600
Capital and reserves:			
Share capital			100,000
Profit and loss account			44,600
			144,600

The Budget Committee have derived the following trading forecasts for the 6 months ended 31 December 1992:

	Sales in Units	Purchases £	Wages and Salaries £	Overheads exc. deprec. £	Purchase of Fixed Assets £	Issue of 20,000 £1 Shares £	Dividends £
May	4,000	12,000	8,000	7,000			
June	4,200	13,000	8,000	7,000			
July	4,500	14,000	8,000	7,000			
August	4,600	18,000	10,000	7,000			
September	4,800	16,000	10,000	7,000		20,000	
October	5,000	14,000	10,000	8,000			10,000
November	3,800	12,000	12,000	8,000	30,000		
December	3,000	12,000	12,000	8,000			

You are given the following information:
1. The selling price in May 1992 was £6 per unit and this is to be increased to £8 per unit in October. 50% of sales are for cash and 50% on credit to be paid two months later.
2. Purchases are to be paid two months after purchase.
3. Wages and salaries are to be paid 75% in the month incurred and 25% in the following month.
4. Overheads are to be paid in the month after they are incurred.
5. The fixed assets are to be paid for in three equal instalments in the three months following purchase.
6. Dividends are to be paid three months after they are declared and the receipts from the share issue are budgeted to be received in the month of issue.
7. Fixed assets are depreciated 10% per annum on a straight line basis on those assets owned at 31 December 1992.
8. Closing stock at the beginning of the period under review was equal to the previous two months purchases. At 31 December 1992 it was equal to three months purchases.

Required:
(a) Prepare the following budgets for the 6 months ended 31 December 1992:
   (i) cash budget
   (ii) budgeted profit and loss account
   (iii) budgeted balance sheet
(b) Comment upon the results, highlighting those areas that you wish to draw to the attention of the Budget Committee.

(AAT Cost accounting and budgeting)

9.2 Company Z is preparing budgets for the coming year. 120,000 direct labour hours will be 100% level of expected productive time, but a flexible budget at 90%, 110% and 120% is required so that cost allowances can be set for these possible levels.
Budgeted cost details:
1. *Fixed cost per annum*

	£
Depreciation	22,000
Staff salaries	43,000
Insurances	9,000
Rent and rates	12,000

2. *Variable* costs

Power	30p per direct labour hour
Consumables	5p per direct labour hour
Direct labour	£3.50 per direct labour hour

3. *Semi-variable costs*
Analysis of past records, adjusted to eliminate the effect of inflation, shows the following:

		Direct Labour Hours	Total Semi-Variable Cost
Last year	1988	110,000	330,000
	1987	100,000	305,000
	1986	90,000	280,000
	1985	87,000	272,500
	1984	105,000	317,500
	1983	80,000	255,000

Required:
A cost budget at 100% and flexed to show cost allowances at 90%, 110% and 120% of expected level.

(*AAT Cost accounting and budgeting*)

9.3 A nursing home, which is linked to a large hospital, has been examining its budgetary control procedures, with particular reference to overhead costs.

The level of activity in the facility is measured by the number of patients treated in the budget period. For the current year the budget stands at 6,000 patients and this is expected to be met.

For months 1 to 6 of this year (assume 12 months of equal length) 2,700 patients were treated. The actual variable overhead costs incurred during this six month period are shown below:

Expense	£
Staffing	59,400
Power	27,000
Supplies	54,000
Other	8,100
Total	148,500

The hospital accountant believes that the variable overhead costs will be incurred at the same rate during months 7 to 12 of the whole year.
Fixed overhead costs are budgeted for the whole year as follows:

Expense	£
Supervision	120,000
Depreciation/financing	27,000
Other	64,800
Total	372,500

Required:
(a) For months 7–12 of the above year present an overhead budget. You should show each expense but should not separate individual months. What is the total overhead cost per patient which would be incorporated into any statistics?
(b) The home actually treated 3,800 patients during months 7–12, actual variable overhead was £203,300 and fixed overhead was £190,000. In summary form, examine how well they exercised control over their overhead.
(c) Interpret your analysis and point out any limitations or assumptions.

(*ACCA Certified Diploma*)

Questions without answers

Answers to these questions are published separately in the Teacher's Manual.

9.4 A manufacturing company has the following budgeted costs for one month, which are based on a normal capacity level of 40,000 hours. A departmental overhead absorption rate of £4.40 per hour has been calculated, as follows:

Overheads item	Fixed	Variable per hour
	£000	£
Management and supervision	30	–
Shift premium	–	0.10
National insurance and pension costs	6	0.22
Inspection	20	0.25
Consumable supplies	6	0.18
Power for machinery	–	0.20
Lighting and heating	4	–
Rates	9	–
Repairs and maintenance	8	0.15
Materials handling	10	0.30
Depreciation of machinery	15	–
Production administration	12	–
	120	

Overhead rate per hour: variable		1.40
fixed		3.00
total		£4.40

During the month of April, the company actually worked 36,000 hours producing 36,000 standard hours of production and incurred the following overhead costs:

	£000
Management and supervision	30.0
Shift premium	4.0
National insurance and pension costs	15.0
Inspection	28.0
Consumable supplies	12.7
Power for machinery	7.8
Lighting and heating	4.2
Rates	4.2
Repairs and maintenance	15.1
Materials handling	21.4
Depreciation of machinery	15.0
Production administration	11.5
Idle time	1.6
	175.3

You are required to:

(a) prepare a statement showing for April the flexible budget for the month, the actual costs and the variance for each overhead item;

(b) comment on each variance of £1,000 or more by suggesting possible reasons for the variances reported;

(c) state, for control purposes, with reasons to support your conclusions:
   (i) whether (b) above is adequate; and
   (ii) whether the statement prepared in respect of the request in (a) above could
        be improved, and if so, how.

(CIMA Cost Accounting)

9.5 Sparks Engineering Ltd manufactures three types of product for the building industry. Budgeted sales of the products, known as D, O and T, for budget period I are:

Product	Quantity	Price
D	3,000	£60
O	7,000	£70
T	5,000	£80

Materials used in the manufacture of the company's products are:

Component ref. no.	1234	1317	1425	2197
Component unit cost	£2	£3	£4	£5
Quantities used				
D	5	3	1	2
O	4	4	2	3
T	3	2	1	5

Two types of labour are used, viz. Assemblers and Wirers, the standard unit times for each product being

	Assemblers (hourly rate £0.5)	Winders (hourly rate £0.6)
D	3 hours	1.5 hours
O	4 "	2 "
T	5 "	2.5 "

Production overhead which is absorbed into product costs on a direct labour hour basis, is budgeted as follows:

	£
Building occupancy	30,050
Equipment utilization	16,100
Personnel services	12,150
Materials handling	9,310
Production planning and control	9,790

Selling and Distribution costs budged for the period are:

	£
Representation	101,300
Sales Office	30,100
Advertising and Publicity	29,100

and are charged to products in proportion to the sales income of the period.
Stocks at the beginning of Period I are expected to be

Finished goods	Quantity	Unit cost £
D	1,000	39
O	3,000	51
T	2,000	51

Components		
1234	40,000	2
1317	20,000	3
1425	10,000	4
2197	30,000	5

The company plans an increase of 10% in the quantities of finished stocks held at the end of Period I, and a reduction of 20% in the quantities of component stocks.

You are required to:
(a) prepare budgets for
    (i)   sales (in quantity and value),
    (ii) production quantities,
    (iii) material usage in quantities,
    (iv) material purchases (in quantity and value),
    (v) direct labour utilization and cost.
(b) prepare a statement showing the valuation of finished stocks at the end of Period I, and
(c) prepare a budgeted Profit Statement for the period, showing the amount of profit contributed by each product.

(ACCA Cost Accounting)

9.6 Your company's sales division is split on a regional basis, north and south. The sales budget had been set at the following levels for the current year. Your company sells only one product with the budgeted price set higher in the south than in the north:

	Budgeted Units	Price	Budgeted Revenue
Northern region	150,000	£10	£1,500,000
Southern region	180,000	£12	£2,160,000
Total	330,000		3,660,000

Actual sales for the year turned out to be 350,000 units of which 40% were in the northern region. The total revenue for the northern region was £1,470,000 and for the southern region was £2,310,000. The budgeted and actual cost was £9 per unit.

The Sales Director has asked you to analyse the above figures before he has a meeting with the Sales Managers of the northern and southern regions.

Required:
(a) Prepare profit statements to show budgeted profit, actual profit and total sales margin variance for each region and for the company as a whole for the year under review.
(b) Prepare sales margin price variances and sales margin quantity variances for each sales region and reconcile to the total sales margin variances calculated in (a) above.
(c) Analyse the above results for the Sales Director, highlighting possible reasons for the variances and action that should be taken.
(d) Outline the methods by which the standards set in a budget for sales volume and sales price will be arrived at.

(AAT Cost accounting and budgeting)

Appendix 1

The annual budgeting process

An outline of the sequence in a manufacturing entity.
Numbers are for identification in the activities - they are not an indication of the sequence.

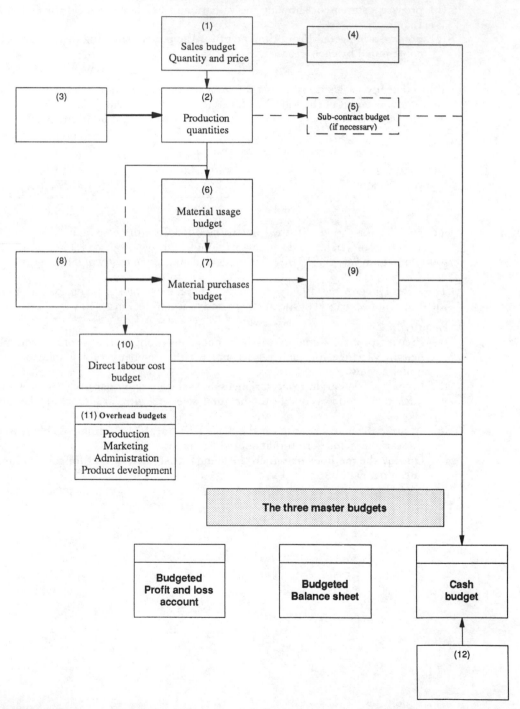

10 ▷ Management of working capital

Objectives

After you have completed this chapter, you should be able to:

- use accounting ratios to calculate the net operating cycle and use this to establish the amount of funding needed for investment in working capital
- describe various techniques and procedures for ensuring that working capital is properly controlled (excluding stock, which was covered in Chapter 4)
- evaluate the effect of changing the credit terms offered to customers, such as a longer credit period to increase sales and cash discounts in order to accelerate cash flows
- construct spreadsheet models that evaluate the effect on cash flow and profit when credit terms are varied

Introduction

Many students for whom this book is intended will already have studied how to calculate and interpret accounting ratios. The subject of accounting ratios is often included in modules on finance and accounting in the context of assessing financial performance. These students also tend to spend some time working on things such as cash budgets, often as part of an assignment on presenting a business plan in order to obtain finance. The two things (accounting ratios and cash budgeting) are often seen as two separate techniques, yet they are very much interrelated when it comes to working capital budgeting.

The monthly cash budget is often used as a technique for estimating the amount of funding required to finance working capital. However, there is no need to do this because the same information can be obtained by using the concept of the net operating cycle (sometimes called the net cash cycle), which makes use of accounting ratios. The monthly cash budget should really be seen as a tool for planning and control.

This chapter also introduces some simple techniques that can be used to evaluate the effect of offering cash discounts to accelerate cash flows and for increasing sales income by offering a longer credit period. The various sections on constructing computer spreadsheet models assumes that readers already have some 'hands-on' experience of using one of the popular spreadsheet packages. If this is not the case, you will find it quite interesting to come back to the examples in this chapter after sorting out how a spreadsheet works.

10.1 The need for working capital

Most business projects require the company to obtain funds for investment in two areas:

1. fixed assets, such as the plant and machinery needed to produce the goods or services for sale
2. working capital (stocks and debtors, less trade creditors)

The reason why investment in working capital is necessary in most cases is because there will be a time lag between the receipt of goods from a supplier and the receipt of cash from customers for the sale of those goods. For example, in the case of a manufacturing entity there will be a considerable time period between receipt of a batch of raw materials from a supplier and the time that money arrives from the sales of the finished product made from those raw materials. During the whole of this period, the company will have to pay all of its operating costs and will probably have to pay its suppliers before any money is received from its customers.

Investment in working capital is a 'necessary evil' for many companies. Entrepreneurs call it 'dead money' because the investment in working capital does not actually add value to anything (except in the case of maturing stocks such as timber, whisky and champagne). If more money is invested in fixed assets the company can produce more products for sale, but if more money is invested in working capital it does not produce more of anything Consequently, companies aim to keep the amount invested in working capital as low as is possible. The amount of working capital needed will depend on two things: the level of trade and the length of net operating cycle for that trade. Managers must watch both things; for example:

- if trade expands, more money will have to be invested in working capital
- components of the net operating cycle (stock holding period, debtor collection period, less creditor payment period) must be closely monitored and controlled.

By keeping the net operating cycle as short as possible, the amount of investment in working capital can be reduced. If you look at published financial statements of retail supermarkets you will find that their working capital is negative (working capital is effectively financed by their creditors). This is because they sell their goods for cash long before they have to pay their suppliers.

10.2 The net operating cycle

The net operating cycle provides a means of estimating the amount of funding needed to finance the whole operating cycle from the time that stock is received to the time that sales income starts to arrive from debtors.

It is easier to see how it works by setting the explanation in the context of a new business. We will use the following contrived situation:

A new trading company is formed on 1 January and has forecast its results for the first year as follows:

Sales (11 × £40,000)	440,000
Cost of sales	220,000
Gross profit	220,000
Overheads	120,000
Net profit	100,000

The above figures were based on sales of £40,000 per month, purchases £20,000 per month and overheads £10,000 per month. In view of the factors mentioned below, it is only possible to achieve 11 months' sales during the first year.

The following estimates are also made:

Stock holding period (time stock is held before being sold) 1 month
Debtor collection period (time debtors take to pay) 2 months
Creditor payment period (time taken to pay creditors) 1 month
All overheads will be paid in the month they are incurred

Brief

The company wishes to determine the amount of funding needed to finance working capital.

Activity 1

Bearing in mind that this is a new business, identify the month during which cash will first start to arrive from debtors.

The company will therefore need sufficient cash (or overdraft facilities) to get through the first three months' operations before it becomes self-financing from sales income. We could find an answer to the problem by setting out a monthly cash flow statement (for example, by assuming an opening cash balance of zero) or we can use the net operating cycle.

The net operating cycle is used to calculate the total **net outflow** of cash during that cycle. There are two types of payment to be made during this period, one for purchases and one for overheads. The purchases are subject to one month's credit, the overheads are on a cash basis. It will therefore be necessary to calculate net operating cycles for each type of cash outflow.

Activity 2

Complete the table below. This requires you to enter the time period (in months) in both columns (purchases and overheads) for the stock holding period and the debtor collection period. The creditor payment period is a minus figure but it relates solely to 'purchases'. There is no creditor payment period for overheads.

Net operating cycle	Purchases (months)	Overheads (months)
Stock holding period		
Debtor collection period	————	————
Less creditor payment period	————	– ————
Net operating cycle		

By relating the net operating cycle to the forecast annual trading figures, it is possible to find the total funding needed to finance working capital. This company needs sufficient finance to enable it to pay for two months' purchases and for three months' overheads.

Activity 3

Calculate the total funding required by completing the following computation:

Purchases (for 2 months)	£
Overheads (for 3 months)	£
Total	

This is simply a convenient way of expressing the fact that the company needs sufficient cash to fund two months' payments to suppliers and three months' payments for overheads, before it starts to receive cash from sales. The same figure could have been determined by the somewhat longer route of setting out a cash flow forecast for the first three months based on the assumption that the opening cash balance was zero. You can prove this for yourself by working through the following activity.

Activity 4

Prepare a cash flow forecast for this example by completing the table set out below. This table has been extended into the fourth month (April) so that you can see how the overdraft starts to reduce as the sales income is received.

Monthly cash flow forecast	Jan	Feb	Mar	Apr
Receipts: Cash from debtors				
Total receipts				
Payments: To creditors for purchases For overheads				
Total payments				
Bank balance: At start of month	0			
At end of month				

It is quite interesting to look at the balance sheet at the end of March. You might initially think that the total of stock, debtors, less creditors will amount to £70,000 (equal to the finance provided by the overdraft) but this is not so. The working capital, excluding the overdraft will be as follows:

Stock (1/12 × £240,000)	20,000
Debtors (2/11 × £440,000)	80,000
	100,000
Less creditors (1/12 × £240,000)	20,000
Net total	80,000

If you assume that there were no other transactions during the three month period, then you can see that £70,000 of these net assets have been financed by a bank overdraft. The question is: 'how has the remaining £10,000 been financed?'

Activity 5

See if you can identify (not calculate) the source of funds for the remaining £10,000.

Activity 6

You can prove this by calculating the profit for the three months to the end of March in the space provided below. Remember that there are two months' sales and three months' overheads in this example.

Sales
Less cost of sales

Gross profit

Less overheads

Profit

The balance sheet at the end of March will be as follows:

Current assets:

Stock		20,000
Debtors		80,000
		100,000

Creditors falling due within one year

Trade creditors	20,000	
Bank overdraft	70,000	
		90,000

Net current assets		10,000

Capital and reserves

Profit and loss account		10,000

The terminology used in balance sheets can sometimes lead to a confused way of thinking. In the above example, the figure of £10,000 for 'net current assets' is often treated as synonymous with 'working capital'. Yet the amount invested in working capital is £80,000 and most of this was financed by the bank. If we had thought of the bank overdraft as a source of funds rather than a liability, the balance sheet could have been set out as follows:

Current assets:

Stock		20,000
Debtors		80,000
		100,000

Creditors falling due within one year

Trade creditors		20,000
		80,000

Funded by:

Bank overdraft		70,000
Profit and loss account		10,000
		80,000

This modified version of net current assets shows how easy it is to be misled by including cash (or overdrafts) in the calculation of working capital. One of the accounting ratios that students are often asked to calculate is known as the 'current ratio'. This ratio is simply a matter of expressing the relationship between current assets and current liabilities, and it is found by dividing current assets by current liabilities. If we use the balance sheet figures set out below Activity 6 we would state that the current ratio was 1.1 to 1, which can be found by dividing £100,000 by £90,000.

Activity 7

Calculate the current ratio using the modified version of the balance sheet shown above the previous paragraph (where the bank overdraft is treated as a source of funds rather than a liability).

It is always very difficult to see how information on the current ratio can be used. A classical interpretation is that if the ratio falls from one year to the next, this is an indication that the company is moving towards financial problems. Yet a reduction of the current ratio might be the result of skilful management of current assets such as stock and debtors. You can see, intuitively if not with figures, that if managers are successful in reducing the levels of stock and debtors the current ratio for the year in which that reduction occurred will be lower than it was in the previous year. This should be interpreted as a healthy sign whereas the classical approach suggests that we are supposed to be worried about it.

However, the purpose of this section is not so much concerned with making sense of the current ratio as it is with whether cash balances (or overdrafts) should be included in the concept of working capital. Cash is a general pool of funds, and this pool does not merely ebb and flow with trading transactions. There are many transactions apart from trading that cause cash to increase and decrease.

Activity 8

Make a note here of some of the transactions (apart from routine trading transactions) that will result in cash inflows and cash outflows.

Since cash is generated (or consumed) by both capital and trading transactions, it should be excluded from any consideration of the amount that needs to be invested in working capital. The management of cash (surpluses or deficits) is really a separate issue to the management of the main working capital items such as stock, debtors and creditors.

If we vary the details on which we have been working we can see why retail supermarkets are able to operate on a negative working capital. Assume that the details used in Activity 2 are changed so that we are dealing with a cash sale business. The net operating cycle would be as follows:

Net operating cycle	Purchases (months)	Overheads (months)
Stock holding period	1	1
Debtor collection period	0	0
	1	1
Less creditor payment period	(1)	–
Net operating cycle	0	1

This shows that the company will need sufficient funding to finance one month's overheads and that thereafter it will be self financing from sales income. If the figures were presented in a monthly cash flow statement (assuming a starting cash balance of zero) they would be as follows:

Monthly cash flow forecast	Jan	Feb	Mar	Apr
Receipts:				
Cash from customers	0	40,000	40,000	40,000
Total receipts	0	40,000	40,000	40,000
Payments:				
To creditors for purchases	0	20,000	20,000	20,000
For overheads	10,000	10,000	10,000	10,000
Total payments	10,000	30,000	30,000	30,000
Bank balance:				
At start of month	0	(10,000)	0	10,000
At end of month	(10,000)	0	10,000	20,000

As you can see, the company is starting to build up cash surpluses at the rate of £10,000 per month after February. It is incumbent upon managers to decide how these cash surpluses are invested. There is no point in leaving them as uninvested cash. If we assume that the £20,000 surplus at the end of April is invested in fixed assets (perhaps some kind of expansion of the retail facilities) the balance sheet at the end of April will be as follows:

Fixed assets		20,000
Current assets		
Stock (1 month)	20,000	
Creditors falling due within one year		
Creditors	20,000	
		0
		20,000
Financed by:		
Profit and loss account:		
Sales (3 × 40,000)	120,000	
Cost of sales (3 × 20,000)	60,000	
Gross profit	60,000	
Overheads (4 × 10,000)	40,000	
		20,000

In the above example, the current ratio is 1:1. It does not require a great deal of imagination to see that if the stock holding period were reduced to (say) half a month, there would be £20,000 cash received in January, resulting in a cash balance of £40,000 by the end of April. If this is all invested in fixed assets, the current assets would be stock of £10,000 and current liabilities would be creditors of £20,000. There would be a current ratio of 0.5:1 (which is fairly typical of most retail supermarkets), as follows:

Fixed assets (investment of surplus cash)		40,000
Current assets		
Stock (1/2 month)	10,000	
Creditors falling due within one year		
Creditors	20,000	
		(10,000)
		30,000
Financed by:		
Profit and loss account		
(3.5 × (40,000 − 20,000)) − (4 × 10,000)		30,000

The important points to be learned from this series of exercises are:

- the amount invested in working capital is dependent upon the net operating cycle and the level of trade
- firms aim to keep the net operating cycle as short as possible in order to maximize funds available for investment in resources that actually generate income

- if trade increases, the level of debtors will increase. For example, if the level of credit sales in Year 1 is £120,000 and the credit period granted is one month, we would expect debtors at the end of the year to be (1/12 × £120,000) £10,000. If credit sales during the next year were doubled to £240,000 we would also expect debtors to double to (1/12 × £240,000) £20,000
- a cash surplus (or overdraft) should not be treated as a part of the working capital because it represents a general pool of funds that is affected by cash flows outside of the day-to-day trading transactions
- the current ratio as used in financial analysis is ambiguous; interpretation of the current ratio is impossible without knowledge of the operating cycle and without making reference to the cash flow statement (as published by most companies)

10.3 Management of debtors

There are three factors to consider:

1. credit control and debt collection procedures
2. extending credit periods to increase sales
3. accelerating cash inflows by offering cash discounts.

Debt collection and credit control

It should be apparent from your study of section 10.2 that companies need to exercise some kind of control over the granting of credit and over debt collection. If debtors exploit the granting of credit by not paying on the due date the company will be denied funds that could be invested in profit earning activities. Strictly speaking, the cost to the company of its investment in debtors is the cost of capital but you might find it difficult to grasp this concept until you study Chapter 12. For the time being you can think of the cost of capital as being related to the amounts paid to those who have provided the capital such as shareholders and lenders.

In Chapter 4 you gave some thought to the cost of capital in relation to the cost of holding stock. This was presented in the context of why it is necessary for companies to control their stock holding levels. The same considerations apply to the cost of holding debtors, and for the need to control the level of debtors.

Activity 9

Make a note here of some of the procedures that companies could adopt to exercise control over the granting of credit and collection of debts.

Extending credit to increase sales

There is little doubt that customers do see the extension of credit as an incentive to buy. You have probably seen eye-catching notices on shop fronts saying something like: 'buy now, pay in three-months' time'. This kind of trading has become more common in recent times as companies grapple with the problem of finding ways out of a recession. The increase in sales will provide benefits in the form of increased contribution from the additional sales, but there is a cost.

Activity 10

Try to identify three types of cost associated with granting an extended credit period. One of these (perhaps the most costly) was mentioned in the previous section on debt collection.

1.

2.

3.

The cost of holding additional debtors is only one element in the equation. Increased trade might entail holding additional stocks, although this could be ameliorated by some kind of JIT stock management. The cost of holding additional stocks is usually compensated to some extent by an increase in the total level of credit granted by suppliers. The provision of finance in the form of trade credit is often seen as cost free – there can be a cost but we will ignore that for the time being.

In order to evaluate whether an extension of credit is likely to be beneficial, it is necessary to compare the contribution earned on additional sales with the additional costs. We will work on the following simplified example:

- Current annual sales: £1.200,000
- Contribution to sales ratio: 25%
- Current credit period: 1 month

The company's cost of capital is 20%. The company estimates that if the credit period were extended to 2 months there would be a 10% increase in annual sales. The additional trade would result in stock holding levels being increased by £8,000 and there would be additional creditors of £6,000. At the current level of sales, bad debts are approximately 1% of sales. This is expected to increase to $1^{1}/_{2}$% of sales under the new credit arrangements. There will be no increase in administration costs.

The task

Evaluate whether the proposal to increase the credit period is likely to be beneficial to the company.

Activity 11

The first step is to calculate the increase in profit. This will consist of the additional contribution earned from the additional sales, less the **increase** in the cost of bad debts:

Contribution from additional sales   £
Less:
Increase in bad debt expense   £
_____

Increase in profit

We now need to calculate the cost of the additional investment in working capital. In this example there is an increase in debtors, an increase in stocks, less an increase in creditors.

Activity 12

Calculate the additional amount invested in working capital. Ignore the incidence of bad debts when doing this calculation and assume that all customers will take advantage of the extended credit period.

Increase in debtors   £
Increase in stocks

_____

Less increase in creditors

_____

Increase in amount invested in working capital

The cost of financing the additional £122,000 is (.20 × £122,000) £24,400. The relevant figures can now be summarized as follows:

Increased profits from additional sales	22,200
Financing costs	24,400
Net benefit or (cost)	(2,200)

In this example, the figures suggest that the proposal is not beneficial but managers could take the view that the net cost of £2,200 falls within an acceptable range of error and decide to go ahead in any case. If you are familiar with the use of a spreadsheet you could try setting up a model based on the details for this example and making the percentage increase in sales as a variable input. If you do this, you will find that the proposal becomes beneficial when the increase in sales is 11% or more, and this is fairly close to the estimates made.

The example as a spreadsheet model

You will have to skip the activity in this section if you are not familiar with the way that spreadsheets work. You can always return to it at some later time. In the spreadsheet shown in Figure 10.1, the shaded cells represent those where the amounts were entered from the keyboard. The unshaded cells contain formulae and they return amounts according to the formula entered in each cell. The model relates to the above example and was designed to see what would happen by varying the input for cell C7, the percentage increase in sales (set at 10% in the example below). It can also be used to see the effect of varying other inputs such as number of months in debtors and the forecast bad debts percentage.

Fig. 10.1

	A	B	C
1		Current	Proposed
2	Sales	1,200,000	1,320,000
3	CSR	0.25	0.25
4			
5	Months in debtors	1	2
6			
7	Sales increase %		0.1
8	Bad debts %	0.01	0.015
9			
10	Additional contribution		30,000
11	Additional bad debts		7,800
12	Additional profit		22,200
13			
14	Additional debtors		120,000
15	Additional stock		8,000
16	Additional creditors		(6,000)
17			122,000
18			
19	Cost of capital	0.2	24,400
20			
21	Net benefit/-cost		(2,200)

Activity 13

Identify the formula that would have been entered in each of the following cells. Ignore the symbol that might have to precede each formula (such as @ or –) because this will depend on the spreadsheet package being used.

C2:   C11:

C10:   C14:

Offering cash discount to accelerate cash flows

In some ways the evaluation of a proposal to offer cash discounts is the reverse of how we evaluated the increase in sales by offering more generous credit terms. The basic approach is to compare the cost of the discount with the benefit gained by releasing funds. This benefit can be viewed either as a saving in the cost of capital or as the income that can be earned by investing the released funds at the cost of capital. In some cases there could be further variables to take into account; for example, the offer of a cash discount might result in a different level of sales and of bad debts. In the following example we will assume that there is no change in the level of sales demand and no change in the level of bad debts:

- Current annual level of sales : £1,200,000
- Current average debt collection period: 2 months

The company proposes to offer a cash discount of 2% for early settlement. The discount can be deducted if debtors pay within 15 days. It is estimated that one-half of the company's customers will take advantage of this discount. There will be no increase in debt collection costs and no increase in the level of sales. The company's cost of capital is 24%.

The task

Evaluate whether the proposal will be beneficial to the company.

The first step is to calculate the amount of funds that will be released by a reduction in debtors. Prior to introduction of the cash discount, debtors will average (2/12 × £1,200,000) £200,000 throughout the year. We now need to establish the average level of debtors if the discount is offered. One-half of the sales are to customers who will take 15 days credit, the other half will be to customers who take 2 months' credit. You can assume that 15 days is the same as half a month in the calculations for the following activity. Remember that debtors in this activity represent the gross debtors prior to deducting the discount.

Activity 14

Calculate the estimated total level of debtors if the cash discount is offered. You can do this by adding the following:

Debtors with 15 days (half a month) outstanding   £

Debtors with 2 months outstanding   _____

    Total

The amount of funds released will therefore be as follows:

Debtors prior to cash discount scheme	£200,000
Debtors after discount scheme	125,000
	75,000

The funds released of £75,000 can be used to earn (or save) the company 24% of £75,000 and this amounts to (£75,000 × .24) £18,000 per annum.

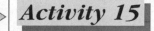

Activity 15

Calculate the annual cost of the discount. This is simply 2% of half the annual sales.

In this case the proposal appears to be beneficial. There is a benefit to the company of £18,000 at a cost of £12,000.

The example as a spreadsheet model

In setting up a spreadsheet on the above example, it would be helpful if it were constructed in such a way as to see the effect of varying the cash discount rate and varying the proportion of debtors who might take advantage of the discount. The example in Figure 10.2 is not necessarily the most sophisticated model but it does allow a number of inputs to be varied for the 'what if' experiments. Three of the cells have been shaded for identification in the activity.

Fig. 10.2

	A	B	C	D
1		Existing	Proposed	Gain
2	Annual sales	1,200,000	1,200,000	
3	Proportion of debtors taking:			
4	Full credit terms	100%	50%	
5	Cash discount terms	N/A	50%	
6				
7	Months in debtors for customers taking:			
8	Full credit terms	2	2	
9	Cash discount terms	N/A	0.5	
10				
11	Discount rate		2%	
12				
13	Average debtors	200,000	125,000	75,000
14	Cost of capital	24%		
15				
16	Gain through investment of funds released			18,000
17	Annual cost of discount			12,000
18	Net benefit/-cost			6,000

Activity 16

The formula entered in cell C5 (shaded) was designed to respond to changes in the input for cell C4. Identify the formulae that would have been entered in the following cells:

C5:

C13:

D17:

A more sophisticated way of evaluating the effect of offering cash discounts is to use a discounted cash flow (DCF) approach. DCF is covered in Chapter 12 but it is presented there in the context of long-term (capital) investment appraisal. It should, however, be possible for you to see how the general principles could be applied to debtor management after completing a study of Chapter 12.

10.4 Trade credit

Trade credit is a source of short-term finance. It is often assumed that trade credit is cost-free because suppliers do not charge interest for the period that the amount remains unpaid. This tends to lead to a general belief that it makes good business sense to delay payment as long as possible, perhaps beyond the due date. This belief is not entirely well founded: trade credit can have a cost for the following reasons:

- suppliers might offer a discount for early settlement; if this is not taken there is a cost equal to the lost discount
- some suppliers do charge interest on amounts not paid within the normal credit terms
- delaying payment beyond the due date can cause a loss of supplier goodwill and might result in that creditor refusing to supply further goods or services
- if a company acquires a reputation as a bad payer its credit rating will deteriorate, thus making it more difficult to obtain credit elsewhere

It is difficult to quantify costs such as loss of goodwill and loss of credit rating. It is, however, possible to quantify the cost of lost discounts.

Evaluation of lost discount

When creditors offer a cash discount for early settlement, the company has two options: it can pay the full amount charged at the end of the normal credit period, or it can pay a smaller amount at the end of the period to which the cash discount terms apply. If it chooses not to pay early, the cash that it would have had to pay at that time will remain invested in the business. This amount will remain invested in the business for the period between the date of early settlement and the normal settlement date. Evaluation of the lost discount can be based on a comparison of two amounts:

1. the amount that would have been paid if the cash discount were taken, and
2. the full amount of the invoice **less** the income that would be earned by retaining the amount in 1 and leaving it invested until the normal due date.

This might be easier to see by using an example.

Example

A company has an invoice of £10,000 outstanding. The normal credit terms are for payment within 60 days but the supplier offers a cash discount of 2% for settlement within 10 days. The company is able to invest funds that give a return of 25% per annum.

Activity 17

Calculate the amount that the company will pay if it accepts the cash discount terms.

If the amount in Activity 17 is not paid, it will remain invested in the business for another (60–10) 50 days and the company will be able to earn income on this at the rate of 25% per annum.

Activity 18

Calculate the amount of income earned on investing £9,800 for 50 days at the rate of 25% per annum.

The comparison between the two options is therefore as follows:

	Accept	Refuse
Amount paid	£9,800	£10,000
Less income earned on cash retained		336
Net cost	£9,800	£9,664

In the circumstances described in the example, the cash discount will be refused. It is possible to use a formula to estimate the implied interest cost of refusing cash discounts. This can then be compared to the company's own rate of return on investments. In the above example, the implied interest cost is approximately as follows:

$$\frac{2}{98} \times \frac{365}{50} = 15\%$$

As you can see, this is somewhat less than what the company earns on its own investments.

The example as a spreadsheet model

Readers who are familiar with spreadsheets will know that financial models are not designed to produce a single answer to a unique problem. They are set up so that some inputs can be varied to see what would happen when these inputs are varied. In designing a model for the above example, it might be useful to know what the answer would be if the credit periods were different to the 10 and 60 days given, or if the discount rate and investment rate were different to those given, or if the invoice was for a different amount. In the example given in Figure 10.3, the amounts in cells B1 to B5 were all entered from the keyboard. The remaining figures (in the block C7 to D11) are the results of formulae entered in those cells. Some of the formulae are quite simple, for example D7 is merely a reference to B1 and the formula in cell C7 is B1 − (B3 × B1).

Fig. 10.3

	A	B	C	D
1	Invoice amount	10,000		
2	Normal credit terms (days)	60		
3	Discount offered	2%		
4	Discount credit terms (days)	10		
5	Company's return on investment	25%		
6			Accept	Refuse
7	Amount paid		9,800	10,000
8	Less income earned from			
9	investing £9,800 for 50 days			336
10				
11	Net cost		9,800	9,664

Activity 19

Identify the formula that would have been entered in the shaded cell D9.

Activity 20

As a final activity for this chapter you could set up a spreadsheet model for this example on the lines suggested. After you have done this, deal with the following:

All variables are to remain the same as the original example except for the normal credit period of 60 days. Ascertain from your model the length of normal credit at which there is virtually no difference in net cost between paying early or taking the full credit term. After you have done this, prove that the implied interest cost in that case is (roughly) 25% (the same as the company's return on investments) by using the formula given after Activity 18.

Summary

The key learning points in this chapter can be summarized as follows:
- in most companies there are two major areas where funds are invested: fixed assets and working capital
- the amount of funds required for investment in working capital will depend on the net operating cycle and the level of trade
- if the volume of trade increases, working capital will increase proportionately

- firms aim to keep the amount invested in working capital as low as possible by keeping the net operating cycle as short as possible
- the length of net operating cycle can be reduced by operating JIT stock management techniques, by strict credit control on debtors and by making use of trade credit
- sales can be stimulated by offering more generous credit terms; the effect on profit can be evaluated by comparing the increased contribution with the cost of carrying a larger amount of debtors and (possibly) a higher bad debt expense
- cash flows from debtors can be accelerated by offering cash discounts; the effect on profit can be evaluated by comparing the cost of the discount with the income earned on the funds released
- trade credit is not necessarily cost-free, the cost of not taking cash discounts is one example of the cost of trade credit
- the financial effect of not accepting cash discounts for early settlement can be evaluated in one of two ways: (i) by calculating the implied interest rate and comparing this to the company's return on capital, or (ii) by comparing the cash discounted payment with the full payment less the income that could be earned on the cash retained between the two settlement dates
- delaying payment beyond the due date might involve the company in the hidden cost of suppliers refusing to make further suppliers and a loss of credit rating
- spreadsheet models are only useful if they are constructed in such a way as to show what would happen to the results if one of the inputs to that model was changed

Activity 1
April

Activity 2

	Purchases	Overheads
Stock holding period	1	1
Debtor collection period	2	2
	3	3
Less creditor payment period	(1)	–
Net operating cycle	2	3

Activity 3

Purchases $2/11 \times 220{,}000$ (or $2 \times 20{,}000$)	40,000
Overheads $3/12 \times 120{,}000$ (or $3 \times 10{,}000$)	30,000
Total	70,000

Activity 4

Monthly cash flow forecast	Jan	Feb	Mar	Apr
Receipts:				
Cash from debtors	0	0	0	40,000
Total receipts	0	0	0	40,000
Payments:				
To creditors for purchases	0	20,000	20,000	20,000
For overheads	10,000	10,000	10,000	10,000
Total payments	10,000	30,000	30,000	30,000
Bank balance:				
At start of month	0	(10,000)	(40,000)	(70,000)
At end of month	(10,000)	(40,000)	(70,000)	(60,000)

Activity 5
The profit earned on the sales (included in debtors).

Activity 6

Sales (2 × 40,000)	80,000
Cost of sales	40,000
Gross profit	40,000
Less overheads (3 × 10,000)	30,000
Profit	10,000

Activity 7

100,000/80,000 = 1.25:1.

Activity 8

Cash inflows from: share issues, issues of loan stocks, sale of fixed assets, investment income. Cash outflows from: repayment of capital (this is usually repayment of loans although it can include a redemption of share capital), purchase of fixed assets, payment of taxation, payment of dividends.

Activity 9

Seeking trade references, or credit ratings from credit rating agencies. Setting credit limits. Strict follow-up routines when debts become overdue. Stopping supply of further goods until outstanding debts are paid.

Activity 10

You might have listed the following:
1. Opportunity cost of capital tied up in increased debtors.
2. Increase in bad debt expense.
3. Increase in administration costs.
(You might have mentioned the matter discussed in the text following this activity – if so, give yourself a bonus point!)

Activity 11

Note the following:
Sales will increase by (.1 × £1,200,000) £120,000.
Bad debts expense will increase by (.015 × £1,320,000) − (.01 × £1,200,000) £7,800.

Contribution from additional sales (.25 × £120,000)	30,000
Less increase in bad debts expense (see above)	7,800
Increase in profit	22,200

Activity 12

Current debtors are 1/12 × £1,200,000	100,000
New debtors will be 2/12 × £1,320,000	220,000
Increase	120,000
Increase in debtors (as above)	120,000
Increase in stocks	8,000
	128,000
Less increase in creditors	6,000
Increase in amount invested in working capital	122,000

Activity 13
C2: B2+(C7 × B2)
C10: C3 × (C2 − B2)
C11: (C2 × C8) − (B2 × B8)
C14: (C2 × C5/12) − (B2 × B5/12)

Activity 14

Debtors with 15 days outstanding (0.5/12 × £600,000)	25,000
Debtors with 2 months outstanding (2/12 × £600,000)	100,000
Total	125,000

Activity 15
$600,000 \times .02 = £12,000$.

Activity 16
C5: 1 − C4
C13: (C4 × C2 × C8/12) + (C5 × C2 × C9/12)
D17: C11 × C5 × C2

Activity 17
$98\% \times £10,000 = £9,800$.

Activity 18
$£9,800 \times .25 \times 50/365 = £336$ (rounded).

Activity 19
B5 × (B2 − B4)/365 × C7

Activity 20
It occurs (roughly) at 40 days. The interest rate is:

$$\frac{2}{98} \times \frac{365}{(40-10)} = 25\% \text{ (rounded)}$$

Questions for self assessment

Answers to self-assessment questions are given at the end of the book.

10.1 The following information has been extracted from the accounts of Hardings Ltd for the year to 31 March 1989:

Trading items	£000
Sales	1,620
Purchases	930
Cost of goods sold	900

Summarized balance sheet at 31 March 1989

	£		£
Fixed assests at cost	400,000	Share capital	400,000
Less: Accumulated	170,000	Retained profit	142,500
depreciation	170,000		
	230,000		542,500
Investments	50,000		
Stock*	150,000		
Trade debtors*	180,000	Trade creditors*	77,500
Bank balance*	10,000		
	620,000		620,000

*Assume that each of these balances remained steady over the 12 months to 31 March 1989.

There is a strong demand for the goods traded in by Hardings Ltd, and an expansion plan is currently being put into operation. Plant costing £150,000 is to be purchased and paid for in June 1989 and, from 1 July, the scale of trading operations is expected to increase by 25%. Each of the components of the operating cycle, in days, is to remain unchanged. The present bank balance is just sufficient to support the current level of operations, and the company's bank has agreed to provide overdraft finance to meet cash requirements arising over the forthcoming 12 months.

The following information has been extracted from the forecast profit and loss account of Hardings Ltd for the year to 31 March 1990:

Profit and loss account extracts, year to 31 March 1990

	£000
Trading profit before depreciation:	
April–June	30
June March	130
	160
Less: Depreciation	60
	100
Add: Extraordinary profit on the sale (1 June 1989) of the investments shown in the above balance sheet	15
	115

Required:
(a) Calculate for the financial year to 31 March 1989, in days:
    (i) the rate of stock turnover
    (ii) the rate of collection of debts
    (iii) the rate of payment of creditors
    (iv) the cash operating cycle.
(b) Calculate the *additional* working capital requirement which results from the implementation of the expansion proposals.
(c) Calculate the overdraft requirement on 1 July 1989 (assume that the whole of the *additional* working capital requirement arises on 1 July 1989 for the purpose of this calculation).
(d) Prepare Hardings' forecast balance sheet as at 31 March 1990.
(e) Assess, briefly, the financial implications of the plans for expansion from the viewpoint of a lending bank.

Notes:
 (i) *Ignore interest payable on any bank overdraft.*
 (ii) *Ignore taxation.*
(iii) *Assume a 360 day year for the purpose of your calculations. No dividends are to be paid for the year to 31 March 1990.*

(CIB Accountancy)

10.2   International Electric plc at present offers its customers 30 days credit. Half the customers, by value, pay on time. The other half take an average of 70 days to pay. It is considering offering a cash discount of 2% to its customers for payment within 30 days.

It anticipates that half of the customers who now take an average of 70 days to pay, will pay in 30 days. The other half will still take an average of 70 days to pay. The scheme will also reduce bad debts by £300,000 per year.

Annual sales of £365 million are made evenly throughout the year. At present the company can borrow from its banks at 12% per annum.

Required:
(a) Calculate the approximate equivalent annual percentage cost of a discount of 2% which reduces the time taken by debtors to pay from 70 to 30 days. (This part can be answered without reference to the narrative above.)
(b) Calculate debtors outstanding under both the old and new schemes.
(c) How much will the scheme cost the company in discounts?
(d) Should the company go ahead with the scheme? State what other factors, if any, should be taken into account.
(e) Outline the controls and procedures a company should adopt to manage the level of its debtors.

(ACCA Certified diploma)

10.3   Linpet was incorporated on 1 June 1989. The opening balance sheet of the company was as follows:

	£
Assets	
Cash at bank	60,000
Share capital	
£1 ordinary shares	60,000

During June the company intends to make payments of £40,000 for a freehold property, £10,000 for equipment and £6,000 for a motor vehicle. The company will also purchase initial trading stock costing £22,000 on credit.

The company has produced the following estimates:

(i) Sales for June will be £8,000 and will increase at the rate of £3,000 per month until September. In October sales will rise to £22,000 and in subsequent months sales will be maintained at this figure.

(ii) The gross profit percentage on goods sold will be 25%.

(iii) There is a risk that supplies of trading stock will be interrupted towards the end of the accounting year. The company, therefore, intends to build up its initial level of stock (i.e. £22,000) by purchasing £1,000 of stock each month in addition to the monthly purchases necessary to satisfy monthly sales. All purchases of stock (including the initial stock) will be on one month credit.

(iv) Sales will be divided equally between cash and credit sales. Credit customers are expected to pay two months after the sale is agreed.

(v) Wages and salaries will be £900 per month. Other overheads will be £500 per month for the first four months and £650 thereafter. Both types of expense will be payable when incurred.

(vi) 80% of sales will be generated by salesmen who will receive 5% commission on sales. The commission is payable one month after the sale is agreed.

(vii) The company intends to purchase further equipment in November 1989 for £7,000 cash.

(viii) Depreciation is to be provided at the rate of 5% per annum on freehold property and 20% per annum on equipment. (Depreciation has not been included in the overheads mentioned in (v) above.)

Required:

(a) Outline three reasons why a business would wish to hold some of its assets in the form of cash or short-term equivalents.

(b) State why a cash budget is required for a business.

(c) Prepare a cash budget for Linpet Ltd for the six month period to 30 November 1989.

(ACCA *Certified diploma*)

10.4 The following forecasts are provided in respect of Grassington Ltd for 1994:

	£000
Sales	2,700
Purchases	1,800
Cost of goods sold	1,830
Average trade debtors outstanding	300
Average trade creditors outstanding	160
Average stocks held	305

All purchases and sales are made on credit, and trading transactions are expected to occur at an even rate throughout the year.

Required:

(a) Calculation of the cash operating cycle.

(b) The bank are seeking a reduction of £20,000 in the company's overdraft. Indicate the various ways that this can be achieved through the management of working capital and demonstrate the effect of your suggestions on the cash operating cycle.

(*based on CIB Accountancy*)

Questions without answers

Answers to these questions are published separately in the *Teacher's Manual*.

10.5 The finance director of Pondwood Ltd wishes to prepare an estimate of next year's working capital requirements.

Sales for the next year are expected to be 85,500 units at a basic unit price of £50. Direct materials, direct wages and direct energy costs are expected to be £15.51 per unit, £17.35 per unit and £4.95 per unit respectively. Administrative salaries are forecast to be £264,000, and distribution and other overheads a total of £92,000.

Corporate taxation is at a rate of 35%, payable one year in arrears.

The current year's profit before taxation, after deducting interest payments of £118,000 for the company's overdraft, is £311,000.

Pondwood offers its customers a 2½% cash discount for payment within 14 days. On average 40% of customers take this discount, and the remainder take an average of 10 weeks to pay for their goods.

Stocks of raw materials equivalent to 4 weeks usage are held, and finished goods equivalent to 8 weeks demand. The production process takes an average of 4 weeks. Work in progress is valued at the cost of materials for the full period of the production process and the cost of wages and energy for half the period of the production process. Pondwood is allowed 8 weeks credit from its suppliers of raw materials and 6 weeks credit for distribution and other fixed costs. Energy bills are payable quarterly in arrears.

The company pays wages one week in arrears and salaries one month in arrears (one month may be assumed to be 4 weeks).

Pondwood's existing overdraft facility has recently been extended to cover the next financial year. The interest rate payable on the company's overdraft has remained at 11% per year during the past year, and is not expected to change during the foreseeable future. The company has utilized its full overdraft facility during the past year.

Required:
(a) Evaluate whether, on the basis of the above information, the company's overdraft facility is likely to be large enough to finance the company's working capital needs for the next year.

State clearly any assumptions that you make.

A monthly cash budget is not required as part of your evaluation.
(b) What other information would be helpful in the assessment of the company's overdraft requirements?

(ACCA Financial Management)

10.6 Worral Ltd is a wholly owned subsidiary of Grandus plc. Grandus has always allowed its subsidiaries considerable freedom of action, but the board of directors of Grandus are concerned about Worral's recent performance and working capital management. As a result Grandus's board of directors has given the managers of Worral one year in which to increase the company's current ratio to at least the industry average, without adversely affecting other aspects of the company's performance.

Worral's managers are considering three possible alternative courses of action:
(i) Increase long-term loans by £300,000 and use the proceeds to reduce the company's overdraft.
(ii) Offer a cash discount of 3% for payment in 14 days. The normal terms of sale allow 60 days credit. All sales are on a credit basis. If the cash discount is offered 50% of customers are expected to take it, and bad debts are expected to be halved. The annual cost of administering the cash discount scheme would be £30,000.
(iii) Use the services of a non-recourse factoring company at a commission of 2.5% of turnover and finance charges of 3% over bank base rate on funds advanced immediately. Worral would take the full finance facility available on all credit sales, and would use the proceeds to reduce current liabilities. The use of a factor is expected to result in credit management cost savings of £135,000 per year.

Bank base rate is 11%. Worral pays 2% above bank base rate for its overdraft.

Summarized financial details of Worral Ltd

	1984	1985	1986	1987	Industry Average 1987
	£000	£000	£000	£000	
Turnover	8,234	8,782	8,646	9,182	–
Profit after tax	486	492	448	465	–
Current ratio	1.84	1.61	1.52	1.48	1.60
Acid test	0.97	0.93	0.90	0.84	0.95
Gearing	75.4%	74.6%	79.2%	85.8%	75%
Bad debts/sales	0.5%	0.9%	1.2%	1.5%	0.5%
Collection period (days)	60	73	92	107	60

Summarized balance sheet as at 31 December 1987

	£000	£000
Fixed assets		3,200
Current assets:		
Stock	2,100	
Debtors	2,684	
Cash	90	
		4874
Less: Current liabilities:		
Overdraft	1,650	
Other	1,643	
		3,293
		4,781
Financed by:		
Shareholders' funds		3,461
12% long-term loan 2008–12		1,320
		4,781

The long-term loan is from Grandus plc. Long-term loans to subsidiaries are charged at their current cost to Grandus. Grandus's 12% £100 debentures 2008–12 are currently trading at £82.75.

Required:
Critically evaluate the three suggestions and recommend which should be selected. All relevant calculations must be shown. The effects of taxation may be ignored.

(ACCA *Financial Management*)

10.7 Control of working capital is a vital part of short-term financial management.

Required:
Explain the means by which a manufacturing company may seek to maintain the optimum levels of:
(a) stocks of raw materials, work in progress and finished goods.
(b) trade debtors.

(ACCA *Certified diploma*)

10.8 Designer Dresses Limited is a small company to be formed by James and William Clark to sell an exclusive range of dresses from a boutique in a fashionable suburb of London. On 1 January 1989 they plan to invest £50,000 cash to purchase 25,000 £1 shares each in the company. Of this £30,000 is to be invested in new fittings in January. These fittings are to be depreciated over 3 years on the straight line basis (their scrap value is assumed to be zero at the end of their lives). A half year's depreciation is to be charged in the first six months. The sales and purchases forecast for the company are as follows:

£000	Jan	Feb	Mar	Apr	May	June	Total
Sales	10.2	30.6	30.6	40.8	40.8	51.0	204.0
Purchases	20.0	30.0	25.0	25.0	30.0	30.0	160.0
Other costs*	9.0	9.0	9.0	9.0	9.0	9.0	54.0

*These include wages but exclude depreciation.

The sales will all be made by credit card. The credit card company will take one month to pay and will deducts its fee of 2% of gross sales before paying amounts due to Designer Dresses. One month's credit is allowed by suppliers. Other costs shown above do not include rent and rates of £10,000 per quarter, payable on 1 January and 1 April. All other costs will be paid in cash. Closing stock at the end of June is expected to be £58,000.

You should ignore taxation. For your convenience you are advised to work to the nearest £000.

Required:
(a) Prepare a cash forecast for the 6 months to 30 June 1989.
(b) Prepare a forecast profit and loss account for the same period.
(c) Prepare a forecast balance sheet at 30 June 1989.
(d) Comment briefly on the financial prospects of Designer Dresses. You should refer both to its profitability and liquidity.

(ACCA *Certified diploma*)

11 ▷ Relevant costs and short-term decisions

Objectives

After you have completed this chapter, you should be able to:

- explain why costs and revenues that are relevant to profit measurements are not necessarily relevant for making decisions
- apply the general principle that because decisions affect future events, the relevant costs (and revenues) are the future cash flows arising from those decisions
- evaluate various types of decision problem by identifying the relevant costs and revenues applicable to each problem
- describe and apply the concept of opportunity cost
- evaluate various types of decision problem by using the concept of contribution for finding an optimum solution

Introduction

In some ways the title of this chapter is misleading because we will be trying to identify both relevant costs and relevant revenues when helping managers to make decisions. It would, however, be wrong to use a title such as *'relevant information'*, because this implies a much wider subject than is covered by the contents of this chapter. A study of relevant information should include various 'qualitative' aspects of decision making, whereas we will be concerned mainly with searching for the relevant figures.

The decision problems in this chapter are all 'short-run' decisions, they are usually concerned with maximizing profits in the immediate future. Long-term decision making is a separate subject. The quantitative techniques used for helping managers with long-term decisions are covered in the next chapter. But the two subjects are closely linked. When you come to study investment appraisal in Chapter 12 you will find the quantitative techniques are very easy to learn – they amount to little more than multiplying and adding. The skill of presenting managers with information for long-term decisions is not so much a matter of being able to do the calculations but in selecting the relevant inputs for those calculations. This includes selecting relevant costs and revenues in much the same way as we do for short-term decisions.

11.1 Relevant costs: General principles

Cost recording systems tend to be dominated by the need to report profits and assets to the shareholders. Traditional accounting information does not usually help managers to make decisions about what to do in the future. Decisions affect what happens in the future; the past has happened and cannot be changed by anything. The relevant quantitative data that will help managers to make decisions often includes both costs and revenues. It is almost impossible to provide a general rule that can be applied to all decision problems, but the following definition works in the majority of cases:

> *Relevant costs, and relevant revenues, are future cash flows that will arise as a direct consequence of the decision.*

You must keep in mind that although a cost (or revenue) might not be relevant to the decision, it could well be relevant to profit measurement – but that is a different problem. Sometimes, you might feel tempted to tabulate data for decision making in the form of a profit statement. This might not necessarily result in managers making bad decisions (although it could) but it does mean that you are not thinking in terms of relevant costs and revenues. Consider this in relation to the following example.

Example

A company holds an item of stock which had cost £600 to buy. This stock item has been damaged and can either be sold now for £500, or it can be repaired at a cost of £20 and sold for £560. There are no other options open to the company.

In this particular case the details are so simple that a manager would know the best course of action (repair and sell) without requiring any kind of evaluation from the accountant. But if we were to ask someone who had not studied this subject to set out the relevant information in a way that would help with the decision, it is more than likely that the following kind of computation would be prepared:

		Sell damaged £500		Repair and sell £560
Sale proceeds		£500		£560
Less:				
Original cost	600		600	
Repair cost	nil		20	
		600		620
Loss		100		60

The above would be a natural response to the request for numerical information because we are so accustomed to thinking in terms of profit measurement. As it happens, no harm would be done in this case because the statement will enable the manager to make the best choice (repair and sell to minimize the loss). But when you look at the statement it does contain information that is not relevant to the decision.

Activity 1

Identify the information that is not relevant to this decision.

There are two ways of justifying why this information is irrelevant. In the first place (and this is the most important point) it is a past cost that cannot be changed by a decision affecting the future. Secondly, you will notice that the same amount (£600) appears under each alternative, indicating that it is not affected by the decision (in this case because it is a past cost). Non-relevant costs are sometimes described as those that do not change as between the alternatives, but this is not always as helpful as thinking in terms of future cash flows arising as a direct consequence of the decision.

One way of producing relevant information for the above decision problem is to use an incremental approach, similar to the way in which we produced a solution for the dairy products manufacturer in Chapter 6 (Section 6.4). A presentation in this form could be as follows:

	Sell damaged	Repair and sell	Incremental gain/(loss)
Future cash inflow	£500	£560	£60
Future cash outflow	nil	(20)	(20)
Future net inflow	500	£540	£40

This shows (something that we knew from the start of this simple example) that future income from repairing and selling is £40 greater than the future income of selling as damaged stock. Despite the simplicity of the example, it does illustrate how past costs are irrelevant in decision making. Accountants refer to them as 'sunk costs' because the money has been spent and any choice of action for the future cannot alter the amount that has been spent in the past.

The following is a list of the general principles that you should follow when identifying relevant costs and revenues for decision problems:

- relevant costs and revenues are cash flows
- only future cash flows are relevant in decisions; past (or sunk) costs are not
- depreciation is an accounting allocation of a past cash flow and is irrelevant
- only incremental cash flows are relevant, any cost that will continue to be incurred, with or without the decision, is not relevant
- committed costs are costs that the company will have to incur in the future as a result of a current commitment and if they cannot be changed by the decision they are not relevant

The list must be interpreted with care. There is a fairly common misconception among some students that fixed costs are not relevant to decisions. But if you look at the above list again, nowhere does it suggest that fixed costs are irrelevant. Future cash flows that arise as a direct consequence of a decision might be classified as fixed costs or variable costs; either way, they will be relevant to the decision.

Example

Recent profit statements for a branch show significant losses. Central management are considering whether or not to close the branch. The budgeted profit statement for the next accounting period is as follows:

Sales		£600,000
Variable cost of sales		480,000
		120,000
Fixed costs:		
Share of national advertising	50,000	
Share of central office expenses	60,000	
Branch manager's salary	30,000	
Branch rent and rates	20,000	
Sundry expenses of the branch	10,000	
		170,000
Loss		(50,000)

It is estimated that if the branch is closed, central office expenses can be reduced by £5,000. The branch manager would be entitled to a redundancy payment of £3,000. The rental agreement for the premises is such that it can be rescinded at a moment's notice. It is forecast that some customers (due to customer loyalty) will switch to shopping at a nearby branch of the same company and that this nearby branch will obtain 10% of the turnover of the closed branch (at the same margin).

Activity 2

Review the above details and identify which costs and revenues **are relevant** to the decision. Do not try to solve the problem at the moment but you might wish to note the amounts for some of the relevant costs and revenues on your own paper.

The basic approach to producing relevant information to help managers with the above decision (should the branch be closed or not?) is to consider what would happen to future cash flows if the branch is closed. Students are usually told to solve this type of problem by comparing the lost contribution with the fixed costs saved. But this is merely a convenient way of looking at how future cash flows will change as a result of making a decision to close the branch. For example, if the branch is closed:

- cash inflows from 90% of the sales are lost but cash outflows for 90% of the variable costs will not occur (the lost contribution)
- cash outflows on central office expenses will be reduced by £5,000
- the cash outflow for branch manager's salary will not occur but there will be a cash outflow for the redundancy payment
- there will be no cash outflow for branch rent, rates and general expenses

---

Activity 3

Evaluate whether it will be beneficial to close the branch by completing the following statement of relevant costs and revenues:

Change in future cash flows as a result of closing the branch:

Lost contribution

Fixed costs saved

11.2 Opportunity cost

In some cases, the relevant cost might be the opportunity cost. Opportunity cost is an unusual concept of cost in the sense that it never has been, nor ever will be, recorded as a cost in the books. It can be defined as a benefit (usually profit) forgone as a result of choosing a particular choice of action.

In some cases, an opportunity cost approach is merely another way of solving a problem that could have been solved by using a traditional relevant cost approach. For example, an opportunity cost approach could have been used for the first example in section 11.1, although it requires a certain amount of mental gymnastics to see it. If such an approach had been taken, the analysis could have been as follows:

There are two choices: (i) sell damaged for £500, and (ii) sell for £560 after spending £20 on repairs.

	Sell damaged choice (i)	Repair and sell choice (ii)
Cost of not choosing (ii) = the lost net revenue from (ii) (£560 – £20)	£540	
Cost of not choosing (i) = lost revenue from choice (i)		£500

Since the lowest cost is choice (ii) (repair and sell) this would be the best decision. But this is an unnecessary complication to a simple problem. Sometimes an opportunity cost will be used in long-term investment problems. Consider the following Activity.

Activity 4

A company owns the freehold of some premises that cost £40,000 many years ago. At the moment this property is leased to another company but the lease will end shortly. The company owning the freehold is considering using it for a business project that will require an investment in working capital of £10,000. If the property is not used for this project it could be sold for £100,000. For the purposes of investment appraisal, it will be necessary to determine how much has been invested in this project. Make a note of the total amount of capital invested at the start of this project.

The same kind of concept is used when trying to work out a minimum price for a particular job or contract. The term '**minimum price**' is a technical expression, meaning a price that will just cover the relevant costs. You can practise using this idea in the following Activity.

Activity 5

A company intends to make an offer for a contract that will take two years to complete. This contract will involve using a particular machine which originally cost £200,000 five years ago. The machine is being depreciated in the accounting records on a straight line basis over 10 years. It is a highly specialized piece of equipment and if it is not used on this contract it will have to be sold. It is estimated that its current scrap value is £40,000 but if it is used on this contract it will have a scrap value of £30,000 at the end of the contract. How much should be charged to the contract for the use of this machine if the company is trying to work out a minimum price?

11.3 Developing skills through practice

The general principles outlined in the previous two sections should enable you to solve almost any type of problem involving relevant costs. This does not mean that you will find all problems easy; each one has its own idiosyncrasies. But if you use the basic approach of considering how future cash flows will change as a result of the decision, you should be able to work out an appropriate solution. The following example contains a fair amount of detail, but you should be able to solve it in about 5 to 10 minutes. It is based on a past exam question set by the Association of Accounting Technicians.

Example

A company has completed an order for a customer who has gone into liquidation before taking delivery. This customer had paid a non-returnable deposit of £3,000. The sales manager has finally found a potential customer who will buy the product if certain conversion work is undertaken.

The company has already spent £20,000 on manufacturing the product, and the following information relating to the proposed conversion work is collected:

	£
Materials required at cost	2,000
Direct wages – 4 workers	2,000
Variable overhead	400
Depreciation	1,000
Foreman	150
Fixed production overhead	800
	6,350

It is company policy to price its products at 25% mark-up on cost, and accordingly a price of £32,937.50 (£20,000 + 6,350 + 6,587.50) would be quoted to the potential customer.

Notes:
1. The materials that are to be used on the conversion are in stock. The material could be used in the production of another product in place of material that the company would otherwise have to buy at a cost of £4,000.
2. Four workers would be required to complete the conversion. They would be taken from a department that is currently working well below full capacity.
3. The conversion work will require the use of machinery that cost £120,000 8 years ago. It has an estimated life of 10 years. Depreciation is charged on a straight line basis.
4. The conversion work will be supervised by a foreman who is currently employed by the company. The foreman receives a salary equivalent to £1,500 per month. It is estimated that the conversion will occupy 10% of the foreman's time.
5. It is company policy to charge production with a proportion of general fixed overheads at an absorption rate of 40% of material costs.
6. The conversion will take one month.
7. In its existing condition, the product could be sold as scrap for £1,000.

Some students tend to be put off by the amount of detail in these problems. This is a pity because they are usually quite easy to solve if you have understood the basic principles. They are also quite interesting, and the 5 or 10 minutes that you invest on the next activity will be time well spent.

Activity 6

You are required to calculate the 'minimum price' for this conversion. You can do this by completing the following schedule. For each item, include a note to explain your figures.

£

Materials

Direct wages

Variable overhead

Depreciation

Foreman

Fixed production overhead

Any other costs

Minimum price

The calculation of a minimum price in Activity 6 suggests that any price in excess of £5,400 would be a benefit to the company. We can test the truth of this by assuming that the converted product is offered at a price of £6,000. This should provide the company with a benefit of (6,000 – 5,400) £600 when the conversion option is compared to the option of scrapping the existing product. The figures can be set out as follows:

		Scrap		Convert
Income:				
Already received		3,000		3,000
Conversion sale proceeds		nil		6,000
Scrap sales		1,000		nil
		4,000		9,000
Costs:				
Earlier expenditure	20,000		20,000	
Incremental costs of conversion	nil		4,400	
		20,000		24,400
		(16,000)		(15,400)

As you can see, the company will gain £600 (16,000 – 15,400) if it chooses to convert at a price of £6,000 instead of scrapping the existing product. This gain will not be apparent from any of the accounting measurements in the books, but that does not mean it will not occur.

11.4 Contribution and decision making

The concept of contribution (difference between sales price and variable costs) was used in Chapter 2 in the context of short-term forecasting. You might also recall that the distinction between fixed and variable costs was used in Chapter 2 to provide relevant information on a production strategy problem which is usually labelled as the 'high-tech/low-tech' option. In this chapter we will see how contribution is used to help managers with other kinds of decisions. Some of these problems can be solved by a simple application of the concepts; others require you to learn specific techniques. Three types of problem where contribution provides a key to relevant information for short-term decisions are as follows:

1. pricing decisions for 'special orders' when the company has, or does not have, spare production capacity
2. optimum product mix when one of the factors of production is in short supply
3. closing a business segment.

You have already worked on a problem involving a decision to close a business segment in Activities 2 and 3. The problem was presented there in the context of considering future cash flows although the approach used was to compare the lost contribution with the fixed costs saved.

Prices for special orders

The way in which we use the concept of contribution for this type of problem is merely a convenient way of considering future cash flows that will arise as a direct consequence of a decision. A special order is one that falls outside of the company's normal terms of trade and will, therefore, involve the company in quoting (or accepting) a special price. Our approach to helping managers with this problem will depend on whether or not the company has spare production capacity. The basic approach is as follows:

- **Spare capacity:** any price in excess of the variable cost will be a benefit to the company.
- **No spare capacity:** an opportunity cost approach can be taken. The opportunity cost of diverting existing resources to the special order is represented by the lost contribution from normal production.

Activity 7

A crisp manufacturer is operating at 80% capacity by producing 20,000 packets of crisps each period. Total production costs for the last period were £8,000, resulting in a total cost per packet of crisps of (£8,000/20,000) £0.40. The costs of £8,000 include £3,000 that are considered to be fixed costs.

A national retail supermarket has offered to place a special order to buy 5,000 packets per period at a price of £0.30p per packet.

Should the company accept this order?

Make a note here of any qualitative factors the company should consider.

Activity 8

Evaluate the opportunity cost if the following circumstances applied to the company in Activity 7:

The output of 20,000 packets represents full capacity. The crisps are normally sold to shops at a price of £0.50 per packet. It decides to accept the special order from the supermarket.

Operating at full capacity is only one of many constraints that affect the quantities that a company is able to produce. Some of the more interesting problems on special orders are related to situations where production capacity is limited due to a shortage of a production resource such as raw materials. These can still be solved by using the opportunity cost approach but you will appreciate the situation better after studying the following section.

Limiting factor decisions

If a company produces a range of products and the production capacity is limited because of a shortage of resources, the company will need to establish an optimum product mix (which products, and how many of each product, it should make). In this book we will be using a simple technique that can be used only if there is a single constraint, such as a shortage of raw materials, or a shortage of machine hours. In cases where there is a combination of several constraints (such as a shortage of raw materials and machine hours) it is necessary to use a mathematical technique known as linear programming. The subject of linear programming is outside the scope of subjects covered by this book.

The technique used for solving the problem of a single constraint is quite easy to learn. You will see this by working on the following example.

Example

Boxer Ltd manufactures two types of cupboard. One cupboard has two doors, the other has three. The doors are all of the same type and are purchased direct from a special supplier. They doors are somewhat special and are in popular demand. The supplier has indicated to Boxer Ltd that it can only supply 120 doors during the next period. There is no other source of supply for these doors.

Boxer Ltd's selling prices and variable costs (including the doors) are:

	Two-door cupboard	Three-door cupboard
Selling price per unit	£100	£120
Variable cost	68	78
Contribution	32	42

Boxer Ltd needs to work out an optimum production plan for the next period.

Activity 9

If you had not been made aware that there was some kind of technique to be used in this situation, what would be your intuitive reaction to the above? Should Boxer Ltd make two-door or three-door cupboards?

Assume that Boxer Ltd considers that the best plan is to make three-door cupboards because the contribution is higher. We can show that this was the wrong decision by comparing the total contribution that would be earned if the 120 doors were used to make three-door cupboards and compare this to the total contribution that would be earned by making two-door cupboards.

Activity 10

Calculate the total contribution that would be earned if all of the 120 doors were used to make:

1. Three-door cupboards

2. Two-door cupboards

Activity 10 shows that the intuitive reaction based on highest contribution per cupboard provides the wrong answer. Since doors are a constraint on what Boxer Ltd can produce, we should have approached the problem by considering the contribution earned for each door used. This technique is sometimes labelled as 'highest contribution per unit of limiting factor'. If we had used it in the case of Boxer Ltd we would have approached the problem as follows:

	Two-door cupboard	Three-door cupboard
Contribution per unit	£32	£42
Usage of scarce resource (doors)	2	3
Contribution per unit of scarce resource	£16	£14
Preferred order of production	1st	2nd

Sorting out the preference order, based on the highest contribution per unit of scarce resource used, is usually a first step. In most of these problems there are likely to be market constraints that set a limit on the quantities to be produced for one or more of the products. We can see how this affects Boxer Ltd by assuming that the market for two-door cupboards is limited to 48. It is quite easy to see the optimum product mix in this case because after making 48 two-door cupboards there will be (120 – 96) 24 doors left over. This will enable Boxer Ltd to make 8 three-door cupboards.

In a problem that involves more than two products, it will be necessary to set up some kind of schedule to keep track of the scarce resource used. After producing the maximum quantity of the first choice product there will be a quantity of resources available for the second choice product. After producing the maximum of this product there will be a balance of resources for the third choice, and so on. There will come a point where the balance of resources is not sufficient to cover the entire planned quantity for the next product in the pecking order of preferences. Production quantities of that product will be limited by the balance of resource available (as for the 8 three-door cupboards of Boxer Ltd). You can practise preparing the schedule by completing the next activity for Boxer Ltd. Following this, there is a final activity where you will have to apply the complete technique to a more realistic problem.

Activity 11

Complete the table below. This is intended to be for the above case of Boxer Ltd where the market for two-door cupboards is limited to 48.

Preferred order	Product type	Production quantity	Scarce resource used	Balance of scarce resource
				B/f 120
1st	Two-door			
2nd	Three-door			

Details for the final activity

A company produces three products but the number of machine hours available is limited to 33,000 hours. Details of each product are as follows:

	Product A	Product B	Product C
Selling price per unit	£40	£60	£66
Variable cost per unit	£30	£40	£30
Machine hours per unit	4	10	12
Maximum sales (units)	2,000	1,000	2,000

Activity 12

In the space below, determine the optimum product mix for this company. Remember to find the preferred order of products first, then set up a schedule to find the quantities of each that could be produced given the market constraints and the constraint that machine hours are limited to 33,000.

As with most of the problems dealt with in this chapter, we have concentrated on the quantitative aspects. There will be a number of qualitative issues to consider, particularly with optimum product mix problems, because the sales of one type of product will suffer if a complementary product is withdrawn. However, the main role of accounting in cases of problem solving is to produce figures that will help managers to evaluate their options.

Summary

The key learning points in this chapter can be summarized as follows:

- routine accounting measurements for financial accounting can rarely be used by managers for making decisions
- relevant costs and revenues for short-term decisions are the future cash flows that will arise as a direct consequence of the decision
- the same concept will be used when identifying relevant cash flows for long-term investment appraisal
- an opportunity cost is a benefit forgone as a result of choosing a particular course of action

- a minimum price is a price that will just cover the relevant costs
- in many cases, the future cash flows can be identified in terms of contribution (a net cash inflow representing the difference between sales income and variable cost)
- if a company has spare capacity, any price in excess of variable cost will contribute to profits
- if a company is operating at full capacity, or production quantities are constrained by other factors, special prices should be evaluated by using an opportunity cost approach
- the opportunity cost of diverting resources to the special order is represented by the lost contribution from normal production
- if there is a single resource constraint, optimum product mix problems can be solved by using a technique that measures the contribution per unit of limiting factor used for each type of product
- all decision problems involve a consideration of qualitative factors in addition to the quantitative factors

Activity 1
The original cost of £600.

Activity 2
The relevant costs and revenues are:

- 90% of the sales and 90% of the variable costs.
- The share of central office expenses to the extent of the £5,000 saving.
- The branch manager's salary and the redundancy payment.
- Branch rent and rates.
- Branch sundry expenses.

Note that the share of national advertising and the share of central office expenses (apart from the £5,000 saving) are not relevant to the decision. They have either been incurred (such as the advertising) or they will continue to be incurred even when the branch is closed.

Activity 3

Lost contribution (90% of £120,000)		£108,000
Fixed costs saved:		
Central office expenses	5,000	
Branch manager's salary	30,000	
Branch rent and rates	20,000	
Branch sundry expenses	10,000	
		65,000
Periodic loss if branch is closed		43,000
Add redundancy payment		3,000
Loss in next period		46,000

Activity 4

Freehold property (the opportunity cost)	100,000
Working capital	10,000
	110,000

Activity 5
By using the machine on this contract the company will receive £30,000 when the machine is sold instead of its current sales value of £40,000. There is, therefore, an opportunity cost of (40,000 – 30,000) £10,000 as a result of using it on the contract.

Activity 6

Materials – opportunity cost of not using it for other product	4,000
Direct wages – no incremental cash outflow	nil
Variable overhead – an incremental cash outflow	400
Depreciation – an accounting allocation of a sunk cost	nil
Foreman – no incremental cash outflow	nil
Production overhead – no incremental cash outflow	nil
Other costs:	
Opportunity cost of being denied scrap sale proceeds	1,000
Minimum price	5,400

Note that the amount originally spent is a sunk cost and that the amount received as a non-returnable deposit is sunk revenue.

Activity 7

The variable cost per unit is (£5,000 ÷ 20,000) £0.25 per packet. Since the price offered is £0.30 per packet, there will be a contribution to profit of £0.05 per packet and the offer can be accepted.

Points to be considered could include: the price is very close to the variable cost and any gain will depend on the accuracy of the costing. What will happen to the sales of crisps in other shops if it is known that they can be obtained cheaper from the supermarket?

Activity 8

The opportunity cost is as follows:

Contribution from sales to the supermarket 5,000 × (30p – 25p)	£250
Contribution lost by not being able to sell to ordinary shops 5,000 × (50p – 25p)	£1,250
	£1,000

Activity 9

Probably three-door cupboards (because the contribution per unit is higher).

Activity 10

1. Three-door cupboards (40 × £42)	£1,680
2. Two-door cupboards (60 × £32)	£1,920

Activity 11

Preferred order	Product type	Production quantity	Scarce resource used	Balance of scarce resource
				B/f 120
1st	Two-door	48	96	24
2nd	Three-door	8	24	0

Activity 12

Product	A	B	C
Contribution per unit	£10	£20	£36
Usage of scarce resource (machine hours)	4	10	12
Contribution per hour	£2.50	£2.00	£3.00
Preferred order	2nd	3rd	1st

Production schedule:

Product	Quantity	Hour usage	Balance of hours Max 33,000
C	2,000	24,000	9,000
A	2,000	8,000	1,000
B	100	1,000	–

? Questions

Questions for self assessment

Answers to self-assessment questions are given at the end of the book.

11.1 A business is considering whether to supply a store with goods on a one-year contract to the value of £70,000, although the costings established for the contract suggest that a loss would result:

Contract Costing

	£	£
Material for the goods:		
Material C		14,000
Material F		7,000
Operating labour		30,000
Supervisory labour		12,000
Depreciation of machinery		10,000
General overheads		21,000
Total cost		94,000
Revenue		70,000
Loss		24,000

The following information is established:
i) Material C is already in stock, having been purchased some time ago at a cost of £14,000. It cannot be used for any other purpose, and if not used on this contract would have to be disposed of at a cost to the business of £2,000.
ii) Material F was bought for £7,000 last year. It could be used on existing orders as a substitute for Material X which is not in stock and which would cost £9,000 to buy.
iii) Operating labour would consist of three workers who would be transferred from other departments in the business. These workers earn £200 per week each. Their place in the other departments would be taken by three new employees working on a one-year contract who would each be paid £220, including necessary overtime. Assume 50 weeks per year.

iv) The cost of supervisory labour – £12,000 – is an allocation of part of the salary of a supervisor who is in overall charge of several production lines.

v) The machinery which would be used to produce the toys was purchased 9 years ago at a cost of £100,000, with an estimated life of 10 years. The depreciation charge in the costing represents the charge for the final year of the machinery's life. The machinery has been idle for some time, and if not used on this order the machinery would be scrapped for a revenue of £2,000. After use on this contract the machinery would have no value, and would have to be disposed of at a cost estimated at £1,500.

vi) General overheads represent an allocation to the contract of part of the firm's total overheads, based on an absorption rate of 100% of material costs. There are no specific general overheads which the contract would incur.

Required:
Give your recommendation whether on financial grounds the contract should be undertaken.

Your calculations must be supported by clear statements of the reasons why a particular figure is included or excluded, and of any assumptions that you make.

(AAT Final)

11.2 The production manager of your organization has approached you for some costing advice upon project X, a one-off order from overseas that he intends to tender for. The costs associated with the project are as follows:

	£
Material A	4,000
Material B	8,000
Direct labour	6,000
Supervision	2,000
Overheads	12,000
	32,000

You ascertain the following:
i) Material A is in stock and the above was the cost. There is now no other use for Material A, other than the above project, within the factory and it would cost £1,750 to dispose of. Material B would have to be ordered at the cost shown above.

ii) Direct labour costs of £6,000 relates to workers that will be transferred to this project from another project. Extra labour will need to be recruited to the other project at a cost of £7,000.

iii) Supervision costs have been charged to the project on the basis of 33$\frac{1}{3}$% of labour costs and will be carried out by existing staff within their normal duties.

iv) Overheads have been charged to the project at the rate of 200% on direct labour.

v) The company is currently operating at a point above break even.

vi) The project will need the utilization of machinery that will have no other use to the company after the project has finished. The machinery will have to be purchased at a cost of £10,000 and then disposed of for £5,250 at the end of the project.

The production manager tells you that the overseas customer is prepared to pay up to a maximum of £30,000 for the project and a competitor is prepared to accept the order at that price. He also informs you that the minimum that he can charge is £40,000 as the above costs show £32,000 and this does not take into consideration the cost of the machine and profit to be taken on the project.

Required:
(a) **Cost the project for the production manager clearly stating how you have arrived at your figures and giving reasons for the exclusion of other figures.**

(b) Write a report to the production manager stating whether the organization should go ahead with the tender for the project, the reasons why and the price, bearing in mind that the competitor is prepared to undertake the project for £30,000.

Note: The project should only be undertaken if it shows a profit.

(c) State four non-monetary factors that should be taken into account before tendering for this project.

(AAT Final)

11.3 Small company

Author's guidance notes: The following question involves a special order in a situation where production capacity is constrained by a limit in the supply of raw materials. It is possible to solve the problem by treating materials as a limiting factor but this is not the easiest approach. The most logical way is to use the concept of an opportunity cost. In this case the opportunity cost of diverting existing resources to the special order is the lost contribution from normal production. It is an interesting problem, where the solution appears quite simple after you have managed to sort out how it should be resolved.

A small company is engaged solely in the automated production of a standard product by a special extrusion process. The direct material cost of each product is £8, machine time is 1 hour per unit. The direct labour cost is embraced within other variable costs which amount to £2 per machine hour. The availability of the raw material is of concern to the management of the company. There seems no way to increase the available quantity above £80,000 per month. There are no capacity or labour problems in fully utilizing the monthly quantity. Sales demand at £20 per item is very heavy. Fixed overhead, based on the volume indicated above, is £4 per hour.

A potential customer has approached the company with a special order worth £8,000 for a one off product using the same material. The quantity of material required will cost £3,520 and the necessary machine time of 500 hours is available. A special component costing £600 will need to be purchased by the company to adapt its extrusion equipment. This is easily assembled and dismantled, but it results in £80 of material being wasted due to the interruption of the production run.

Required:

(a) Distinguish between:
  (i)   variable cost and fixed cost,
  (ii) opportunity cost and sunk cost.

(b) Tabulate the expected results per unit and per month if the standard product only is made.

(c) What contribution is offered by the special order? Should the company accept the order? What minimum price would you apply to the order? Explain your answer.

(ACCA Certified diploma)

11.4 National Fandango plc

Author's guidance notes: The following A Level question requires a computation of an optimum product mix when raw materials are a constraint. The total supply of raw materials is given in £s rather than some kind of physical measure such as doors, kilos or square metres. There is no fundamental difference between measurements in £s and measurements in physical units. You can solve the problem by working in terms of a contribution per £1 of material.

National Fandango plc produce four products, each on separate production lines within the factory complex. The company is at present preparing plans for both production and sales for the next year end. The budget figures reveal the following:

Budget details for year ending 31 May 1989

	Products			
	Renon	Stim	Lench	Croux
Maximum production (units)	30,000	30,000	30,000	30,000
Unit revenue and cost details:	£	£	£	£
Selling price	75	99	129	168
Variable costs:				
Material	27	36	51	60
Labour	24	30	36	54
Overhead	12	15	18	27

In addition to the above, management have established from suppliers of raw material that because of extraction difficulties being experienced a maximum of £3,000,000's worth of raw material can be supplied in the above period. There are no alternative sources of supply for this material, which is the only one used in each of the above products. The budgeted fixed overhead cost for the period has been forecast at £1,000,000.

Required
(a) Using all of the above information, calculate the product mix which will maximize the budgeted profit for the year ending 31 May 1989.
(b) Using your findings in (a) above prepare the budgeted profit and loss account for the year ending 31 May 1989.
(c) Explain any reservations that National Fandango plc may have is using the product mix calculated in (a) during the year ending 31 May 1989.

(AEB A Level)

Questions without answers

Answers to these questions are published separately in the *Teacher's Manual*.

11.5 You are given below the production plan and costs for the month of August 1986 of Robson Ltd, a small precision engineering firm.

Product	M	N	P	R
Selling price				
£ per unit	£40	£50	£25	£35
Direct labour hours				
per unit	4	6	2	3
Raw material				
£ per unit	7	14	5	10
Variable overhead costs				
£ per unit	8	6	8	6
Allocated fixed costs				
£ per unit	4	5	2	6
Plan for August				
Number of units	100	500	250	400

The direct labour work force, which is paid at £3 per hour, has been under considerable pressure due to volume of work. This has culminated in a confrontation between management and the work force whereby the work force have indicated their intention to walk out for one week during the four week month of August. The above original plan represents full utilization of all available hours. There is no opportunity for sub-contracting or overtime.

Required:

(a) Compute the profit that would be achieved by the original plan.

(b) Compute the production plan which would maximize profit for August if the 'walk-out' did take place as threatened. Determine the maximum profit achieved by your plan and briefly discuss any qualitative factors which should be considered.

(ACCA Certified diploma)

11.6   Symbols Ltd

Author's guidance note: The following problem requires an evaluation of a situation where the company can solve its production capacity problems by sub-contracting. The cost of sub-contracting is represented by the difference between the sub-contract price and the variable costs saved. Sub-contracting saves the company from having to use its own machine hours (the limiting factor) and so you need to think in terms of the cost per unit of limiting factor saved in order to determine a preferred order of products for sub-contracting.

Symbols Ltd manufacture three products, Alpha, Beta and Gamma, the standard costs of which are as follows:

	Alpha	Beta	Gamma
	£	£	£
Materials	21	14	21
Labour:			
Machinists			
(@ £1.50 per hour)	6	9	3
Assemblers			
(@ £1.00 per hour)	3	4	2

The company's fixed overheads for the forthcoming year (commencing 1st January) are expected to amount to £100,000.

The marketing director has estimated that demand for the forthcoming year will be:

Alpha	6,000 units at a selling price of £50 each
Beta	10,000 units at a selling price of £45 each
Gamma	8,000 units at a selling price of £40 each

but the production director has pointed out that machine capacity is currently 88,000 hours per annum, although this will increase to 120,000 hours per annum when the new plant (already on order) is delivered. However, this will not be during the year for which the budget is being prepared. The production director, anticipating the problem, has located a general engineering firm who are equipped to undertake work of appropriate quality and have quoted the following prices for production of the company's products on a sub-contracting basis:

Alpha	£40 per unit
Beta	£36 per unit
Gamma	£32 per unit

Required:

(a) Advise the managing director how the services of the sub-contractor should be used to enable Symbols Ltd to meet the expected demand for its products in the most profitable manner, and show full details of the calculations upon which your advice is based.

(b) Prepare a statement showing the profit to be expected if your advice is followed.

(c) Briefly explain the reasoning you have applied in making your recommendation.

(ACCA Costing)

11.7 The manager of a small business has received enquiries about printing three different types of advertising leaflet. Information concerning these three leaflets is shown below:

Leaflet type	A	B	C
	£	£	£
Selling price, per 1,000 leaflets	100	220	450
Estimated printing costs:			
Variable, per 1,000 leaflets	40	70	130
Specific fixed costs, per month	2,400	4,000	9,500

In addition to the specific fixed costs a further £4,000 per month would be incurred in renting special premises if any or all of the above three leaflets were printed.

The minimum printing order would be for 30,000 of each type of leaflet per month and the maximum possible order is estimated to be 60,000 of each leaflet per month.

Required:

(a) (i) Examine and comment upon the potential profitability of leaflet printing. Make whatever calculations you consider appropriate.

    (ii) Assuming that orders have been received to print each month 50,000 of both Leaflet A and Leaflet B calculate the quantity of leaflet C which would need to be ordered to produce an overall profit, for all three leaflets, of £1,800 per month.

(b) It is possible that a special type of paper used in printing the leaflets will be difficult to obtain during the first few months. The estimated consumption of this special paper for each type of leaflet is:

    Leaflet A 2 packs per 1,000 leaflets
    Leaflet B 6 packs per 1,000 leaflets
    Leaflet C 16 packs per 1,000 leaflets

Advise the manager on the quantity of each leaflet which should be printed in order to maximize profit in the first month, if 50,000 of each type of leaflet have been printed, there remains unfulfilled orders of 10,000 for each type of leaflet and there are 170 packs of special paper available for the rest of the month.

(c) 'If the manager of the above business wastes ten packs of special paper then the cost to the business of that waste is simply the original cost of that paper.'
Critically examine the validity of the above statement.

(ACCA Certified diploma)

Capital project appraisal

Objectives

After you have completed this chapter, you should be able to:

- discuss the various techniques used for assisting managers with capital expenditure decisions, and explain the strengths and weakness of each method
- perform the basic calculations using four different techniques
- explain what is meant by the 'time value of money' and illustrate how this concept is used in techniques that are based on discounted cash flow
- explain how 'net present value' is linked to the cost of capital
- describe the problems associated with determining the cost of capital for use in net present value calculations
- calculate the 'weighted average cost of capital' (WACC) from appropriate data
- describe what is meant by 'financial risk' and demonstrate how changes in the level of gearing might affect the WACC
- describe what is meant by 'marginal cost of capital' and explain why this might not necessarily correspond to the interest rate on loans obtained to finance the project
- calculate a rate for the cost of equity that takes account of some of the rudimentary expectations of shareholders

Introduction

Companies receive funds from the providers of capital and invest these funds in business projects. The directors must select business projects that will enable the company to reward the providers of capital with the return they are expecting. Those who provide the risk capital (the ordinary shareholders) expect more from the company than a regular dividend from the annual profits; they expect to see their investment increase in value.

The practice of entrusting money (or wealth) to someone with the expectation that they will make it grow through trade is much older than many of us imagine. The parable of the talents in the New Testament is one example of how it was practised 2,000 years ago. Putting this into a modern business context, we can understand why it is often stated that one of the primary objectives of a company should be to maximize shareholder wealth. A great deal of the economic theory underlying the 'net present value' technique (see section 12.5) rests on the assumption that maximizing shareholder wealth is the company's primary objective.

A decision on the best way of using shareholders' funds for investment in business projects is, therefore, a serious matter and a great deal of research has been done to develop techniques that will help mangers with this kind of decision. Most of this research has been devoted to the net present value technique. It is a vast subject and there are very many text books that deal solely with the subject of investment appraisal.

If you are studying this at a foundation level, you must not think of the subject as being able to perform calculations. There is nothing complicated in any of the mathematics; most of the calculations are nothing more than multiplying and adding. It is more important that you develop your skills in being able to select and use the relevant data. You will not be able to do this very well unless you understand the various concepts and theories. The level of material chosen for this chapter should be suitable for both complete beginners and for those who might have studied some aspects of the subject previously. The four sections at the end of the chapter (sections 12.7 to 12.10) might take the subject a little beyond the stage expected in a foundation text book. This additional material has been included for the benefit of students on certain types of management course, but most students should find it useful because it deals with practical issues and also with some aspects of investment theory.

12.1 A profile of the subject

All capital projects involve investing a known sum of money now in order to secure returns from that investment in the future. In business projects, the return might be the contribution earned from sales created by an investment in physical assets such as plant and machinery, or it might be a reduction of costs such as where a company buys its own delivery fleet instead of paying for the services of an external carrier. In some cases the investment might be in something intangible, such as an advertising campaign designed to increase future sales.

In most cases the business project will have an estimated life cycle, and the returns will be a series of benefits received throughout the life of that project. The returns will be measured either in terms of profits or cash, depending on the investment appraisal technique being used. The only amount known with certainty is the investment; future returns have to be estimated.

There are four basic techniques used in investment appraisal:

1. accounting rate of return
2. payback
3. net present value
4. internal rate of return

Accounting rate of return (ARR) is the only technique that measures future returns in the form of profits. These profits are then expressed as a percentage of the amount invested. The concept of a percentage return on the amount invested is a familiar one to most managers. You can probably recall how we used it in Chapter 8.

The payback method is a simple technique that takes account of how long it will take for the stream of future cash flows to repay the initial investment. It goes some way to helping managers to assess the risks involved because projects with a short payback period are less risky than those where the payback period is longer.

Net present value (NPV) is the superior technique although there is a tendency for managers to treat it with suspicion. Some of this mistrust might be related to a misunderstanding of the theory, which is hardly surprising since it requires very many hours of study on an advanced course in financial management to make sense of all of the concepts involved. NPV is based on cash flows. It considers the time value of money (see later), and considers the returns expected by the providers of capital. The subject is sometimes called 'discounted cash flow' (DCF) although this misrepresents the technique because DCF is merely a description of the mathematics involved.

Internal rate of return (IRR) is another technique that recognizes the time value of money and is based on the mechanics of discounted cash flow. The result of the calculation is not given as a value but as a percentage. Although managers tend to be more comfortable with an indicator given in percentage terms, the underlying theory of IRR is far less sound than that for NPV. In some cases there will be no conflict between IRR and NPV in the sense that they would both lead to the same decision being taken. In other cases, however, NPV will recommend one course of action and IRR another. In these cases the company should be guided by the NPV advice because there are certain flaws in the IRR technique.

12.2 Accounting rate of return

When you calculated the return on capital employed (ROCE) in Chapter 8 you expressed the profits for one period as a percentage of the capital invested for that period. The capital was based on the amount invested at the end of the period, although we could have used the capital at the start of the period or the average capital for the period. In capital project appraisal we are not looking at a single year, we are considering the profits for a series of years over the life cycle of the project. Since ARR is expressed as an annual rate, the normal practice is to calculate the average annual profits and express this amount as a percentage of the capital invested.

Average profits

The calculation of average annual profits is simple arithmetic but you need to be careful in selecting the right data. Profits are not the same thing as cash. At the very least, profits will be after deducting depreciation on the assets used. In some cases the profit figures given to you are calculated after deducting accounting apportionments of existing fixed costs. It is important that you make sure that these are excluded from the calculation because the profits that we use in ARR calculations are the additional profits that the company will earn as a result of the investment. If the apportioned fixed costs will be incurred even if the project is not undertaken, they are not relevant to the decision.

Example

A company is considering a business project that will have a four-year life and for which the following figures have been prepared:

	Contribution	Fixed costs	Profit
Year 1	£20,000	£2,000	£18,000
Year 2	£25,000	£2,000	£23,000
Year 3	£40,000	£3,000	£37,000
Year 4	£15,000	£2,000	£13,000

Fixed costs include an amount of £1,000 per annum as an apportionment of the costs of a central services department. The central services department will not incur any additional costs if the company takes on this project. Depreciation has not been taken into account in the above. The project requires an investment in plant and machinery of £80,000 and it is estimated that the plant will have a scrap value of £40,000 at the end of the project. The amount of additional working capital needed to support this project is estimated at £2,500 and this should remain fairly constant throughout the four years.

Activity 1

Calculate the average annual profits to be used in the calculation of ARR.

There are two common bases for measuring the capital invested: the initial capital (the amount invested at the start of the project) and the average capital. Neither of these has more merit than the other; they are simply different bases. The initial capital is quite easy to see: in the above example it is represented by the £80,000 invested in plant and the £2,500 invested in working capital.

A high proportion of students miscalculate the average capital when they are asked to do it for the first time. On balance, the learning process is more time-efficient if you are allowed to make the mistake (assuming you do) rather than read through some kind of explanation designed to point you in the right direction.

Students looking at this for the first time tend to question why the two figures are added and why the numerator is two instead of the number of years in the project. You must keep in mind that we are trying to find an average; we are not calculating depreciation. When you calculated the average profits you added four figures and divided by four. If you are trying to find the average of two figures you add them and divide by two. In some of your previous studies you might have calculated something called the stock turnover ratio. If you used the average stock for that calculation, what did you do? You added the stock at the start of the year to the stock at the end of the year and divided by two.

If you are still not convinced, imagine what the figures would be if £80,000 was invested at the start of the project and it was still worth £80,000 at the end. If you deducted the closing investment from the opening, there would be no investment in the project – which cannot be right. If you add the two figures and divide by two, there will be £80,000 invested throughout the project – which does seem right.

Having calculated ARR we need to think about how it can be used. Most companies decide on what is usually called a 'hurdle rate'. The hurdle rate is a predetermined percentage that all new projects must exceed if they are to be accepted. The hurdle rate in most cases will be linked to the company's cost of capital (see later). For example, if a company calculates that the providers of capital require a return of 15%, it will not undertake any projects where the ARR is less than 15%. In cases where a company has identified two (or more) investment opportunities, the ARR will assist managers in choosing the most profitable.

A discussion of investment appraisal often centres around the advantages and disadvantages of each method. There are several advantages and disadvantages in using ARR for investment appraisal but some of these might be difficult to appreciate until after you are able to compare it with the other methods. However, you might be able to see some of them now.

Activity 4

See if you can identify two advantages and two disadvantages of using ARR for investment appraisal.

Advantages	Disadvantages
1.	
2.	

12.3 The payback method

Payback is a simple technique that is very popular with managers. The calculation is simply to work out the length of time that it takes for the future stream of cash flows to repay the initial outlay. This period of time is known as the payback period. It is usually expressed in years and a decimal part of a year. Future cash flows should exclude any cash flows that are not relevant to the decision, such as the annual apportioned costs of £1,000 in the previous example. In payback calculations, future cash flows are assumed to occur at an even rate throughout each year.

Activity 5

Refer to the details above Activity 1 and work out the length of time that it takes for the future cash flows to repay the initial investment of £82,500.

In the same way as companies set a hurdle rate for ARR, they might also set a predetermined maximum payback period for project acceptance. For example, a company might have a policy of rejecting all investment opportunities unless the estimated future cash flows from the project show that the initial investment will be repaid within (say) three years. In cases where a company has to make a choice out of two (or more) competing investments, it will choose the one with the fastest payback period, providing it satisfies the predetermined payback period criterion.

Maximum acceptable payback periods tend to rather short, typically not more than five years. The future is always uncertain but the further we peer into the future the less certain we can be about what will happen. A company will be taking a risk if it is relying on receipts that it expects to receive beyond (say) the next five years. In this way the payback method provides some kind of initial filter for rejecting projects that carry an unacceptable risk. The word 'risk' has a technical meaning in investment appraisal and it is another aspect of the subject that has been subject to a great deal of research. In a crude sense, risk is related to the uncertainty of future returns.

Despite the simplicity and popularity of the payback method, it suffers from a number of problems that you will discover by working through a few activities.

Details for the next activity

A company has identified two investment opportunities, each requiring an initial outlay of £50,000. The company can undertake only one of these investments. Estimated cash inflows from each project are as follows:

	Project 1	Project 2
Year 1	£4,000	£10,000
Year 2	£10,000	£30,000
Year 3	£20,000	£40,000
Year 4	£40,000	£5,000
Year 6	£80,000	–
Year 7	£40,000	–

Activity 6

State (in your own words) why the payback method might lead the above company into making a bad investment decision.

In the technical language of investment appraisal, this problem is usually described by stating that the payback method ignores receipts beyond the payback period.

Details for the next activity

A company has identified two investment opportunities. Each project has a three-year life and each requires an initial outlay of £20,000. The company can undertake only one of these investments. Estimated cash inflows from each project are as follows:

	Project 3	Project 4
Year 1	£5,000	£15,000
Year 2	£15,000	£5,000
Year 3	£6,000	£6,000

Activity 7

There is nothing in the payback method to help managers with making a choice; each project repays the initial outlay in two years. State, giving reasons, which of the two projects you would recommend the company to undertake.

In reaching this conclusion you have recognized (even if only intuitively) the time value of money. The time value of money is something that is ignored by the simple payback method that we have been using up to now. You have also taken account of your own intuitive reaction to the subject of risk. You felt more comfortable with Project 4 because most of the money comes in during Year 1 and this is likely to be more certain than the projections for Year 2.

It is possible to modify the payback method by recognizing the time value of money, but you need to be familiar with the mechanics of discounted cash flow in order to see how it works. This modified version is usually called the 'discounted payback method' because all future receipts are discounted to their 'present value' and the payback period is calculated by using the discounted values. The discounted payback method would have selected Project 4 in Activity 7. For the time being, however, you should try to think about the advantages and disadvantages of the basic payback method.

Activity 8

See if you can identify two advantages and two disadvantages of using the basic payback method for investment appraisal.

	Advantages	Disadvantages
1.		
2.		

12.4 Time value of money and DCF arithmetic

The time value of money

Some of the underlying economic theory that supports the net present value (NPV) technique is based on the concept that money has a time value. The usual way of getting students to think about this is to state that £100 received today has a higher value than £100 to be received in one year's time and then invite them to suggest why they think this is so. A natural first reaction to this is to think in terms of inflation. After all, inflation erodes the value of money so if we had the £100 today we could buy more with it than with the £100 that we get in one year's time. But as it happens, the economic theory of the time value of money is not related directly to the problem of inflation. Money will still have a time value, even if there is no inflation.

Assume that you live in a society where there is no inflation. Try to describe (in your own words) why £100 received today has a higher value than £100 to be received in one year's time. There are two basic ways of explaining it; one is based on the concepts used by economists, the other is more pragmatic. Either explanation will do.

Most of the theory on investment decisions relates to the idea that investment rates are compensation for the sacrifice of immediate consumption. This concept also helps to explain how inflation must be recognized in the DCF calculations. You will learn more on this in section 12.7 but for the time being we will ignore inflation. If a person is prepared to sacrifice the immediate consumption of goods worth £100 providing they are compensated for this sacrifice by being allowed (without additional outlay) to consume goods worth £120 in one year's time, we can say that this person's time rate is 20%. An economist would refer to the 20% as that person's 'preferred marginal time rate'.

The word 'marginal' is quite important when you come to study this in more detail because the preferred time rate for each individual will vary with a number of factors. For example, in order to entice a person to part with more money than they have already given up, it might be necessary to increase the compensation rate. The marginal time rate is the rate that will entice that person to part with their next increment of capital. It is marginal in the sense that it represents the rate required on the top slice of that person's total investments. A person's preferred marginal time rate is not only affected by the amounts already invested but by other factors such as age. It seems that as we get older we need more financial inducement to convince us to part with our next slice of money.

In more practical terms we can think of the time rate as an interest rate. If someone is prepared to part with £100 today in order to have £120 to spend in one year's time we would say that the interest rate being sought by this person is 20%. The £100 represents the initial investment, the £20 represents the interest and the £120 represents the terminal value after one year. If we wanted to find the present value of the £120 to be received in one year's time, we would refer to the 20% as the discount rate.

DCF arithmetic

The arithmetic for discounting is nothing more than compound interest in reverse. If you wanted to find the terminal value after two years of £100 invested today at 10% compound interest there are two ways of doing the computation. You could either add the first year's interest to the £100 and then add the second year's interest to the value at the end of the first year

(£100 plus the interest), or you could use a formula. If you took the two step approach, your figures could be as follows:

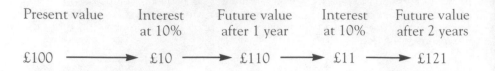

Present value	Interest at 10%	Future value after 1 year	Interest at 10%	Future value after 2 years
£100 →	£10 →	£110 →	£11 →	£121

If we use the compound interest formula the £100 is multiplied by $(1 + 0.1)^2$. The 0.1 in the brackets is the interest rate and the power number of^2 is the number of years. If we tidy up the formula for this example it becomes $£100 \times 1.1^2$. If you have a calculator with a power function (on some calculators this is labelled as x^y, on others you need to press the 'INV' button and then X) you can do the arithmetic. You will find that it gives the answer of £121. The two ways of doing the arithmetic can be illustrated as follows:

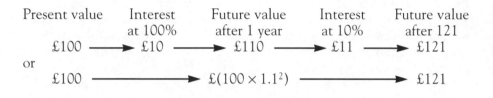

Present value	Interest at 100%	Future value after 1 year	Interest at 10%	Future value after 121
£100 →	£10 →	£110 →	£11 →	£121

or

£100	→	$£(100 \times 1.1^2)$	→	£121

But in discounted cash flow calculations we work in the opposite direction. We will be given the future value and then be asked to calculate the present value of that amount. There are three ways in which we could do this, although they are all based on the same arithmetic. In the above example, if we were given the future value of £121 at the end of two years and asked to find its present value assuming an interest (or discount) rate of 10% we could divide the £121 by 1.1^2. If you do this on your calculator you will find the answer is £100.

The second way is to alter the arithmetic slightly. You might have learned in your mathematics lessons that $1/2$ is the same as 2^{-1}. If you did not learn this it does not matter, you can either accept it or prove it on your calculator as follows: enter the number 2, then invoke the power function, then enter 1, then change the sign to a minus by pushing the +/− key, then press = and the answer should be 0.5 (thus proving that $1/2$ is the same as 2^{-1}). The reason for mentioning this will be apparent in a moment. But for now you should be able to see that instead of dividing £121 by 1.1^2 we could multiply it by 1.1^{-2}. If you can do this on your calculator (don't forget to change the 2 to a minus) you will find that the answer is £100.

The third way is to use a discount table. If you calculate 1.1^{-2} on your calculator you will find that it comes to 0.826446281. If you look at the discount tables in the Appendix you will see that the discount factor for 10% after 2 years is given as 0.826. Discount tables are usually published as either three figure or four figure tables. If you multiply £121 by 0.826 you will find that it comes to £99.946, which to the nearest significant figure is £100. (If you multiply it by 0.826446281, as found on your calculator, it comes to exactly £100.) We can illustrate the mechanics of the three ways of discounting as follows:

Present value		Future value
£100 ◄————— $(£121 \div 1.1^2)$ ◄——— £121
£100 ◄————— $(£121 \times 1.1^{-2})$ ◄——— £121
£100 ◄————— $(£121 \times .826)$ ◄——— £121

In exams you are advised to use discount factors from the discount tables. At least you now know how they work and are less likely to misuse them.

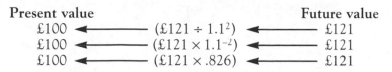

Activity 10

A person will only make further investments providing they can earn a return of 20% or more. An offer has been made to this person to invest £1,000 now for a return of £1,600 to be paid back in 3 years' time. Work out whether this person will be enticed to make the investment. You must use discounting techniques (either on your calculator or by using the discount tables) and then explain why the person would, or would not, make the investment.

12.5 NPV calculations

We usually look at NPV calculations in the context of helping managers to make decisions regarding investments in business projects. A company is a legal person (not a human being) and so it does not have a preferred marginal time rate, but its shareholders do. In fact, each shareholder will look at this differently but because of market mechanisms (which we will not go into here) we can think of shareholders as a single body expecting a particular rate of return from the company. Consequently, we need to think of the company as an intermediary between the providers of the capital and the investment of that capital in business projects.

The return expected by those who provide capital to the company is called the 'cost of capital'. Calculating a single rate for the cost of capital (particularly when there is more than one type of capital) is a subject of much debate and controversy. Some of the more important aspects of this are dealt with in sections 12.8 to 12.10. For the purposes of this present section we will assume that the cost of capital is known. If we discount the future cash flows from a business project using the cost of capital as the discount rate, we should be able to establish whether the return is sufficient to service the cost of capital.

In setting out NPV calculations a few conventions are used. The time of making the investment is known as 'Year 0' (meaning now), cash outflows are prefixed with a minus sign (−) and cash inflows are prefixed with a plus sign (+). If we were to set out a calculation of NPV for the situation described in Activity 10, it would appear as follows:

	Cash flow	Discount factor	Present value
Year 0	−£1,000	1.000	−£1,000
Year 1	0	0.833	0
Year 2	0	0.694	0
Year 3	+ £1,600	0.579	+ £926
		Net present value	−£74

Note the following: the present value of an amount of money held today is equal to its face value and so the discount factor is 1. The third column is headed 'present value' and includes the discounted value of all cash outflows and inflows throughout the life of the project. The expression 'net present value' means the sum of all the plus and minus amounts. In simple problems there will be one cash outflow (the investment) followed by a series of cash inflows. In more realistic problems (particularly when taxation is taken into account) there will be some years during the life of the project when the cash flow for that year is negative.

In NPV calculations for business projects it is always assumed that the yearly cash inflows arrive in one lump sum at the end of the year (notice how this differs from the assumption in payback). Although this is unrealistic, the computations would be unnecessarily complex if any other assumption were made.

Calculation of the NPV for a business project leads to the following decision criteria:

- If the NPV is negative, reject the project. A negative NPV indicates that the returns will not be sufficient to service the cost of capital. You can see this by referring to Activity 10 and the NPV calculation above.
- If the NPV is positive, accept the project. The returns are greater than the cost of capital and provide a surplus that will (theoretically) increase shareholder wealth (see below).
- If there is a choice to be made among competing projects, accept the project with the highest NPV.
- If the NPV is zero, accept or reject the project. Theoretically there is nothing wrong with accepting it (the return equals the cost of capital) if no other investment opportunities with a positive NPV can be found.

It is possible to produce theoretical models that show how shareholder wealth will increase by the amount of the positive NPV. These models are used to justify some of the underlying concepts of the NPV technique but they only work on the assumption that all shareholders have access to information on the proposed investment. We will not be looking at these models here although you should realize that if one of the objectives of the company is to maximize shareholder wealth, the directors should accept projects with the highest positive NPV.

If you have not had any previous practice at doing NPV calculations you could work on the example used for Activities 1, 2 and 3. It is quite an interesting example because it will force you to select the relevant cash flows. As with any investment appraisal method, the relevant cash flows are those that would arise if the company decides to take on the project. Apart from eliminating the annual £1,000 charge, you will have to bring in the cash flows that arise at the end of Year 4 when the plant is sold and the working capital is released.

Activity 11

Work out the NPV for the project used for Activities 1, 2 and 3, using a cost of capital of 15% (discount tables are provided in the Appendix). Use the following format:

	Cash flow	Discount factor	Present value
Year 0			
Year 1			
Year 2			
Year 3			
Year 4			
		Net present value	

There are a number of other topics to learn in relation to NPV and these are dealt with later in the chapter. The topics covered are as follows:

- **Inflation and taxation** – section 12.7
- **Average cost of capital** – section 12.8
- **Average and marginal cost of capital** – section 12.9
- **Cost of equity** – section 12.10

12.6 Internal rate of return

The internal rate of return (IRR) is another discounted cash flow technique but it provides an indicator in the form of a percentage instead of a value. It is completely different to the ARR because it deals with cash flows (not profits) and attempts to measure the interest rate being earned on the investment by considering the timing and amounts for each subsequent cash flow.

The rate of return (the actual rate itself) produced by IRR calculations is a slippery concept to describe. The classical explanation is that it is a discount rate that produces a net present value of zero. Although this is true, it is not much help to someone who is trying to understand the information being implied by the IRR. Unfortunately, if we wish to be precise with any other kind of description, the language can be almost as incomprehensible as the classical explanation. An explanation that gives a reasonable idea of the IRR is that it represents the true interest rate earned on an investment over its life cycle.

If the life of the project is for one year only, and there is one cash inflow at the end of that year, it is possible to see the IRR by observation or from a simple calculation. If the project was for an investment of £100 now and it ends one year later with a cash inflow of £120, we can see that the rate of interest is 20%. You can even test the truth of the classical explanation of IRR by discounting the £120 at 20% to see if it gives a NPV of zero (but you know it will). When the cash inflows are for more than one year, it is not possible to see the IRR by observation, nor is it possible to find the rate by a simple calculation. Consider the following example of a project with a two-year life.

Example

An amount of £10,000 is placed in a bank deposit account. At the end of year one an amount of £6,300 is withdrawn. The account is closed at the end of the second year by a withdrawal of £5,170.

We can see that the total interest is (6,300 + 5,170 – 10,000) £1,470 but it is spread over two years and the amount invested during the second year was less than in the first year. The rate of interest being earned is actually 10% because the figures were contrived to make it 10%. But it is impossible to see this by observation and there is no simple way in which it can be calculated. Now that we are told it is 10% we can see what happened on the deposit account. The figures would have been as follows:

Initial investment	£10,000
Interest for Year 1	1,000
	11,000
Withdrawn at end of Year 1	6,300
Balance at end of Year 1	4,700
Interest for Year 2	470
Withdrawn at end of Year 2	5,170

Although this is for a deposit account (where the interest rate will be known) you can easily relate it to a business project where there was an investment of £10,000 and a cash inflow of £6,300 at the end of Year 1 and a cash inflow of £5,170 at the end of Year 2 (the end of the project). In order to calculate the IRR on such a project, we would need to find a discount rate that produces a net present value of zero. We know that this rate is 10% in the above case.

Activity 12

Prove that a discount rate of 10% will give a NPV of zero by completing the following table for the above example.

	Cash flow	Discount factor	Present value
Year 0	– £10,000	1	
Year 1	+ £6,300	0.9091	
Year 2	+ £5,170	0.8265	
		Net present value	

In business projects we will not know the IRR, and our problem will be to find it. There are several ways of doing this. The two most popular are:

- Use a spreadsheet. Most spreadsheet packages have a built-in IRR function. You will have to include a 'guess rate' in the formula because these programs work by doing iterative calculations (at split-second speed) until the NPV works out at zero.
- Trial and error using discount tables. The idea is to calculate two NPVs using two different rates and then interpolate between them.

It always seems rather futile to ask students to calculate IRR in an exam because it does not test very much other than whether you have been able to remember how it is done. In practice, we would always use a spreadsheet and you should do this if you are working on a course assignment that requires a calculation of IRR.

The trial and error method is really a left-over from the days before computer spreadsheets. It is easier to see how the interpolation arithmetic works if one of the rates chosen gives a positive NPV and the other a negative NPV. This is not essential because any two rates will do; it simply makes it easier to understand the explanation.

We can see how it works if we assume that our two guess rates for the deposit account example (above) were 8% and 12%. If you work out the NPV at 8% you will find that it comes to + £265. If you then work it out at 12% you will find that it comes to − £254. At this point we know that the IRR is somewhere between 8% and 12%

There is a formula that you have to use for these manual calculations. It can look quite frightening when it is set out in the form of symbols, but all it is does is to add to the lower rate (in our case, 8%) a fraction of the difference between the two rates used. This fraction is found as follows:

$$\frac{\text{NPV at the low rate}}{\text{The range (in £s) between the two NPVs}}$$

In our example, this fraction is 265/519, which amounts to roughly one-half. To find the IRR we would add one-half of the difference between 8% and 12% (2%) to the low rate of 8%. Although this does amount to 10% in our example, you must accept that the method will give only an approximate rate. A lot depends on the range between the two rates used; in the above illustration we used rates that were 2% either side of the true rate and so our calculations were bound to be fairly accurate.

In case you have to use the formula it is normally set out as follows:

$$A \quad + \quad \left[\frac{C}{C-D} \quad \times \quad (B-A) \right]$$

where A is the lower discount rate, B is the higher discount rate, C is the NPV at the low rate and D is the NPV at the high rate.

As stated earlier, there is no point in using this formula if you have access to a spreadsheet, it should be used only when it is necessary to calculate IRR manually. Spreadsheets use a different approach to finding IRR, although you do have to include a guess rate in the IRR formula. This rate can be any low positive number such as 1%. The program will then discount the cash flows at repeated increments of this rate until the NPV is returned as zero. The iterative calculations are then stopped and the cell in which you entered the formula will display the discount rate at which this occurred.

The IRR of a project can be compared to the company's cost of capital. If IRR is less than the cost of capital the project should be rejected. In many cases IRR will lead to the same accept/reject decision as the NPV method, but there can be conflicts. In cases where a company is considering a choice between mutually exclusive projects, the ranking of projects (which project is the best) can differ as between IRR and NPV.

There are various ways of showing how the IRR method can be modified to remove this conflict but the exercise is somewhat academic. There seems to be little practical point in modifying IRR so that it provides the same conclusion as NPV, managers could make their decision on the basis of NPV in the first place. You might have to study this on a more advanced course but at a foundation level it is sufficient to be aware that IRR does sometimes give incorrect rankings and that managers should be guided by NPV. There is no doubt that NPV is the superior of the two DCF methods, but to understand why requires additional study that you probably do not need to undertake at this stage.

The following sections take the subject of NPV a little further. You will have to be guided by your syllabus (or tutor) in deciding whether they need to be studied. They are all quite interesting topics and, if you have the time, are worth studying even if they do fall outside the scope of your syllabus.

12.7 Inflation and taxation

The subject of inflation is presented here in the context of NPV, although it is equally applicable to any DCF method. Taxation is also explained in relation to NPV but since it represents a cash flow it should be taken into account in all methods based on cash flows. It can also be applied to ARR but this will depend on whether the company wishes to determine the ARR before tax or after tax.

Inflation

In order to understand the impact of inflation on NPV calculations, you need to recall the idea that investment rates can be seen as compensation for the sacrifice of immediate consumption. Money by itself is of very little use; it is desirable mainly because it gives the owner power to consume goods and services. If people are prepared to sacrifice immediate consumption providing they are compensated by being allowed to consume more later, the rate of compensation offered must enable them to consume the extra quantity they are seeking. We must think now about the impact of inflation and how it erodes the value of money in terms of its purchasing power.

Market rates of interest (those that can be obtained through capital markets) include an amount that reflects current rates of inflation. In Activity 13, the person being asked to part with the £100 would endeavour to find an investment that gave a return of 26%. The 26% is known as the 'money' rate (or market rate). The rate of 20% is called the 'real' rate because it is this rate that measures the real amount of extra goods that the person can consume.

The relationship between the money rate, inflation rate and real rate can be reduced to an equation The following abbreviations (with the rates from Activity 13 for illustration) are normally used:

MR = money rate	26%
IR = inflation rate	5%
RR = real rate	20%

The equation, together with the relevant figures from Activity 13 set out underneath, is as follows:

$$(1 + IR) \quad \times \quad (1 + RR) \quad = \quad (1 + MR)$$
$$1.05 \quad \times \quad 1.2 \quad = \quad 1.26$$

When we gather information for NPV calculations, it is likely that we will know the inflation rate and the money rate. We will have to determine the real rate from these two (you will see why in a moment). This can be done by rearranging the above the equation to give the following formula:

$$1 + RR = \frac{1 + MR}{1 + IR}$$

In gathering data for NPV calculations, the future cash flows will be expressed in terms of today's prices. There are two ways of recognizing how inflation affects this data:

- we could inflate all future cash flows by an inflation factor and then discount these using the **money rate** as a discount rate – this would be a cumbersome exercise
- we could express all future cash flows at today's prices and then discount these using the **real** rate as a discount rate – this is less cumbersome because we can use the data originally gathered.

Both methods give exactly the same answer. You can see this by doing the two calculations for an amount of £10,000 to be received in 2 years' time using the rates in Activity 14.

Activity 15

A project includes an amount of £10,000 to be received after two years from now. The amount of £10,000 is expressed in terms of today's prices. Using the real rate of 5% found from Activity 14, calculate the present value of this £10,000.

If we had taken the other approach (inflating the future receipt) the amount of £10,000 would be inflated to (£10,000 × 1.05^2) £11,025 by the end of Year 2. We can then discount this using the money rate of 10.25%. You cannot do this using the discount tables because no discount factor is given for this rate. If you do it on your calculator (£11,025/1.1025^2) you will find that it comes to £9,070, which is the same as your answer in Activity 15.

The normal practice is to express future cash flows at today's prices and use the real rate as the discount rate – less arithmetic is involved with this approach. If you have to cope with this in an exam and cannot remember the formula, you will get some marks by simply deducting the inflation rate from the market rate to derive a real rate (television and radio reporters sometimes do this when talking about real rates). Although it does not give quite the right answer, it is fairly close to the real rate and is better than ignoring inflation completely.

Taxation

Another factor that we cannot ignore (except in the classroom sometimes) is taxation. There is no doubt that the tax department will want a share of the profits. The tax that companies pay on their profits is called corporation tax. It is levied at a rate on the 'taxable profit', which is not quite the same thing as accounting profit. There are a number of factors that cause taxable profit to differ from accounting profit, but the most significant in the context of investment appraisal is that the depreciation charged in arriving at accounting profit is not an allowable expense for tax purposes.

The tax rules do, however, make provision for an annual deduction from profits for capital expenditure on most assets. These rules grant what is known as a 'writing down allowance' (WDA), which must be calculated at a rate specified by tax legislation. The writing down allowance on plant and machinery is calculated at the rate of 25% on the reducing balance. When the asset is sold, the difference between the sale proceeds and the tax written down value is treated as an allowance or income, depending on the circumstances. If the asset is sold for less than the tax written down value, the difference is given as an allowance called a balancing allowance. If it sold for more than the tax written down value the difference is treated as income called a balancing charge. You will see how this works in a moment.

The rate of corporation tax depends on the level of profit. At the time of writing this edition, for a company whose total profit (as computed for corporation tax purposes) exceeds £1,500,000 the rate of corporation tax is 33%. For a company where the total profit does not exceed £300,000 the rate is 25%. Between the two profit levels there is something called marginal relief, which is meant to smooth effective rates from 25% to 33% although the formula does not always work. The corporation tax on the profit for an accounting year is payable nine months after the end of that year. As you can imagine, this causes a cash outflow in the year following the one in which the cash inflow occurs.

Although interest payments are deductible in arriving at total profit for tax purposes, this aspect can be ignored when calculating cash outflows for tax payments. A loan cannot be related to any specific project, it forms part of the company's total pool of capital. Since loan interest represents a part of the cost of capital, the tax relief on interest paid is taken into account when calculating the cost of capital. You will see how this works in section 12.8.

We can see how taxation affects cash flows by working on the example used for Activities 1, 2 and 3. The investment in plant and machinery was £80,000 and it was estimated that the plant would be sold for £40,000 at the end of the project. The capital allowance computation for tax purposes (based on 25% of the reducing balance) is as follows:

Year 1	Cost of plant	80,000
	Writing down allowance	20,000
	balance c/f	60,000
Year 2	Writing down allowance	15,000
	balance c/f	45,000
Year 3	Writing down allowance	11,250
	balance c/f	33,750
Year 4	Sale proceeds	40,000
	Balancing charge	6,250

The taxable profits based on relevant cash flows less capital allowances for Years 1 to 4 are as follows

	Year 1	Year 2	Year 3	Year 4
Contribution less relevant fixed costs	19,000	24,000	38,000	14,000
Less capital allowances	20,000	15,000	11,250	
Add balancing charge				6,250
Taxable profits/(losses)	(1,000)	9,000	26,750	20,250

If we assume that the company pays corporation tax at the rate of 33%, the project causes the following increase or decrease in tax liabilities for each year:

	Year 1	Year 2	Year 3	Year 4
Increase/(decrease) in tax liabilities	(£330)	£2,970	£8,827	£6,682

Because corporation tax is payable nine months after the accounting date, these amounts will be reflected in the cash flows for the year following that to which they apply. This means that cash flows will extend into Year 5. The complete computation of cash flows is as follows:

	Year 1	Year 2	Year 3	Year 4	Year 5
Contribution less fixed costs	19,000	24,000	38,000	14,000	–
Taxation	–	330	(2,970)	(8,827)	(6,682)
Sale of plant				40,000	
Working capital				2,500	
Cash inflow/(outflow)	19,000	24,330	35,030	47,673	(6,682)

As you can see, taxation makes a considerable difference to the pattern of cash flows.

Activity 16

Work out the revised NPV (after taking taxation into account) using the discount rate of 15% as used in Activity 11 and then compare the result to Activity 11.

	Cash flow	Discount factor	Present value
Year 0			
Year 1			
Year 2			
Year 3			
Year 4			
Year 5			
		Net present value	

12.8 Average cost of capital

Companies usually obtain their capital in at least two forms, equity (ordinary shareholders) and loans. The cost of financing each of these two forms of capital will differ. The return expected by ordinary shareholders will be greater than the return expected by those who lend money to the company. This is because ordinary shareholders provide the risk capital and the rate of return that they expect will take account of their perception of this risk. Lenders, on the other hand, see their investment as relatively safe and there is no lack of certainty over the return they will receive because the rate is usually fixed in advance.

Consequently, the total pool of capital in a company is likely to be a mixture of different types of capital and each type has its own unique cost. Yet we have to identify a single rate for the cost of capital when calculating the NPV of business projects. One solution to this problem is to calculate an average cost of capital. This average takes account of the relative amounts for each type of capital. For example, if 3/4 of the capital consists of equity shareholders expecting a return of 12%, and the remaining 1/4 consists of loan capital costing 4%, the average cost of capital is (3/4 × 12% + 1/4 × 4%) 10%. Notice how the proportions for each type of capital provide a 'weighting' when calculating the average. The cost of 10% in this example is called the 'weighted average cost of capital' and it is usually known by the acronym WACC (pronounced 'wack').

The actual calculation of WACC is straightforward, but there are difficulties in establishing the cost of each type of capital. The main problem is concerned with the cost of equity. We will be taking a fairly naive view of the cost of equity in this section; the more advanced aspects are covered in sections 12.9 and 12.10.

When calculating the cost of each type of capital we have to ignore the 'nominal' values recorded in the books. These nominal values are simply a means of providing a legal description of the capital, they are not values in any economic sense. If the nominal value of an ordinary share is 25p and it is being traded in the market place at £2.00, the 25p is irrelevant, it is simply a way of giving a name to the share. Anyone wishing to buy a share in this company (from another shareholder) will have to pay £2.00 and since they are investing £2.00 we need to look at the rate of return they are expecting as a percentage of this market value.

Equity shareholders do not contract with the company for any specified rate of return; the rate they are expecting is signalled through the share price. In this section we will assume that the rate of return expected can be judged by comparing the latest dividend payment with the market value of the share. You will see later how this assumption has to be modified.

Activity 17

A company's issued share capital consists of 100,000 ordinary shares of 25p each. The company has just paid out a dividend of 40p per share. Immediately after the dividend was announced, the share price in the stock market moved to £4.00 per share. Calculate the rate of return that shareholders in this company are expecting.

In the case of loan capital, there is a rate of interest specified in the loan agreement. In the case of loans obtained from a financial institution (such as a bank) we can use this rate of interest in the calculation of WACC. But a company can issue loan stocks to the general public and this loan stock is bought and sold through the capital market in the same way as shares. These loan stocks are usually called 'debentures' and they are often traded in multiples of £100 in nominal value. Debentures have a nominal value in the same way as shares, and this nominal value is unlikely to be the same as the market value.

When the debentures were first issued, the rate of interest would have been fixed by reference to prevailing interest rates for that type of stock. This rate of interest is a fixed percentage of the **nominal value** and so when market interest rates change, the market value of debentures will change. The market value will move to a point where the interest being paid on the nominal value gives a return to the investor that is compatible with current interest rates. As with ordinary shares, we have to refer to the market value of loan stocks to determine the rate of return required by those who invest in this type of stock.

Activity 18

The company in Activity 17 had also issued a nominal amount of £100,000 5% loan stock many years ago when investors in this type of stock would have been content with a return of 5%. The current market price for this stock is £50 for stock with a nominal value of £100. Calculate the rate of return required by investors in this type of stock.

There is one further aspect of loan interest that needs to be considered here. The company in Activity 18 will have to pay out £5,000 as interest but its corporation tax liability will be reduced because interest is deducted from total profit for tax purposes. If this company pays corporation tax at the rate of 33%, its tax bill will drop by (£5,000 × 0.33) £1.650. This tax saving must be taken into account when calculating the cost of interest. This does not apply to dividends because dividends are not treated as an expense when calculating taxable profit. The cost of loan capital in Activity 18 was calculated as 10% but this was before tax relief. After taking tax relief into account, the true cost to the company is (0.67 × 10%) 6.7%. (You could also have found this be expressing the net amount paid out of (£5,000 – £1,650) £3,350 as a percentage of the total market value of £50,000.)

Now that we have the cost of each type of capital for this company, we can see how its WACC would be calculated. There are various ways of setting out the numbers. The easiest to understand is probably as follows:

Type of capital	Total nominal value	Total market value	Payout (div/int)	
25p ordinary shares	£25,000	£400,000	£40,000	
5% loan stock	£100,000	£50,000	£3,350	(net of tax)
		£450,000	£43,350	

The total amount paid out (dividends and interest) to service the total pool of capital is then expressed as a percentage of the total market value of that capital. The WACC of this company is (43,350/450,000) 9.63%. Notice how this ignores the nominal value of capital.

We could have found the same answer by using the market value of each type of capital as a weighting for the cost of that particular capital. If we use this approach the computation is as follows:

Equity 400,000/450,000 × 10% = 8.89%
Loans 50,000/450,000 × 6.7% = 0.74%

WACC   9.63%

There are a number of conceptual problems associated with using WACC as a basis for calculating a discount rate, but they are not discussed in this book. Most of the companies who carry out investment appraisal by using the NPV technique use WACC as a basis for the discount rate. The final two sections are concerned mainly with the cost of equity, in particular how equity shareholders respond to changes in the level of loans taken on by a company.

12.9 Average and marginal cost of capital

Current capital and additional capital

Our calculations for the average cost of capital (WACC) in section 12.8 were based on the existing capital of a company. Such a rate will be used as the discount rate in NPV calculations when the company intends to use its existing capital resources to finance a new project.

In many cases, however, the company will be considering a new investment project for which additional funding is required. This additional funding has its own cost and also changes the existing average cost of capital. The cost of the additional capital is known as the **marginal cost of capital**; it is marginal in the sense that it represents the cost of the next increment of capital.

There are two ways of appraising a new project when additional finance is to be raised. One is to discount the projected cash flows at the marginal cost of capital. If this produces a positive NPV the project must be earning a return in excess of the marginal cost of capital and should be accepted. The alternative approach is to discount the projected cash flows using the WACC that will apply after taking on the new capital.

Financial risk

Unfortunately, the marginal cost of capital is often misunderstood and, as a result, the WACC after taking on the new capital is also misunderstood. In order to see the problem we need to view it through the eyes of the ordinary shareholders. We need to think about how they will react if the new capital taken on by the company is in the form of loans. If this happens, the company's gearing level will increase. The word 'gearing' is a reference to the proportion of capital in the form of loans. When a company's gearing level increases, the ordinary shareholders will perceive a greater financial risk in their investment. As a result, they will expect a higher return in order to compensate for the higher risk.

The term 'risk' has a special meaning in investment appraisal. Most investments are risky but since some are more risky than others, it is conceivable that there might be some way of quantifying risk to help investors to manage their portfolio of investments. Various ways of measuring risk have been devised and although it is an extremely interesting subject, it is not appropriate to discuss them in this book. You can, however, get some idea of how the term 'risk' is used by dealing with the following activity.

Activity 19

You have the opportunity to make an investment. You have a choice between two types of investment – we will call them investment A and investment B. The prospects for each investment have been assessed as follows:

- Investment A: the return is expected to be between 10% and 12%
- Investment B: the return is expected to be between 1% and 80%

Which of these two investments carries more risk?

If you were now to explain your choice in commonsense terms, you would say that you noticed the rate of return on Investment A was fairly certain, whereas the rate of return on Investment B is not so certain. It was the absence of certainty in Investment B that affected your assessment of its risk. At a more scientific level you have measured the variability (or volatility) of the possible returns and noticed that it is much greater for Investment B than it is for Investment B. It is the susceptibility to fluctuations in possible returns that lies at the heart of risk measurement. The wider the range, the greater the risk.

We can now get some idea of how risk assessment is affected by gearing. This particular risk is called 'financial risk' because it is affected by the way in which a company is financed. It can be distinguished from what is known as 'business risk', which stems from the type of trade undertaken.

The financial structures of two companies operating in the same line of business are as follows:

	Company A	Company B
Ordinary shares of £1 each	5,000	1,000
Reserves	5,000	1,000
	10,000	2,000
10% loan capital	–	8,000
	10,000	10,000

You will notice that Company A is 'ungeared' and Company B is 80% geared (80% of its total capital is in the form of loans).

The earnings before interest and tax for each company are the same. The results for two consecutive years (using a tax rate of 35% for convenience) are as follows:

	Company A		Company B	
	Year 1	Year 2	Year 1	Year 2
Earnings before interest and tax	1,200	900	1,200	900
Interest	—	—	800	800
	1,200	900	400	100
Taxation (35%)	420	315	140	35
Earnings available for equity	780	585	260	65

Notice that earnings before interest and tax (usually abbreviated to EBIT) have dropped by 25% in both companies.

You will also notice a considerably higher fluctuation of earnings available for equity in Company B in comparison with Company A. In order to appreciate the effect of these variations, we need to consider how they will be viewed through the eyes of individual shareholders. A suitable basis for this exercise could be **earnings per share**. In this example, the earnings per share is a simple calculation; earnings available for equity are simply divided by the number of equity shares (5,000 in A and 1,000 in B).

Activity 20

Calculate the earnings per share for each company for both years. Make a note of the percentage fall (between the two years) on earnings per share for each company.

Notice how earnings per share (EPS) responds to changes in EBIT. A fall of 25% in EBIT causes the ungeared company's EPS to fall by 25%. In Company B, a fall of 25% in EBIT causes EPS to fall by 75% (three times the rate of Company A). In fact it would only require a 33.3% fall in the EBIT of Company B for EPS to drop by 100%.

It is this vulnerability to a wider fluctuation of returns that will cause Company B's shareholders to perceive a much greater risk in their shares by comparison to Company A. The real impact of this as far as each company is concerned is related to the cost of capital. Company B shareholders will expect a much higher return than those of Company A in order to compensate for the higher risk. These higher expectations will be signalled through a lower share price in Company B by comparison to Company A.

Activity 21

Scenario

A company's existing capital consists entirely of equity shares. It has been calculated that the existing cost of equity is 18%. A new project has been identified for which additional financing will be required. The company can obtain sufficient loan funds at a gross cost of 10% (net cost after tax relief of 6.7%) and intends to finance the project by means of this loan. If the loan is taken on, the company's gearing ratio (based on market values) will change from 100% equity to 70% equity, 30% loans.

Thinking problem

The marginal cost of capital is not 6.7% (the cost of the next increment of capital). State why this would be so.

It is the response of equity to changes in the gearing ratio that has resulted in many thousands of words being written on the subject of the cost of capital. There are basically two schools of thought:

- the traditional view (an unscientific belief)
- the Modigliani and Miller hypothesis

Both bases are inconclusive. The important point that you must recognize when discussing this subject (e.g. in exams) is that the marginal cost of capital is not necessarily the same as the rate that will have to be paid to the new providers of capital. The marginal rate (when loans are taken on) must recognize the additional return expected by the equity shareholders to compensate for the increased financial risk which they perceive in their investment.

Marginal and average cost of capital: The traditional view

As gearing levels increase, equity shareholders perceive a greater risk and demand a higher return. These return expectations are signalled through the share price. Up to a point, the cheaper debt capital will compensate for the increase in the cost of equity, and initially WACC will fall. However, there will be a point at which the additional demands required by equity will more than offset the gains of using cheaper debt capital. At this point, WACC will start to rise.

This suggests that there should be an optimum gearing level (the point at which WACC is at its lowest) but there are no scientific studies to enable such a point to be calculated. The way in which equity will respond to changes in gearing is merely an intelligent guess.

The calculations for WACC adopting the traditional view can be illustrated by using the following (entirely contrived) data:

Capital structure		Cost of equity	Cost of debt	WACC
100% Equity		15%	–	15.0%
80% Equity	20% Debt	16%	10%	14.8%
60% Equity	40% Debt	17%	10%	14.2%
40% Equity	60% Debt	23%	10%	15.2%
20% Equity	80% Debt	40%	10%	16.0%

On a line graph, the above rates for WACC would appear as shown in Figure 12.1.

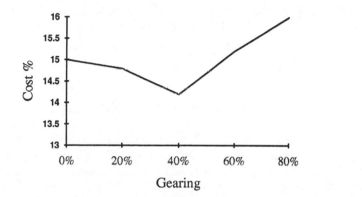

Fig. 12.1

We will now use some of the above details to illustrate the marginal cost of capital (the cost of the next increment of capital). We will do this by seeing what happens if the new capital causes the company's capital structure to move from a 40% gearing level to a 60% gearing level.

On the face of it, the marginal cost of capital appears to be the 10% on the new capital plus the extra (23 – 17) 6% to be paid to equity. But the true cost will be related to the amount being paid out on the new capital, plus the extra amount needed to be paid out to keep the equity shares at their current market value. To see this, we need to assume total market values of the two types of capital before the new capital is obtained. We will assume the following:

Position prior to taking on new debt capital:

	Market value	Cost	Payout
Equity	£600,000	17%	£102,000
Debt	£400,000	10%	£40,000
	£1,000,000		£142,000

WACC at this point is (142,000/1,000.000) 14.2%, as shown in the above schedule.

We are assuming that new debt capital is taken on so that gearing becomes 40% equity and 60% debt. If the market value of equity is to be maintained at £600,000, the new capital structure will be:

	Market value
Equity	600,000
Debt	900,000
	1,500,000

We have already said that at this level of gearing the equity shareholders will require a return of 23%. If the company does not increase its current payout to the equity shareholders, the equity share price will drop to a point where the payout of £102,000 becomes 23% of the market value. This point is reached when the total market value of equity falls to (102,000 ÷ .23) £443,478.

In order to keep the market value of equity shares at £600,000 the company will have to pay dividends equal to 23% of £600,000. If it does this, the new position is as follows:

	Market value	Cost	Payout
Equity	£600,000	23%	£138,000
Debt	£900,000	10%	£90,000
	£1,500,000		£228,000

Notice how WACC is now (228,000/1,500,000) 15.2%, as shown in the original schedule.

We can now see the marginal cost of the new capital by relating the extra payout as a percentage of the additional capital.

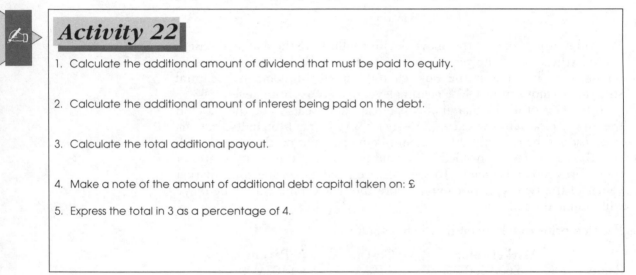

Activity 22

1. Calculate the additional amount of dividend that must be paid to equity.

2. Calculate the additional amount of interest being paid on the debt.

3. Calculate the total additional payout.

4. Make a note of the amount of additional debt capital taken on: £

5. Express the total in 3 as a percentage of 4.

Any new project financed by the additional £500,000 loan must produce a yield in excess of 17.2% in order to be acceptable. We can, therefore, either use the 17.2% as a discount rate in NPV calculations to see if it gives a positive NPV (indicating that the return exceeds 17.2%), or we can find the IRR of the project to see if it is greater (or less) than 17.2%.

Average and marginal cost of capital: The Modigliani and Miller hypothesis

It is this subject that has attracted most of the attention in academic circles. We cannot possibly make sense of all the mathematics and suggested proofs of the theory. We will simply consider what it tries to tell us regarding WACC in response to changes in gearing levels. This, in turn, will give an indication of how equity will move.

The original hypothesis, which has been subject to many arguments and counter-arguments, ignores taxation. It suggested that the cost of equity ought to be a positive linear function of the gearing ratio. In other words, as gearing levels increase, the cost of equity will increase by a constant factor (known as the risk premium) and WACC will remain constant irrespective of the gearing ratio.

The following set of figures show what would happen (in an imaginary case) if the hypothesis is valid:

Capital structure		Cost of equity	Cost of debt	WACC
100% Equity		15.00%	–	15%
80% Equity	20% Debt	16.25%	10%	15%
60% Equity	40% Debt	18.33%	10%	15%
50% Equity	50% Debt	20.00%	10%	15%
40% Equity	60% Debt	22.50%	10%	15%
20% Equity	80% Debt	35.00%	10%	15%

On a graph, the three types of capital cost (equity, debt and WACC) would be as shown in Figure 12.2.

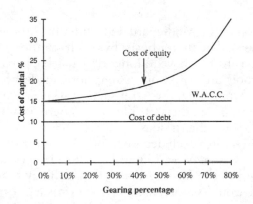

Fig. 12.2

You can now use this example to calculate marginal cost of capital – using the new rates for cost of equity:
Position prior to taking on new debt capital:

	Market value	Cost	Payout	
Equity	£600,000	18.33%	110,000	(see below)
Debt	£400,000	10%	40,000	
	£1,000,000		150,000	

The decimal for cost of equity is 3 recurring. Notice that WACC at this point is (150,000/1,000,000) 15%.

Position after taking on new debt and maintaining market value of equity at £600,000 (to be completed during the activity):

	Market value	Cost	Payout
Equity	£600,000	22.5%	
Debt	£900,000	10%	
	£1,500,000		

Activity 23

First complete the above tabulation. After doing this, calculate the marginal cost of capital, and make a note of your calculations in the space provided in this box. After doing the calculation, make an observation.

1. Calculation of marginal cost of capital:

    additional payout

    additional capital

2. Observation:

The above explanation of the Modigliani and Miller hypothesis is based on their original analysis. The hypothesis by itself cannot disprove the traditional view; it has to be viewed alongside what happens in practice. The arithmetical proofs are based on assumptions made by the authors regarding a certain type of market transaction (known as 'arbitrage' trading) which might or might not happen. There is no conclusive empirical evidence to show that it does.

The original hypothesis also excluded taxation. When taxation is brought into the model it shows that WACC will be at its cheapest with 99% of the total capital being in the form of loans. It is unlikely that any public company in the UK would be prepared to take on such a high level of gearing (gearing levels tend to be around 33%). The situation is different in Germany where companies are financed almost entirely by bank loans. One of the advantages of this is that the cost of capital is known with certainty, making long-term planning much easier than it is in UK, where funding is equity based. Companies can never be sure what will happen on the equity market but they are aware of the signals that might affect shareholder action such as profits, dividends and gearing levels.

12.10 Cost of equity

When calculating WACC there is usually no difficulty with the cost of fixed interest capital such as preference shares and loans. The main problem relates to the cost of equity. In order to feel comfortable with some of the concepts, we need to play around with a little mathematics. If you are already familiar with the arithmetic of annuities and perpetuities, you can skip some of the following subsections. If you are not (and tend to be put off my mathematics) there is no need to worry because we can use some of the keys on your calculator, assuming that it has keys for brackets and power numbers.

Some of the basic arithmetic

The mathematical formulae relate to annuities and perpetuities. These are derivatives of the compound interest formula. You don't need to worry about the derivation of the formulae; you need to see how and why they are used.

The term 'annuity' is used to describe a situation where the future stream of cash flows are for an equal amount to be received (or paid) at regular intervals. Despite the name 'annuity' (which seems to suggest 'each year') the regular interval can be any period, such as one month or one year. In investment appraisal calculations, we are usually looking at a future stream of regular cash inflows, but the monthly repayments of a mortgage, or monthly repayments under a hire purchase agreement, are payments of annuity. In fact you can use the formula to find out what your monthly mortgage repayments should be.

We will start by using the normal discounting arithmetic that you have already learned.

Activity 24

Find the present value of three receipts of £100 to be received at the end of the next three years, using a discount rate of 10%. You can do this by completing the following tabulation. The discount factors have been included to save time.

	Cash inflow	Discount factor	Present value
Year 1	£100	.909	
Year 2	£100	.826	
Year 3	£100	.751	

Now we will see if we can find a short cut.

Activity 25

Review your calculations in Activity 24 to see if you can spot an approach that would have speeded up the calculations. Make a note of it here.

The total of the three discount factors could have been found from an annuity table. An example of an annuity table is given in the Appendix. The numbers in these tables are cumulative discount factors which can be used when the future stream of cash flows are for equal amounts at regular intervals.

Activity 26

Locate the factor that could have been used for Activity 25 and note it here.

The formula used to calculate the annuity factors is repeated here as follows:

$$\frac{1 - [(1 + r)^{-n}]}{r}$$

The symbol 'n' means the number of periods (years in our example) for which the amount will be received, and 'r' is the discount rate. It looks complicated, but you'll be surprised just how quickly you can learn to use it, providing you make use of the less frequently used keys on your calculator. We will try it for the details used in Activities 24 to 26. The sequence of key depressions is important. For most calculators it is as follows:

Key	Purpose
1	Entering the 1 at the start of the formula
– (minus)	
(	Opens the brackets
1.1	Entering 1 plus discount rate
x^y	To the power of (this might be INV and then X)
3	The three years
+/–	To change the 3 to –3
)	Close brackets. This gives the intermediate result of the amounts in brackets
=	The total of 1 – (the product of the bracketed figures)
÷	
.1	Dividing the amount by r

The answer should be 2.486851991. The factor in the annuity table is 2.487 because these tables are rounded to the nearest three decimal points.

Now we will try using it to solve two problems. In the first of these you could use the annuity tables; this might be quicker until you become accustomed to using the formula. You cannot use the tables for the second problem because they do not give enough future periods.

Activity 27

Someone has been given the choice of either being paid £3,000 now, or £400 per year over the next 10 years (i.e. £4,000 in total). This person could invest the money received at 10%. Which option is best. All you need to do is find the present value of the 10 instalments of £400, and compare it to the £3,000.

If you want to calculate the monthly repayments on an ordinary repayment mortgage, all you do is divide the amount borrowed by the present value of an annuity – using the number of months for 'n' and the monthly interest rate for 'r' in the formula.

If you wanted to do the calculation as a series of key depressions you would have to use more brackets in order to produce the discreet sums in the progression of the calculation. You might make a mistake here because you have to remember how many brackets you have opened and ensure that you use the same number of closing brackets. To avoid this you can do the calculations in separate stages.

Activity 28

Roy and Jenny borrow £40,000 on a monthly repayment mortgage. The repayment term is 20 years. The interest rate is 12% per annum. Calculate the monthly repayments. Do two preliminary calculations and note the results here:

1. Monthly interest rate (simply 0.12 divided by 12):

2. Present value of an annuity using this interest rate and a term of (20 × 12) 240 months:

3. Now divide the result of the calculation into £40,000.

Perpetuities

If the equal sums are to be received into an indefinite future (to infinity) their total present value becomes:

$$PV = \text{the recurring amount} \times \frac{1}{r} \quad \text{or} \quad \frac{\text{recurring amount}}{r}$$

You might be puzzled by this but it can be rationalized by noting that as the number of periods ('n') gets closer to infinity, then the result of the bracketed formula $((1 + r)^{-n})$ gets closer to zero. The fraction, with the figures in brackets already calculated, would be:

$$\frac{1 - 0}{r}$$

You can experiment with this on your calculator. You don't need any brackets. Use a rate of 10% (.1) and then calculate 1.1^{-40}, and then 1.1^{-5000}. When you feel like some self-amusement, try finding the number of periods where the calculator changes from giving a result to giving a zero (this will depend on the capabilities of your calculator).

Dividend valuation model

Theoretically, shareholders see the value of their investment as the present value of a stream of future dividends to be received from that investment.

It is possible to demonstrate mathematically (which we will not do – you will have to accept it) that this future stream of dividends stretches to infinity. This implies that if we know the dividends expected, and the rate of return expected, we can determine the capital value of the share. This is known as the 'dividend valuation model'.

Activity 29

Equity shareholders in a particular type of industry expect a 12% return on their investment. A dividend of £0.60 has just been announced by a particular company. Calculate what the market price of the equity shares in this company is likely to be.

In cost of capital calculations, we use the same components but in a different way because we are trying to find the rate of return expected. We know the market price of the share and we know the dividends; from these two we can calculate the rate of return expected by equity. It is simply a matter of rearranging the figures as follows:

$$\text{If market value} = \frac{\text{dividend}}{\text{rate of return expected}}$$

$$\text{then return expected} = \frac{\text{dividend}}{\text{market price}}$$

Activity 30

Rearrange the arithmetic in Activity 29 to find the rate of return expected, assuming that we are given the market price of £5.00 per share.

The next step in trying to understand the formula for calculating cost of equity is to understand something about 'cum-div' and 'ex-div' share price quotations.

A share price quoted as **cum-div** means that the price includes two elements:

- its true capital value (present value of future dividend receipts to infinity)
- the right to receive the whole of the next dividend

A share price quoted as **ex-div** relates to the true capital value only; in other words, it does not include the right to receive the next dividend.

For most of a company's accounting year, its shares are traded cum-div. They go ex-div at about two to four weeks prior to the payment of the dividend. This is to give the company an opportunity to close its share register at a certain date and prepare the dividend cheques for all the shareholders on the register at the point. Any share transfers during the period from when the register was closed to the time that the dividend is paid are not recorded in the share register and so the purchaser of shares during this period buys them at an ex-div price because the new owner will not get the next dividend.

The reason for pointing this out is that in cost of capital calculations we are usually given share prices that are quoted cum-div, whereas the capital value need for the calculation is the ex-div value – being the true capital value of the future stream of dividends.

In Activity 29, the price of £5.00 which we calculated would have been the ex-div value. The actual market price of this share cum-div would be its ex-div value plus the whole of the next dividend, i.e. (£5.00 + £0.60) £5.60. So if we were given the cum-div price of £5.60 in a cost of capital calculation, we would have to reduce it to its ex-div price. This is easily achieved; we simply knock off the whole of the impending dividend per share. The arithmetic can be set out as follows:

$$\text{Return expected } \frac{60p}{£5.60 - £0.60} = 12\%$$

The next step requires making use of a little bit of notation. At the start of a company's financial year, shareholders will not know what the next dividend is going to be, but as a starting point we can assume it will be the same as last year. On this assumption the 60p above can be represented by the symbol D_0 (the dividend at the present time). At this stage the formula is as follows:

$$\text{Return expected} = \frac{D_0}{\text{Ex-div price}}$$

But shareholders normally expect some growth in their dividends and would expect to get more than 60p at the end of the year.

Activity 31

See if you can think of the information that shareholders in a company might use to estimate a likely growth rate on the dividends.

Activity 32

See if you can identify a growth rate in the following series of total dividends paid by a company:

	1992	1993	1994
Dividends paid	80,000	88,000	96,800

It will not be so precise as this in most cases. There is some arithmetic that can be used to calculate growth rates over a period of past years but most shareholders will rely on observing signals rather than doing complicated arithmetic.

Assuming that there is some information for estimating growth rates, we will use the symbol 'g' to represent that rate. The dividend that was given the symbol D_0 represented the dividend that was received (or announced) today. With a growth rate of 'g' this dividend will become $D_0 \times 1 + g$ by the end of the next year. This is usually expressed as D_1 meaning the dividend expected at the end of the next year. We have not quite finished with the series of steps to give us a formula for cost of equity based on the dividend valuation model, but we are nearly there. We will use what we have so far in the next activity.

Activity 33

A summary of the details relating to the previous activities is established as follows:

- Current impending dividend 60p
- Market price currently quoted £5.60 (always assume share prices are quoted cum-div unless you are told they are ex-div)
- Dividend growth rate expected 10%

Calculate cost of equity using D_1 as the numerator instead of D_0. Don't overcomplicate the denominator, it's the same as before.

Notice how the ex-div price in this case is found by deducting the impending dividend of 60p. This is because the amount of 60p would have been part of the cum-div price. In cases where the cum-div price is given some time after payment of the last dividend, it will be necessary to deduct the next dividend expected, based on perceived growth rates.

In order to explain how the arithmetic that we have used up to now resolves into the formula that you must eventually use, it would be necessary to explain something that was deliberately skipped earlier in this section. This was where we avoided the arithmetical models that explain how shareholders see the capital value of their investment as the present value of a future stream of dividends stretching to infinity. If these models had been presented we would now have to change them slightly to recognize that this future stream of dividends is perceived as dividends that will grow by a constant factor each year.

I am assuming that most students for whom this book is intended will be quite content simply to accept the formula. There is always some satisfaction in making sense of how a formula is derived but on balance it is more important that you learn how to use it. The above notes and activities should enable you to find the right inputs for the formula and enable you to discuss the concepts on which it is based.

The formula you should use for cost of equity based on the dividend valuation model is as follows:

$$\text{Cost of equity} = \frac{D_1}{\text{Market value ex-div price}} + g$$

Activity 34

Use the formula to calculate cost of equity for the details in Activity 33.

The formula used in Activity 34 is usually called 'Gordon's growth model'. This is not the end of the subject on the cost of equity, although it is as far as we will go in this book. The dividend valuation model tends to be a somewhat naive model because it considers dividends as the sole determinant of share values. Share values are influenced by many factors, perhaps the most important is the company's earnings.

There are also various risk factors that we have not considered. We have looked at financial risk (in relation to gearing) and realized that the subject is inconclusive. There is also a problem of business risk that affects share values. Business risk is related to the type of business project that a company undertakes, and we looked at one aspect of this in Chapter 2 when considering operational gearing. But the subject is quite vast. It is also very interesting and includes many fascinating theories. I hope that one day you will have an opportunity to study the subject in more detail. In the meantime, good luck with your foundation studies and in the exams.

Summary

The key learning points in this chapter can be summarized as follows:

- companies accept money from investors and invest this money in business projects with a view to compensating the investors from the returns earned on these business projects
- there are four basic methods of investment appraisal: accounting rate of return, payback, net present value and internal rate of return
- each of these methods is based on the incremental cash flows (or profits) that would arise as a result of taking on the investment
- accounting rate of return expresses the average incremental profits as a percentage of the capital invested (either the initial capital or the average capital) and compares this to a hurdle rate set by the company
- payback is based on the length of time that the future stream of cash flows will repay the original investment
- discounted payback is based on the same idea except that the future receipts are discounted to their present value
- net present value discounts future cash flows by using the cost of capital as a discount rate

- if the net present value of all cash flows is positive, the project can be accepted because it will be earning a return that exceeds the cost of capital
- theoretically, if shareholders have information of the project the total market value of shares will be increased by the amount of the positive NPV
- internal rate of return is the discount rate that gives a net present value of zero and represents the rate of interest being on the project over its life cycle
- if the decision rule under IRR conflicts with that under NPV, the decision should be based on NPV because there are flaws in the concept of IRR
- the effect of inflation is recognized by discounting future cash flows expressed in today's prices at the real rate (money rate with an adjustment to remove the element of inflation)
- taxation alters the pattern of cash flows
- when a company's capital consists of different types of capital, the cost of capital is usually based on the weighted average cost of capital
- the marginal cost of capital is the cost of taking on the next increment of capital; this cost consists of the amount to be paid on the new capital plus the amount needed to maintain the value of equity
- risk is related to the variability of returns, financial risk relates to the variability of returns that is caused by the level of gearing
- there are no conclusive studies to show the optimum level of gearing ('optimum' meaning when WACC is at its lowest)
- the cost of equity is subject to many concepts and theories, most companies calculate the cost of equity using the dividend valuation model
- the dividend valuation model recognizes that shareholders perceive a rate of growth in dividend payments

Activity 1

Total profits for four years shown in the table are £91,000 but this includes an irrelevant cost of (4 × £1000) £4,000 and so the relevant profits before depreciation for the four years are (91,000 + 4,000) £95,000. Total depreciation is £40,000. Total relevant profits are, therefore, £55,000. Average annual profits are (55,000 ÷ 4) £13,750.

Activity 2

13,750/82,500 = 16.67%.

Activity 3

Initial capital is	£82,500
Capital at end of project	£42,500
	£125,000

Average capital (125,000 ÷ 2) £62,500. (You could also have found this by taking the average of £80,000 and £40,000 for the plant (£60,000) and adding the £2,500 for working capital that was invested throughout the four years.)
ARR on this basis is (13,750/62,500) 22%.

Activity 4

Advantages include: it is based on a concept that managers understand; it takes account of estimated income for the whole project (payback does not do this); the percentage return can be compared to a predetermined hurdle rate set by the company.
Disadvantages include: it is ambiguous (e.g. capital can be either initial capital or average capital); it is based on accounting profit, which is more subjective than cash; it ignores the time value of money.

Activity 5

The relevant cash inflows, and the cumulative amounts, are as follows.

		Cumulative
Year 1 (20,000 – 1,000)	19,000	
Year 2 (25,000 – 1,000)	24,000	43,000
Year 3 (40,000 – 2,000)	38,000	81,000
Year 4 (15,000 – 1,000)	14,000	95,000
At end of Year 4 (40,000 + 2,500)	42,500	137,500

Payback occurs during Year 4. Payback period is 3.11 years (i.e. 3 years plus (1,500/14,000) of a year).

Activity 6

The payback method suggests selection of Project 2 where payback occurs during Year 3. It occurs during Year 4 on Project 1, yet the total cash inflows from Project 1 are much greater than those from Project 2.

Activity 7

Project 4, because most of the money is received in the first year.

Activity 8

Advantages include: it is simple to use and easily understood by managers; it allows managers to assess some of the risks involved in a project.

Disadvantages include: it ignores receipts beyond the payback period; it ignores the time value of money (unless modified to discounted payback).

Activity 9

1. If the £100 is received now it can be invested to earn interest. By having to wait one year we lose the opportunity of earning that interest.
2. If the £100 is not received now we have lost the opportunity of being able to consume goods and services. People are prepared to sacrifice current consumption providing they can increase future consumption.

Activity 10

The present value of £1,600 to be received in 3 years' time, discounted at a rate of 20%, is £1,600 × 0.579) £926. The investment will not be made because to earn 20% interest this person would not be prepared to invest more than £926 in the project. (Instead of this explanation, you could have said that the return is less than 20%.)

Activity 11

	Cash flow	Discount factor	Present value
Year 0	−82,500	1	−82,500
Year 1	+19,000	0.870	+16,530
Year 2	+24,000	0.756	+18,144
Year 3	+38,000	0.658	+25,004
Year 4 (14,000 + 42,500)	+56,500	0.572	+32,318
		Net present value	+9.496

Activity 12

Present values of receipts are: Year 1 £5,727; Year 2 £4,273; total = £10,000.

Activity 13

With inflation at 5%, goods worth £100 today are equal to goods worth £105 in one year's time. This person wants to consume an extra 20% of £105 which is £26. The £26 is 26% of the current amount of £100.

Activity 14

1.1025/1.05 = 1.05. The real rate is 5%.

Activity 15

£10,000 × 0.907 = £9,070.

Activity 16

	Cash flow	Discount factor	Present value
Year 0	−82,500	1	−82,500
Year 1	+19,000	0.870	+16,530
Year 2	+24,330	0.756	+18,393
Year 3	+35,030	0.658	+23,050
Year 4	+47,673	0.572	+27,269
Year 5	−6,682	0.497	−3,321
		Net present value	−579

Notice that a project that would have been accepted when tax was ignored (Activity 11) should now be rejected because the NPV is negative when tax is taken into account.

Activity 17

40/400 = 10%.

Activity 18

The interest paid on stock with a nominal value of £100 is £5. This represents (5/50) 10% of the market value. The answer is 10%.

Activity 19

Investment B.

Activity 20

Company A: EPS Year 1 (£780/5,000) 15.6p; Year 2 (£585/5,000) 11.7p, a fall of (3.9/15.6) 25%.
Company B: EPS Year 1 (£260/1,000) 26p; Year 2 (£65/1,000) 6.5p, a fall of (19.5/26) 75%.

Activity 21

The cost of equity will increase in recognition of the higher financial risk.

Activity 22

1. £138,000   £102,000 = £36,000
2. £90,000 – £40,000 = £50,000
3. £36,000 + £50,000 = £86,000
4. £500,000
5. 86,000/500,000 = 17.2%

Activity 23

£75,000/£500,000 = 15%, the same as before the capital structure was changed (which is what you would have expected from the hypothesis).

Activity 24 £

Year 1 £100 × .909	90.90
Year 2 £100 × .826	82.60
Year 3 £100 × .751	75.10
	248.60

Activity 25

You could have multiplied one amount of £100 by the total of the discount factors. £100 × 2.486 = £248.60.

Activity 26

The annuity factor is given as 2.487. The discrepancy between this and Activity 24 results from the fact that the individual discount factors have been rounded to three decimal points. If you work through the annuity formula according to the guidance that follows this activity, you will find that the correct annuity factor is 2.486851991.

Activity 27

£400 × 6.145 = £2,458. It would be better to accept the £3,000 now.

Activity 28

1. 0.01% per month
2. 90.8194
3. £440.43 per month

Activity 29

£0.60/0.12 = £5.00

Activity 30

£0.60/£5.00 = 12%

Activity 31

Growth in past dividends. Perhaps announcements by the directors.

Activity 32

They are growing at the rate of 10% per year.

Activity 33

Note that 60p × 1.1 = 66p. Cost of equity is, therefore, 0.66/(5.60 − 0.60) 13.2%.

Activity 34

(0.66/5.00) + 0.1 = 23.2%

Note a substantial difference between this and the original rate of 12% (Activity 30) when growth expectations were ignored.

Questions for self assessment

Answers to self-assessment questions are given at the end of the book.

12.1   (a) Essential to an understanding of the investment appraisal techniques of payback, accounting rate of return and net present value is the role of depreciation.

Required:
Explain how you would treat depreciation in a computation for each of the above appraisal techniques giving reasons for your decisions.

(b) Company TH Ltd is considering investing in one of two mutually exclusive projects. Both projects would require an investment of £150,000 at the commencement of the project and the profile of returns is as follows:

	Project 1		Project 2	
	Profit	Cash-flow	Profit	Cash-flow
	£	£	£	£
Year 1	40,000	60,000	30,000	54,000
Year 2	30,000	50,000	20,000	44,000
Year 3	25,000	45,000	15,000	39,000
Year 4	35,000	55,000	25,000	49,000
Year 5				74,000

You are told that the machinery associated with Project 1 will be sold for £70,000 at the end of year 4 and the machinery associated with project 2 will be sold for £30,000 at the end of year 5.
The company's cost of capital is 15%.

Required:
Determine for both projects the:
(i)   Payback period.
(ii) Accounting rate of return.
(iii) Net Present Value.
and advise which project should be invested in, giving your reasons.

(c) You have been asked by a manager at TH Ltd why you might need the expected disposal proceeds of the capital investment at the end of the project for any investment appraisal technique as the capital investment has already been depreciated.

Required:
Clearly answer the manager's query identifying which investment appraisal technique, if any, utilizes the disposal proceeds of a capital investment at the end of a project.

(AAT Final)

12.2   Your company is considering investing in its own transport fleet. The present position is that carriage is contracted to an outside organization. The life of the transport fleet would be five years, after which time the vehicles would have to be disposed of.
The cost to your company of using the outside organization for its carriage needs is £250,000 for this year. This cost, it is projected, will rise 10% per annum over the life of the project. The initial cost of the transport fleet would be £750,000 and it is estimated that the following costs would be incurred over the next five years:

	Drivers' Costs £	Repairs & Maintenance £	Other Costs £
Year 1	33,000	8,000	130,00
Year 2	35,000	13,000	135,000
Year 3	36,000	15,00	140,000
Year 4	38,000	16,000	136,000
Year 5	40,000	18,000	142,000

Other costs include depreciation. It is projected that the fleet would be sold for £150,000 at the end of year 5. It has been agreed to depreciate the fleet on a straight line basis.

To raise funds for the project your company is proposing to raise a long-term loan at 12% interest rate per annum.

You are told that there is an alternative project that could be invested in using the funds raised, which has the following projected results:

Payback: 3 years
Accounting rate of return: 30%
Net present value: £140,000

As funds are limited, investment can only be made in one project.

Note: The transport fleet would be purchased at the beginning of the project and all other expenditure would be incurred at the end of each relevant year.

Required:
(a) **Prepare a table showing the net cash savings to be made by the firm over the life of the transport fleet project.**
(b) **Calculate the following for the transport fleet project:**
    (i)   Payback Period
    (ii) Accounting rate of return
    (iii) Net present value (using a discount rate of 12%).
(c) **Write a short report to the Investment Manager in your company outlining whether investment should be committed to the transport fleet or the alternative project outlined. Clearly state the reasons for your decision.**
(d) **Discuss briefly whether 12% was an appropriate rate for the cost of capital.**

(*AAT Final, modified – part (d) added*)

12.3 R. Jones (Salford) Limited has just received a quotation for £4,470 for installing cavity wall insulation in its office building during December 1987. You ascertain the following information:

Its fuel bill in 1987 for heating the office is expected to be £10,000.
The bank has recently offered a loan at 12% per year.
Fuel prices are expected to increase at 5% per year.
The scheme is expected to save 10% of the fuel bill.

In 6 years, the firm is planning to move to another area, so it has decided to base its initial evaluation on a 6 year project life. Because of the uncertainties involved, it has also decided to ignore any effect of the improvement on the sale value of the building. The firm requires a risk premium of 2% above its cost of bank borrowing for investments of this type.

Assume that all cash flows arise at the end of the year in which they occur.
Ignore taxation.

Required:
(a) **Calculate for the project:**
    (i)   The payback period (to the nearest year)
    (ii) Its net present value
    (iii) Its approximate internal rate of return.
(b) **Comment on the advantages and disadvantages of each of the three methods which appear in part (a). State which method is likely to give the best answer.**

(*ACCA Certified diploma – modified*)

12.4 Fellingham PLC has 20 million Ordinary £1 shares in issue. No shares have been issued during the last four years. The company's earnings and dividends record taken from the historic accounts showed:

Year	1	2	3	4
Earnings per share	11.00p	12.40p	10.90p	17.20p
Dividend per share	10.00p	10.90p	11.88p	12.95p

At the Annual General Meeting for year one the Chairman had indicated that it was the intention to consistently increase annual dividends by 9%, anticipating that on average this would maintain the spending power of shareholders and provide a modest growth in real income.

In the event, subsequent average annual inflation rates, measured by the general index of prices, have been:

Year	2	3	4
	11%	10%	8%

The Ordinary shares are currently selling for £3.44, ex the year four dividend.

Required:

(a) Comment upon the declared dividend policy of the company and its possible effects upon both Fellingham PLC and its shareholders, illustrating your answer with the information provided.

(b) What cost of equity capital is implied for Fellingham PLC by the use of the dividend model:

$$K \begin{bmatrix} \text{cost of} \\ \text{equity} \\ \text{capital} \end{bmatrix} = \frac{D_0[1+g]}{P_0} + g$$

in which D = dividend, P = share price, and g = annual rate of dividend growth?

(ACCA *Certified diploma*)

Questions without answers

Answers to these questions are published separately in the *Teacher's Manual*.

12.5 Beacon Chemicals plc is considering the erection of a new plant to produce a chemical named X14. The new plant's capital cost is estimated at £100,000 and if its construction is approved now, the plant can be erected and commence production by the end of 1986. £50,000 has already been spent on research and development work. Estimates of revenues and costs arising from the operation of the new plant appear below:

	1987	1988	1989	1990	1991
Sales price – £ per unit	100	120	120	100	80
Sales volume – units	800	1,000	1,200	1,000	800
Variable costs – £ per unit	50	50	40	40	40
Fixed costs £000's	30	30	30	30	30

If the new plant is erected sales of some existing products will be lost and this will result in a loss of contribution of £15,000 per year over its life.

The accountant has informed you that the fixed costs include depreciation of £20,000 per annum on the new plant. They also include an allocation of £10,000 for fixed overheads. A separate study has indicated that if the new plant was built, incremental overheads, excluding depreciation, arising from its construction would be £8,000 per year.

The plant would require additional working capital of £30,000.

For the purposes of you initial evaluation ignore taxation.

Required:
(a) Prepare a statement of the incremental revenues, costs and net cash flows arising from a decision to build the plant.
(b) Calculate the payback period to the nearest year.
(c) Compute the net present value of the project using an 8% discount rate.
(d) Write a short report to the managing director recommending acceptance or otherwise of the project. Explain the reasons for your recommendation and state what further investigations may be necessary.
(e) Should companies take taxation into account when they evaluate investment proposals? Explain your answer.

(ACCA Certified diploma)

12.6 Silicon Limited over the past 4 years has spent £3 million on developing a new silicon chip. It is now faced with three mutually exclusive choices:
  (1) It can manufacture the chip itself in which case the plant will cost £5 million. This will be spent at the end of December 1987. Additional working capital of £2.1 million will be required when production commences at the start of 1988. Sales and selling prices are expected to be as follows:

	1988	1989	1990	1991	1992
Number sold – (000s)	100	100	100	80	80
Sales price – (£ per unit)	120	120	120	100	90

  Silicon usually depreciates plant of this type over 5 years using the straight line method and assumes a zero scrap value. Variable costs are expected to be £65 per unit and fixed costs, including depreciation, £3 million per year.
  (2) Sell the know-how to a major international firm for a single payment of £3.1 million, receivable at the end of December 1987.
  (3) Sell the know-how for a royalty of £10 per unit. Anticipated sales of chips would be as shown above.
If choice (2) or (3) are taken, then the company will not manufacture the chips itself. Silicon estimates that its weighted average cost of capital is 12%. You should assume that sales revenue and costs occur at the end of the year in which they arise. Ignore taxation.

Required:
(a) Calculate the cash flows relevant to a decision whether or not to manufacture the chips. You can ignore choices 2 and 3 for this part of the answer.
(b) Calculate the net present value of each option.
(c) What other factors should be taken into account before a decision is made? What would your decision be?

(ACCA Certified diploma)

12.7 Arkwright Mills PLC is considering expanding its production of a new yarn code name X15. The plant is expected to cost £1 million and have a life of 5 years and a nil residual value. It will be ready for operation before 31 December 1984 and the initial period will be used to build up stocks. £500,000 has already been spent on development costs of the product and this has been charged to revenue in the year it was incurred. The following profit and loss statements for the new yarn are forecast:

	1985	1986	1987	1988	1989
	£M	£M	£M	£M	£M
Sales	1.2	1.4	1.4	1.4	1.4
Costs, including depreciation	1.0	1.1	1.1	1.1	1.1
Profit before tax	0.2	0.3	0.3	0.3	0.3

Tax is charged at 33% and paid 1 year in arrears. Depreciation has been calculated on a straight line basis. A capital allowance of 25% of the reducing balance is available and the company has substantial taxable profits. Additional working capital of £0.6 M will be required at the beginning of the project. You should assume that all cash flows occur at the end of the year in which they arise.

Required:

(a) Prepare a statement showing the incremental cash flows of the project relevant to a decision concerning whether or not to proceed with the construction of the new plant.

(b) Compute the Net Present Value of the project using a 10% discount rate.

(c) Compute the discounted payback period to the nearest year. Explain the meaning of this term.

(d) Define Internal Rate of Return and state how you would calculate it for an Investment Project. (No calculations are required.)

(e) Prepare a short note explaining why net present value is superior to payback.

(ACCA *Certified diploma, tax rates and allowances updated*)

12.8 Blunsden Electronics plc is considering replacing one of its machines with more modern equipment. The existing machine has unit costs of production as follows:

	£
Labour	50
Maintenance	30
Depreciation	20
Apportioned overheads	100
	200

The new machine will have the following cost structure:

	£
Labour	20
Maintenance	20
Depreciation	40
Apportioned overheads	40
	120

Overhead costs are apportioned on the basis of labour cost. Maintenance is regarded as a variable cost. The cost of the new machine is £200,000 and development costs of £100,000 have already been spent. The new machine will be more flexible than the old machine, enabling working capital to be reduced by £50,000 after the new machine has been installed. You should assume that this saving lasts only for the life of the new machine.

The level of overheads for the firm will remain unchanged as a consequence of introducing the new machine. The potential output of the new machine will be 25% higher than for the old machine. However, for the foreseeable future production will be constrained by market conditions to the current level of 2,000 units per annum. The lives of both the new and old machines are expected to be 5 years from today's date and their scrap values at that date, zero.

The company aims to achieve a target debt ratio of 40% (equity 60%:debt 40%). A bank has offered the company a loan at 10% per annum to finance the project. Cost of equity is estimated at 13%.

You can ignore taxation in your calculations.

Required:

(a) Prepare a statement showing those incremental cash flows of the project that are relevant to a decision concerning whether or not to proceed with the purchase of the new plant.

(b) Compute the cost of capital which should be used to discount the cash flows of the project.

(c) Write a short note explaining your answer to (b), stating what other rate you might have used and why the one you have chosen is preferable.
(d) Compute the net present value of the project.
(e) Write a short report on the project giving your recommendations and stating what additional information you would require.

(ACCA Certified diploma)

Present Value Table

Present value of 1 i.e. $(1 + r)^{-n}$
where r = discount rate
$\quad\quad n$ = number of periods until payment

Discount rates (r)

Periods (n)	1%	2%	3%	4%	5%	6%	7%	8%	9%	10%	
1	0·990	0·980	0·971	0·962	0·952	0·943	0·935	0·926	0·917	0·909	1
2	0·980	0·961	0·943	0·925	0·907	0·890	0·873	0·857	0·842	0·826	2
3	0·971	0·942	0·915	0·889	0·864	0·840	0·816	0·794	0·772	0·751	3
4	0·961	0·924	0·888	0·855	0·823	0·792	0·763	0·735	0·708	0·683	4
5	0·951	0·906	0·863	0·822	0·784	0·747	0·713	0·681	0·650	0·621	5
6	0·942	0·888	0·837	0·790	0·746	0·705	0·666	0·630	0·596	0·564	6
7	0·933	0·871	0·813	0·760	0·711	0·665	0·623	0·583	0·547	0·513	7
8	0·923	0·853	0·789	0·731	0·677	0·627	0·582	0·540	0·502	0·467	8
9	0·914	0·837	0·766	0·703	0·645	0·592	0·544	0·500	0·460	0·424	9
10	0·905	0·820	0·744	0·676	0·614	0·558	0·508	0·463	0·422	0·386	10
11	0·896	0·804	0·722	0·650	0·585	0·527	0·475	0·429	0·388	0·350	11
12	0·887	0·788	0·701	0·625	0·557	0·497	0·444	0·397	0·356	0·319	12
13	0·879	0·773	0·681	0·601	0·530	0·469	0·415	0·368	0·326	0·290	13
14	0·870	0·758	0·661	0·577	0·505	0·442	0·388	0·340	0·299	0·263	14
15	0·861	0·743	0·642	0·555	0·481	0·417	0·362	0·315	0·275	0·239	15

	11%	12%	13%	14%	15%	16%	17%	18%	19%	20%	
1	0·901	0·893	0·885	0·877	0·870	0·862	0·855	0·847	0·840	0·833	1
2	0·812	0·797	0·783	0·769	0·756	0·743	0·731	0·718	0·706	0·694	2
3	0·731	0·712	0·693	0·675	0·658	0·641	0·624	0·609	0·593	0·579	3
4	0·659	0·636	0·613	0·592	0·572	0·552	0·534	0·516	0·499	0·482	4
5	0·593	0·567	0·543	0·519	0·497	0·476	0·456	0·437	0·419	0·402	5
6	0·535	0·507	0·480	0·456	0·432	0·410	0·390	0·370	0·352	0·335	6
7	0·482	0·452	0·425	0·400	0·376	0·354	0·333	0·314	0·296	0·279	7
8	0·434	0·404	0·376	0·351	0·327	0·305	0·285	0·266	0·249	0·233	8
9	0·391	0·361	0·333	0·308	0·284	0·263	0·243	0·225	0·209	0·194	9
10	0·352	0·322	0·295	0·270	0·247	0·227	0·208	0·191	0·176	0·162	10
11	0·317	0·287	0·261	0·237	0·215	0·195	0·178	0·162	0·148	0·135	11
12	0·286	0·257	0·231	0·208	0·187	0·168	0·152	0·137	0·124	0·112	12
13	0·258	0·229	0·204	0·182	0·163	0·145	0·130	0·116	0·104	0·093	13
14	0·232	0·205	0·181	0·160	0·141	0·125	0·111	0·099	0·088	0·078	14
15	0·209	0·183	0·160	0·140	0·123	0·108	0·095	0·084	0·074	0·065	15

Annuity Table

Present value of an annuity of 1 i.e. $\dfrac{1 - (1 + r)^{-n}}{r}$

where r = interest rate
n = number of periods

Interest rates (r)

Years (n)	1%	2%	3%	4%	5%	6%	7%	8%	9%	10%	
1	0·990	0·980	0·971	0·962	0·952	0·943	0·935	0·926	0·917	0·909	1
2	1·970	1·942	1·913	1·886	1·859	1·833	1·808	1·783	1·759	1·736	2
3	2·941	2·884	2·829	2·775	2·723	2·673	2·624	2·577	2·531	2·487	3
4	3·902	3·808	3·717	3·630	3·546	3·465	3·387	3·312	3·240	3·170	4
5	4·853	4·713	4·580	4·452	4·329	4·212	4·100	3·993	3·890	3·791	5
6	5·795	5·601	5·417	5·242	5·076	4·917	4·767	4·623	4·486	4·355	6
7	6·728	6·472	6·230	6·002	5·786	5·582	5·389	5·206	5·033	4·868	7
8	7·652	7·325	7·020	6·733	6·463	6·210	5·971	5·747	5·535	5·335	8
9	8·566	8·162	7·786	7·435	7·108	6·802	6·515	6·247	5·995	5·759	9
10	9·471	8·983	8·530	8·111	7·722	7·360	7·024	6·710	6·418	6·145	10
11	10·37	9·787	9·253	8·760	8·306	7·887	7·499	7·139	6·805	6·495	11
12	11·26	10·58	9·954	9·385	8·863	8·384	7·943	7·536	7·161	6·814	12
13	12·13	11·35	10·63	9·986	9·394	8·853	8·358	7·904	7·487	7·103	13
14	13·00	12·11	11·30	10·56	9·899	9·295	8·745	8·244	7·786	7·367	14
15	13·87	12·85	11·94	11·12	10·38	9·712	9·108	8·559	8·061	7·606	15

Years (n)	11%	12%	13%	14%	15%	16%	17%	18%	19%	20%	
1	0·901	0·893	0·885	0·877	0·870	0·862	0·855	0·847	0·840	0·833	1
2	1·713	1·690	1·668	1·647	1·626	1·605	1·585	1·566	1·547	1·528	2
3	2·444	2·402	2·361	2·322	2·283	2·246	2·210	2·174	2·140	2·106	3
4	3·102	3·037	2·974	2·914	2·855	2·798	2·743	2·690	2·639	2·589	4
5	3·696	3·605	3·517	3·433	3·352	3·274	3·199	3·127	3·058	2·991	5
6	4·231	4·111	3·998	3·889	3·784	3·685	3·589	3·498	3·410	3·326	6
7	4·712	4·564	4·423	4·288	4·160	4·039	3·922	3·812	3·706	3·605	7
8	5·146	4·968	4·799	4·639	4·487	4·344	4·207	4·078	3·954	3·837	8
9	5·537	5·328	5·132	4·946	4·772	4·607	4·451	4·303	4·163	4·031	9
10	5·889	5·650	5·426	5·216	5·019	4·833	4·659	4·494	4·339	4·192	10
11	6·207	5·938	5·687	5·453	5·234	5·029	4·836	4·656	4·586	4·327	11
12	6·492	6·194	5·918	5·660	5·421	5·197	4·988	4·793	4·611	4·439	12
13	6·750	6·424	6·122	5·842	5·583	5·342	5·118	4·910	4·715	4·533	13
14	6·982	6·628	6·302	6·002	5·724	5·468	5·229	5·008	4·802	4·611	14
15	7·191	6·811	6·462	6·142	5·847	5·575	5·324	5·092	4·876	4·675	15

Suggested answers to self-assessment questions

Chapter 1

1.1 (a) In terms of accounting profit, it will not pay to close Department 3 unless this results in saving more than £6,000 on general overheads. At the moment Department 3 is contributing £5,000 towards the total profit of the firm. This contribution will be lost if the department is closed. It is quite likely that the total of general overheads will remain the same after closing Department 3 and so the £6,000 apportioned to this department will simply be included in the amounts apportioned to the other two departments.

(b) Probably in the ratio of each department's floor area.

(c) The contribution of £5,000 will be lost and total profits will be (£32,000 – £5,000) £27,000. The figures could have been set out in various ways such as:

Total contribution from Departments 1 and 2	£60,000
Less general overheads	33,000
Profit	27,000

(d) There might be a loss of custom in the other departments. Some shoppers might be attracted to the store because of the existence of Department 3 and are likely to buy goods in other departments. How will the shopping area and other facilities for that department be used? Are there any redundancy costs that need to be considered?

1.2 The total fixed costs for the period can be found from $100,000 \times £12 = £1,200,000$.

(a) Sales $80,000 \times £30$		2,400,000
Less variable costs $80,000 \times £10$		800,000
		1,600,000
Fixed costs		1,200,000
Profit		400,000

(Note that this could have been found from: 80,000 × (£30 – £10) less £1,200,000.)

(b) At this level of sales, profit will equal 100,000 × £8 (the profit per unit). The £800,000 could have been found from the following:

Sales 1000,000 × £30		3,000,000
Less variable costs 100,000 × £10		1,000,000
		2,000,000
Fixed costs		1,200,000
Profit		800,000

(c) Sales 120,000 × £30		3,600,000
Less variable costs 120,000 × 10		1,200,000
		2,400,000
Fixed costs		1,200,000
Profit		1,200,000

(Or 120,000 × £20 less 1,200,000.)

1.3 (a) (i) The total marginal cost of production is (£20,000 + £10,000) £30,000. Since 30,000 units were produced, the marginal cost per unit is (£30,000 × 30,000) £1.00 per unit.

(ii) The fixed factory overhead cost per unit is (£15,000 × 30,000) £0.50. The absorbed cost per unit is as follows:

Marginal cost (as above)	£1.00
Factory overheads absorbed	.50
Absorbed cost per unit	£1.50

(b) There are 5,000 units in stock and so closing stock on a marginal cost basis is (5,000 × £1) £5,000 and on an absorbed cost basis it is (5,000 × £1.50) £7,500. Computation of profit under each basis could be as follows:

(i) With closing stock valued at marginal cost:

Sales		100,000
Manufacturing costs:		
Raw materials	20,000	
Direct labour	10,000	
Factory overheads	15,000	
	45,000	
Less closing stock	5,000	
		40,000
		60,000
Selling and administration		35,000
Profit		25,000

(ii) With closing stock valued at absorbed cost:

Sales		100,000
Manufacturing costs		
(as above)	45,000	
Less closing stock	7,500	
		37,500
		62,500
Selling and administration		35,000
Profit		27,500

Note that the profit using absorbed cost for valuation of closing stock is £2,500 higher than when a marginal cost basis is used. The absorbed cost basis treats (5.000 × £0.50) £2,500 of fixed factory overheads as an asset (as part of stock) to be carried forward to the next year.

Chapter 2

2.1 (a) £240,000 ÷ (£40 – £25) 16,000 pairs of shoes.
(b) 25,000 – 16,000 = 9,000 pairs. As a percentage this is (9,000/25,000) 36%.
(c) Variable costs become £27 and contribution £13 per unit. Contribution required is (£240,000 + £20,000) £260,000. Answer £260,000 ÷ £13 = 20,000 pairs.
(d) Fixed costs become (£240,000 + £30,000) £270,000. New selling price is (£40 × 1.125) £45. Contribution per unit becomes (£45 – £25) £20. Answer £270,000 ÷ £20 = 13,500 pairs.

2.2 Company A

Working (high/low)	Low	High	Increase	
Activity (sales value)	£220,000	£280,000	£60,000	
Total costs	£199,000	£244,000	£45,000	(75% × sales)
Less variable costs				
75% of sales	£165,000	210,000		
Fixed costs (balance)	£34,000	£34,000		

(a) Contribution required (£34,000 + £42,000) £76,000. Contribution to sales ratio is 25%. Answer £76,000 ÷ 0.25 = £304,000.
(b) Contribution will be (£188,000 × 0.25) £47,000. Profit will be (£47,000 – £34,000) £13,000.
(c) Assumptions include: no change in price levels between the two years; no change in sales mix between the two years; no factors affecting fixed costs between the two years.

2.3 Cavalaire Ltd, workings:
Depreciation: Method 1 (£200,000 ÷ 5) £40,000 per year. Method 2 (£80,000 ÷ 5) £16,000 per year.
Total fixed costs: Method 1 (£60,000 + £40,000) £100,000. Method 2 (£29,000 + £16,000) £45,000.
Contribution per unit: Method 1 £60 – £35 = £25. Method 2 £60 – £45 = £15

(a) Break-even points:
Method 1: £100,000 ÷ £25 = 4,000 units.
Method 2: £45,000 ÷ ££15 = 3,000 units.

(b) Workings:
Method 1: Capital invested (£200,000 + £40,000) £240,000. Target profit (£240,000 × 0.20) £48,000. Contribution required £100,000 + £48,000 = £148,000.
Method 2: Capital invested (£80,000 + £40,000) £120,000. Target profit (£120,000 × 0.20) £24,000. Contribution required £45,000 + £24,000 = £69,000.

Answer:
Method 1: £148,000 ÷ £25 = 5,920 units.
Method 2: £69,000 ÷ £15 = 4,600 units.

(c) Additional figures for the discussion could include the DOG ratio. This requires calculating the level of sales at which profits are equal under each method. Profits will be equal when the additional contribution per unit from Method 1 of (£25 – £15) £10 covers the additional fixed costs under Method 1 of (£100,000 – £45,000) £55,000. Equilibrium is, therefore, achieved at (£55,000 ÷ £10) 5,500 units. At this level the cost and profit structures are as follows:

		Method 1		Method 2
Sales (5,500 × £60)		330,000		330,000
Variable costs	192,500		247,500	
Fixed costs	100,000		45,000	
		292,500		292,500
EBIT		37,500		37,500

DOG ratios are:
Method 1: (330,000 – 192,500) ÷ 37,500 = 3.67 times.
Method 2: (330,000 – 247,500) ÷ 37,500 = 2.2 times.

Students could have included a profit/volume graph plotting the contribution from each method.

The discussion should include the following points:

- Method 1 carries greater risk than Method 2 because EBIT under Method 1 is much more sensitive to changes in the level of sales. A 10% increase in sales will cause EBIT under Method 1 to change by (3.67 × 10%) 36.7 %, whereas EBIT under Method 2 will change by (2 × 10%) 20%.
- A further aspect of risk in Method 1 is that it breaks even at a higher level of sales than for Method 2.
- A decision over which method to adopt will depend on how confident managers are regarding estimates of sales demand. If demand is likely to be for the maximum production capacity of 10,000 units, Method 1 offers the higher return on capital invested.

2.1 Giles Radio

(a) (i) Initial investment:

Premises (opportunity cost)	120,000
Refurbishment costs	30,000
Stock ($1.5 \times .8 \times 40,000$)	48,000
	198,000

(ii) Fixed costs:

Annual running costs (assumed fixed)	44,000
Depreciation ($30,000 \div 5$)	6,000
	50,000

Contribution to sales ratio = 20%

Sales level to break even $50,000 \div .2$	250,000

Check:

Sales	250,000
Cost of sales (80%)	200,000
Contribution	50,000
Fixed costs	50,000
Profit	0

(iii) Forecast profit:

Sales ($12 \times 40,000$)	480,000
Cost of sales ($480,000 \times .8$)	384,000
Gross profit (which = $.25 \times 384,000$)	96,000
Running costs and depreciation	50,000
Forecast profit	46,000

(iv) Margin of safety:
   $(480,000 - 250,000) \div 480,000 = 48\%$.

(v) Level of sales required to achieve profit of 20% of initial investment:

Required profit ($.2 \times 198,000$)	39,600
Sales required ($39,600 + 50,000$) $\div .2$	448,000

Check:

Sales	448,000
Cost of sales ($80\% \times 448,000$)	358,400
Gross profit ($.25 \times 358,400$)	89,600
Fixed costs (as before)	50,000
Profit	39,600

(b) Points to mention: The project appears to be viable. Based on projected sales the return on initial capital is (46/198) 23%, compared to the company's target rate of 20%. The margin of safety is quite high. If actual sales are less than projected sales by anything greater than ((480 – 448) ÷ 480) 7%, the return will be less than the target rate of 20% on initial capital.

Chapter 3

3.1 Rumbles Ltd

(a) (i) The managing director has noticed that sales increased by 7,000 units and, therefore, expected the profit to increase by the additional contribution on these units. The contribution per unit is (£20 – £12) £8 and the increase expected was 7,000 × £8 = £56,000.

(ii) To comply with financial accounting regulations, the accountant will value opening and closing stocks on the basis of absorbed cost. This amounts to (£12 + £6) £18 per unit. The accountant's profit statements will, therefore, be as follows:

	Period 2 £	Period 2 £	Period 3 £	Period 3 £
Sales		220,000		360,000
Cost of sales:				
Opening stock	90,000		198,000	
Variable cost of production	204,000		156,000	
Fixed production overheads	90,000		90,000	
	384,000		444,000	
Less closing stock	198,000		108,000	
		186,000		336,000
Profit		34,000		24,000

(iii) The effect of valuing stock on the basis of absorbed cost is to carry fixed overheads forward from the period when they were incurred to the period when the goods are sold. In Period 2 closing stocks exceed the opening stocks by 6,000 units, which means that the fixed overheads charged against sales are reduced by (6,000 × £6) £36,000. In Period 2, the reverse occurs. Opening stocks exceed closing stocks by 5,000 units which means that the cost of sales will include an amount of (5,000 × 6) £30,000 in excess of the fixed overheads of £90,000 incurred in that period.

(b) Various types of statement could be prepared. The following is an example that shows the difference quite clearly:

	Period 2	Period 3	Difference
Sales	220,000	360,000	140,000
Variable cost of sales	(132,000)	(216,000)	(84,000)
Contribution	88,000	144,000	56,000
			Director's expectation
Fixed overheads:			
Incurred in period	90,000	90,000	
Brought forward in opening stock	30,000	66,000	
Carried forward in closing stock	(66,000)	(36,000)	
Included in cost of sales	54,000	120,000	(66,000)
Contribution less the amount for fixed costs included in cost of sales	£34,000	£24,000	(£10,000)

3.2 A description of all five terms in part (a) can be found in the chapter. A discussion of (b) (i) can be based on the text following the CIMA definitions of prime cost and marginal cost on page __.

(ii) On the face of it this statement appears to be true but it does contain a great deal of imprecise language (probably a deliberate ploy by the examiner). In the first place we need to know how the terms 'absorption costing' and 'marginal costing' are being used. Are they a reference to the book-keeping system, or a reference to the basis for stock valuation. On the assumption that they relate to bases for stock valuation, the following questions need to be answered: What is meant by 'in full'? If it means that the absorbed cost of a product includes all factory overheads (even if fixed) then the statement is true. But if it means that the absorbed cost of a product recognizes all overheads, including those beyond the factory floor, the statement is not true. What is meant by 'variable costs'? If this is a reference to variable production costs, the statement is true. But if it includes variable costs beyond the factory floor (such as sales commissions and delivery costs) the statement is not true.

3.3 After completing the book-keeping, the trial balance prior to the transfer of items to the profit and loss account is as follows:

	Debit £	Credit £
Raw materials control (18 items)	90	
Finished goods control (97 items)	970	
Debtors	3,800	
Creditors		1,850
Bank	5,084	
Administration expenses	50	
Sales		300
Cost of sales (150 + 6)	156	
Share capital		12,000
Profit and loss account		4,000
Fixed assets	8,000	
	18,150	18,150

Profit and loss account for the period		
Sales	300	
Cost of sales	156	
Gross profit	144	
Administration expenses	50	
Profit before tax	94	

Balance sheet at end of period		
Fixed assets		8,000
Current assets		
Stock (90 + 970)	1,060	
Debtors	3,800	
Bank	5,084	
	9,944	

Current liabilities			
Trade creditors		1,850	
Net current assets			8,094
			16,094
Share capital			12,000
Profit and loss account (4,000 + 94)			4,094
			16,094

Chapter 4

4.1 Note that there appears to be a loss of stock of 100 boxes. This is not apparent until you attempt to reconcile the balance on the stock account. Total purchases were 2,100 boxes, total sales were 1,500 boxes, closing stock is given as 500 boxes. The cost of these losses should be taken out of stock at the price that would have been used for an issue on the last day of the period.

Costs per box are as follows:

Purchase date	£
13 January	36
8 February	38
11 March	40
12 April	35
15 June	28

(a) (i) FIFO

Sales date	Cost price	£	Total
10 February	200 at £36	7,200	
	300 at £38	11,400	18,600
20 April	100 at £38	3,800	
	500 at £40	20,000	23,800
25 June	100 at £40	4,000	
	300 at £35	10,500	14,500
30 June (losses)	100 at £35		3,500
Cost of sales			60,400
Cost of stock	500 at £28		14,000
Cost of yarn purchased			74,400

(ii) LIFO

Sales date	Cost price	£	Total
10 February	400 at £38	15,200	
	100 at £36	3,600	18,800
20 April	400 at £35	14,000	
	200 at £40	8,000	22,000
25 June	400 at £28		11,200
30 June (losses)	100 at £28		2,800
Cost of sales			54,800

	Cost of stock	100 at £36	3,600	
		400 at £40	16,000	19,600
	Cost of yarn purchased			74,400

(iii) AVCO

Transaction	Boxes in stock	Total cost	Average price	Cost of sales
at 10 February	600	£22,400	37.3333	
Sold	500	18,667		18,667
Balance	100	3,733		
Purchases				
March/ April	1,000	38,000		
at 20 April	1,100	41,733	37.94	
Sold	600	22,764		22,764
Balance	500	18,969		
Purchases June	500	14,000		
at 25 June	1,000	32,969	32.97	
Sold + losses	500	16,485		16,485
Closing stock	500	16,484		
Total cost of sales				57,916

Note that closing stock plus cost of sales = cost of purchases of £74,400.

(b) The effect on profit can be set out as follows:

	FIFO	LIFO	AVCO
Sales	67,200	67,200	67,200
Cost of sales	60,400	54,800	57,916
Gross profit	6,800	12,400	9,284
Other expenses	2,300	2,300	2,300
Profit	4,500	10,100	6,984

Students could be expected to make comments in respect of the following: Effect of accounting policy on cost of sales. LIFO would not be acceptable in this case because 400 out of the 500 boxes in stock are being valued at a cost of £40 each whereas the latest selling price is only (£15,200 + 400) £38 per box. The purchase on 11 March could have been delayed until 12 April if Mr G was aware that there might be a fall in price. The goods were not needed on 11 March. Stock losses are quite substantial, suggesting poor internal control over stocks. Profit as a percentage of capital invested (assuming that the FIFO basis is adopted) amounts to £4,500/(£40,000 + £14,000) 8.33% for six months (16.67% per annum). The investment in working capital (£14,000) assumes that there are no debtors.

4.2 Atlas Limited
(a) (i) FIFO   £

Issues on 6 June (1,000 × £4) + (1,500 × £5)	11,500
Issues on 14 June (500 × £5) + (1,500 × £5.50) + (1,500 × £4.50)	17,500

Closing stock (1,500 × £4.50) £6,750

(ii) LIFO

Issues on 6 June (1,500 × £5.50) + (1,000 × £5)   13,250
Issues on 14 June (3,000 × £4.50) + (500 × £5)   16,000

Closing stock (1,000 × £4) + (500 × £5) £6,500

(iii) AVCO

Transaction	Quantity	Total cost	Average price	Cost of issue £
At 6 June	4,500	22,250	£4.9444	
Issue 6 June	2,500	12,361		12,361
Balance	2,000	9,889		
Receipt 12 June	3,000	13,500		
	5,000	23,389	£4.6778	
Issue 14 June	3,500	16,372		16,372
Closing stock	1,500	7,017		

(b) (i) The square root of (2 × £100 × 80,000 ÷ £0.25) is 8,000 units. The EOQ finds an optimum point between two opposing costs – cost of ordering stocks and cost of holding stocks.

(ii) On the basis of no delivery lead time and no buffer stock (as mentioned in the question) the average stock is 4,000 kilos. This can be reasoned as follows: if stock is ordered in quantities of 8,000 kilos the maximum stock level is 8,000 kilos and the minimum is zero kilos. If stock is used at an even rate throughout the period the average stock on hand throughout that period will be one-half of 8,000 kilos.

(iii) 80,000 ÷ 8,000 = 10 orders.

(c) Buffer stocks are held in order to avoid running out of stock before the next supply arrives. There are various ways of calculating buffer stocks, including the use of probability factors. A common practice is to ensure that re-order levels are set so as to allow for the maximum lead time and maximum usage during that lead time. Lead time is the length of time that occurs between the point when the first action is taken to replenish stocks and when those new stocks arrive. The cost of having to hold both buffer stocks and lead time stocks can be reduced by a 'just-in-time' purchasing policy. This involves establishing close links with suppliers for small and frequent orders, often against a bulk contract. Ideally this cooperation requires the supplier to deliver an order as soon as existing stocks of the purchaser run out.

4.3 Ordering schedule:

Number of orders	1	2	3	4	5	6
Order quantity	600	300	200	150	120	100
Average quantity in stock	300	150	100	75	60	50
Cost of average stock	£720	£360	£240	£180	£144	£120
Ordering costs	£6	£12	£18	£24	£30	£36
Holding costs	£144	£72	£48	£36	£29	£24
Total costs	£150	£84	£66	£60	£59	£60

The above schedule shows that the economic order quantity is 120 units. This requires orders to be placed five times per year. This could have been found from the EOQ formula. The square root of (2 × 6 × 600 ÷ 0.48) gives an EOQ of 122 units.

(b) The problems in determining EOQs result from the assumptions inherent in the EOQ model itself. These are discussed on page 102.

4.4 The analysis requires a schedule similar to the following:

Output in units	Labour cost	Overheads per day	Labour and overheads	Cost per unit
Current level				
15	£42.00	£32.00	£74.00	£4.93
New scheme				
16	£46.72	£32.00	£78.72	£4.92
17	£50.66	£32.00	£82.66	£4.86
18	£54.72	£32.00	£86.72	£4.82
19	£58.90	£32.00	£90.90	£4.78
20	£63.20	£32.00	£95.20	£4.76

The above schedule shows the labour and overhead cost per unit. It assumes that there will be no increase in the number of rejects at the higher levels of output. The schedule shows that it will be worthwhile negotiating this scheme with employees since it results in a reduction of unit costs.

Chapter 5

5.1
(a)

	Basis	Dept 1	Dept 2	Maintenance	Canteen
Specific costs:					
Labour		60,000	70,000	25,000	15,000
Consumables		12,000	16,000	3,000	10,000
Heat and light	Floor space	4,000	4,800	2,000	1,200
Rent and rates	Floor space	6,000	7,200	3,000	1,800
Depreciation	Book value	15,000	12,000	2,000	1,000
Supervision	Employees	12,000	9,000	3,000	–
Power	Kilowatt hours	9,000	8,000	2,000	1,000
Service department totals				40,000	30,000
Apportion canteen	Employees	15,000	11,250	3,750	(30,000)
Apportion maintenance	Service hours	25,000	18,750	(43,750)	
Total		158,000	157,000		

(b)   Machine hour rate for Department 1: £158,000/6,320 = £25 per machine hour.
Labour hour rate for Department 2: £157,000/7,850 = £20 per labour hour.
(c)   Department 1: £155,000 – (6,000 × £25) = £5,000 under-absorbed.
Department 2: £156,000 – (7,900 × £20) = £2,000 over-absorbed.
(d)   A blanket rate (or factory-wide) rate is not appropriate because the demands made on production facilities by individual products will differ between the two production departments. In the above example, the costs of Department 1 appear to be driven by the number of machine hours. The cost driver in Department 2 is assumed to be labour hours. If a blanket rate were used, what activity would be used as the cost driver? Adoption of a blanket rate would be a reversal of modern practice which considers that departmental volume based cost drivers result in departmental blanket rates. The overheads need to be analysed further and associated with the activities that cause the costs.

5.2

(a)

	Machining	Assembly	Paint shop	Engineering	Stores	Canteen
Overheads	180,000	160,000	130,000	84,000	52,000	75,000
Canteen	27,000	17,000	13,000	10,000	8,000	(75,000)
Stores	24,000	18,000	12,000	6,000	(60,000)	
Engineering	45,000	30,000	25,000	(100,000)		
Total	276,000	225,000	180,000			

The following bases have been used for apportioning costs of the service cost centres:

    Canteen: number of employees
    Stores: number of orders
    Engineering: number of service hours.

Machine hour rate for machine shop: £276,000/9,200 = £30 per machine hour.
Labour hour rate for the assembly department: £225,000/11,250 = £20 per labour hour.
Labour cost rate for paint shop: £180,000/£45,000 = 400%.

(b) Machine shop: £290,000 – (10,000 × £30) = £10,000 over-absorbed.
Assembly department: £167,000 – (7,800 × £20) = £11,000 under-absorbed.
Paint shop: £155,000 – (4 × £35,000) = £15,000 under-absorbed.
(c) Overhead absorption rates need to be predetermined for various reasons. Some costs, such as maintenance, can vary significantly from one month to the next. If actual overheads were used, the unit costs would be greater in some months than in others. This lumpiness can be smoothed by estimating a total amount for the whole year. The actual cost of some overheads will not be known until after the units have been made and, perhaps, sold. Changing technology has resulted in most production methods being highly automated. In these circumstances, overheads have become the largest single element in the cost of a product. Existing overhead absorption bases (as in this question) lump all overheads together in production departments and use a single volume-based activity (such as labour hours) to absorb overheads. Research has shown that overheads are driven by many activities, some of which relate to the diversity of products. Volume-based absorption rates do not give an accurate measure of the resources being used by each product. For example, in the above schedule engineering costs have been allocated to departments on the basis of the number of hours spent in each department. It might be found that the cost of engineering services in the machine shop is driven by the number of set-ups and that some products require more set-ups than others. Activity-based costing recognizes this by collecting overheads by activity rather than by production department.

5.3 Hospital
(a) Total overheads for the whole hospital are £11,500,000. In-patient days for the whole hospital are 25 × 10,000 = 250,000. The overhead absorption rate is (£11,500,000/250,000) £46 per in-patient day.

(b)

	General		Geriatric
Direct costs (as detailed)	£5,000,000		£6,000,000
In-patient days	(5,000 × 10) 50,000	(100 × 200)	20,000
Direct costs per in-patient day	£100		£300
Add overheads per in-patient day (a)	46		46
Total per in-patient day	£146		£346

(c)   The total overheads of the entire hospital are charged to all departments using a single volume-based activity driver (in-patient day). This makes no attempt to identify the individual activities that drive the overhead costs, or the diversity in the way that the support activities are used for the different types of patient. For example, the administration costs presumably include the cost of running the admissions department where the demands on the services provided will differ as between general surgery (where there is a large volume of short-stay patients) and the geriatric department where there are fewer patients staying in hospital for long periods of time. The same argument can be applied to all facilities included under overheads. It does not make sense to use a broad average when there is such diversity in the type of treatment provided.

Cost information of the type presented provides very little to help managers with cost control, other than being used for a comparison between budgeted costs and actual costs. The analysis of costs is much too general to draw attention to the cost of specific activities and, therefore, cannot be used for any kind of long-term planning aimed at reducing costs. Some of the information might be appropriate for the purposes of funding.

(d)   Activity-based costing will involve identifying the different activities that drive the costs in each department. For example, the total administration costs will result from various activities that include the following: admissions, discharges, day care, and casualty. These particular activities are likely to be driven by the number of patients (irrespective of how long they stay in the hospital) and so a cost per patient could be determined. Cost of cleaning (assuming this does not relate to laundry) is likely to be driven by the number of wards and so a rate per ward should be used. There is not sufficient information in the question to provide numeric examples but we could assume that administration includes £1,500,000 that can be associated with the cost of admissions. Using the total number of admissions of 10,000 as given, cost of admissions would be £150 per patient.

5.4 ABC for Insurance Company

(a)   Total premium income:

Regular (70,000 × £50)	£3,500,000	
Super (10,000 × £100)	1,000,000	
	4,500,000	

Total overheads (given) £900,000
Overhead absorption rate (£900,000/£4,500,000) = £0.20 per £1 of premium income
Unit overhead costs:

Regular £50 × £0.20	£10
Super £100 × £0.20	£20

(b)   Activity-based costing:

Cost drivers:

Selling costs: customer visits $(1 \times 70{,}000) + (5 \times 10{,}000) = 120{,}000$ visits.

Underwriting: adjustments $(1 \times 70{,}000) + (8 \times 10{,}000) = 150{,}000$ adjustments.

Computing: enquiries $(2 \times 70{,}000) + (6 \times 10{,}000)$ 200,000 enquiries.

Premium collection: number of policies $(70{,}000 + 10{,}000)$ 80,000 policies.

Activity-based application rates:

Selling $(£360{,}000/120{,}000)$ £3.00 per visit.

Underwriting $(£300{,}000/150{,}000)$ £2.00 per adjustment.

Computing $(£140{,}000/200{,}000)$ £0.70 per enquiry.

Premium collection $(£100{,}000/80{,}000)$ £1.25 per policy.

Unit costs	Regular	Super
Selling	$(1 \times £3.00)$ £3.00	$(5 \times £3.00)$ £15.00
Underwriting	$(1 \times £2.00)$ £2.00	$(8 \times £2.00)$ £16.00
Computing	$(2 \times £0.70)$ £1.40	$(6 \times £0.70)$ £4.20
Premium collection	£1.25	£1.25
Total	£7.65	£36.45

(c)   Product costs are more meaningful under ABC than traditional absorption methods because they recognize the demands made by each product on the various support activities. This is important for companies that produce a diversity of products where each one has a relatively short life cycle. ABC directs attention to the activities that cause costs and this might lead to a more cost-efficient product (or process) design.

5.5 Simultaneous equations

(a) $A = £4{,}200 + 0.05B$

$B = £2{,}400 + 0.10A$

$A = £4{,}200 + 0.05 (£2{,}400 + 0.10A)$

$A = £4{,}200 + £120 + 0.05A$

$0.995A = £4{,}320$

$A = £4{,}342$

$B = £2{,}400 + (0.10 \times £4{,}342)$

$B = £2834$

(b)   Two other methods that could have been used are as follows:

1.   Repeated apportionments: under this method, service department costs are repeatedly apportioned in the specified ratios until the amount for one of the service departments becomes insignificant. This amount is then apportioned to production cost centres in the relative ratios of those cost centres for the type of cost concerned. The end result is similar to the simultaneous equation method.

2.   Stepped apportionment (not explained in the text): service department costs are apportioned in a specified sequence. The service department that provides most services to other service departments is apportioned first, then the next, and so on. Each apportionment ignores any share that should be attributed to a service department whose costs have been apportioned in a previous step. Costs are simply apportioned over the remaining departments in the ratios for those departments.

Author's note: This kind of arithmetic has lost its relevance in modern practice. If companies are still using departmental absorption rates (in contrast to ABC rates) the figures are entered on a computer spreadsheet that is designed to carry out the apportionment. But it might be another 10 years or so before we can be sure that this kind of question has been expunged from the examination syllabus.

Chapter 6

6.1 *Note:* If part (a) of the question is answered by treating direct labour, variable overhead and fixed overhead as a single 'conversion' cost, this would then have to be split into its separate elements for part (b). Less work is involved if the table of equivalent production is based on each element of cost. Total production of finished goods is represented by the number sold plus the number in stock.

	Direct materials	Direct labour	Variable overhead	Fixed overhead
Costs	£714,000	£400,000	£100,000	£350,000
EUs:				
Finished goods	98,000	98,000	98,000	98,000
Work in progress	4,000	2,000	2,000	2,000
	102,000	100,000	100,000	100,000
Cost per EU	£7.00	£4.00	£1.00	£3.50

(a) (i) Cost of goods sold 90,000 × (£7 + £4 + £1 = £3.50)   £1,395,000
   (ii) Closing stock of finished goods 8,000 × (£7 + £4 + £1 = £3.50)   124,000
   (iii) Work in progress (4,000 × £7) + (2,000 × (£4 + £1 + £3.5)   45,000

            Total production costs (as per question)   1,564,000

(b) (i) Marginal cost of goods sold 90,000 × (£7 + £4 + £1)   £1,080,000
   (ii) Closing stock of finished goods 8,000 × (£7 + £4 + £1)   96,000
   (iii) Work in progress (4,000 × £7) + (2,000 × (£4 + £1)   38,000
         Fixed overhead treated as a cost for the period   350,000

            Total production costs   1,564,000

It is also acceptable to add the fixed overhead cost of £350,000 to the marginal cost of goods sold to give a total manufactured cost of goods sold of £1,430,000.

6.2 ATM Chemicals

Quantities:

Input units		25,000
Normal losses	1,000	
Finished goods	15,000	
Work in progress	6,000	
	22,000	
Abnormal losses (balance)	3,000	

	Material	Labour	Overhead	Total
Costs	£62,000	£44,000	£63,000	
Less scrap value of normal losses	2,000			
	£60,000	£44,000	£63,000	£167,000
EUs:				
Finished goods	15,000	15,000	15,000	
Abnormal losses	3,000	3,000	3,000	
Work in progress	6,000	4,000	3,000	
	24,000	22,000	21,000	
Cost per EU	£2.50	£2.00	£3.00	£7.50

Cost allocation:

Finished goods 15,000 × £7.50		£112,500
Abnormal losses 3,000 × £7.50		22,500
Work in progress (6,000 × £2.50) + (4,000 × £2.00) + (3,000 × £3.00)		32,000
Total (as above)		£167,000

Scrap stock consists of (3,000 + 1,000) 4,000 kilos at £2.00 per kilo	£8,000

6.3 BI plc

(a) Total weight produced was 240 tonnes. Common costs will be apportioned at the rate of (£144,000/240) £600 per tonne.

	Product X	Product Y	Product Z
Sales of refined products	£75,000	£72,000	£72,000
Costs:			
Common costs apportioned	60,000	36,000	48,000
Further processing	30,000	18,000	12,000
	90,000	54,000	60,000
Profit/(loss)	(£15,000)	£18,000	£12,000

(b) Incremental amounts:

	Product X	Product Y	Product Z
If sold after refining	75,000	72,000	72,000
If sold at split-off point	45,000	60,000	56,000
Incremental revenue	30,000	12,000	16,000
Incremental costs	30,000	18,000	12,000
Incremental profit/(loss)	–	(6,000)	4,000

On the basis of this analysis, it will benefit the company to sell Product Y without further processing and Product Z should be refined. Product X can be sold either after the initial process or refined without altering total profits. In all three cases it has been assumed that further processing costs are avoidable by not carrying out the additional processes.

(c) Common costs are unlikely to be relevant to very many decisions except for those that are influenced by the total amount incurred (such as a decision to close down the plant completely). Common costs that have been apportioned to individual products are irrelevant to decisions on those individual products. Such apportionments are purely arbitrary and done only for the purposes of stock valuation when preparing the financial accounts.

6.4 Poultry farmer
(a) Chick rearing section:

Quantities:

Chicks purchased		1,000
Transferred to egg laying	850	
Normal losses	100	
	———	
		950
		———
Abnormal losses (balance)		50
		———

	Purchase cost	Feed	Wages/ overhead	Total
Costs	£180	£1,044	£968	£2,192
EUs				
Transferred to egg laying	850	850	850	
Abnormal losses	50	20	30	
	———	———	———	
	900	870	880	
	═══	═══	═══	
Cost per EU	£0.20	£1.20	£1.10	£2.50

Cost allocation:

Transferred to egg laying section 850 × £2.50	£2,125
Abnormal losses (50 × £0.20) + (20 × £1.20) + (30 × £1.10)	67
	———
	2,192
	═══

(b) Market value of goods produced:

	Eggs	Carcases
Sales	£5,750	£1,750
Closing stocks		
Eggs 2,400/12 × £0.50	100	
Carcases 200 × £2.50		500
Total	5,850	2,250

Sales values are given; we need to determine gross profit in order to ascertain cost. Total market value of production is (£5,850 + £2,250) £8,100. Total cost of production is £6,885. Cost, therefore, represents (6,885/8,100) 85% of market value. Gross profit is 15% of sales.

Stock valuation:

Eggs:	Sales value (as above)	£100
	Less profit margin	15
		———
	Cost	85
		═══
Carcases:	Sales value (as above)	£500
	Less profit margin	75
		———
	Cost	425
		═══

(c) This question is impossible to answer. The problem with joint product costing is that there is no scientific way of establishing the cost of the individual products that emerge from the joint process. Consequently, it is impossible to assess the profitability of either product. Any accounting apportionment of joint costs is arbitrary and is done for the purposes of stock valuation. The focus of attention on joint products should be to ensure that the process as a whole is profitable.

(d) Incremental revenue:

		per hen
If sold as carcases at end of first process		£2.50
Income from further processing:		
Egg sales 120/12 × £0.50	5.00	
Sale of carcase	1.50	
		6.50
		4.00
Incremental costs		3.60
Incremental contribution		£0.40
Incremental fixed costs (per year)		£600

Incremental profit will depend on the number of hens kept in the further egg laying section. It will be necessary for Mr Boggin to keep an additional (£600/£0.40) 1,500 hens each year in the further egg laying section in order to break even. Each hen in excess of this will contribute an additional £0.40 to profit. At the moment, Mr Boggin keeps (2 × 900) 1,800 hens each year. If the same number are kept in the further egg laying section, the increase in profit will amount to (300 × £0.40) £120.

Chapter 7

7.1 Gimmet, workings:

			£
1.	Budgeted sales	10,000 × £12	120,000
	Standard cost	10,000 × £9	90,000
	Budgeted margin	10,000 × £3	30,000

2.	Actual sales:		
	Additional units sold £1,500/£3 = 500		
	Budgeted sales		120,000
	Additional sales (500 × £12)		6,000
	Adverse price variance		(1,000)
			125,000

3.	Actual material cost		
	Standard cost 10,500 × £6		63,000
	Less favourable price variance		(1,268)
	Add adverse usage variance		400
			62,132

4.	Actual wages cost		
	Standard cost 10,500 × £2.40		25,200
	Less favourable efficiency variance		(240)
	Add adverse rate variance		780
			25,740

5. Actual fixed overheads

Overheads absorbed 10,500 × £0.60	6,300
Less favourable volume variance	(300)
Add adverse expenditure variance	200
	6,200

(a) Profit statement:

Sales		125,000
Less manufacturing costs:		
Raw materials	62,132	
Labour	25,740	
Fixed overheads	6,200	
		94,072
Actual profit (per question)		30,928

(b) Sometimes an adverse variance for one factor results from the properties of a dependent factor for which a favourable variance is reported. For example, in the above the material usage variance is adverse whereas the material price variance is favourable. It could be that more materials than standard were used because they were of sub-standard quality.

7.2 In the following answers, the areas are described by starting with the letter in the bottom left corner of each rectangle and moving in a clockwise direction.

(a)

(i)   Since all variances are adverse, the standard cost must be represented by the smaller of the two main rectangles: X U V Y.

(ii) Actual cost must be represented by the larger of the two rectangles: X R T Z.

(iii) Wage rate variance relates to all hours worked and so it must be represented by the area: U R T W.

(iv) Labour efficiency variance is measured at standard rate and so it must be represented by the area: Y V W Z.

(v) The total labour cost variance is represented by the area outside of the standard cost rectangle (as described in (i) above). It can be identified by the area: Y V U R T Z.

Students should note that the small rectangle in the top right corner (V S T W) is the area that is sometimes called the joint rate/efficiency variance. By tradition, it is always included in the rate variance (or price variance in the case of materials).

(b) They might represent something that can be exploited by the company; they might result from a faulty standard; they might help to explain a related adverse variance.

7.3 B Limited

(a) Standard cost for one unit:

	£
Direct material 20 × £10	200
Direct labour 12 × £5.50	66
Fixed overheads 12 × £900,000/60,000	180
	446

(b) Cost variances: £

Direct materials total cost variance

		£
4,800 units of finished product should cost (4,800 × £200)		960,000
Actual material cost		1,050,000
Adverse variance		90,000

Material price variance:

		£
100,000 kg should cost (100,000 × £10)		1,000,000
Actual cost		1,050,000
Adverse variance		50,000

Material usage variance:

	kg	£
4,800 units should use (4,800 × 20)	96,000	
Actually used	100,000	
Adverse quantity variance	4,000	
Adverse quantity variance at standard price (4,000 × £10)		40,000

Direct labour total cost variance:

		£
4,800 units should cost (4,800 × £66)		316,800
Actual cost		310,000
Favourable variance		6,800

Direct labour rate variance:

		£
62,000 hours should cost (62,000 × £5.50)		341,000
Actual cost		310,000
Favourable variance		31,000

Direct labour efficiency variance:

	hours	£
4,800 units should take (4,800 × 12)	57,600	
Actually took	62,000	
Adverse time variance	4,400	
Adverse time variance at standard rate 4,400 × £5.50		24,200

Total overhead cost variance:

		£
Overheads incurred		926,000
Overheads absorbed 4,800 × £180		864,000
Adverse variance		62,000

Overhead expenditure variance:

		£
Budgeted overheads		900,000
Actual overheads		926,000
Adverse variance		26,000

Overhead capacity variance:
This is nil: 60,000 machine hours were budgeted and 60,000 were used.

Overhead efficiency variance:

The standard overhead absorption rate is £900,000/60,000 £15 per hour.

	Machine hours	
4,800 units should take 4,800 × 12	57,600	
Actually took	60,000	
Adverse time variance	2,400	
Adverse time variance at standard rate (2,400 × £15)		36,000

(c) Reconciliation statement

Standard cost of actual production:	
Direct materials	960,000
Direct labour	316,800
Fixed overhead (4,800 × £180)	864,000
	2,140,800

Cost variances	Favourable	Adverse	
Material price		50,000	
Material usage		40,000	
Labour rate	31,000		
Labour efficiency		24,200	
Overhead expenditure		26,000	
Overhead efficiency		36,000	
	31,000	176,200	145,200
Actual cost			2,286,000

(d) Material price variance: price increases after the standards were set; lack of control in buying department.
Material usage variance: standard set too high; inefficient production.
Labour rate variance: standard incorrectly set; expected wage increase not implemented.
Labour efficiency variance: employment of low grade labour (which might explain favourable rate variance); poor control of labour.

7.4 Dour Ltd

(a) The actual sales price was (£112,500/15,000) £7.50 per chair.
The standard variable cost per chair (£3 + £2) £5.00 per chair.
The standard margin is (£8 – £5) £3.00 per chair.

Sales price variance is 15,000 × (£8.00 – £7.50)	£7,500	adverse
Sales margin volume variance 3,000 × £3	£9,000	adverse

(b)
Labour rate variance	£2,000	adverse
Labour efficiency variance	£6,000	favourable

(c)
Material price variance	£11,000	adverse
Material usage variance	£1,000	favourable

(d) Reconciliation report:

			£
Budgeted contribution 18,000 × £3			54,000
Deduct adverse sales margin variances:			
Sales price		7,500	
Sales volume		9,000	
			16,500
			37,500

Cost variances	Favourable	Adverse	
Labour rate		2,000	
Labour efficiency	6,000		
Material price		11,000	
Material usage	1,000		
	7,000	13,000	6,000
Actual contribution			31,500

(e) Despite a reduction in sales price, the company was unable to meet its targeted sales volume of 18,000 chairs. The forecasts might have been too optimistic. Fashions might have changed. If part of the market was for garden use, demand might have been affected by the weather. The two labour cost variances suggest that a higher rate of pay has encouraged greater efficiency. They could also be explained by employing staff with better skills than those that were envisaged at the time when the standards were set. The two material cost variances suggest that materials used were of a higher quality than originally planned and this has led to less wastage.

Chapter 8

8.1 *Tutorial note:* In a question like this you will find it worthwhile to set out a calculation of the revised budgeted profit, and of the actual profit, before working on the variances. This will help you to become familiar with the detail and also provides 'goal post' figures for the reconciliation statement. This approach is used in the workings given here. These assume that the variance on promotional expenses should be treated as a planning variance.

		£	£
Revised budgeted profit:			
Sales 10,000 units at £9.50			95,000
Marginal cost of sales:			
Production 12,000 units:			
Materials 42,600 square metres at £0.65		27,690	
Direct labour 8,000 hours at £3.30		26,400	
Variable overhead 8,000 hours at £2.40		19,200	
		73,290	
Less closing stock 2,000 × £6.1075		12,215	
			61,075
Budgeted contribution			33,925
Fixed overhead		16,800	
Promotional expense		15,000	
			31,800
Revised budgeted profit			2,125

Actual profit/(loss)		
Sales 8,500 × £9.50		80,750
Marginal cost of sales		
Wages	26,500	
Materials	27,000	
Variable overheads	20,150	
	73,650	
Closing stocks 2,000 × £6.1075	12,215	
		61,435
Actual contribution		19,315
Fixed overheads	17,100	
Promotional expense	15,000	
		31,100
Actual loss		(12,785)

Reconciliation statement

	Favourable	Adverse	
Original budgeted profit			10,000
Planning variances:	Favourable	Adverse	
Promotional expenses	2,050		
Sales price 10,000 × £0.50		5,000	
Wage rate 8,000 × £0.30		2,400	
Material usage (42,600 − 37,200) × £0.65		3,510	
		10,910	
Less increase in cost of closing stock			
2,000 × (£6.1075 − £5.615)		985	
	2,050	9,925	7,875
Revised budgeted profit (as above)			2,125

Operating variances:			
Sales volume variance 1,500 × (£9.50 − £6.1075)		5,089	
Material price variance (£26,156 − £27,000)		844	
Material usage (37,275 − 40,240) × £0.65		1,927	
Labour rate (£28,050 − £26,500)	1,550		
Labour efficiency (7,000 − 8,500) × £3.30		4,950	
Variable overhead spending (£20,400 − £20,150)	250		
Variable overhead efficiency (7,000 − 8,500) × £2.40		3,600	
Fixed overhead spending (£16,800 − £17,100)		300	
	1,800	16,710	14,910
Actual profit (as above)			12,785

Workings can be determined from the bracketed figures. The first figure in brackets for each cost variance is related to the standard amount (either quantity or value).

8.2 A standard hour is a measurement of work, not a measurement of time. For example, in the question 1,800 lawn mowers were produced. The standard time allowed for each lawn mower is 10 hours and so the production of lawn mowers represents 18,000 standard hours of work. The concept of a standard hour can be used either for overhead absorption or for measuring performance ratios. For the manufacturer of garden equipment, the following can be determined:

	Standard hours
Budgeted standard hours for the period:	44,000
$(2,000 \times 10) + (8,000 \times 1) + (8,000 \times 2)$	
Standard hours for goods produced	50,000
$(1,800 \times 10) + 8,000 \times 1) + (12,000 \times 2)$	

Productivity ratios
Production volume ratio 50,000/44,000 = 113.6%
Efficiency ratio 50,000/43,000 = 116.3%
Capacity ratio 43,000/44,000 = 97.7%
(Note that 97.7% of 116.3% = 113.6%)

8.3 Two Divisions

(a) Operating ratios	Division A	Division B
Return on investmen	15%	20%
Operating profit to sales	30%	5%
Asset turnover rate	0.5 times	4 times
Reconciliation	$0.5 \times 30\% = 15\%$	$4 \times 5\% = 20\%$

(b) **First calculate residual income:**
(i) With cost of capital at 12%

Operating profit of division	120,000	20,000
Imputed interest	96,000	12,000
Residual income	24,000	8,000

(ii) With cost of capital at 18%

Operating profit of division	120,000	20,000
Imputed interest	144,000	18,000
Residual income	(24,000)	2,000

These calculations show the folly of making comparisons between two completely different types of divisional activity. Division A is capital intensive. By comparison to Division B, its products have a higher profit margin but the amount of sales produced by each £1 of assets is less. Division B is less capital intensive. Its products have a lower profit margin than Division A but the amount of sales produced by each £1 of capital is greater.

With the cost of capital at 12%, Division A generates more residual income than Division B. But since Division A is more capital intensive than Division B, the situation will differ when the cost of capital increases to 18%. Division B will still be providing some residual income whereas Division A produces none.

These results suggest that neither method is ideal for measuring divisional performance. The company must decide whether it is attempting to measure the performance of managers, or if it is attempting to evaluate whether it is worthwhile continuing to operate each division. Assessing the performance of divisional managers might best be served by considering various non-financial indicators. Evaluating whether the investment in a division is worthwhile should be done on the basis of the discounted present value of future cash flows. (Discounted cash flow for investment appraisal is covered in Chapter 12.)

8.4 Workings:
In order to apportion indirect costs on the basis of turnover, the following percentages (rounded) could be used:

	Turnover £m	%
Foods	37.5	45
Clothing	24.0	28
Electric	22.5	27
	84.0	100

The relative floor space of each department can be based on the percentages found from the existing apportionment of indirect costs, as follows:

	Indirect costs £m	%
Foods	2.1	21
Clothing	3.6	36
Electric	4.3	43
	10.0	100

(a) Operating report based on John Smith's ideas (all figures in £m):

	Foods	Clothing	Electric
Turnover	37.5	24.0	22.5
Cost of sales	30.6	16.5	15.2
Direct costs	2.4	2.7	6.4
Indirect costs	4.5	2.8	2.7
Operating profit/(loss)	0	2.0	(1.8)

(b) The existing basis of apportionment is consistent with generally accepted accounting practices but the information has limited value for management decisions because of its arbitrary nature. It might be more useful to managers if the 'charge' for joint facilities were based on an 'opportunity cost'. This type of approach would charge each department with a cost represented by the income that has been lost by not being able to hire out the relevant shop floor facilities to an outside contractor (see Chapter 11).

(c) The problem with raising prices is that although the contribution ratio is increased, the volume of sales might fall. The effect on contribution of lowering or raising prices cannot be judged without considering the likely impact on sales volume. A better approach is to treat floor space as a limiting factor and to ensure that floor space is allocated to products that earn the highest contribution per unit of limiting factor (see Chapter 11 for the arithmetical approach to this type of problem).

(d) The current contribution per 1% of floor space for each department is as follows:

	Contribution £m	% of floor space	Contribution per 1% of floor space
Food	4.5	21	£214,000
Clothing	4,8	36	£133,000
Electric	0.9	43	£21,000

By giving up 10% of the floor space used by electric, the company will lose a contribution of (10 × £21,000) £210,000. Against this the company will receive £270,000 from the cosmetics retailer. Since there appears to be a net gain of (270,000 − 210,000) £60,000, the project should be given further consideration.

8.5 Citadel group

(a)

	Division 1 £m	Division 2 Electric £m	Computer £m	Total £m
Capital employed (profit/return)	80.0	10.0	20.0	30.0
Profit before interest and tax	14.4	1.6	6.2	7.8
Interest at 15%	12.0	1.5	3.0	4.5
Residual income	2.4	0.1	3.2	3.3

(b) A statement on which division is the most profitable will depend on what criterion is used to identify profitability. Division 1 earns more profit than Division 2. Division 2 has a higher residual income than Division 1. This recognizes the cost of using the capital employed in each division. The rate of return on capital employed is higher in Division 2 than it is in Division 1. Residual income is usually considered the best criterion. Any indicator that is based on accounting values for capital employed is suspect when historical costs are used because these do not reflect the current value of capital employed.

(c) The manager of Division 2 might be tempted to improve ROCE by closing the electrical components activity. This would raise ROCE to 31%, whereas at the moment it is (7.8/30) 26%. But this would reveal a fall in residual income from £3.3m to £3.2m and it is for reasons such as this that central management prefer to reward divisional managers on the basis of residual income.

Chapter 9

9.1 Freewheel

(a) (i) Monthly cash budget:

	Jul	Aug	Sept	Oct	Nov	Dec
Receipts:						
From customers:						
Cash sales	13,500	13,800	14,400	20,000	15,200	12,000
Credit sales	12,000	12,600	13,500	13,800	14,400	20,000
Share issue			20,000			
Total receipts	25,500	26,400	47,900	33,800	29,600	32,000

Payments:

To Suppliers	12,000	13,000	14,000	18,000	16,000	14,000
Wages paid:						
for current month	6,000	7,500	7,500	7,500	9,000	9,000
for previous month	2,000	2,000	2,500	2,500	2,500	3,000
Overheads	7,000	7,000	7,000	7,000	8,000	8,000
Fixed asset						10,000
Total payments	**27,000**	**29,500**	**31,000**	**35,000**	**35,500**	**44,000**
Balance b/f	3,000	1,500	(1,600)	15,300	14,100	8,200
Balance c/f	1,500	(1,600)	15,300	14,100	8,200	(3,800)

(ii) Budgeted profit and loss account:

Sales		177,800
Costs of sales:		
Opening stock	25,000	
Purchases	86,000	
	111,000	
Closing stock	38,000	
		73,000
Gross profit		104,800
Wages and salaries	62,000	
Overheads	45,000	
Depreciation	8,500	
		115,500
Loss before tax		10,700
Dividends		10,000
Reduction of accumulated profits		20,700

(iii) Budgeted balance sheet at 31 December 1992

Fixed assets (£126,000 + £30,000 – 8,500)		147,500
Current assets:		
Stock	38,000	
Debtors	27,200	
	65,200	
Creditors: amounts due within one year		
Trade creditors	24,000	
Other creditors	41,000	
Bank overdraft	3,800	
	68,800	
Net current liabilities		3,600
Total assets less current liabilities		143,900
Capital and reserves		
Share capital		120,000
Profit and loss account (44,600 – 20,700)		23,900
		143,900

(b) Matters that need to be discussed with the budget committee include:

1. Sales are decreasing yet the plan on stocks is to increase them from two months' purchases to three months' purchases. Is this really necessary? In times of recession, the normal practice is to run down existing stocks, not to increase them. Running down existing stocks will conserve liquid funds (by reducing purchases) and reduce the overdraft of £3,800 at the end of December.
2. The budgeted figures indicate a trading loss. What action should be taken to remedy this? Can sales be increased or can costs be reduced?
3. Because there is budgeted a loss for the period the dividend is being paid out of accumulated profits earned in previous years.
4. The cash position will deteriorate when the remaining instalments for the purchase of fixed assets are paid.

9.2 Company Z

	90% £	100% £	110% £	120% £
Depreciation	22,000	22,000	22,000	22,000
Staff salaries	43,000	43,000	43,000	43,000
Insurance	9,000	9,000	9,000	9,000
Rent and rates	12,000	12,000	12,000	12,000
Power	32,400	36,000	39,600	43,200
Consumables	5,400	6,000	6,600	7,200
Direct labour	378,000	420,000	462,000	504,000
Semi-variable costs:				
Variable	270,000	300,000	330,000	360,000
Fixed	55,000	55,000	55,000	55,000
Total	**826,800**	**903,000**	**979,200**	**1,055,400**

The 'high/low' method (see Chapter 2) gives a variable element for the semi-variable costs of £2.50 per direct labour hour. The fixed element (£55,000) is derived as a balancing figure.

9.3 Nursing home

Notes and assumptions: The number of patients has to be used as the cost driver since there is no other information in the question for flexing the variable costs. The budgeted number of patients for months 7 to 12 is assumed to be (6,000 − 2,700) 3,300. Budgeted variable cost per patient for the first six months is found by dividing the costs for the first six months by 2,700 (the number of patients treated).

(a) Overhead budget for months 7–12:

Variable overhead:		£	£ per patient
Staffing		72,600	22
Power		33,000	10
Supplies		66,000	20
Other		9,900	3
		181,500	55
Fixed overhead:			
Supervision	60,000		
Depreciation/financing	93,600		
Other	32,400		
		186,000	
Total overhead		367,500	

Overhead cost per patient £367,500/3,300 = £111.36. Care should be taken over how this amount is used because the fixed overhead cost per patient depends upon the number of patients treated.

(b) Variance report for months 7–12:

	Original budget	Flexed budget	Actual results	Variance
Number of patients	3,300	3,800		
	£	£	£	£
Variable overhead	181,500	209,000	203,300	5,700 (F)
Fixed overhead	186,000	186,000	190,000	4,000 (A)
	395,000	393,300	1,700	1,700 (F)

(c) The data supplied was not sufficiently detailed to give any meaningful analysis. Expenses were given under broad subheadings and a single volume-based cost driver (number of patients) has been used. This has resulted in broad averages that are almost meaningless. For example, the cost of power is shown as £10 per patient yet the amount spent on each patient for electricity will depend on the length of each patient's stay in the nursing home. The cost of power per patient was also based on the costs for the first half of the year but because this type of cost is seasonal it is unlikely to occur at the same rate during the second half of the year.

The above variance report shows that the total spending on variable overheads was less than the budgeted expenditure. This is impossible to interpret because the amount spent was given as a single total of £203,300. The same limitation applies to fixed overheads. The adverse variance on fixed overheads might suggest that costs were not properly controlled, but a more detailed investigation might reveal that some of these costs contain an element that does vary with the level of activity.

Chapter 10

10.1 Hardings Ltd

(a)

		Days
(i)	Stock turnover (150,000/900,000 × 360)	60
(ii)	Debtors collection (180,000/1,620,000 × 360)	40
(iii)	Creditors payment (77,500/930,000 × 360)	(30)
(iv)	Cash opreating cycle	70

(b) Working capital requirements:

	At 31/3/89	Additional (× 0.25)	Total
	£	£	£
Stock	150,000	37,500	187,500
Debtors	180,000	45,000	225,000
Creditors	(77,500)	(19,375)	(96,875)
Totals	252,500	63,125	315,625

(c) Overdraft requirements:

Investment:

Plant		150,000
Working capital (as above)		63,125
		213,125

Less:		
cash from operations (April–June)	30,000	
sale of investments	65,000	
		95,000
		118,125
Less opening balance		10,000
		108,125

Note that in this case the profit of £30,000 is the same as cash since there is no change in the level of items in working capital.

(d) Forecast balance sheet

Fixed assets (550,000 – 230,000)		320,000
Current assets		
Stock	187,500	
Debtors	225,000	
Bank	21,875	
	434,375	
Creditors falling due within 1 year:		
Trade creditors	96,875	
		337,500
		657,500
Share capital		400,000
Profit and loss account		257,500
		657,500

Note:

Closing bank balance:		
Overdraft required	108,125	
Less cash from operations	130,000	
Balance	21,875	

(e) The cash requirements are clearly short term and there seems to be no reason why a bank should not support the scheme. The forecasts show that the overdraft will be repaid by 31 March 1990. Even if post-expansion results do not come up to expectations, and results are similar to the first three months of operations, there will be a positive cash flow of £90,000 leaving a bank overdraft of only £18,125 at the end of the year.

10.2 International Electric plc

(a) Approximate equivalent annual percentage cost:

The discount is 2% for an advance in cash settlement of 40 days. The annual equivalent of this is approximately $365/40 \times 2\% = 18.25\%$. Note that a more precise rate can be found from the formula $100 \times (1.02^{9.125} - 1) = 19.81\%$ (the power number of 9.125 is found from 365/40).

(b) Outstanding debtors:

	£m
Old Scheme:	
$30/365 \times 0.5 \times £365m$	15.0
$70/365 \times 0.5 \times £365m$	35.0
	50.0
New scheme:	
$30/365 \times 0.5 \times £365m$	15.0
$30/365 \times 0.5 \times 0.5 \times £365m$	7.5
$70/365 \times 0.5 \times 0.5 \times £365m$	17.5
	40.0

(c) Cost of discount: all existing customers who pay within 30 days (one half) will be entitled to the discount, as well as one half of the remaining half. This means that the total cost will be $3/4 \times £365m \times 2\% = £5.475m$.

(d) Total costs and benefits are as follows:

	£000
Bank interest saved (£50m − £40m) at 12%	1,200
Bad debts saved	300
	1,500
Cost of discounts (as in (c))	5,475
Excess of costs over gains	3,975

The scheme is not, therefore, beneficial to the company. The above analysis ignores any savings in administration costs. Any savings in administration costs resulting from fewer debt chasing routines tend to be offset by additional work in collecting discounts deducted by customers who were not entitled to them.

(e) Debtor management involves: credit references, credit limits, debt chasing routines, and refusing to supply customers who have exceeded their credit limit. These matters are discussed more fully in the text.

10.3 Linpet

(a) Cash (or cash equivalents) are held for three basic purposes:
  1. Transactions: cash is required to meet the day-to-day commitments.
  2. Speculation: the company can respond quickly to new opportunities.
  3. Precaution: to meet unexpected obligations or cope with interruptions of normal cash flows due to unforeseen circumstances.

(b) Cash budgets are basically a tool for planning and control. For planning purposes, they enable the company to estimate when surpluses and deficits will arise. For control purposes, actual cash flows are compared to budget so that any significant variances can be investigated and appropriate action taken.

(c) Cash budget for six months to 30 November 1989

	Jun	Jul	Aug	Sep	Oct	Nov
Receipts:						
Cash sales	4,000	5,500	7,000	8,500	11,000	11,000
Credit sales	–	–	4,000	5,500	7,000	8,500
	4,000	5,500	11,000	14,000	18,000	19,500
Payments:						
Freehold	40,000					
Vehicles	6,000					
Equipment	10,000					7,000
Wages	900	900	900	900	900	900
Overheads	500	500	500	500	650	650
Purchases	–	29,000	9,250	11,500	13,750	17,500
Commission	–	320	440	560	680	880
	57,400	30,720	11,090	13,460	15,980	26,930
Balances:						
Opening	60,000	6,600	– 18,620	– 18,710	– 18,170	– 16,150
Closing	6,600	– 18,620	– 18,710	– 18,170	– 16,150	– 23,580

10.4 Grassington

(a) Cash operating cycle:	Days
Stock (305/1,830 × 365)	61
Debtors (300/2,700 × 365)	41
	102
Less creditors (160/1,800 × 365)	32
	70

(b) Three options open to the company are:
1. Reduced debtors by £20,000
2. Reduce stocks by £20,000
3. Increase creditors by £20,000

The effect of each of these on the cash operating cycle is as follows:
1. The reduced debtor collection period will be (280/2,700 × 365) 38 days. The debtor collection period in (a) is 41 days. The cash operating cycle will be reduced by (41 – 38) 3 days.
2. The reduced stock holding period is (285/1,830 × 365) 57 days. The stock holding period in (a) is 61 days. The cash operating cycle will be reduced by (61 – 57) 4 days.
3. The increased creditor payment period is (180/1,800 × 365) 36 days. The creditor payment period in (a) is 32 days. The cash operating cycle will be reduced by (36 – 32) 4 days.

Chapter 11

11.1 One-year contract

The relevant costs of the contract are as follows:		£
Material C (disposal cost save(d)		(2,000)
Material F (cost of buying Material X)		9,000
Operating labour (incremental cost)		33,000
Supervision (no incremental cost)		–
Depreciation (allocation of sunk cost)		–
General overheads (no incremental cost)		–
Machine:		
opportunity cost = lost sale proceeds	2,000	
incremental cost = cost of disposal	1,500	
		3,500
Total relevant costs		43,500
Contract price		70,000
Contribution		26,500

Since there will be a net increase in future cash flows of £26,500, the contract should be accepted.

11.2 Project X

(a) Relevant costs of the contract:

	£
Material A (cost saving)	(1,750)
Material B (incremental cost as shown)	8,000
Direct labour (incremental cost)	7,000
Supervision (no incremental cost)	–
Overheads (no incremental cost)	–
Machinery (net incremental cash flow)	4,750
Total incremental costs	18,000
Contract price	30,000
Contribution	12,000

(b) The report should include the following points:
1. The original cost of £32,000 (excluding cost of machinery) is based on an absorption costing approach and does not reveal the increase in future cash flows that would arise if the project is undertaken.
2. The incremental costs that result from taking on the project amount to £18,000.
3. If a price of £30,000 is tendered, there will be a net increase in future cash inflows of £12,000. If the company is operating at above the break-even level, the whole of this £12,000 will be reflected in accounting profit.
4. The minimum price (a price that covers relevant costs) is £18,000. Any price in excess of £18,000 will be a benefit to the company.

(c) Non-monetary factors could include: time-scale of the project and capacity to complete it; whether any specific training is required; advice needed for dealing with overseas customers.

11.3 Small company

(a) (i) The terms 'variable cost' and 'fixed cost' are a reference to the way that total costs for a period will respond to changes in the level of activity. Variable costs are those where the total amount for a period will depend upon the level of activity: as activity increases, so the total cost increases. Fixed costs are those that remain at the same level irrespective of the level of activity. The activities that cause total variable costs to change are known as cost drivers, and there are very many different kinds of cost driver. The problem of identifying cost drivers will depend on the type of organization. In simple cases (such as a retailer), sales activity is likely to be the sole cost driver. In complex organizations there are many different kinds of activity that cause total costs to change.

(ii) 'Opportunity cost' and 'sunk cost' are terms that are used to identify costs when producing information to help managers make decisions. An opportunity cost is a benefit forgone as a result of taking a particular course of action. It is an unusual concept of cost in the sense that although it is identified as a cost for making decisions, it is never recorded as a cost in the accounting records. A sunk cost is a cost that has already been incurred. Although sunk costs are relevant for the purposes of profit measurement, they are not relevant to making decisions because they cannot be changed by a decision. However, past costs are sometimes used as a guide to future costs.

(b) The current output is limited by the quantity of materials available and so maximum current output is (£80,000/£8) 10,000 units. This represents 10,000 machine hours.

	£ per unit	£ per month
Direct material	8	80,000
Variable cost	2	20,000
	10	100,000
Sales	20	200,000
Contribution	10	100,000
Fixed costs	4	40,000
Profit	6	60,000

(c) The contribution offered by the special order is:

Direct material (£3,520 + £80)	3,600
Variable cost (500 × £2)	1,000
Component	600
	5,200
Price offered	8,000
Contribution	2,800

The opportunity cost of diverting £3,600 of material to this order is as follows:

Contribution from this order	2,800
Lost contribution from standard products that could be made with this material:	
£3,600/£8 × £10	4,500
Net loss of contribution	1,700

The minimum price should, therefore, be (£8,000 + £1,700) £9,700. At this price the company will be indifferent as between producing regular products or taking on the special order.

11.4 National Fandango plc

(a) Optimum product mix

	Renon	Stim	Lench	Croux
	£	£	£	£
Selling price	75	99	129	168
Variable costs	63	81	105	141
Contribution per unit	12	18	24	27
£s of material used	27	36	51	60
Contribution for each £1 of material used	£0.44	£0.50	£0.47	£0.45
Preferred order	4th	1st	2nd	3rd

	Production quantity	Material used	Balance available
			£3,000,000
Stim	30,000	£1,080,000	£1,920,000
Lench	30,000	£1,530,000	£390,000
Croux	6,500	£390,000	nil
Renon	nil		

(b) Budgeted profit statement

Sales (30,000 × £99) + (30,000 × £129) + (6,500 × £168)	£7,932,000
Variable costs	
(30,000 × £81) + (30,000 × £105) + (6,500 × £141)	6,496,500
Budgeted contribution	1,435,500
Fixed costs	1,000,000
Budgeted profit	435,000

(c) The product mix calculated in (a) takes a strict arithmetic approach. This might not be the optimum mix if the sales of some products are dependent upon the sales of others. For example, the arithmetic suggests that no Renon should be produced yet the sales of other products might depend upon Renon being available. This reservation applies also to the reduction in output of Croux.

Chapter 12

12.1 (a) The payback and net present value methods of investment appraisal are based entirely on cash flows. Depreciation is not a cash flow, it is an accounting allocation that spreads the net result of two cash flows over several accounting periods. The two cash flows involved are the payment for the asset and the sale proceeds at the end of the project. These will be included in the cash flows for payback and net present value according to the time that they occur. The difference between these two figures is spread over the life of the project as depreciation when calculating the accounting rate of return.

(b) (i) Payback for Project 1 is 2.9 years and for Project 2 it is 3.3 years.
(ii) Accounting rate of return: answers depend on whether initial investment or average investment is used.

Based on average investment:
Project 1: £130,000/4/£110,000 = 30%
Project 2: £140,000/5/£90,000 = 31%

Based on initial investment:
Project 1: £130,000/4/£150,000 = 22%
Project 2: £140,000/5/£150,000 = 19%

(iii) Net present value
Project 1:

Time	Cash flow	Discount factor	Present value
Year 0	−150,000	1	−150,000
Year 1	+60,000	0.869	+52,140
Year 2	+50,000	0.756	+37,800
Year 3	+45,000	0.659	+29,655
Year 4	+125,000	0.571	+71,375
		Net present value	+ 40,970

Project 2:

Time	Cash flow	Discount factor	Present value
Year 0	−150,000	1	−150,000
Year 1	+54,000	0.869	+46,926
Year 2	+44,000	0.756	+33,264
Year 3	+39,000	0.659	+25,701
Year 4	+49,000	0.571	+27,979
Year 5	+104,000	0.497	+51,688
		Net present value	+ 35,558

The company should undertake Project 1 in preference to Project 2. Project 1 carries less risk than Project 2 since the original investment is repaid over a shorter period of time. The net present value of Project 1 is also greater than Project 2. Net present values are an indication of the amount by which the total market values of shares will increase if the project is accepted.

(c) The disposal proceeds are needed for the following purposes:
- calculation of depreciation for the accounting rate of return
- calculation of average investment for accounting rate of return
- cash inflows at the end of the project for NPV and payback calculations.

12.2 Transport fleet

(a) Net cash savings:

	Year 1 £	Year 2 £	Year 3 £	Year 4 £	Year 5 £
Carrier's charges	250,000	275,000	302,500	332,750	366,025

Cash costs of own fleet					
Drivers	33,000	35,000	36,000	38,000	40,000
Repairs	8,000	13,000	15,000	16,000	18,000
Other costs	10,000	15,000	20,000	16,000	22,000
	51,000	63,000	71,000	70,000	80,000
Net savings	199,000	212,000	231,500	262,750	286,025

(Depreciation excluded from cash outflows is at the rate of £120,000 per annum.)

(b) (i)

Payback	**Cash flow**	**Cumulative**
Year 1	199,000	
Year 2	212,000	411,000
Year 3	231,500	642,500
Year 4	262,750	905,250

Payback occurs during Year 4 at a point when cash of £107,500 has been saved out of a total saving of £262,750. Total payback period is 3.41 years.
(ii) Accounting rate of return: total cash savings over the 5 years are £1,191,275. Total depreciation is £600,000. Total increase in profit is (1,191,275 – 600,000) £591,275. Annual average is (591,275/5) £118,255. Average investment is (£750,000 + £150,000 ÷ 2 = £450,000. Accounting rate of return on average investment is (£118,255/£450,000) 26.3%. Accounting rate of return on initial investment is (£118,255/£750,000) 15.8%.

(iii) Net present value:

	Cash flow factor	Discount value	Present
Year 0	−750,000	1	−750,000
Year 1	+199,000	0.893	+177,707
Year 2	+212,000	0.797	+168,964
Year 3	+231,500	0.712	+164,828
Year 4	+262,750	0.636	+167,109
Year 5	+436,025	0.567	+247,226
		Net present value	+175,834

(c) The report should include the following points: The alternative project has a higher accounting rate of return and a slightly shorter payback period than the transport fleet proposal. Management should, however, be guided by the net present value calculations since this is the superior technique. This shows that the transport fleet proposal will produce greater returns for the company and its shareholders than the alternative project. If the payback period is seen as an indicator of risk, there is very little difference between the two options.
(d) The company has probably used the rate of 12% on the assumption that it represents the marginal cost of capital. This is a naive view because it ignores how equity shareholders will react to the higher gearing levels. It will be necessary to increase the payout to equity shareholders in order to maintain the present market value of their shares. If the company intends to base the discount rate on the marginal cost of capital (instead of the weighted average cost of capital) the additional payout to equity shareholders forms a part of that marginal cost.

12.3 R. Jones (Salford) Ltd

Cash savings are represented by 10% of the fuel bill over the next six years, as follows:

Year	Fuel bill without insulation £	Saving with insulation £	Cumulative savings
1988	10,500	1,050	
1989	11,025	1,102	2,152
1990	11,576	1,158	3,310
1991	12,155	1,215	4,525
1992	12,763	1,276	5,801
1993	13,400	1,340	7,141

(a) (i) Payback occurs roughly at the end of Year 4.
(ii) Net present value works out at +£73 using a discount rate of (12 + 2) 14%.
(iii) The internal rate of return is approximately 14.6% (14.56984% using a spreadsheet).
(b) See relevant sections of the text.

12.4 Fellingham plc

(a) The shareholders' perception of dividend growth rates has an important bearing on the market value of the share. Shareholders take account of various factors when trying to predict dividend growth rates. In this case there was an announcement by the chairman (three years ago) to maintain a growth rate of 9% each year. The growth rate of 9% is confirmed by the sequence of dividends paid since the announcement was made.

A dividend growth rate of 9% has not been sufficient in this case to compensate shareholders for the effects of inflation, which was higher than 9% for two out of the three years. For a shareholder to match income with inflation the dividends needed to be as follows:

Year 2: 10.00p × 1.11	11.10p
Year 3: 11.10p × 1.10	12.21p
Year 4: 12.21p × 1.08	13.19p

The company is paying out a very high percentage of its profits as dividend. The total earnings per share for the 4 years is 51.50p and dividends per share for the same period amount to 45.73p. This is a distribution of 90% of earnings calculated on a historical cost basis. It is quite likely that dividends are being paid out of capital if profits are adjusted for the rate of inflation being suffered by the company. In Year 3 the dividend is not covered by current profits. It is unlikely that the company will be able to maintain the 9% growth rate unless there is some improvement in profitability.

(b) Assuming a dividend growth rate of 9%, the cost of equity is 13.1%. The calculation is as follows:

$$\frac{12.95 \times 1.09}{£3.44} + 9\%$$

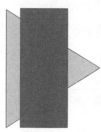

Index